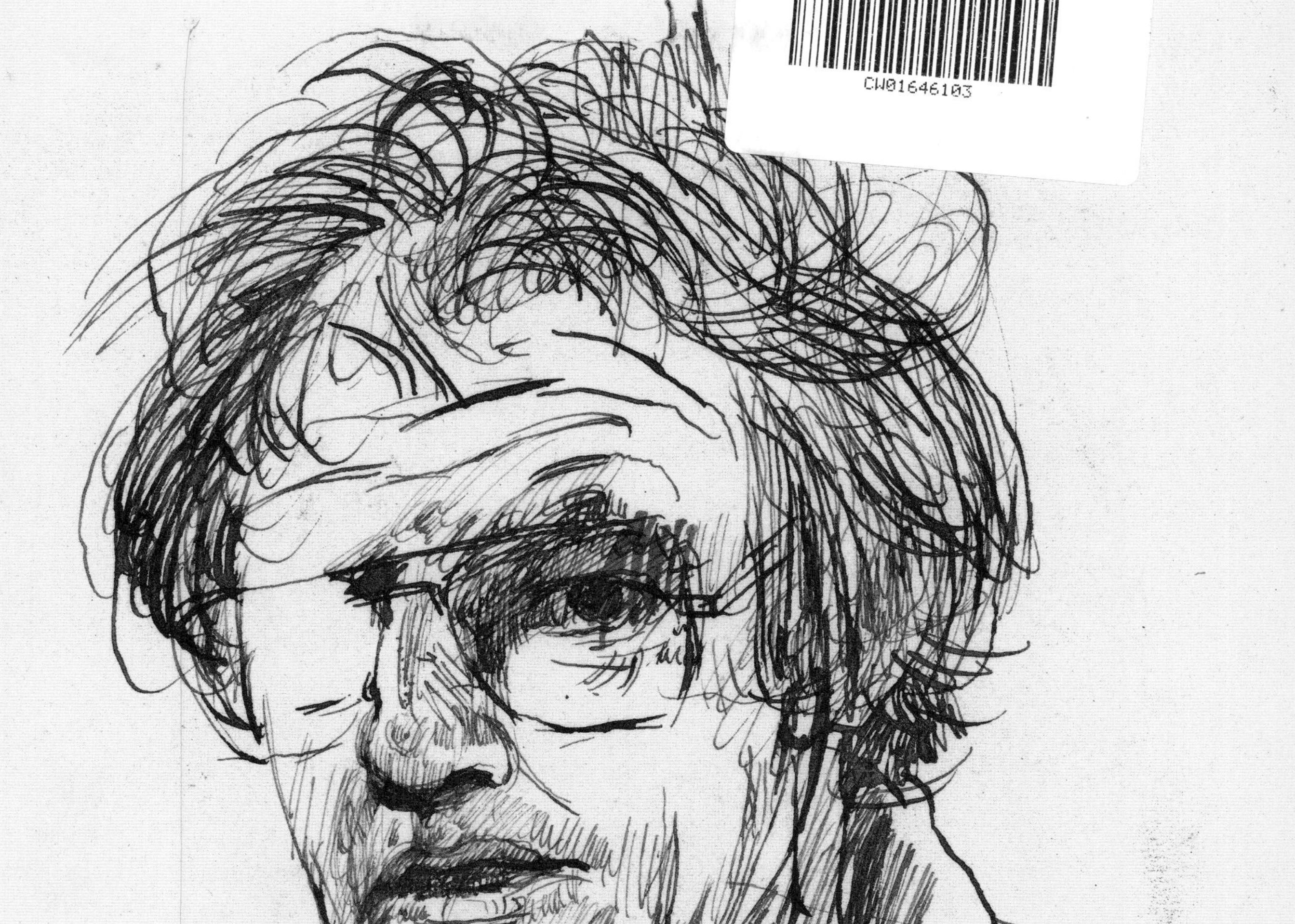

22·8·76.

Its always worst in the morning.

LIGHT AND DARK

The Autobiography of Ken Howard

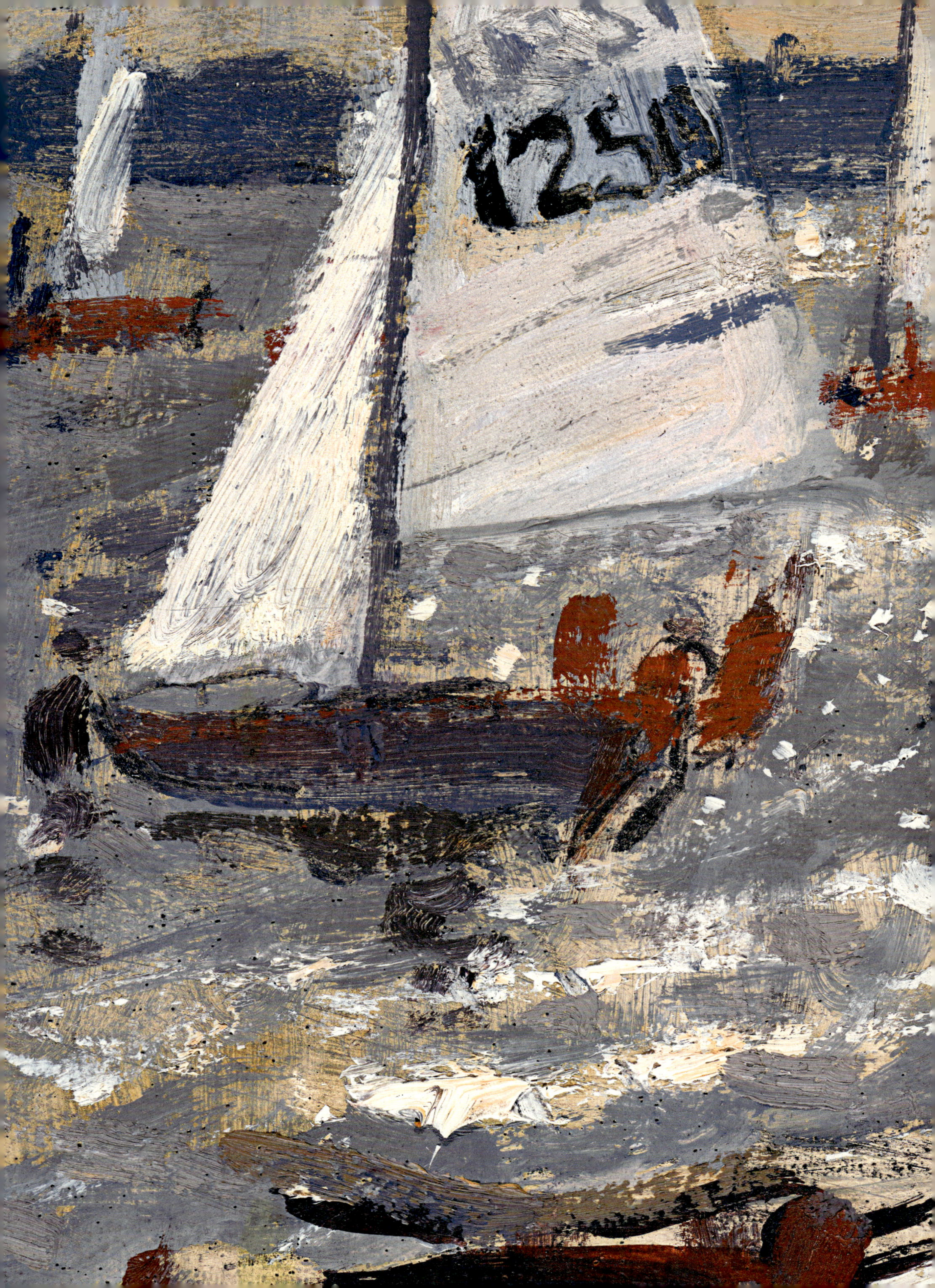

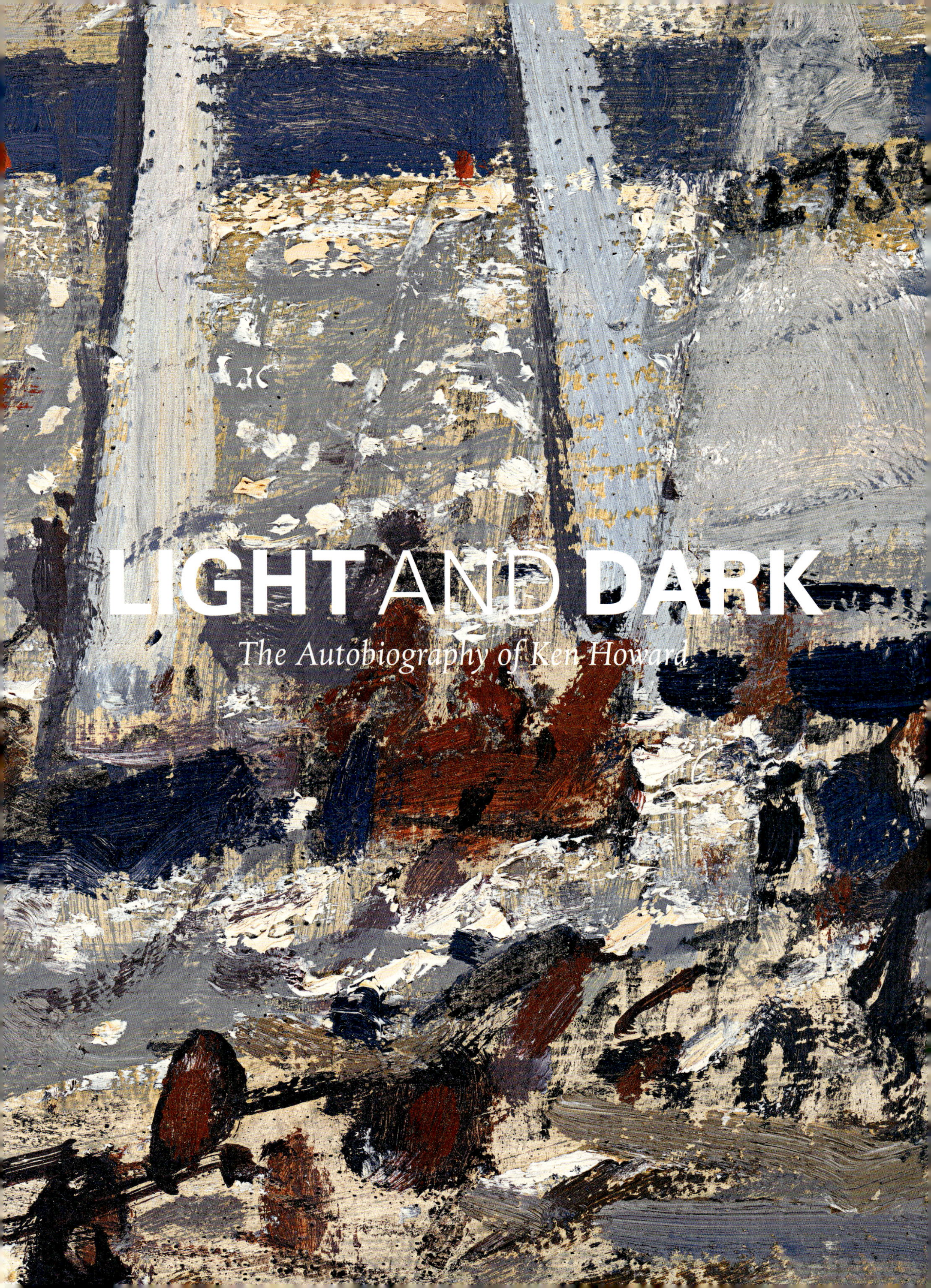

LIGHT AND DARK

The Autobiography of Ken Howard

Royal Academy Publications
David Breuer
Beatrice Gullström
Carola Krueger
Sophie Oliver
Peter Sawbridge
Nick Tite

Editor
Catherine Bradley

Designer
Kathrin Jacobsen

Colour Origination and Printing
EBS

The artist would like to acknowledge with thanks Richard Green Gallery, in particular Sophie Drury; Bertolutti Dora Howard; Chales Roff; and Stan Veygus for providing images reproduced in the book.

British Library Cataloguing-in-Publication Data
A catalogue record of this book is available from the British Library

ISBN 978-1-905711-89-5

Distributed outside the United States and Canada by Thames & Hudson Ltd, London.

Distributed in the United States and Canada by Harry N. Abrams, Inc., New York

Contents

Hindsight, inevitable in planning one's memoirs, can be a dangerous thing. Its influence is insidious, distorting perceptions of long-gone events and those who shaped them. When writing this book, therefore, I have tried as far as possible to remember things as they were – or as I saw them at the time.

A short time ago I was at a party and talking to a friend about a particular autobiography that I had read. 'Oh, you must also read the autobiography of this person's wife, at one stage in his life,' she replied, and it struck me that we all, inevitably, tell stories from our own perspective. When I was young I saw a very good film by the Japanese film-maker Akira Kurosawa called *Rashomon*. This incredible film was, very simply, about a robber who attacks a husband and his wife while they are travelling through Japan; he rapes the wife and kills the husband, as far as I can remember. The important part of the film was that it was based upon each character's remembrances of what took place.

While I have been putting these ideas down, I thought 'Wouldn't it be incredible if I had been able to include, for instance, how Chrissie remembered our life together? Or how Annie remembered our life together?' In other words to do in a book the same sort of thing that Kurosawa had done as a film, because our own memories of events are undoubtedly subjective – and even impersonal recollections are not always objective.

One of the difficult parts of creating this book is that life does not develop in a logical straight line – particularly for an artist. Certain aspects and themes, such as women, work and travel, continue throughout one's life, intermingling and affecting each other. An autobiography describes life in progress, therefore there is no logical beginning and end. So although this book has a broadly chronological sweep, it does weave backwards and forwards on occasion, for example in the chapter on portraits, which ranges across several decades. It does end with the present, however, and my life with my wife Dora, who I am fortunate enough to have with me. My hope is that in the course of the book I give enough information for readers to come to their own conclusion about my life – a life that has been driven by the need to paint.

From a very early age I wanted to paint for a living, though I had no ambition to be particularly innovative. I wasn't going to revolutionise anything. I don't believe that art should necessarily be about revolution – it should be more about evolution. I realised early in life that this was the direction I wanted to take, and became more interested in making art and refining my visual language. If I had added one small brick to the wall of perception, then I believed that I had achieved something.

I have always believed one does not choose to be an artist. There is no choice: it is something you have to do, and I often jokingly describe it as an illness. Drawing and painting is a way of seeing, a way of revealing the world. At first you seek to discover this vision for yourself; later on you hope to reveal that world to others.

Painting is an obsession, and those in its grip are not easy to live with. Partners and families have to understand that obsession in a painter, to accommodate it and not be jealous of it. It is not a question of loving one thing more than the other: they are completely different forms of love.

An artist's work will always be an expression of that individual and his or her life. As the title of this book suggests, life is full of light and dark, sun and shadow, and we all have experience of both. As humans we encounter fulfilment and devastating loss, joy and suffering, and it is this rich tapestry that finally colours one's work.

Ken Howard

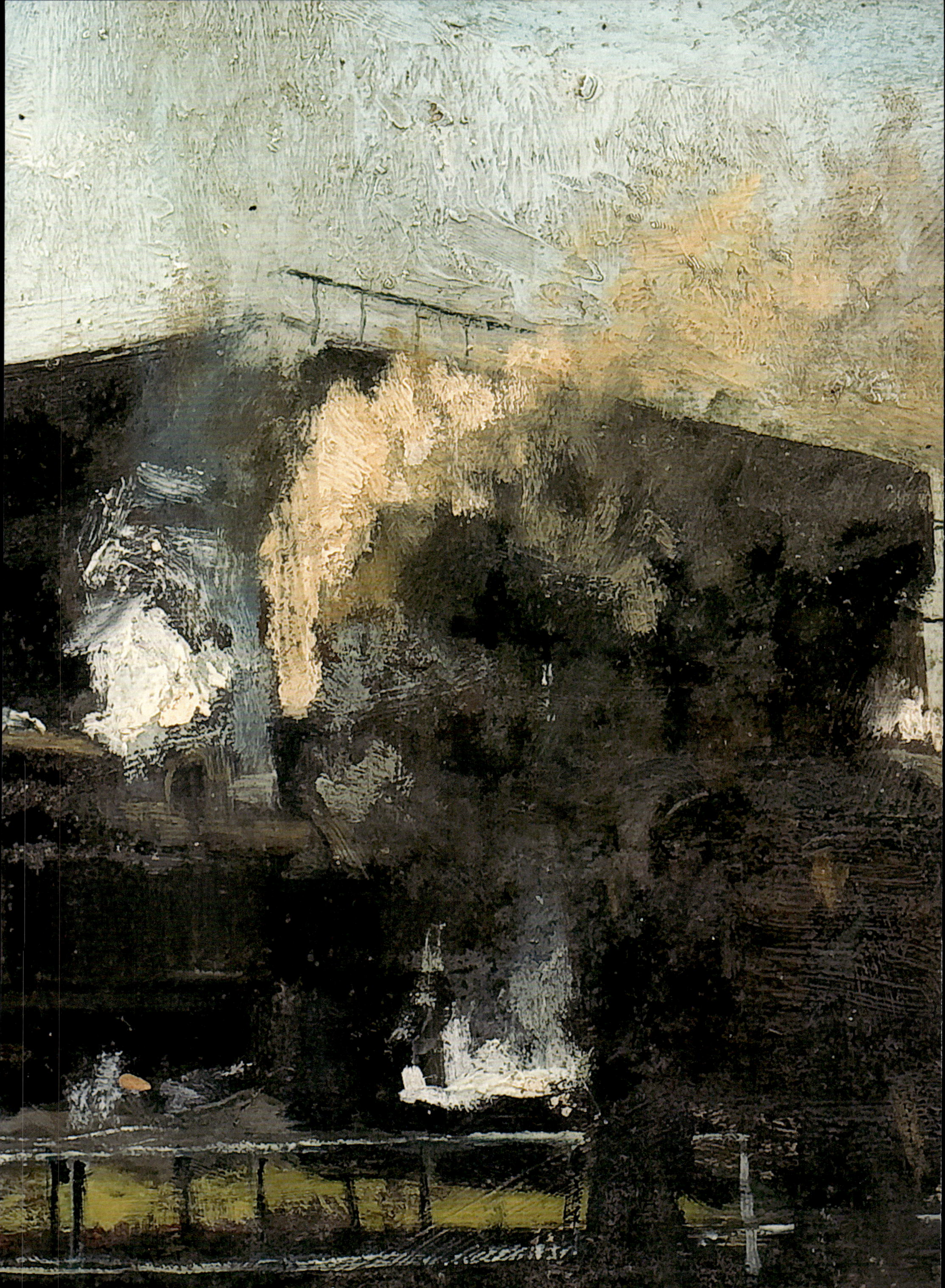

1 Early Years

Neasden Sidings II, *c.* 1953
Oil on canvas, 30 x 40 cm

This small canvas summed up for me all that was beautiful and mysterious about industrial north London. When steam railway disappeared it was the end of an era for me, which I didn't rediscover until many years later when I worked in India.

I was born by Caesarean section on 26 December 1932 at two o'clock in the morning – in other words, two hours after Christmas Day. It was an expensive arrival. When the midwife told my mother that she needed a Caesarean section, my mother objected that she couldn't possibly afford the eight pounds it cost (in those days there was certainly no social assistance or national health system in place). However, the midwife assured her that without the operation either the baby, my mother or both of us would die. And seeing that there was no choice, and the midwife said the council would pay for the doctor, he was duly summoned. The midwife omitted to mention that the council would have to be repaid the money after my birth, at the rate of two shillings and sixpence per week.

As my father had been out of work for a year and a half at the time of my birth, this was a considerable amount of money. My mother had to go out and clean in offices and in people's houses in order to raise the money each week to pay the council back. Yet despite my parents' circumstances – and the severe global depression – 1932 was a good year to be born. I realised years later in life that when you are born is crucial for the way your career, if that's what it can be called, will develop. I have got to know many people in my life who were just as talented as I was, but who had been born in a different time-frame and so had never really earned a living painting, sculpting or in other creative areas. Many artists had their careers interrupted by war, and by the time they returned circumstances had changed – either they had married and were starting families or there wasn't work in art circles. Most turned to teaching, going into grammar schools and so forth, and they were never able to earn their living painting. For those who tried to do so, there were very few galleries around and very few people buying pictures in postwar Britain. The Royal Academy, for example, didn't really start selling in a big way until the mid-1980s, which was about the time I got elected.

So although it didn't seem so at the time, 1932 was a good year in which to be born. When I came to the age of eleven, for example, I was able to go to the grammar school through passing the eleven-plus exam. When I reached sixteen, the postwar Labour government awarded me a grant for the massive amount of £1.40 a week to continue my studies, as my father and mother had no money. That £1.40 gave me opportunities previously impossible for those from a working-class background. By the time I had finished studying in 1959 the art schools were expanding, and as I had been to the Royal College of Art it was relatively easy to get work teaching in an art school.

Ten years later, when I gave up teaching, the economy was booming, with plenty of work being commissioned to illustrate books, magazines etcetera, and as

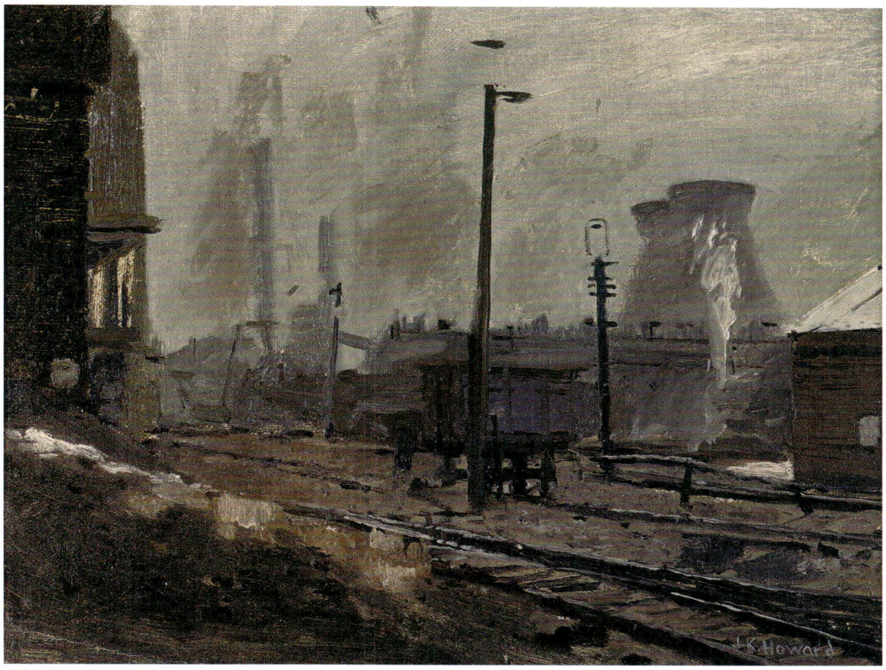

I could draw quite well I was able to earn a living doing that. One of the high points of my career was illustrating many of the telephone directories issued throughout the United Kingdom (see page 164). When I decided to stop both my teaching and my illustration work, I was fortunate that galleries were opening all over London. There were probably a dozen galleries in London when I was studying in the 1950s, but at the beginning of the 1970s and through the '80s they were sprouting everywhere – sometimes for tax reasons, sometimes because people really wanted to open a gallery and the opportunity was there. So I was able to pick up with a gallery fairly quickly. I then got elected to the Royal Academy at the right time in my life, by which point I was earning a good living painting. Eventually I went to probably the best gallery in London. Yet had I been born only ten years earlier, the war would have disrupted my studies and none of these things would have been set into place.

Certainly I had far more opportunities than my father, who had been born into a large, working-class Lancashire family at a time when there was no question of university or any further study. He was put to work in the local mill, then did an apprenticeship for a fitter, or some form of engineering apprenticeship, and became a fitter himself. He came down to London, like many other young men in the 1920s, looking for work, and was taken on by Handley Page, probably one of the biggest aircraft manufacturers in Britain at that time. He had lodgings in Cricklewood, at the side of the railway sidings there; in fact it was in Cricklewood that I was born, and the sidings would prove crucial to me in my early days as a painter. It was because of his 'digs', as they were called, that he met my mother – a friend of my father's landlady who came to visit – and fairly quickly my parents got married.

My father was a good man. I loved him dearly and never in the course of our life together – he was 67 when he died, and I was about 45 – did we have bad words together. In fact we were more like brothers than father and son. I suppose we tended in the end to gang up on my mother, who was far more ambitious and in many ways, I suppose, dissatisfied with the life that my father had given her. My father was a completely unambitious man, I'm pleased to say, and therefore when I said to him later in life that I wanted to study art, there was no question of him saying 'Oh, you can't do that, you must go to university' or 'You must get a proper job'. He just looked at me and said, 'Eee son, if that's what tha wants to do, tha better do it. I've only got one thing to say and that's I haven't got any money, and so you are going to have to earn a living doing this thing.' He didn't really appreciate the implications of this, and certainly at that age I did not have a clue what he meant. All I knew was that the one thing in life I wanted to do was to draw and paint, and therefore it was logical to assume that I would be able to earn a living in this way.

My father never tried to teach me very much – he wasn't that sort of man – but one of the few bits of advice he did give me, which I'll always remember, was that 'if tha can't say owt good about a bloke, say nowt'. He lived by that completely: I only once heard him say something negative about another human being, and that was Winston Churchill. My father hated him with a passion. I didn't really understand it at the time, but later in life, of course, I realised that Churchill's politics had affected my father's early life as a working-class boy very much. He never forgave him, and during the war, when Churchill was such a hero to many people, my father never said anything positive about him. But Churchill was the only man that I ever heard my father speak critically about.

Though not an ambitious man, my father did work within the union movement and became a shop steward in the engineering union. I don't think he was particularly interested in politics, only in trying to help his fellow working man to have a decent living, and he became a shop steward and fought to that end. I remember how he spoke vehemently against the system called piecework, in which you got paid according to what you produced. He was dead against this because as soon as you were able to manage a reasonable amount of production per hour, he said, employers cut your rates so that you had to produce even more for the same amount of money. He was very conscious of the class system, and I seem to remember when I was young, from conversations with my mother, that at one stage my father had been a member of the Communist Party; it wasn't really approved of at that time, and it wasn't spoken about very much. He then became a strong Labour supporter, which he remained for the rest of his life. My own allegiances were more varied. Like many young men I started off as a Socialist supporter, along with my mother, and then became a Lib Dem and eventually did touch on Conservatism.

My mother said that my father would have turned in his grave had he thought his son had voted for the Conservative Party. In retrospect, of course, I completely understand my father's position. He never, ever in his life, even by the time he left London in the 1960s, earned anything approaching twenty pounds a week, and I'm sure that when I was very young and he got a new job after a period of unemployment, he was on a very low wage.

In fact one of my earliest memories as a schoolboy was my father coming home every evening, worn out and tired, and on Fridays handing my mother his pay packet. My mother would take a ten shilling note out of that packet and give it back to my father, and that was his pocket money for the week. The rest of that money, what little there was, was handled by my mother, and everything was put away weekly. The electricity was put away weekly, as was the rent, later the mortgage – as my parents were eventually to buy the house we lived in. Money was definitely a concern, fuelling another of my earliest memories of my father – seeing him come in with ten Wild Woodbines, all he could afford for a week. They were very small, very thin cigarettes, wrapped in a small paper container rather than a packet. He would sit at the table with a mat and a sharp razor and carefully cut the ten Wild Woodbines in half to make twenty, small and thin as they were. This meant he could have three cigarettes each day – one after breakfast, one after lunch and one in the evening – and they were one of his great pleasures. His smoke remained a passion to the end of his life, by which time I suppose he was probably smoking 40 cigarettes a week (although he didn't die from any smoking-related disease). He would also take my mother to the cinema once a week and that would be another two shillings out of his ten gone. What my father did with the remaining six shillings I am not quite sure.

When I was older we would always go for a drink on a Friday night, and he would buy me a half of lager or something similar. It struck me many years later that my father had worked himself to death in the factory: he died when he was only 67, without ever earning a decent living wage. I realised in later life that I paid more in tax in a year than my father earned in the whole of his working life. It seems a terrible thing to know that he worked hard at something he didn't really enjoy – I know that for sure – while I earn my living doing just what I want to do.

My mother was a Scot, born in Edinburgh. Like my father, she came from a large working-class family, and her father was a farm manager at a farm called Goga Mains, just outside Edinburgh. I always thought it sounded rather grand when I was young, but he wasn't well off, bringing up a family of six on a low wage. As soon as my mother was sixteen, or possibly even younger, she was dispatched to London in service – a common practice at the time. She worked for the director of

Harrods in Hendon, a slightly posher area close to where we lived in Cricklewood. My mother hated it and ran away after a few weeks. She went home to Edinburgh, whereupon her mother just put her straight back on a train, telling her, 'You will go back to London and you will continue that job because we can't keep you and feed you here.' When one thinks back to that sort of time, relative to the life that I have experienced, such conditions seem hard to believe.

My mother was like many wives of working men at that time – ambitious for their children, and I think probably somewhat disappointed that their husbands hadn't achieved more, without realising that it was virtually impossible for them to do so. The opportunities were very seldom there – I don't say never, but very seldom – and they certainly hadn't had the chance of an education that those only one generation later, like myself, enjoyed.

If my father was my friend, my mother was my inspiration, and I loved her dearly for it. Not necessarily at the time – in my young years she could be very impatient – and she never really understood what I was doing, trying to be a painter. It came home to me very clearly many, many years later when I went to visit her in Hull, where she was living with my sister. Like all working-class mothers of that period, they never ever said anything positive to their sons. They were afraid, in their way, that their sons would get 'too big for their boots', as they termed it, and move away from their social background. I longed for my mother to say something positive, especially as my father certainly did. Just before he died I remember we went to a civic lunch in Plymouth, where I had a big exhibition. On the way out my father just looked at me and said, 'Ee, son, tha's done all right.'

My mother could never bring herself to do so. Even at the end of her life when I went to visit her, by which time much had happened, and I thought at last that my mother must say something positive. It had been quite a good year – I had painted the Queen, had an exhibition; I had been elected to the Royal Academy and I was on the television that evening. We sat and watched the programme and at the end I didn't say a word, waiting for her to react first. She slowly turned to me and said, 'Och, Ken, I wish you'd done something worthwhile with your life.' I wasn't the least bit offended by this, but found it amusing as it followed the same pattern. My mother would have loved me to have what she would have termed a 'proper job', maybe working in a bank. In fact during the conversation I said to her, 'Like what?' and she replied, 'Oh, I wish you had been a bank manager.' She could have told this to her friends: 'My son's a bank manager.' She never felt she could say to her friends 'My son's an artist' because they all knew that artists were drinkers and womanisers, with no sense of responsibility and so forth. However, I know from what her friends said that in many ways she was still proud of her son, as mothers are.

She had a lovely sense of humour as well. I remember early on in my life she teased me, 'Och, Ken, you're so lucky. If you fell down the loo, you would come up with a bar of chocolate!' She was quite discerning because I have come up with many bars of chocolate in my life; I have been what one would call lucky in many ways. Of course, I could retort, as it's always been said, that the harder I worked, the luckier I got! But it was my mother who instilled in me a Protestant work ethic, if you like. Not very artistic, you may think, but I have to admit that the painters, writers, artists and sculptors that I have known who have earned a living from their chosen career have always been disciplined and worked, while those that have been, so to speak, artistic have sometimes not fulfilled the potential that was there. You can't make rules about these things. They are always going to be broken, just as one can't expect that people who produce good work are necessarily good people, or that those producing bad work are bad people. Very often bad people create very good work and good people make very bad work. Nevertheless, it's nice when it does work out.

My mother didn't only instil a work ethic in me – she worked very hard herself. From the very beginning of my life I remember her going out to work. During the war she worked in a factory. After the war she went out and did housework in order to support her children, my sister and myself, and to help out

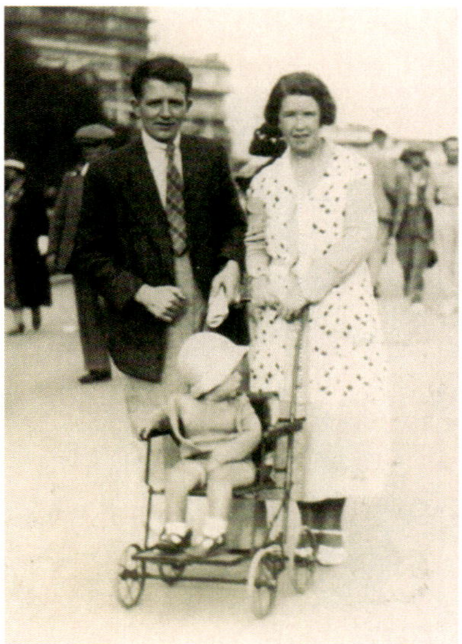

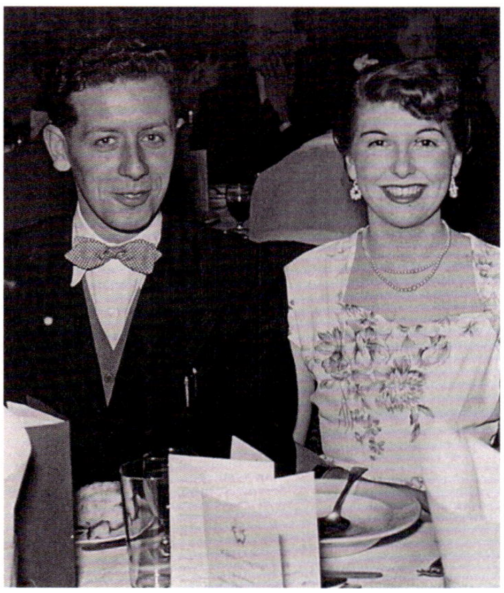

Left
My mother and father with me in a pushchair at the seaside, probably Clacton or Southend, *c.* 1934. I was always a lazy child as far as walking was concerned; even years later in the Boy Scouts I still wanted people to carry me.

Right
My sister Jean with Jimmy Love at the Willesden Cycling Club Dinner in 1949. He was a very good cyclist and had been in the British Olympic team in London the previous year.

with my father's meagre earnings. She also worked very hard in the house. We always had lodgers who needed feeding and bed and breakfast, on top of the work she did out of the house. My mother certainly had a strong work ethic herself, but it didn't kill her at an early age, unlike my father; she lived to be 84.

I had one sister, Jean, two years older than myself. We never really understood each other and were completely different as siblings, as is very often the case. Jean had an enormous amount of talent. I often remember thinking that she could have done anything in her life if she had decided to concentrate on it, but she didn't have the ability to stick at anything. In the end she became rather resentful because she felt that I had all the opportunities, whereas in fact my parents, particularly my mother, had been meticulous in making sure that we both had the same chances. If I wanted to learn the piano, my sister also had to have piano lessons, although she would then give them up. When I went to grammar school and my sister didn't get through her eleven-plus, she went on to what was called in those days technical college. My parents were determined that she would have as much opportunity as I did.

She was, in fact, quite a difficult person. Had she been born now she would have been diagnosed as schizophrenic, but unfortunately in those days she was just considered difficult. When she was nice, she was very, very nice – but when she was bad, wow! did you know it. I can remember from my early childhood the sense of the volcano about to blow up in the house. It would happen over several days, but you knew it was coming and it was very disruptive when it did. I suppose, looking back, it did sometimes coincide with new moons or whatever, but there was no thought of giving her medication as would happen now. Unfortunately, when she was 54, and after three previous attempts, Jean finally took her life.

She was, in many ways, a very sad person, but when she was happy she could live life to the full. She loved sports and dancing, and she was very attractive when she was young. However, she put on a lot of weight later and I think became disillusioned with most things in life, which was very sad. We were never very close – I don't know whether that was because we were brother and sister, or because we had completely different interests. There may also have been a certain amount of jealousy between us, but whatever the reason my sister and I never really related. But of course it was a dreadful shock when she did commit suicide, not so much to me but to my mother, who never really got over it.

So this was the family into which I was born. After arriving by Caesarean section I cried for a year – at least that's what my mother told me. We were living in a flat in a little street called Alder Grove in Cricklewood. I often joke and say that I was born between two railway sidings, one at Cricklewood and one at Neasden;

in fact I was, and it was this environment that made me a painter. I cried for the first year, and the only thing that my mother could do was put me down at the bottom of the garden in my pram to howl away. She had to do this because the landlady didn't really want children in the house anyway. The midwife or the district nurse, which they had even in those days, knew just to go straight down the garden when she visited; on her return she would say to my mother, 'He's still crying but don't worry, he'll get over it.' In contrast my sister had been a very, very good child. She had never cried at night or been disruptive; she was, as my mother put it, the perfect child until she was one year old, whereas for my first year I was the worst child you could possibly imagine. However, my habit of crying all the time saved me from nearly dying in my first year. My mother heard me go quiet and came down the garden to find my sister stuffing silver paper into my mouth as hard as she could. Whether it was that she wanted to stop me crying, we will never know, but she could easily have killed me, although I'm sure that was not her intention. At the end of that first year I settled down, eventually becoming a slightly obnoxious, but on the whole nice little boy of whom all my aunts and uncles said, 'What a nice little boy he is.' Of course, the more you heard that, the more you wanted to be a nice little boy. There is nothing like encouragement in this life.

As with most people, I suppose, I have only a few vague memories about my first five years. I suppose that is why I decided to write down my memories at this stage of my life. I have just been reading a book on Walter Sickert, one of my heroes, and noted that at the end of his life he rather lost his marbles, becoming unable to remember very much or appreciate what was going on. I realised that eventually the same thing might happen to me, and therefore decided to write down a few memories of my lifetime, which has been, in many ways, very eventful.

For those first few years I do remember very little, but one of my early memories is of my father sleeping in the chair at the end of his day's work. I always remember that he seemed to be in a very high chair and to be a very big man. In fact, as I realised later, he wasn't a very big man, and I still have one of the chairs in my studio in Cornwall. Of course, I was a very small child to whom all adults seemed very large; my early memory would have been from the floor, looking up at my father. I see small children now holding on to chairs and can myself remember quite clearly the seat of a chair being above my head. The table above it seemed to be extremely high. Such visual memories come quite naturally to me, I suppose, as I have tended all my life to be a visual person.

I seem to remember my childhood as a happy time, although I can also remember lying in bed at night and hearing my parents argue downstairs, often

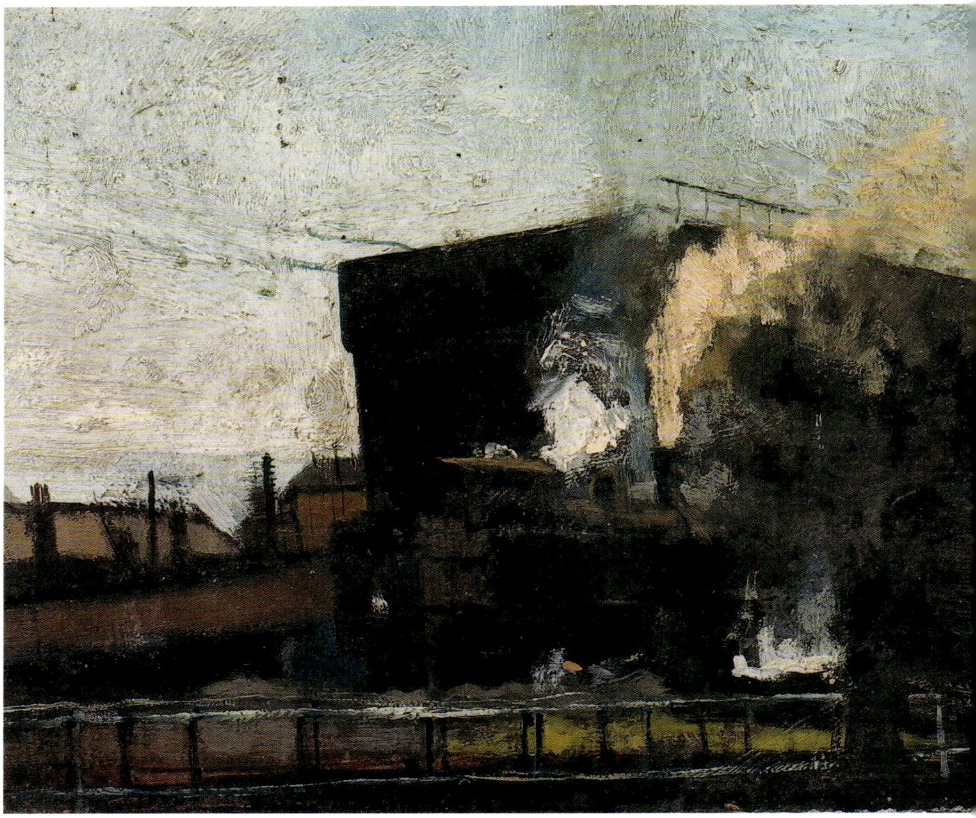

Neasden Sidings, ***c.*** **1952**
Oil on board, 25 x 67 cm

This is one of many paintings I made of industrial north London, where I was born. For me, the area was full of excitement. I could smell it, hear it, feel it and touch it – and I wanted to reveal its beauty to people with preconceived ideas about industrial landscapes. Revelation is what art should be about.

with their voices raised – without any idea of what they were talking about or arguing about. I know it was because of my sister, as she really did provoke my father, who in turn took a lot of provoking. I also have a very early memory of walking round the corner with two suitcases, my sister and my mother, probably aged three or four. We waited at the bus stop for the bus to come. My mother had left my father but she realised, even before the bus came, that there was nowhere to go. She had no money, where could she take us? She picked up the cases and we went home. I didn't realise it at the time, but later on, although I heard my parents arguing, the one thing I didn't want them to do was separate. I was selfish, like all children: I wanted my home, with both my mother and father. I wanted a normal childhood, and if it was sometimes disrupted by argument then so be it.

Later on my parents both mellowed and by the time they began to get to middle age, they were living together in a reasonably harmonious way. My mother still loved to nag my father, but he just seemed to 'turn off his hearing aid' – not that he actually had one – and would just carry on in his quiet, non-confrontational manner.

It's funny how things come into your mind regarding one's childhood. I can remember being up in my bedroom watching other children playing in the street on a summer's evening and wanting to be out there myself. My mother was very strict, however; I must have been very young and was put to bed at the correct time. I also remember one of the first toys I had – an aeroplane that I had to make myself. It flew by an elastic band which you twiddled around, using the propeller, until the elastic

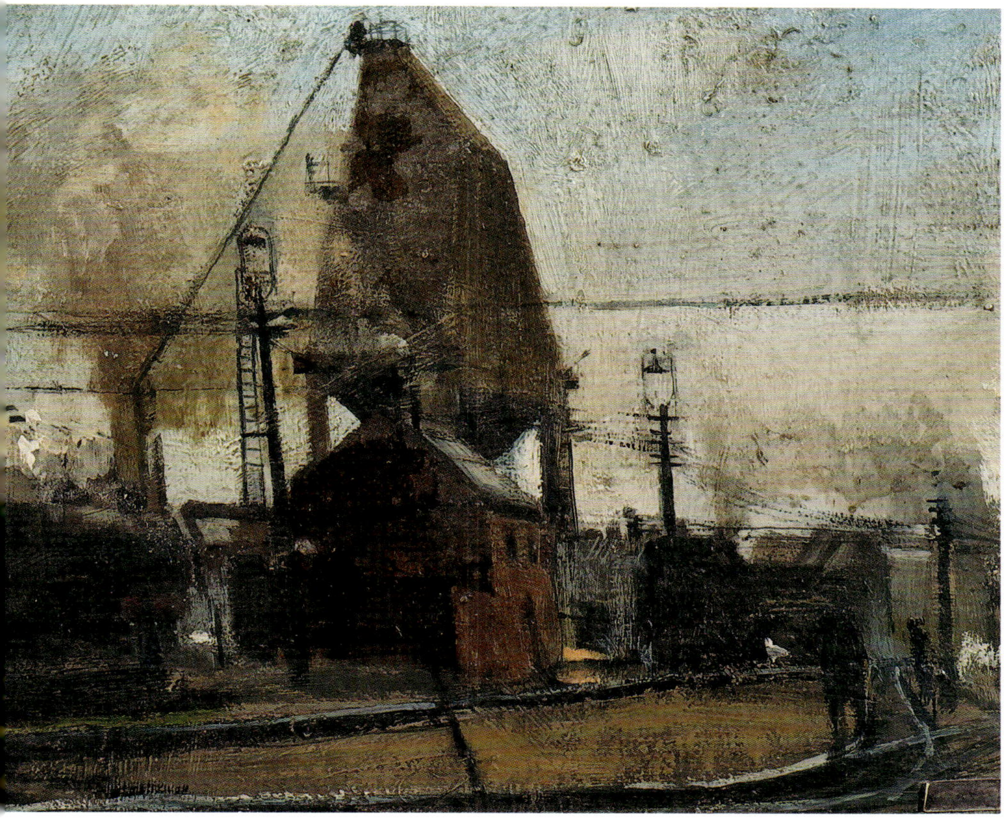

band was very tight, then you let it go and it actually flew. I remember it was quite efficient, the pride of my life, and one of my father's brothers had borrowed it, my favourite uncle. I remember standing at the back door where he was winding this aeroplane up; I was thinking, 'Uncle Billy, you're winding it up too much', but he kept on going. In the end he held it above his head and let it go. It took off, soared to a great height and flew to a great distance beyond the gardens. It must have crashed somewhere in a cabbage patch and I never saw that plane again. It was one of the unhappiest moments of my young life.

I can always remember Christmas quite well, and although we had no money our parents always managed to buy us presents. When we got to a certain age they bought me a three-wheeled bike and my sister a two-wheeled bike, which we discovered at about 4 am, leaping up to see what Father Christmas had left us. We then rode around our bedroom on our bikes, although it was a very small room and how we did it I don't quite know. I do remember my parents coming in and saying, 'Back into bed or the neighbours will think you are coming through the wall.' These are happy memories of childhood, and good to have, but not very distinct recollections.

I suppose I first became conscious that I wanted to paint when I was round about ten years old. I had become interested in the railway yards near me through collecting railway numbers, something little boys did at that stage. I got bored with collecting the numbers, however, and went wandering into the shed – something else that you could just do in those days. There were the odd notices buried in the grass that said 'Trespassers will be prosecuted', but one never paid them any attention. Many years later when painting in a railway yard I decided that I had better do it properly, so I went to see the manager to ask if it was all right to carry on. 'Why did you come and ask me?' he demanded. 'You should have just carried on doing it. I have seen you there for days. Now I have got to put someone with you, otherwise I will be responsible if anything happens to you.' As a child, however, one never even thought about asking permission. You just wandered into the running shed and saw these beautiful trains steaming, almost like animals. The smell was incredible and I remember years afterwards visiting the junction in Delhi. The one thing that struck me straightaway was the smell of the trains, reminding me of those very early days in Cricklewood and Neasden.

By this time we had stopped living in lodgings and – largely through my mother's influence – were renting a house, a relatively new building in Review Road, a street close to the North Circular Road. These houses had been built in the early 1930s. They were terraced, probably twenty houses in a row with perhaps one semi-detached property before the next terrace started, and ours was just about in the middle of the terrace. They were not very prepossessing, but they were home and big enough for parents, two children and at least one lodger, very often two. Round the corner was the North Circular, which today, of course, would be considered a very dangerous thing to have nearby; there are now bridges going across it. Then it was a relatively quiet road, however; in fact I can remember that in the whole of our street there was not one single car. It was a street of working people who simply walked round to the North Circular, where the factories were. My father went to York Shipley, which made refrigeration, but there was also a British Oxygen factory and a Smith's Electrical, which I believe supplied electrical components for cars. There were various other small factories, too, where the men of the area went to work.

Across on the other side of the North Circular was a stretch of water called the Welsh harp. It was a sort of reservoir surrounded by woods, in what is even today an undeveloped area. It was a happy hunting ground for us children and we often went over there to play. One of our games was to make very dangerous rafts which usually tipped up when you tried to get on to them, throwing us into the water. We were afraid to go home wet, so would make a fire in an old oil can and fill it up with some old cuttings of wood, both of which lay around on the site. Then we dried our clothes, thinking that our parents wouldn't know that we had been over to the Welsh harp and fallen into the water. In reality, of course, we were pretty smelly by that time, and they knew damned well what we had been up to.

After surviving my sister's attempt to kill me with silver paper, I nearly came to grief in the Welsh harp. At weekends we would go over there as a family and take a picnic. My sister and I would bathe in the Welsh harp – not the cleanest of water because of the outflow from the factories around the water. However, we didn't think about such things and we often bathed there, me wearing a little knitted green and yellow swimming costume, not pants but a proper knitted costume that I remember quite distinctly. Unfortunately there were potholes under the water that you couldn't see, and one day I slipped into one and I went straight down. I couldn't swim then, and I can still vaguely remember coming up, spluttering and going down again, then being grabbed the second time I came up – I believed at that time you came up three times before you drowned – by my sister. She caught me by the hair and pulled me to the edge of the water to haul me out. So having nearly killed me once, she certainly saved my life the second time.

By this time we were into the war, which began when I was only six. I remember how we all queued up outside the school, where we were given brown paper bags, a large block of chocolate and various other small goodies. Then we were loaded on to coaches and dispatched across various parts of the country; I ended up at Kettering, but all that seems quite vague. The war was a disruptive time for me as I was constantly leaving London and then being brought back again. This was because when the bombing became severe my parents sent me away to relations in Edinburgh or Calne in Wiltshire, I remember, or Nottingham, or wherever brothers or sisters of my parents were living. And when the bombing quietened down again my mother, who obviously wanted the family together, would bring us back and we would have a few more months in London. My father was in a reserved occupation as a fitter; I believe he was involved in building tanks, among other things. Having engineering skills and being of a certain age, he was not called up to fight.

But for me as I grew up the war was an exciting time. I remember quite clearly standing in the street watching the planes fighting in the sky – dogfighting, it was called – and found it very exciting. I didn't know much about the fighting and death. I remember my main concern was that before the war I had become very keen on ice cream, sold by a man who came round on a bicycle with a box on the front. It was a cool-box bicycle and he sold water ices – triangular in shape, with a wonderful blue and white chequered paper wrapping. My one thought during the war was that when it was all over the man would come back with his ice cream and life would return to normal – which of course he never did, as life moves on. At night we would go to the air-raid shelter at the factory where my father worked on the North

Circular Road. This was in the big factory basement and therefore was fairly safe, so all the workers and their families would go. I remember that spending the night there was an enormous adventure. Men played cards and there was a dartboard, women knitted and talked, and children had to take something to do.

I would take my drawing pad and books to copy things out of. I can remember copying a Zeppelin out of some book, but am not sure what it was – a volume of the *Encyclopaedia Britannica*, perhaps, although I don't think we had such things, or a magazine. Anyway, I copied this Zeppelin and everyone gathered round and said, 'Isn't he clever?' At that age I got plenty of encouragement, such as being called a nice little boy and being encouraged to behave well; then, when people said you were clever, I was encouraged to be even better. I am quite convinced that progress in life requires lots of encouragement, and that talent in young people is actually quite easy to stifle. My second wife, who was German, had wanted to paint when she was young. Her father, who was a General – or possibly a Brigadier General – in the German Army, had seen her doing it one day and commented, 'Ah, there was never any talent in our family anyway.' This destroyed her confidence for a long while, but eventually, many years later, she went to art school and became a very fine painter.

After our night in the shelter we would come out when the all clear sounded in the morning. At night a wailing air-raid siren told us to go to the shelter, and in the morning a continuous blast meant it was 'all clear' and safe to come home as the German planes had gone and bombing had stopped. And we would emerge into that very early morning light, looking around to see what had been destroyed and hit during the night. I remember that we had a black cat called Smokey who would come every morning to meet us at the air-raid shelter. My mother would say, 'Ah, the house must still be there because here's Smokey', and we would go home. One of our lodgers refused ever to go into the air-raid shelter, saying that, 'If one of the bombs has got my name on it, it will get me.' So he stayed in bed and slept in the house. Sometimes in the morning we would go upstairs to see how Uncle Ellis was to find him still sleeping in bed. The windows would be blown in and his bed covered in glass, but Uncle Ellis just carried on sleeping as if nothing had happened.

On our way to school in the morning we would see the result of the bombings from the night before. I remember going up to school one morning and discovering that two houses had gone completely – a landmine had dropped and just blown them straight away. Blast was a very strange thing during the war, I remember. It could strike one thing and entirely miss something next to it. That morning I saw those houses completely destroyed, with women's underwear caught in the trees and other household items lying around. Yet in a strange way it didn't shock or greatly disturb me. I had my biscuit tin in my hand, something we all carried to school, and one went on picking up pieces of shrapnel, deciding whether they were pieces of a bomb or a shell or an incendiary. When we got to school we did swaps out of our biscuit tins, trading a tap of a shell for something from a bomb, and the whole thing became a kind of adventure.

By the time the war ended I was nearly thirteen years old and was then more conscious of what had gone on. Although the war didn't always seem very real to me, there were times when it did hit home. I remember that at the end of the war we held street parties to celebrate VE Day (when the war in Europe ended) and VJ Day (when it ended in Japan). The latter, of course, was largely brought about by the dropping of atomic bombs on Hiroshima and Nagasaki. When these things happened I was young and it went over my head – rather as the first photographs of Auschwitz and then Belsen did when they appeared at the end of the war. At that age I was too young for them really to touch and deeply affect me. Only years later when I was working in Germany and went to visit the Belsen camp, where I saw photographs of the mounds where people were buried, did the whole horror of the situation come back to me.

I remember the street parties for VE Day particularly clearly. Trestle tables were placed down the middle of the road and bunting was spread across from the houses. Of course the adults had a great deal to celebrate, although the suffering was by no means at an end. I remember at the VE Day party there was a Mrs Smith who lived three or four doors away from us. Two of her three sons had already been killed in the war and one had survived. At the end of the street party, she received a telegram – and this was on the day the war ended – to inform her that her third son had been killed. Even as a young boy I was touched by this experience, as I knew Mrs Smith quite well; she used to come to her gate and talk to me whenever I was on my way to school. After the war she became rather sad and began to imagine that she had illnesses – maybe this was part of the effect of losing her sons in the war. She used to tell me about these illnesses, until one day when I got home from school and my mother told me that Mrs Smith had committed suicide the previous night. When they did an autopsy on her later, there was nothing wrong with her whatsoever. She was completely healthy and normal, but psychologically she was broken down.

The shelters in the street – long brick shelters with three entrances – lasted to the end of the war and beyond. We used to play in them, but they were very dirty and people peed in them; they weren't very nice at all. As well as these, we all had individual shelters in our gardens, supplied by the government. You could either have a shelter in your garden or you could have one resembling an enormous iron table in your living room. When the siren went off, if you didn't go out to a shelter in the street, you just got under this big iron table – and unless a bomb hit this table directly, you were all right. If the house fell down, this iron table would hold back all the rubble around you and you were therefore saved. Of course at the beginning of the war, before all these sophisticated shelters arrived, you just dived under the stairs because you realised that when a house collapsed they were usually the one part that survived.

The shelters in the gardens, called Anderson shelters, weren't very successful. They were made out of corrugated iron (which I later learned to call 'wriggly tin' when I was working in Northern Ireland). These shelters were dug down into the earth, probably five feet deep, and a square concrete bowl was inserted. Then the corrugated iron shelter was built on to the side of this concrete centre, and the whole structure covered with earth. It looked as though there was a little hill with a door in the front of it in each garden. Of course these inevitably filled up with water; our own Anderson shelter, which we used before we went to my father's factory shelter, regularly had two or three feet of water in it. We children used to quite like it; we would collect minnows and small fish from the local reservoir and put them into the water. But sleeping there at night when it was damp, of course, was not very good for your health. As a child you withstood it and it had no effect, but for older people it must have been a disaster.

I remember it was because of our Anderson shelter that we saved our little house, which, by that time, my parents owned. We were in the Anderson one night – my father, mother, sister and myself – when suddenly the top of the shelter began to glow red. This spread; obviously there was something extremely hot on top of the earth, and the heat was getting through and making the metal glow. My father climbed out of the shelter to see what it was and discovered a burning incendiary bomb on top of the shelter. Looking at the house, he saw something burning through the bathroom window, which was on the first floor (it was a two-storey house). He rushed into the house and up the stairs to find that an incendiary had gone through the roof and landed in the bathroom. Had one not landed on top of the Anderson shelter at the same time, we would never have known and the house would have burned down. These bombs were dropped in sticks, with the result that you probably had about 50 incendiary bombs on a street at any one time.

By this time I had become quite convinced that earning a living from painting was the only thing I wanted to do. Again I didn't have a clue what it was about. We had no art in our house – I always say that the only art in our house was on the top of biscuit tins, and it wasn't very inspiring. I seem to have a vague memory that there was a Constable in the living room – a painting of Brighton beach with a couple of boats drawn up on it, obviously a reproduction. This is one of the first times I remember being conscious of painting, just as one of my early memories of music was of going to a house with loudspeakers up in the corner of the room near the ceiling. I remember sitting there as a little boy thinking that there must be somebody behind that board, playing a saxophone or a trumpet, or whatever instruments were playing the dance music.

When I was young, I thought it had been an advantage being born into a working family because I had the necessity to work. I had seen people already in my young life who didn't have that sort of drive and who, although they had a lot of talent, had never really fulfilled it. Later on I changed my mind, and I still think today that it would have been an enormous advantage to have been born surrounded by good art, painting and furniture, living in a well-designed house and so forth. I think it would probably have honed my aesthetic sensibilities more finely than they have been, but we can't change things and there were various advantages in having to work: it taught one to view art as a necessity, not an indulgence.

Thinking in my mother's terms – I was so lucky that if I fell down the loo, I would come up with a bar of chocolate – I did have several fortunate pieces of encouragement when I was young. One 'bar' came through Mr White, a neighbour and manager of a Dewhurst's butcher's shop in Fleet Street (I remember the name because, funnily enough, I was to work for a Dewhurst's later in my life). Mr White saw me drawing and asked if he could take some of the drawings to show one of his customers. My mother agreed and he took them away. A few days later I received a letter from the art editor of the *Daily Mail*, a God-like figure to me. This must have been in the 1940s – goodness knows what his name was, and he would obviously be long dead by now. In the letter he wrote, 'I think you've really got talent and you must keep doing this thing.' And he sent me one of his own little paintings – a little oil painting on board which, alas, I don't have any more. I remember it very clearly and obviously I remember it as being better than it probably really was, but the fact that this man, the art editor of a national newspaper, had written to me gave me incredible encouragement.

On another occasion the manager of the Queen's cinema at Cricklewood, where we used to go to Saturday morning 'flicks' as we called them, announced that they were going to have an art competition. Several Saturdays later, we all took our works in, and I won the first prize. I went up on to the stage to receive it before the films came up. The manager congratulated me, adding, 'I've always wanted to

An early photograph of me painting in the meat market at Smithfield in London, *c.* 1958. At that time I worked on the spot on a much larger scale, and so I preferred to work on overcast days when the light was more even.

commission a painting of the cinema. Would you do it for me?' Of course I thought 'how wonderful!' and went away and worked like mad on this painting of the Queen's, Cricklewood, making drawings of it and transferring them on to a piece of board. It was a gouache as far as I remember, and when it was finished I went in to the manager's office one Saturday morning. He had completely forgotten that he had asked me to do it, and he obviously wasn't very impressed with what I had done, at which I was rather annoyed. But his reaction didn't discourage me, funnily enough. On the contrary: I'd been encouraged because I had won the prize and he had asked me to do this painting.

So encouragement played a very important part, as did the fact that, although I was very young, I already knew that this was the only thing I wanted to do. However, there was one very bad big hurdle to get over. I had to get to grammar school and had to get my matriculation (a school-leaving qualification), which I knew I wasn't naturally very talented at. I remember when it came to the eleven-plus examination I got very het up about it, so anxious was I to pass. I went and did the exam and then came home to bed, where I stayed for three days with a migraine headache.

At that time my mother suffered very badly from migraine headaches, and it was thought when I was young that I would do so as well. My mother's were eventually cured by an operation to remove nerves on one side of her face, although she always said the consequences of that were worse than the migraines. I am not sure about that, as when she had a migraine she used to retreat into a dark room in the house, obviously in severe pain, and wouldn't come out for a couple of days. From an outsider's point of view I thought it was better to lose the feeling in the side of one's face and not to have the migraines, but she didn't agree. She always said she would never, ever have had it done had she known what was happening.

Fortunately I got through the eleven-plus and was accepted for Kilburn Grammar School. There I spent the next five years waiting to go to art school, wherever it should be. Grammar school wasn't a very happy time, as I told my mother sometime later. She didn't believe me, but I came to dread some of the lessons that I struggled with, such as the compulsory French. I had to get French in order to matriculate, so I knew I had to pass it, come what may. I remember the French master writing on one of my reports, 'You haven't got a snowball's chance in hell of passing in French, Howard.' In fact it did me good: I was so angered by this remark that I thought, 'Well, I'll show you' – and I did in fact scrape through. Although I wasn't very academic as such, I did finish top of the class on no fewer than five occasions, strangely enough. This was because in those days you came top

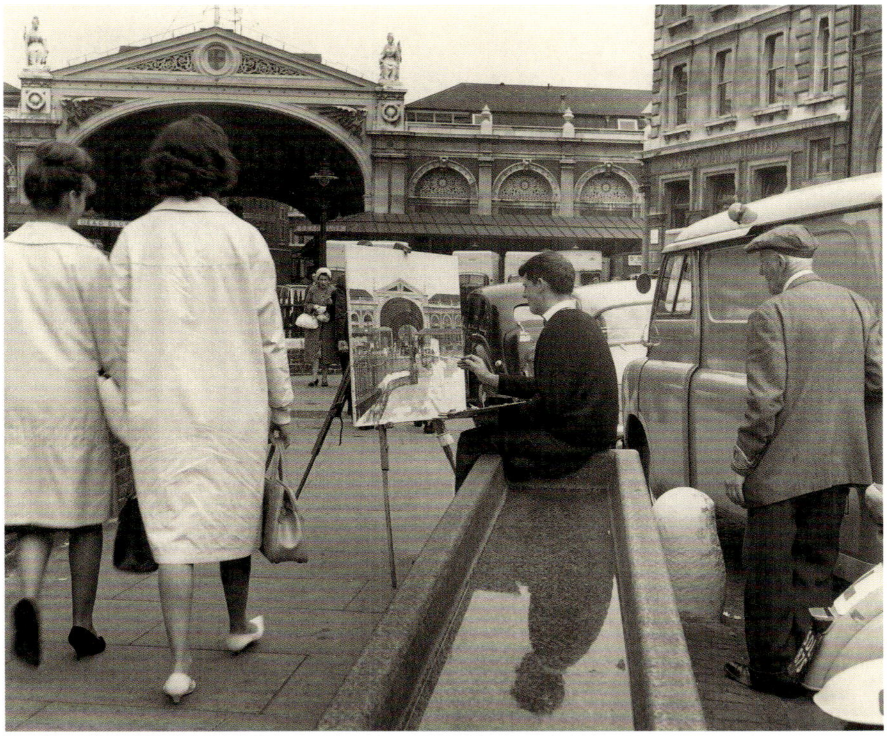

of the class on the average of all your results. I was only average in most subjects, but I was always top in art, finishing up with 98 or 99 per cent. In contrast, the clever boys, the ones who should have been top of the class, got very good marks in maths, but only two per cent in art, so their average went to the dogs. Thus Howard, who got an average mark in maths and wasn't the brightest boy in the class, ended up top. Nevertheless, this didn't kid me that I was really academic, or make me want to do anything other than pursue my aim to get to art school.

It was an aim for which the grammar-school staff in those days had scant sympathy. I now think it's true to a degree that people thought those going to art school were choosing a soft option at which they would never earn a living. I remember the gentlemen who said that I didn't have a snowball's chance in hell of passing French writing on my report one day, 'There are other things in this life than painting, Howard.' 'Maybe so,' I thought when I read it, 'but there is nothing quite as exciting.'

Anyway, I managed to get through my years at grammar school – though I never became a prefect or anything like that. I became the person always called on to do the posters for the various societies, and I was fortunate at that time to have a man as my art master who, in fact, really did affect my life. His name was Bob Whitmore. Rather like those I mentioned earlier, he had been born in the wrong time-frame and had started to make some sort of mark, with some paintings in the Royal Academy, for example, when war had broken out. He went off to the war and by the time he returned he had a couple of children and couldn't really do anything other than take a job as an art teacher. I think, looking back, that Bob was a frustrated man. To me, however, he was a revelation.

Goya and Spanish paintings were among my earliest inspirations, I remember. I read a very good book by Lion Feuchtwanger – a German literary figure who wrote about the lives of artists; I remember that his description of Goya's life was extremely vivid. I was very young and impressionable at the time, and I remember thinking that this was the sort of life that I wanted to lead. Although I knew that was rather romantic and life wasn't going to be anything like that, reading that book still made me recognise somewhere in it the sort of person that I wanted eventually to try and become.

Typical of many people interested in the arts, I wasn't very sporty. I was always the last boy picked for any of the games in the playground. The two best boys were always the captains and at the end, when the last were picked, one would say, 'Ah well, I'd better have Howard.' So I would be taken on for football or cricket as the last, and not very good, choice in the team. I very quickly got discouraged by this, as one does, disappearing instead to the art room at lunchtime, as Bob Whitmore said that I could go in whenever I liked. I did, and Bob then saw that I had some talent and he began to take me a little bit seriously. He said something to me when I must have been about fourteen; I didn't understand at all what he was saying and yet it was to make a complete difference to my life. He told me, 'Howard, if you want to earn your living painting, you've got to do two things: you've got to get to the Royal College of Art and you've got to become a Royal Academician.' I didn't have a clue what either of them meant, but I took Bob's words to heart and decided that I had to get to the Royal College of Art and become a Royal Academician.

I had another experience at that time which had a profound effect and made me realise that if I was going to do this thing, I had to do it seriously. There was an art shop in Kilburn High Street, right by where the number 16 bus stopped, which I used to go home from school on if I didn't cycle. I very often cycled to school, but it was nice to go by bus now and again if you could afford the bus fare. In the middle of the art shop's window I saw a paintbox. It was mahogany, with a wonderful layout of paints and brushes. I remember that it had canvas boards leaning against the open lid and a wonderful mahogany palette. I used to stand and look at it, promising myself that one day I would have a paintbox like that. But it also had a price tag on it, of course, which said 25 pounds – to me an impossible amount of money. At the time my father, I think, was earning eight pounds a week. I remember going home and telling my mother about this box, but with no intention of saying I wanted it. I just described it to her and said, 'One day, Mum, I'm going to have a box like that!' When I got home a couple of days later my mother said to me, with great understatement, 'There is something for you in the living room, Ken.' I went in – and there on the table was this paintbox. My parents had spent three weeks of my father's wages in order to buy me this box when they had great need of many things in the house, such as furniture, carpets and so on. However, they had gone out of their way and realised how important this was to me. Of course it was.

Although I wasn't a very sporty person, my bike was quite an important part of my life – a simple, quick and cheap way of getting from A to B. It also involved me in a nearly fatal accident when I was at grammar school. It's surprising how, when you look back, you realise how many times in your early life you very nearly died. I was cycling home from school with a friend along the North Circular Road; in those days the traffic was nothing like as heavy. We were talking and suddenly our pedals got interlocked and our two bikes threw us off. My friend toppled on to the pavement at the side of the road, and I went sprawling into the middle, with a lorry not too far behind. I crashed down on the road and the lorry driver swung the wheel over, and I can still remember to this day the wheel as it went past my hair. The lorry driver was too shaken to get out because he was quite convinced that as I had disappeared under the front of his vision, he had driven straight over me. It was a pretty scary experience, made worse by the fact that my sister was on a bus going the other way at the time and immediately told my parents. As a result I was banned from riding along the North Circular for what at that time was 'ever again' – but, of course, that changed with time. It is interesting when you look back how often in one's life a quirk of fate kept you alive. For the sake of another inch or two, one way or the other, I would have been dead at the age of thirteen or whatever it was.

Cycling also took up quite a large part of my holidays. I remember that the first holiday I ever took on my own, with two young friends when we were about twelve, was cycling in Devon. We put our bikes on a train and went down to Exeter, got off there and began to cycle around on Dartmoor. It was strange really that our parents didn't worry more about it, as we were still relatively young.

In 1948, when I was fifteen, I cycled from London to Land's End with two boys from my cycling club. We rode back along the south coast to Southampton, and then back up to London – about 500 miles in all. I remember on the first night we cycled from London to Cheddar Gorge, leaving London at 5 pm and reaching Cheddar for breakfast the next morning. We then carried on and travelled down the north coast of Devon. I remember sleeping out on a rainy, wet night in a field near Bude, and eventually we arrived at Land's End. On the return journey we came across a small Cornish village called Mousehole.

I have to explain that I had no previous connections with the West Country. Both my parents had come from the north, my mother from Edinburgh and my father from Lancashire, and the visits, holidays and even wartime evacuations of my childhood had always been in the north. On arriving at Mousehole, I was struck by what a wonderful little village it was, set around a very picturesque harbour. The village was sacked, along with Penzance and Newlyn, by a Spanish raiding fleet in 1595 – seven years after Spain's ill-fated Armada. No development has been allowed in the middle of the village, so it remains exactly as it was rebuilt after this destruction. Only one house survived the sacking and dates back from pre-Armada times.

As we cycled away from the village we encountered a very steep hill, Paul Hill – too steep even for us teenagers, who were fairly fit and good at cycling – so we started to push our bikes up. On the left we came across what looked like a large chapel or church hall. It was fairly derelict, although people were obviously still living in the main house and making some use of the chapel. Outside the door stood a man who was what I then believed to be the epitome of an artist. He wore a fisherman's smock and had a large white beard. As far as I can remember (although I can't be absolutely certain as I started wearing one later and therefore may be imagining things), he also had a black, Borsalino-type hat, typical of what artists wore in those days. Around this man (I later found out he was Nigel Lamborne) were about half a dozen children; they had beautiful little dresses on, as far as I can

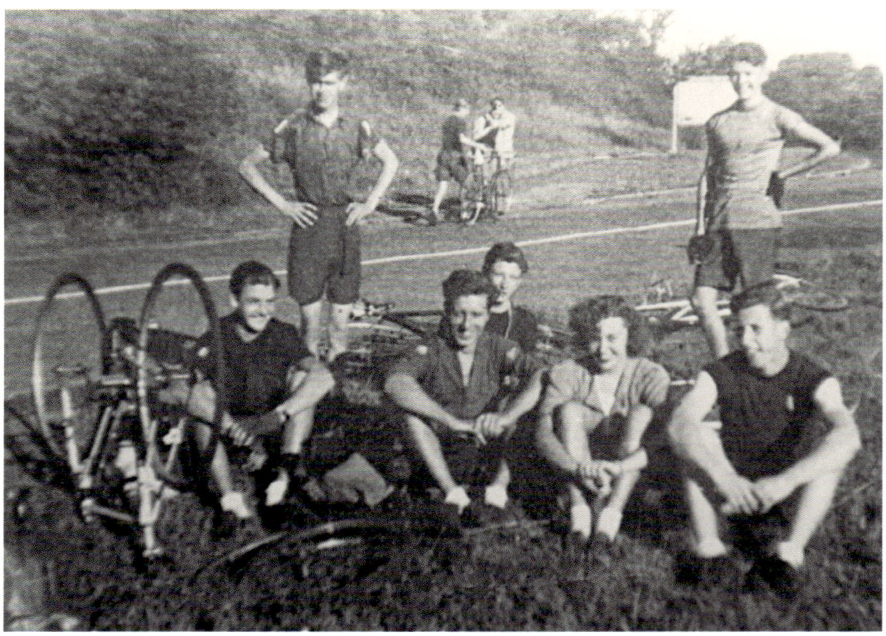

Members of the Willesden Cycling Club on the Watford bypass near Elstree, *c.* 1949. The club held time trials early on Sunday mornings, and the standard was high. Ken Mitchell (far left) went on to race as a professional in Australia, along with Dan Burgess (seated, third from left). Seated second from left is Jimmy Love, a member of the British Olympic team in London in 1948. I am standing on the right, and was not in this league. The only thing I ever won was a first handicap in a ten-mile time trial – not very good.

remember, but no shoes on their feet – it was like a painting by Stanhope Forbes. As we pushed our bikes up the hill and looked at this picturesque scene and peered into the dark depths of the church hall, or village hall perhaps, we realised that it was this man's studio. The ceiling was beginning to collapse and it was in bad repair, but I was fascinated, promising my friends, 'I'm going to be an artist like that one day'. It was before I had gone to art school or been accepted by Hornsey, yet I said that aloud in front of my friends. Many years later I was to buy that self-same studio; it remains my studio to this day.

I've noticed in my life how strange it is that so much happens by accident and coincidence. I think the reason I came to buy a studio there was because my sister married a Mousehole fisherman some years after my first visit. She had been a land girl in Penzance in the war and went on to take up nursing, working at Penzance hospital. At that time she met Bill, her first husband, who was fishing out of Newlyn. My parents came to Cornwall for the wedding and decided to move down there, even though my father wasn't of retirement age. Being a skilled fitter, my father was offered a job at Camborne, in an engineering firm, but when his papers came from London and referred to his union involvement, the job disappeared. They were committed to the move, however, as my father had given up his work in London. To make ends meet he took a job working on the village car park, while my mother served in a local café, and thus they survived.

I visited my parents in Mousehole when they came to live down there and eventually this building came on the market, fortunately at a time when I could afford it. Isn't it strange that I should pass it when I was fifteen and vow that, 'I'm going to be an artist like that one day?' Interestingly I didn't add, 'and I'm going to own that building one day too'.

Another great coincidence happened to me just recently, when I was reviewing a book about William Coldstream. The book spoke a lot about a man called Sam Carter, a former Professor of Perspective at the Slade who eventually became Professor of Perspective at the Royal Academy – the position to which I was appointed in around 2003. As I read the book to prepare my review, it dawned on me that the next-door house in Mousehole, St Clement's Hall (which I had once owned), had been bought recently by a woman in her sixties, with a very old husband. I remembered that his name was Sam, and I then found out that it was Sam Carter himself. So it turned out that I had been appointed Professor of Perspective myself while next door to me, in a house that I had once owned, was living a man who had also been Professor of Perspective at the Royal Academy, two professorships before mine. I had never known Sam Carter, or even heard of him before, and yet by coincidence – out of all the places in England he could have gone to live or where I could have been living – we ended up next door to each other.

Maybe this has got something to do with Cornwall, which is certainly a mysterious place. There's a saying there, 'If you go to live in Cornwall when you are too young, you get pixielated – the pixies get you.' It's all right to go to live in Cornwall when you're older, but although for many it seems a romantic ideal to go and live there, it doesn't necessarily work out when you're young. I always said that the pixies got my parents, and particularly my mother, who, completely out of character, proposed the move to Cornwall in her early sixties. Maybe the pixies had something to do with Sam Carter coming to live at St Clement's Hall, next door to my present studio, St Clement's Studio.

The story of how I became involved with both properties is quite complex. When my father died I bought my parents' cottage from my mother. I gave her a lease for the rest of her life for 1p per year, to give her security, and then carried out major works on the cottage, including the roof. Eventually my mother left Cornwall and went to Hull to live with my sister, against my advice as they had never really got on.

It was at this time that St Clement's Hall, which included the studio, came on the market. The Hall had been the village school and the studio had originally been used for concerts and other performances. As the Hall had a large 'granny flat', my mother agreed to my selling the cottage to finance the purchase of the Hall, which I did in the mid '80s. The wheel had turned full circle, and the studio I had first seen as a boy of fifteen became my West Country place of work. Later I bought the fields around the Hall to prevent development that would have spoiled the village. Many years later I was to sell the Hall, but kept the studio and one of the fields as a garden, building a living area into the studio.

One of my aunts – at least Ina was always known as an aunt, although she wasn't actually the sister of my father or mother – showed me some letters recently which I had written to her when I was quite young, possibly even before grammar school. It was very interesting as all the 'p's, 'd's and 'q's were the wrong way round, every one of them, and obviously I was what these days they call 'dyslexic'. Looking back, I can see various ways in which this showed itself. When I went to grammar school, for example, I loved acting – something not unusual in painters, who often have a penchant for it. I know that Sickert, for instance, initially went on the stage. Yet when I was at grammar school and loved being in the school plays, it was hell to learn the part. I never could. I was always the worst speller in the school, and later, when I was teaching in art schools, the students described me among themselves as the fellow always walking around with a dictionary. (When I had to write reports, I was always looking up the words, even though I was getting on for 30 by this time.) So, obviously, if I had been born today I would have been termed as dyslexic, but when I thought about this I was quite pleased not to have been. If I had been told this I think I would probably have felt a little sorry for myself and made it an excuse for not doing things. However, when I was young no one understood dyslexia; the teachers said I was lazy, and that I must learn to spell, write properly and manage to remember things. And so I did. I can now spell and remember things reasonably well, and I can write reasonably well too.

However, none of these things made my time at grammar school any easier, I must admit. When I got to the Fourth Form, aged fourteen, I decided, against the wishes of my parents and the school, that I wanted to apply for art school early and not do my matriculation. My mother had by this time somewhat mellowed – at least as far as I remember she must have done, because I wasn't refused the chance of doing it. So I went to the art school at Willesden and requested an interview with the head. By this time I had learned all my skills really by copying, both drawings and paintings, learning as I went along. Some of them were quite impressive. I did a copy of *The Laughing Cavalier* by Frans Hals, for example, as one always did in those days, and it was generally accepted as being pretty astonishing. But when I saw the head of the art school, he said, 'Yes, yes, you have got talent, but you've got nothing original here at all. Go away and take your matriculation and then come back. And in that year do something original.'

Naturally I was disappointed. But I went back to grammar school and battled on, finally taking my School Certificate, as the leaving examination was called, in 1949. I managed to get the matriculation required by my mother if I was to go to art school, for which you needed English, Maths, French and two other subjects, apart from Art. The first step had been achieved.

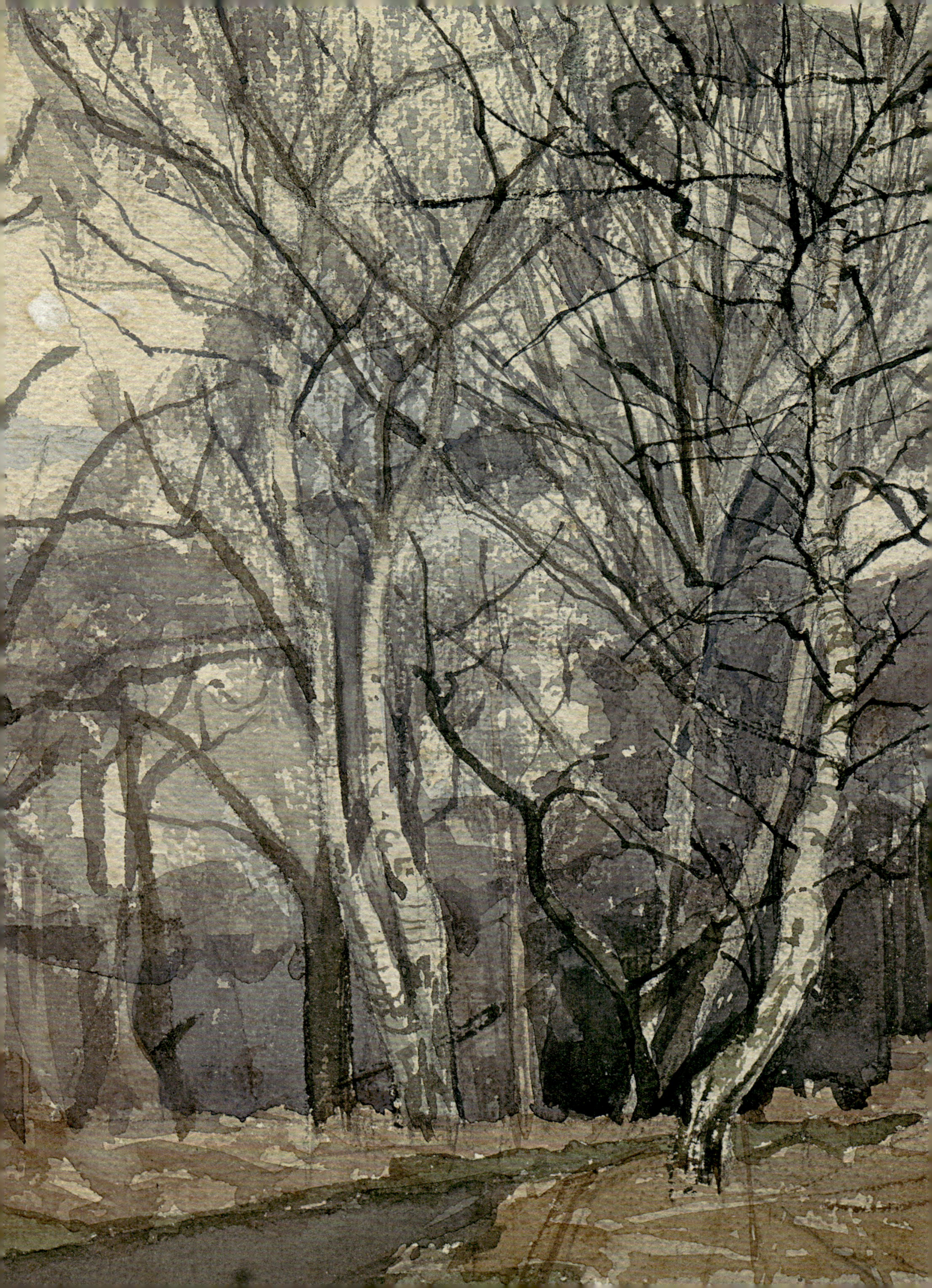

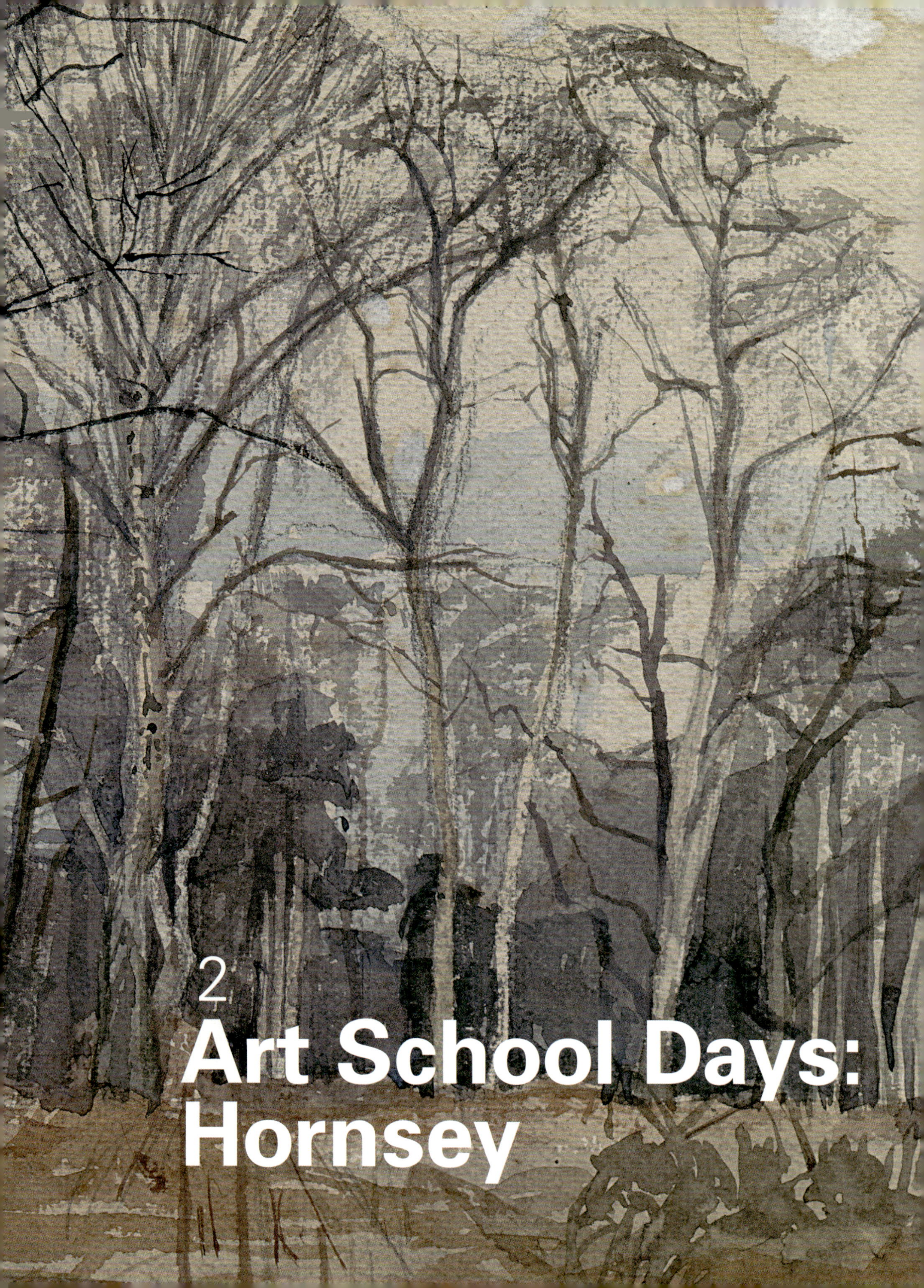

2
Art School Days: Hornsey

Self-portrait, 1952
Oil on canvas, 40 x 30 cm
Royal Academy of Arts, London

While at Hornsey we were set weekend homework and a self-portrait was one such subject. One of my first oil paintings on canvas, it was scraped down with a palette knife. At the time I was very much influenced by the early work of Victor Pasmore. I got to know him many years later when he was elected to the Royal Academy.

I started to live when I was sixteen. I didn't realise it at the time, but once I got to art school it was as if I had come home. For the first time in my life I was really happy – I felt my strength grow and I had success. Although I had a contented childhood, I hadn't particularly enjoyed my years at school. I hadn't been desperately miserable, but I hadn't felt fulfilled or that I was particularly good at anything. In my early teens I had read John Ruskin's *Modern Painters*, in which he said that if a man found what he wanted to do in this life, let him ask no greater blessing. I remember recognising that as true when I read it and realising that I was lucky enough to have found what I wanted to do in this life.

After taking my matriculation I had decided that I didn't really want to go to Willesden. Bob Whitmore, who had by this time become a sort of guru, said that the best art school in London was Hornsey, so I decided to try there. In 1949 I applied for a place at the Hornsey School of Art, presenting a portfolio of work and attending an interview, and was lucky enough to be accepted. It was one of the high points of my life when I received the letter saying I had been awarded a place at an art school.

Art schools then were very different from how they are today. For one thing they were all called schools of art, not colleges of art or parts of universities. They gave Intermediate Certificates and NDDs (National Diplomas in Design) rather than BA or MA degrees, but these were really worth something. When you had gained your Intermediate Diploma you knew that you had a base of drawing, perspective, composition, anatomy – of craft, in essence – and when you studied for your NDD you developed this further. It didn't mean that you were then necessarily an artist. At that time they could almost have called the schools of art 'schools of craft', because that was what they were concerned with teaching.

Hornsey School of Art was situated on Crouch End Hill. It was a Victorian building, like most of the art schools, and had probably been built for the purpose, with high lofty studios. It wasn't particularly big by modern standards – I would say at a guess that there were about 200 students in all, including Intermediate, Diploma and those studying for the Art Teachers' Diploma (ATD). There were then many, many art schools in main cities all over the country, some smaller than Hornsey, established in Victorian times along with libraries, swimming pools, art galleries and parks. They belonged to the era when wealthy Victorians felt that they should provide some cultural and leisure amenities for the working classes, who had earned them so much money at so small a wage.

Later on, of course, following the 1961 Coldstream Report and the recommendations of the Summerson Committee in 1964, some of the smaller

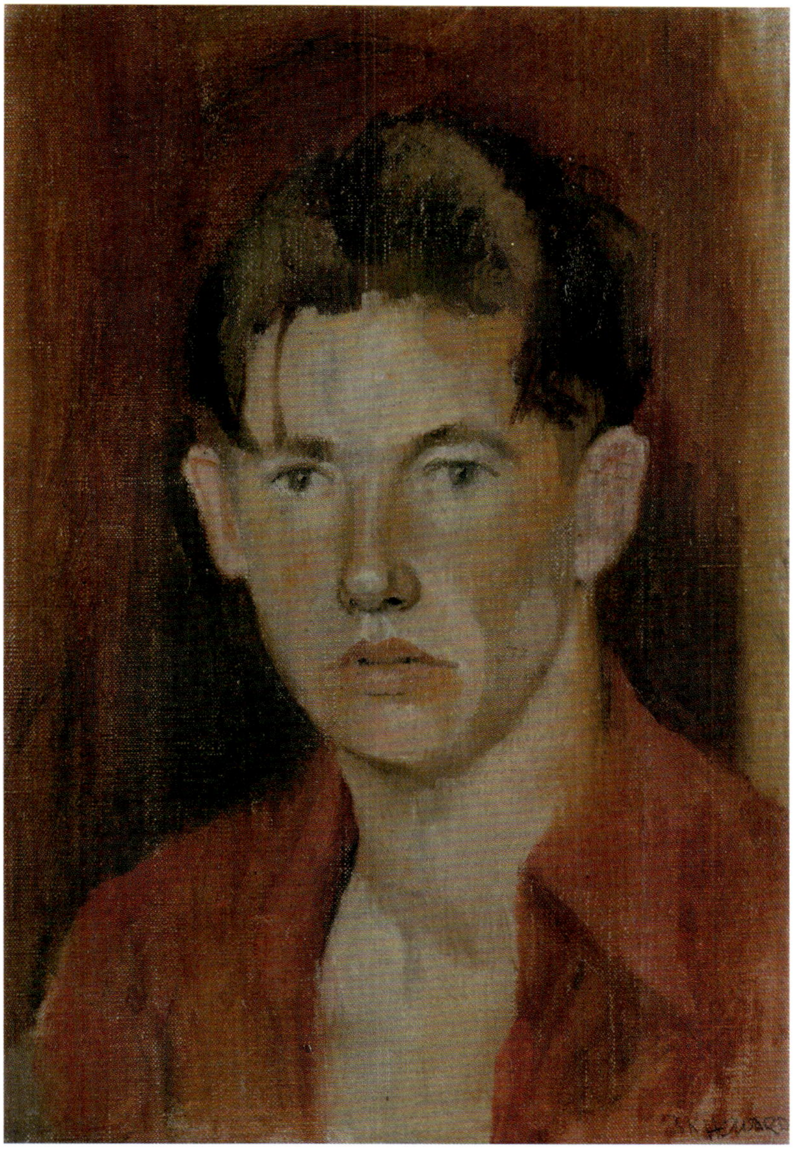

schools closed. A few of the larger ones, such as Hornsey, expanded and became part of Middlesex University. This didn't necessarily improve them as art schools, however. The idea was that there were too many art students with too little work to go to, and therefore their numbers had to be reduced. What happened in effect was that many of the schools were closed and those that remained got the degree course. I believe I am right in saying that there were as many students at the end, but without such a good art-school system as there had been before. The teaching staffs, for example, had in the past been made up of full-time and part-time staff. I don't believe there was much consideration at that time of the actual cost of this. The main thought was what would most benefit the students, and obviously having part-time staff – maybe only teaching two days a week, and doing their own work five days a week – was of great value to students. But the schools also needed full-time members of staff to develop the courses, which were very well organised, so the staff was made up of the two parts. As young students, of course, we didn't really appreciate the staff members who were there. We thought we knew it all and that they were old fuddy-duddies. Years later, for instance, I saw in the Tate one day two beautiful little pictures by a man called Jesse Caste, and I thought, 'Good Lord! I didn't realise that Jesse had work in the Tate.' In the sale rooms I very often saw works come up by people who had taught me at Hornsey, but I had not respected them or realised what fine artists they were. Such is the folly of youth, I suppose.

The first day at Hornsey was an induction day; you came along to sign all your papers, and to be told what the course would be like, and then you came home, returning the next day to start settling down to the nitty-gritty. I must admit I was somewhat disappointed on my first day as I believed, or had at least imagined, that everyone in an art school would look like Augustus John; they would have beards and wear smocks and generally appear very artistic. In reality most people looked like me or like some of the ex-servicemen who were older than I was, but they certainly didn't certainly look like 'artists' – not even the staff. I remember a talk by John Platt, the head of the school, a very good etcher and printmaker who had just come from Harrow School of Art to be head of Hornsey. John Gerald Platt was his full name, but we called him 'JG', and he looked more like a bank manager than an artist. On our first day he called all of the young students about to start at the school into the main studio for a few words. That day he was to say something that has stayed with me forever. He told us, 'Up to now you have been playing at art, you haven't really been serious about it. From now on you are going to eat art, drink art, live art, and your life is going to fit around your art. Your art isn't going to fit around your life. And if you are not willing to accept this fact, you may as well go home now because you are certainly not going to do anything within the arts.' It seemed a little bit severe – it even seemed rather uninspiring at the time, but as time went on I realised that this was true.

In fact such a commitment wasn't to be a negative thing. I firmly believe that life is enriched by having a centre, a core from which everything spreads out. By going to art school I became interested in music, reading, opera, films, all emerging from the centre, my training in drawing and painting at art school.

When we started we were all of differing abilities. At the first life class I attended I sat next to a friend called Bill. I saw immediately that he was a very good draughtsman, and when the teacher came and sat down with him I heard him say, 'Lane, you could take intermediate tomorrow and you would get it.' When he came up to me, by contrast, he sat down, gave me some guidance and just pulled my drawing to pieces. This was with three years to go, and when I looked at Bill's drawing I thought, 'Good Lord! How do I ever approach that sort of quality?'

Yet three years later Bill had not developed his talent. He was dark, he loved the girls and they loved him, and he had not committed himself to his work. Meanwhile those of us who hadn't been very good to begin with, who had needed to work away each day and at evening classes, had gradually developed our abilities. We had moved into the ascendancy, becoming at last, maybe, by the end, the best half-dozen or so students in the school.

After our induction we were given the rest of the day off to wander round the school and look at the departments – the craft department, the drawing studios and the painting studios. Travelling home on the bus I realised that what I had to do above all else was to become as good a draughtsman as the senior students I had seen at work in the life-drawing studios. What I also realised was that I didn't want to paint like any of the senior students who were working in the painting studios. I didn't know why, but I felt sure that what I was looking at wasn't really what I wanted to do. It was what I could only describe as 'art-school art' – not somehow concerned with life, or reality, or all the things that inspired the artists I had begun to be interested in. These were mainly the painters in Spain – Goya, Velázquez, and then those who had followed them and grown out of them, such as Courbet, Corot, Boudin and the Impressionists, and art in England through Sickert. At that very early age (I was still only sixteen) I could see the direction that I wanted to follow. I could also see from the paintings in that room that they had not very much to do with what I thought painting should be about.

I was beginning to realise already that there was a way of seeing. It wasn't necessarily concerned with wanting to put things on walls. It was a way of communicating with yourself via the visual world around you. This way of seeing, and expressing it in paint, must be the key attached to everything that I was going to do. I remember when I was teaching in an art school years later someone asked me, 'Why are you teaching them drawing when they now have cameras?' My reply was short: 'If you can't see the difference between drawing from nature and copying a photograph, you shouldn't be in an art school.' It was fairly soon after that experience that I resigned from teaching.

After my first day in Hornsey, sitting on the 210 bus going from Archway to Golders Green, I also saw very clearly that the one thing I had to find was my own language. Having looked at the paintings in the painting school I realised that there was an 'art-school language' that didn't seem to have much to do with a personal language. I knew the latter was one thing I must find, so that when people saw my paintings, they would say, 'Ah, that's a painting by Ken Howard' – not 'Ah, that's a painting derived from somebody else' or 'Ah, that's a painting describing some particular subject.' The most important thing, I reflected, was finding your own form of expression, your own language that was important to you. It didn't have to be extremely radical, nor should it be extremely derivative. Outside influences had to be put aside; you only had to search within yourself for your own language. Maybe your language wasn't going to change the face of European painting, or the course of any other art form. If you were going to do that, I realised it was in you and you could do it anyway. The main thing, and the hardest, was that you had to find that language.

This did not have to be dramatically innovative, and such was never my ambition. I remember when I was teaching at Harrow School of Art the Senior Lecturer commented one day, 'Howard, you are the oldest young man I've ever known!' Without thinking, I retorted, 'Ah, yes, Ivor – but I'll be the youngest old man you've ever known!' Unfortunately Ivor died several years ago, so I don't know what his feeling would have been now or whether he would have agreed with me that I was the youngest old man. Clearly he believed in a radical approach, and he certainly was an innovative person, but in the end, when one looks back over the whole period, his work did little. It isn't around any more and certainly didn't change any way of seeing anything. The other thing that I had begun to appreciate was that the word 'freedom' was in my mind, which I didn't really understand as yet. I just knew that initially I had to find a freedom in my work, a natural form of expression. I had the sense that it would have to come through in time.

When I went to Hornsey School of Art in 1949, the students broke down into two distinct groups. The first, and the largest, consisted of sixteen-year-old boys and girls who had come straight from grammar and other schools. In those days there was no demand that you had to have GCEs, GCSEs and goodness knows what. The only thing the school selectors were interested in was whether you had a talent, and whether it came out in the interview that you had the right attitude to be at an art school. It helped, of course, if you had matriculated or had the School Certificate because the staff knew that you could use your skills in a teaching job later.

At the other end of the spectrum were the more mature students who had just come out of the services. This was 1949 and National Service was still in operation, producing a group of students who had small grants to enable them to carry on with their studies after they finished their service. I, of course, had also managed to get a small grant because my father's wage was very low. I received the massive amount of £1.40 a week, which now sounds ludicrous but was quite a lot of money at the time. If you think that probably people were earning, with a bit of luck, about £10 a week, then £1.40 was quite a reasonable amount for a student. I imagine that the people who were ex-service received a higher amount because several of them were already married and had children. I paid my parents part of my £1.40 a week to live at home because they needed the money to keep the family going.

It made a very dynamic mixture, at least a very dynamic one for us youngsters, because here were men with far more experience. Although they were only five or six years older than us, they seemed to be extremely mature; they knew how to work hard and play hard and that rubbed off on us. They also seemed to be more advanced intellectually than us and had developed more interesting ideas than we boys and girls who had just come from grammar school.

There were about thirty people in the year, approximately ten boys and about twenty girls. Somehow it was more acceptable then for a girl to go to art school than for a boy who had a living to earn and for whom art school didn't seem to be a good route. In fact I seem to remember that the girls were very often much more talented than the boys. I have often believed that women, by their very nature, their very personality, are in fact more suited to the arts than men, but the boys had much more drive, I suppose. They were hungrier and competitive, aware that this was serious business because at the end they had to make a living out of it. Therefore, it was usually the boys who went on to the Royal College of Art rather than the girls, although girls did too.

Art school also had a profound effect on me because, for the first time, I made close friends with people with similar interests. I realise that when I was younger I was quite influenced by the people with whom I worked, or lived, or studied, or went to school, and it would have been easy to go down several lines in my life. Art school immediately introduced me to like-minded people who were interested in similar things – a love of music, cinema, reading and the arts generally – and therefore I followed a certain direction. I have stayed friends with several of my contemporaries at art school, although my closest friend is in fact Brian Harper, a friend from grammar school. I met Brian again later on in my life whilst we were both doing National Service. He had become a cartographer for the Admiralty, and in fact provided me with one of my early introductions to classical music, in the form of Mahler's *First Symphony*. We formed a close friendship which has lasted for more than 50 years, and I am godfather to his daughter (who also went to art school).

Fairly soon four of us boys bonded together. There were two Johns, John Hunter and John Alcock, plus Douglas Merrett and myself. We started doing things together as a group, and in a way we stayed together for the rest of our lives. Johnny Alcock was a very talented boy who went to the Royal College of Art. He had everything going for him when he suddenly began to develop mental problems

This photograph, taken after I finished studying in around 1961, features many of my friends from my student days. It includes Annie Popham, who became my first wife (centre row, in the striped dress), and myself to the rear, grinning broadly in a dark suit with my hand on a Roman cast head. People commented at that time that I was always smiling.

and tragically took his own life when he couldn't have been more than about 24 or 25. Johnny Hunter, with whom I am still in touch, had a tragic time early on in his life; he married young, but his wife died of cancer after she became pregnant with their first child. Douglas had come to art school initially because he was in love with a girl who was going to art school. She eventually took up with another boy, but Douglas carried on, although he had originally wanted to become an actor, and became an extremely good graphic designer. He went to the Royal College of Art and had a very colourful career, working on graphic design in a large television company. He had a fairly varied personal life, first marrying a very good friend and then divorcing, followed by two unsuccessful marriages. Eventually he met the girl he'd gone to art school to be with right at the very beginning. She was also on her own by that time, and they have lived together ever since. I'm sure such things happen in groups of people from all walks of life, and in fact the evolving dynamics of groups could provide interesting material for books and films. The four of us stayed close during our formative art-school years, and a strain of friendly rivalry grew between us. We fairly soon discovered that we all wanted to try to get to the Royal College of Art, and it helped that we stimulated each other and made each other work – the sight of one of us going to lots of evening classes made the others feel that they should go as well. So we helped and encouraged each other, building a very good friendship between us.

Art-school life, of course, was very different in those days. It seems hard to believe that in 1949 we still got a report at the end of each term which said such things as, 'more quality and less quantity might be a good thing' or 'needs to concentrate more'. Sometimes there would be positive remarks which, of course, inspired you to go on. And it's strange how all my life has reflected that. I have always been someone who produces a very large amount of work because of what interests me in life and my love of changing things. Of course my detractors would say I should produce less, and that there should be more thought and consideration behind it. (I would counter that the great painters I admire, such as Goya, Turner, Monet, all produced very large quantities of work.) The art schools had very active societies and, as I said earlier, the fact that one's life is centred around one's art actually makes life richer – you became interested in so many things as spin-offs. We had a film society where we showed all the early French and Italian realist films; I remember *Bicycle Thieves* long before it hit the main circuits, and a wonderful Jacques Tati film called *Jour de fête*, which eventually became a French classic. We also had music clubs and debating groups, and we even formed a jazz group (much to the disgust of the head of the school, whose initial response to our request

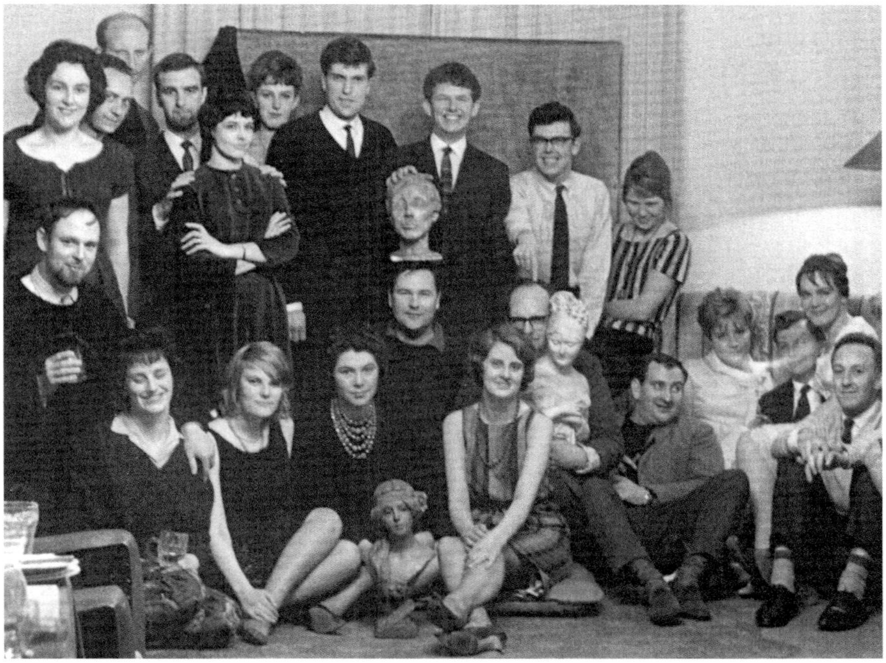

was to call all the students together and proclaim, 'I won't have that muck played in my school.') Nevertheless, he relented and we had our jazz club. Still, the whole temperature, the whole feeling of the art school was, of course, different to what it would be now. There was a strict code of discipline on timekeeping, for example. Even though many of the older students had been on National Service in the Army or the Air Force, and were now married or whatever, John Platt stood at the top of the steps every morning. To any student coming up the steps even half a minute after ten o'clock, he would say, 'If you come to my school, be on time. And if you are late again tomorrow, you can leave.' It was as simple as that. Probably no head could do that today, but then one accepted the discipline, and you were sure to be there at five to ten at the latest the next day.

One of the most active clubs in the school was, of course, the sketch club – a means by which one could show work after the holidays. You were always expected to produce a body of work when you weren't at school, during the holidays, weekends, evenings and so forth. After the main summer holidays there would be a sketch-club exhibition. Everyone put up his or her work in the main studio and an outside critic would come along and spend Saturday afternoon criticising the work.

I seem to remember they were a distinguished group of people. John Berger, then a young art critic and now a very eminent writer, came along and gave us some criticism; I remember he was one of the first critics who ever encouraged me. Others, such as Ruskin Spear, a very good, young, up-and-coming painter, Carel Weight, who was to become Professor of Painting at the Royal College of Art, and the future Royal Academician Robert Buhler used to come along to do these 'crits'. They did in fact go on to the staff at the Royal College of Art, so it sometimes helped at interview that you had come from Hornsey as they were slightly familiar with what you had done.

Parents often came along as well on these Saturday afternoons, which seems very strange now. But they came and listened to the criticism of their sons' and daughters' work – not easy, as these critics were often very hard on us. There wasn't very much of, 'oh, that's nice'. They did very thorough criticisms, taking at least two and a half to three hours going around the work, and at the end the president of the sketch club would have to thank them for their 'very informative crit'. I remember there was once at the sketch club a very large painting by the sketch-club president, then in his last year and widely considered the best painter in the school. His work was probably no more than about 120 cm squared, but in those days it seemed enormous – most of us worked on a fairly modest scale, partly because of the expense, but also believing that something did not necessarily have to be big to be good.

The critic that afternoon was Barnett Freedman, a printmaker and lithographer who was very well-known through the prints he used to have in Lyons Tea Shops all over London at that time. Lyons had been innovative enough to commission good artists to do lithographs and prints for its tea shops, and likewise I became involved doing work for the Post Office, including drawings for its telephone directories (see page 164). Barnett came along and gave a very thorough crit. When he came to this massive canvas in the middle he passed it by and went down all the other pictures. We all believed that he was keeping it to the end because it was the best picture in the exhibition. At the very end of his criticism, however, he walked back to this painting and stood contemplating it for a few minutes. Eventually he turned to the audience and all he said was, 'I only hope this man can play the piano!' It was damning. I don't suppose you could get away with it these days. You would be done for psychological damage or whatever, but in those days you just took it on the chin. As we trained we began to gain enough strength to take that sort of criticism, and then to build on it or try and understand why he said it.

As always when you belonged to such institutions, you finished up running these various groups. I myself became secretary of the sketch club – though fortunately I didn't get quite such a damning report or damaging crit the final time that I showed.

In 1949, of course, we art-school students were interested in what we felt to be – and at the time was – modern art, not on a parochial or English-leaning basis, but including such artists as Stanley Spencer, Gwen John, Whistler, Sickert and, from an American standpoint in those days, people like Ben Shahn. They were social realists and social realism was one of the main movements of the time. It interested us very much, living as we did in industrial north London. And it was really this movement that first made me interested in working in the industrial scene. Obviously a painter paints the life that he is experiencing at the time, and my life then was very definitely based in industrial north London. It was a world of railway sidings, water coolers, power stations and people – little figures rushing off to work. In a way it was a southern equivalent of the northern, Lancashire landscapes of L. S. Lowry.

Also at that time, a movement in England called the Kitchen Sink school was just beginning to happen. It featured such artists as John Bratby and Edward Middleditch, Derrick Greaves and Jack Smith – powerful young painters just out of the Royal College of Art. They were still fairly near to us, and we looked to them for inspiration, rushing into town to see them if there was an exhibition on. Another very strong element was composed of our more avant-garde members of staff, in whom we were interested from a more British point of view really, as some of them were Scots. And there was also a sort of postwar romantic movement, including such people as John Minton and John Craxton, and the Scottish painters Robert Colquhoun and Robert McBride. William Scott, although he didn't fit into that movement, was another painter we looked to and were influenced by, and, of course, there was Lucian Freud. He seemed very young to us, though he must have been in his late twenties, but he was already beginning to make his mark, albeit in a completely different style to how we think of his work today. It was much more refined, analytical, drawing-based. (His work these days is just as much drawing-based as then, but it was a different style.) I remember clearly the paintings he was then doing of Francis Bacon and Johnny Minton – quite astonishing portrait works for a man as young as that.

This was all very, very new to me, coming from a background where there was little art around at home and at grammar school, though we had been encouraged much more along the lines of the great historical paintings of Velázquez, Raphael, Rembrandt and Goya. This was all new, and very exciting. I can remember when there were evening classes to attend, we would leave the school when the main classes finished at four and dash into town to see a show by Craxton and Minton, then rush back to the class and try, I suppose, to use what we had seen there in own our work. I remember one day racing back to the school afterwards; I didn't have an evening class, but I got a girl from our class to take off her shoes and sit for me barefoot. I tried to draw her feet in the style of John Craxton, who at that time was doing these rather large, beautifully drawn feet on the models that he was drawing and painting.

I suppose that it was a little bit naïve in the way that we were influenced, but it was exhilarating and made you feel very much alive. Of course, on a more international level, we were encouraged to be interested in Picasso and Braque and the whole of that French movement. There was even at that time something called the Ecole de Paris, with a young painter in it called Bernard Buffet, who turned out eventually to produce very prosaic, repetitive work. He made an enormous amount of money from it, but in the 1940s he was still hungry, living in a garret in Paris, I imagine, and doing work that spoke of this style. Buffet suffered for his work, which was very intense, and we would rush to the galleries to see if there was anything by him or other painters from the Ecole de Paris.

As for myself, I had already, in a strange sort of way, realised where I wanted to go with my painting. So for me, although I was excited by them, and to a degree did work in a school that was influenced by them, Picasso, Braque and Matisse did not reflect the direction I wanted to go in. I was rather following the line of Cézanne, Degas and Manet, and before that of Corot and Courbet.

One member of staff in particular was very forward-looking. He said to me one day, 'Howard, what you are doing is a complete waste of time. Cézanne said the last word on what you are trying to do, so you may as well start all over again; go out and buy yourself some books, or borrow some books, on Picasso and Braque and begin to think in a different way.' And I looked at him and replied, 'Sir (for that's what we called our members of staff), this is the way I want to paint and this is the way I am going to paint,' and I just carried on doing what I wanted to do. I suppose that's been the story of my life, and that's probably why I have sometimes been heavily criticised by critics.

On the other hand, I think I found a way of seeing that in a strange way has given me a very large public following. I was from the beginning very much a tonal painter. My inspiration came from the Neasden sidings where it was all very much black and white – literally black and white. I remember a member of staff at Hornsey told me, in my second year, 'Howard, you've got no sense of colour whatsoever. You must go down to Spain this summer and paint there, and you will learn something about colour and then come back.' Being a good student I hitchhiked down to Spain, and I worked down there for six weeks. I remember the whole six weeks cost me only £25, including the hitchhiking down to Spain. Unfortunately, when I got back I was painting even more in black and white than when I had gone away, so the trip hadn't produced the results they were looking for.

Working as I did, in the industrial atmosphere of northwest London, I now learned one of my first big lessons. I was painting on Neasden sidings one morning before going to art school (I've always been an early starter) and as I sat there a railwayman was going along to his shed to pick up his train back to Birmingham, or somewhere else – I think the LNER was the line at the time. He stopped and watched me paint. After about five minutes he leaned over and said, 'Sonny, I've walked across this railway yard for 30 years, and for the first time this morning I can see that it is beautiful.' That touched me very deeply. I realised that one of the things I wanted to do in my painting was reveal the world to people, to make others see the world in my terms and to perceive things that they normally wouldn't see. They thought they saw it, they thought they knew what it looked like, and then the artist comes along and expresses his particular vision, enabling them to see it in his terms.

This question of revelation has been with me ever since. Some years later I went to the Tate Gallery to see an exhibition of Whistler's work. I managed to get in early, I can't think now how I did it, but I did, and I went round the exhibition and looked at everything very thoroughly. At ten o'clock the doors were opened and the crowds came in. I suddenly realised that everyone was wearing clothes resembling those in Whistler paintings. When I looked again they were all adopting Whistler poses; then again, and they were forming into Whistler compositions. There were rectangular pictures on the wall with these dark figures standing in front of them. Then, of course, I appreciated that they weren't – they were just ordinary people of the time, wearing contemporary clothes, but after looking at the Whistlers for half an hour I had begun to see the world in his terms; everything in the room seemed to fit into Whistler's image of the world. Once again he had revealed the world to me in his terms.

On another occasion I remember going to the Whitechapel Gallery to see an enormous exhibition of Hockney's work. It was soon after he had become very well-known, sometime in the 1960s after he left the Royal College of Art. When I came out of this exhibition I went into a coffee house for a cup of coffee. It was all chrome, plastic, linoleum and mirrors; I looked around me and thought, 'Why have I never painted somewhere like this before?' Then I suddenly realised that the reason why I had never seen it before as I was seeing it that day was that I had never been looking at Hockney's pictures before. Hockney's vision had revealed this coffee place to me. Three or four days later I had returned to seeing the world in my own terms, though maybe slightly changed by the experience. For me the revelation of showing the world, seeing the world, in a different way is in part I think what painting should be about.

Another instance is the trip to Spain when I was sent to find colour and lived in a simple way for six weeks on £25. I remember I stayed in the Pensión del Principe, near the Puerta del Sol in Madrid. I was with Johnny, one of my four friends from Hornsey, and it seemed wonderful: one shilling and nine-pence for full board –

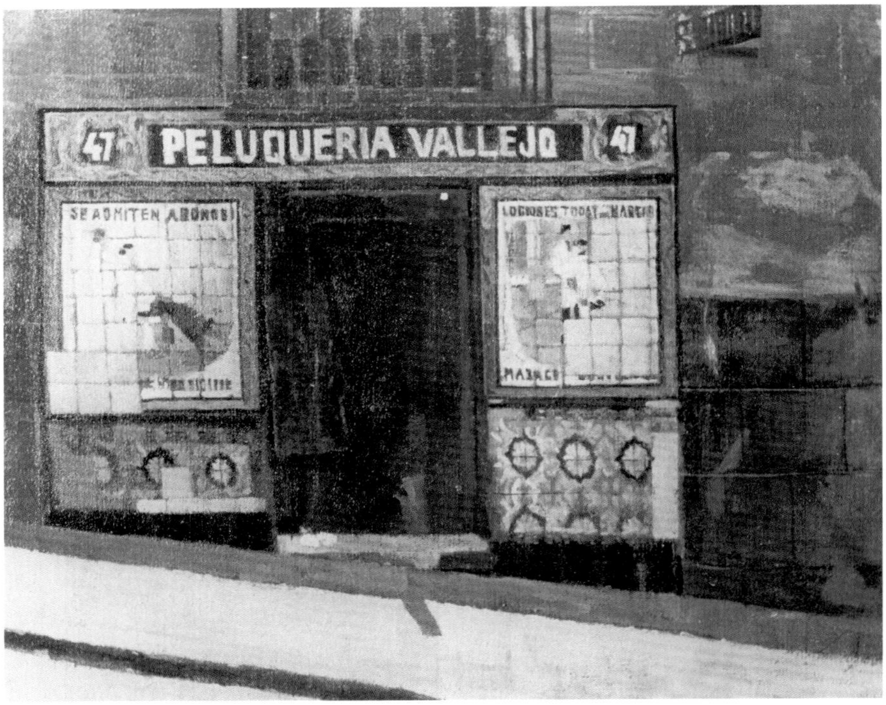

breakfast, an evening meal and a room. As often happens in Spain or Italy, the lady who worked in this *pensión* was obviously the daughter of the family and was never going to get married. She had a moustache, I think, and I seem to remember that one of her legs was shorter than the other, giving her a permanent limp when she walked.

Years later, when I was first married, we went to Madrid. I thought I must show my new young wife the Pensión del Principe where I had been so happy all those years before, but when we went along it was dreadful. It was dirty, the rooms were incredibly basic and the food wasn't very good. I think we stayed one night and then moved on, but in my days as a student it seemed all that I needed when I was travelling – and, of course, at 1/9d a day it was affordable.

Johnny and I worked in Madrid most of the time, painting things such as *peluquerías* – hairdressers' shops – where one would sit out on the street and look through the open doors at the hairdresser working on his customers. I remember the shops were usually surrounded by wonderful ceramic tiles, which fitted in well those days to our concept of a form of social realism. We painted donkeys against dark walls where you had to spot the donkeys, as it were, and various other realist subjects around Madrid. Some years later I bought one of the pictures back in a sale room. I had originally sold it for five pounds, but it cost me something like £600 to get it back.

Spain was a treasure trove for me in many ways. The black paintings and etchings of Goya, *Las Meninas*, the Velázquez portraits, the work of Zurbarán and El Greco all provided very exciting influences. I remember going down to the back streets of Madrid and finding a Goya etching, albeit one that had been scored after a complete set of prints had been taken, but nevertheless still a very fine print of one of *The Disasters of War* – and I couldn't afford it. It was 25 shillings, but that was more than I could afford; it was a very different world in those days. I remember going to the Prado and wanting to see *The Disasters of War* and particularly the *Caprichos* of Goya, by this time one of my great heroes and influences. Even in 1949 you had to ask to see the *Caprichos* as they were considered politically dangerous, and probably *The Disasters of War*, too, and the various other series of etchings that Goya did.

Johnny and I eventually left Madrid and went down to Barcelona. We'd been painting in the shadows, as one had to in Spain because it was so hot and you would just burn up, so we hitchhiked down to Barcelona and decided that before we returned to England we would have one day on the beach. We buried our money belts among our clothes in our wardrobe and went on to the beach. The next day we left our hotel and hit the road. After a while we decided we needed some money and went to our money belts, which we hadn't checked before leaving, to discover that both of us had been robbed. The thieves had very cleverly left just a few pesetas in each belt so we didn't immediately realise when we checked out, 'Good Lord, my money belt's empty.' We therefore had very little money, and although we had planned to hitchhike home, we still needed at least enough to get some meals along the road.

We got over the border at Perpignan and started to hitchhike along towards Avignon to get the main road up to Paris. Unfortunately, it was the day after some murders in the area – I think a French farmer had murdered a family called Drummond – which made hitchhiking in that area impossible. It was all over the news and for a couple of days we couldn't pick up any lifts. Johnny, perhaps a bit more imaginative than me, started to panic that we would never get home. I had on me about the equivalent of 3s 6d and he had the same, so I told him to take my money. 'You get a train along to Avignon, then you'll be able to go to the British Embassy and borrow enough money to pay for your train to get home.' He did this, but I didn't tell him what money I was left with – it was very, very little.

I remember clearly that day hitchhiking or walking along the road and getting together with another hitchhiker. I had half a French baguette and he had a couple of eggs. As we talked, we decided we needed to eat something and discussed what we had between us. We sat down and made a meal, drinking the eggs warm from the shell through a pinhole and dividing the baguette in half. We became close friends, and then walked again for the afternoon.

Eventually I arrived in Avignon at the big crossroads at the main road going up to Paris, and stationed myself by a tree to try and pick up a lift. Both the tree and

Peluquería, 1952
Oil on canvas, 51 x 61 cm

I made this oil study in a back street of Madrid during my visit in 1952, when I was still a student at Hornsey. Like many shops in Madrid, this hairdresser's was covered in wonderful ceramic tiles.

Street Scene, Madrid, 1952
Oil on canvas, 51 x 61 cm

One of my first paintings inspired by light. I painted this canvas in situ in a hot, sunny Madrid street during my visit in 1952, when I was 20. There were roadworks going on in the foreground, which was my initial reason for choosing the subject.

the wall alongside were inscribed with terrible stories like 'I waited here five days without getting a lift' or 'I was stuck here for three days without a lift.' I in my turn was very lucky; a car pulled up and I got in. When we were halfway to Paris the driver stopped for a meal. Of course I had no money, so when the man asked me to join him in the restaurant I had to say no, I wasn't hungry. In fact I was starving, and he said again, 'You must be hungry', which I again denied. He began to get annoyed, saying, 'Look, I've been civil enough to give you a lift. The least you can do is to eat lunch with me.' So I had to explain that I was penniless and I couldn't pay for my own lunch, and he was really upset that I had thought that he was asking or expected me to pay for my meal. So he stood me this great lunch and we talked all the way to Paris. When we arrived he dropped me off and thrust the equivalent of five pounds towards me as I was about to get out of the car. I tried to refuse, saying he had already been too generous, but he chased me along the pavement and forced me to take it. He told me that if I was ever in Paris again, I should come and visit him in his shop on the rue de Berri. Some years later I did visit him when I was in Paris, at his small shop that sold shirts. I remember that he closed it and took me out to lunch – a really warm, wonderful man.

Finally on that trip I got a lift out of Paris with a rather formal Englishman. When I got in, he started to ask me what I did. I replied that I was studying, getting the sense that he thought I should have a proper job. He asked me what I was studying and to avoid telling him 'painting' I said, 'I'm studying the arts.' 'What does that mean – languages and so forth?' So in the end I had to come out with it. 'No, in fact, I'm studying painting.' He really went to town on me about studying something that was useless and goodness knows what – so much so that I was tempted to ask him to stop the car and let me get out. However, I was desperate to get to Calais and I already had my return ticket to get across the Channel. 'Well, I've got to stay in this car,' I thought, so I started to answer him back. I remember giving him, in my very idealistic way, my whole attitude towards the arts and their value to society. I was young and idealistic, but I had a strong political sense and in the end he listened to me. When we got to Calais he stopped and took me into a restaurant where he stood me a big meal. Then he said to me, 'You know, young man, I've never really thought about the arts until today. Now you have made me think about them in a completely different way, and I thank you for it.' For several years after that he always sent me Christmas cards. Unfortunately, typical of youth, I never kept his address, as it would have been lovely to have sent him an invitation to one of my exhibitions a few years later. It was nevertheless a nice experience, and one that I remembered warmly for many years.

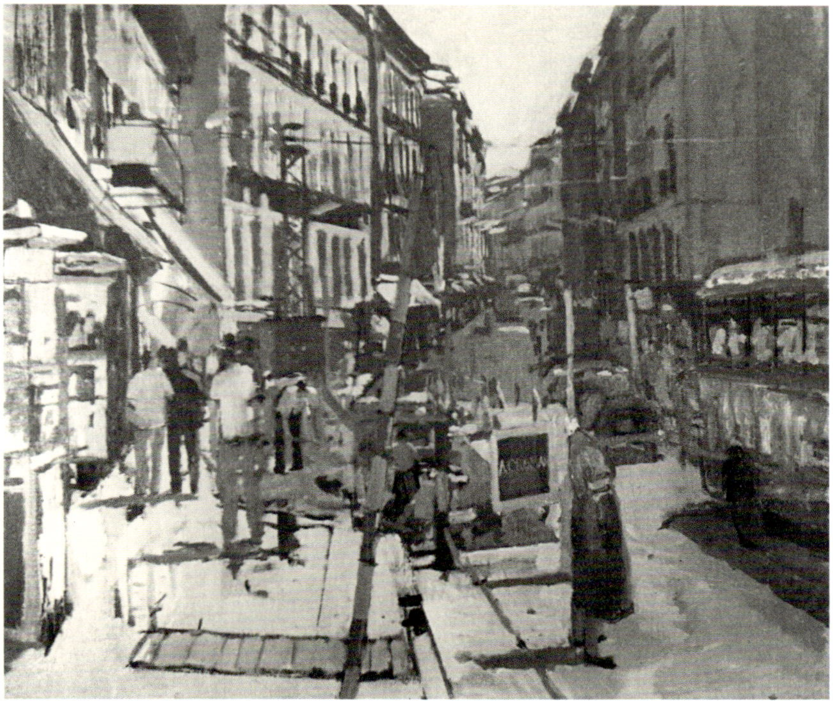

In those days the ticket you bought took you across the Channel and on to a train to Victoria station. I had sent my parents the odd postcard, but not many, yet for some reason my mother and father were there waiting for me when the train drew in to Victoria. They must have known – or guessed, my memory is slightly unclear now – what train I was coming on. As I walked along the platform my mother suddenly burst into tears, saying, 'Oh Lord, you must never travel like that again.' And I realised, belatedly, that my lips were covered in sores caused by the sun and my skin was badly burned. I suppose I must have looked rather a mess, but I hadn't appreciated that at the time. Unhelpfully, I told her that it had been a wonderful six weeks and I wanted to travel again as soon as possible.

I recognised early on at Hornsey that I thought art should be about revelation. The next thing I realised was that in the work I was doing I was concerned with the celebration of life. I loved industrial north London, I loved the power stations with the men pouring out at the end of the day. I loved the railway sidings, the cooling towers, the terraced houses – all of which, of course, were in tune with what was going on at the time, such as the Kitchen Sink school and Edward Middleditch's paintings of Sheffield and the northern towns.

I knew that one could celebrate this sort of environment just as much as a conventionally beautiful scene. Later on, for instance, I worked a lot in Venice and on the beaches of Cornwall – much more obvious landscapes to be celebrated. But the paintings of north London were full of life and drama. I remember some years later I had a show at the same time as an old Academician with whom I was teaching (who is unfortunately no longer with us). My work was based on paintings that I had done at Southall sidings, and my colleague asked, 'Why are you exhibiting those paintings of Southall sidings? Nobody will want them.' I replied that I didn't care, I loved Southall sidings at that moment and that's what I was painting. 'You should be painting gardens,' he said. 'People love gardens and they buy paintings of them.' We both had our shows and I sold all of my paintings of Southall sidings, whereas he sold three or four of his gardens. However, I have to admit that his paintings were considerably more expensive than mine.

If art can be about celebration, I think it can also be about love, and I had realised by then that I really only wanted to paint things that I loved, that I really reacted to. I didn't want to create paintings because people wanted them or because they would sell easily or anything like that. But this is, of course, one of the problems when, later on, you no longer have your teaching, or perhaps can no longer rely on your situation. If you are living entirely by your paintings, there is always the temptation, I suppose, to repeat things because they are popular. I've certainly always tried not to do this, although my detractors would probably say I have. I haven't consciously done it, any more than Monet did when he painted his series of Rouen Cathedral and of the haystacks – even though some critics foolishly said he was painting them because they were commercial. The reality was nothing of the sort. He painted those scenes to show that every moment of every day is different; you could paint one subject for the rest of your life and interpret it in a different way each time. I sometimes wish now, looking back, that I had just taken one subject for the whole of my life and pursued it over the decades. But, of course, it's all very well realising that after many, many years of painting.

Through my constant work at Hornsey and by mixing with other people, I was beginning to resolve what I thought my work should really be about. I had already decided that I needed to find a language, and was seeking to find whatever those elusive words 'freedom' and 'spontaneity' were about. I had realised that my work should be about revelation and celebration. The other thing I was discovering was that I wanted my work to speak to people directly, not with ambiguity, so that when they looked at one of my paintings it communicated with them.

As the months went by at Hornsey School of Art I felt my strengths develop. Life was full. I got up every morning longing to get on my bike and cycle to Hornsey to start another day with the work and the friends and all the experience of being at art school. I even felt at last that I was really living, and fairly soon I began to see my goal. Bob Whitmore had told me that if I wanted to earn a living painting, I had to do two things: get to the Royal College of Art and become a Royal Academician. Although I hadn't appreciated at the time what it meant, now I was beginning to understand. I realised that getting to the Royal College of Art was extremely important. There you would come up against the best students in the country, see the work that they were doing and be pushed along yourself.

Each year at Hornsey there was talk of which final-year students were applying to the College, and of who was going to get in and who wasn't. It's worth remembering that back in the early 1950s there were only three postgraduate schools in England: the Royal College of Art, the Slade and the Royal Academy Schools. I believe it was a very good system because it brought together under one roof the best talents in those three schools. There are now so many postgraduate schools spread throughout the country that there is a little bit of talent here, a little bit of talent there, but no big pool for students to come together and spark off each other. And for me this stimulus was the great advantage of the earlier form of the art-school system.

For some reason the Royal College of Art was the one that we all went to. It was the one that we all wanted to get to, the one in which probably the 30 best students from the art schools round England would finally band together and spark off each other. The Slade was also a very desirable school, with a very high reputation purely from the point of view of fine art, whereas the Royal College had a reputation across the board in the crafts, in the applied arts as well as the fine arts. But still, it was the fine arts that we looked to the College for. The third choice, the Royal Academy Schools, was very definitely third – if you couldn't get into the Slade or the College, you tried to get in there. In retrospect I made a mistake – I wish I had gone for the Royal Academy Schools rather than the Royal College, but when you are young you are swept along on the general belief that there is one place you have to get to. And, of course, it was true that one did connect with some of the best creative people in the country there.

Gradually Hornsey was becoming my whole life. When I got up in the morning I was desperate to get there. We didn't start until 10 am, but the school was a seven-mile cycle ride away and I would very often go to some of my favourite subjects before starting the main ride. For example, I often went to paint in Neasden for an hour or so before starting off, or in Cricklewood, another very inspiring subject.

The days at Hornsey were long. We started at 10 am, but then when the main classes had finished, I believe it was at 4 pm, we would stay on for evening classes. There were life-drawing classes for part-time students every evening, which we could also go to and draw if we wished. So it very quickly got to the stage that one was attending five evening classes a week, on top of those in the day. On Saturday mornings we usually went into London to do what in those days was called outdoor drawing; we would work in markets such as the old Covent Garden, or Smithfield, or the fish market at Billingsgate. In those days, as I say, this was called 'outdoor' drawing, but later on the great terminology discussions turned it into 'environmental studies'. To me it was always outdoor drawing, and when I go out to make studies, I still think of it in those terms.

When evening class finished, at 9 pm, I would quickly get on my bicycle and head for Archway Hill. I knew that every evening a lorry would go up the hill at about 9.20, and I knew that this lorry, which must have been working for a regular firm, would take me round by the North Circular Road. I used to get into its slipstream and peddle like mad, and the lorry would suck me along right round the North Circular through Staples Corner. I would then drop off it and get to my house. I know it was foolish when I think back, but fortunately nothing ever happened and it made the ride home at the end of a long day at the art school much easier. Once I got home my mother would have a large meal ready for me, because naturally I hadn't eaten much during the day.

Money was tight. I paid some of my £1.40 a week to my parents to live at home, and augmented what little was left by getting a job on Friday night and Saturdays. For a long time I worked at the Dewhurst's butcher's shop on the North Circular, where I was paid ten shillings for the Friday night and Saturday and another ten shillings in tips for delivering the meat on a Saturday afternoon, on one of those old butcher's bikes with a large basket at the front over a small wheel. They weren't easy to ride and the area where I had to deliver was quite hilly, but at the end of the Friday night and Saturday I had another pound on top of my grant. It made a difference.

Jobs like that went on right through my studies. I've had a vast range of experience, from being an assistant in a greengrocer's shop for some time to a nightwatchman at factories out at Potters Bar. A lot of the jobs were done in the long holidays, of course, where you needed some work to balance being able to paint for the rest of the holiday. I always used to do the job at the beginning, and as soon as I knew I had earned enough money to see me through to the next term (and grant), I would spend the rest of the time doing what I loved most, which was still drawing and painting. Some of the other jobs I had were very interesting. There was a coach firm, Venture Coaches, just around the corner from where we lived, and I would go there and clean from 11 pm, when the coaches got back from their runs to the coast in the summer, until 2 am. I could walk home in a few minutes and be in bed in time to get enough sleep before work the next day.

Another job I had one summer, I remember, was unloading fruit trains at Victoria station. It was quite reasonably paid. I remember my mother struggled with the fact that I had these really long holidays when I was getting older. Of course neighbours tended to make remarks, and even the milkman would ask, 'When is he going to get a job?', which embarrassed her. So she would nag me to get a job in the summer holidays at least. In the end, even if I didn't really need it because I had accumulated sufficient funds, I would go out and get a job. When I got this one (by which time we actually had a phone in the house) I rang my mother to tell her, 'I've just got a job at Victoria station and I'll be home at six in the morning.' Then, of course, she got very anxious and said, 'You can't possibly do that', after putting me in a position where I more or less had to get a job.

But the work was fun and night work, such as nightwatchman or coach cleaning or unloading fruit trains at Victoria (from ten at night until six in the morning), allowed you still to get a few hours' sleep and have some time to work into the bargain. The job at Victoria was particularly interesting. The others were mainly students and we all worked like mad in gangs unloading peppers, onions or whatever it was that had arrived on the trains from France. You could usually finish by about three in the morning, but, of course, you couldn't clock off until the correct time. I remember there were two ballet students working in my gang, and we used to walk up to Hyde Park from Victoria, climb over the fence for a swim in the Serpentine, then go back and clock off at six. If we'd stayed in the station, we would have ended up playing cards with the full-time men, and we would probably have lost what money we'd earned. I always remember how depressed I was by the physical fitness of the ballet students, who when we got out from swimming did exercises showing incredible control of their muscles and their bodies, while I was still something of a weed. I didn't really do very much sport or exercise, apart from riding my bike every day to Hornsey and back.

Working in a butcher's shop was particularly good because when I finished on a Friday night I could borrow something from the big fridge. Sometimes I would borrow a pig's head or a scrawny chicken, and I would take these home and draw or paint them until the early hours. These were the sort of things that I couldn't normally get hold of to paint, and they typified the type of subject that students felt was really important. The idea of painting flowers or anything conventionally attractive would have seemed an anachronism and something one just shouldn't do. Drawing a scrawny chicken, a pig's head, a pair of boots or something else to do with realism, on the other hand, was something that we were really interested in at that time. The Kitchen Sink school was about such subjects, as was the Ecole de Paris. Early works by Bernard Buffet, for instance, very often featured maybe a dead chicken on a table with various other 'real' things – a knife or a pair of scissors or whatever on the bare wooden table. These paintings tended to be very dramatic and very hungry – not surprising given the sort of world in which we lived. Although life seemed good, and I never felt that I lacked anything, we were, without any doubt, still quite hungry.

Talking of hunger, as I say my mother would put a large meal on the table when I got home because basically I wouldn't have eaten since my big breakfast in the morning. My mother was a great one for a fried breakfast; it was the main meal for my father, and I would join in on that and have a very big breakfast before I went to school. On Mondays I would probably still have enough spare cash to go for an egg-and-chips lunch in the café on the railway bridge above the school (we were fairly unhealthy in what we ate). By Tuesday I would have less money, so I would have a bowl of soup, a roll and a cup of tea at the café. By Wednesday my finances were getting thinner still, so I would usually then just have a bowl of soup and a roll, and no cup of tea. I remember clearly sitting down one Wednesday with my bowl of soup and a roll, and then drinking a whole cup of tea. Only as I was draining the cup did I realise that I hadn't bought one, and there was a rather large builder sitting next to me. What was I to do? There was only one way out. I just gently got up, paid my bill and left – although I often wonder what that builder thought when he turned to take a swig of his tea and found his cup completely empty!

When we stayed on for evening classes we would go down to the canteen and have a cup of tea and maybe a piece of currant cake, and that kept you going through the evening. You were living and enjoying life, so feeling hungry now and again didn't really seem to matter. There was, of course, no question of smoking or drinking, or indulging in any of the things that maybe students these days think they almost have the right to do. This was around about 1952 or 1953, and we had just about enough money to get by. Drugs hadn't even been heard of – fortunately I was of the generation who never had any temptation in that way because there weren't drugs around, at least not commonly available as they are these days.

As well as supplementing my income through working on Friday nights and Saturday, there was also the opportunity to exhibit a little. Every weekend there was an open-air exhibition at Hampstead, which I remember very clearly. In my recollection it was very different from the sort of work that you saw – and still see – on the railings at Hyde Park. The Hampstead Open Air Exhibition was quite a serious business; many students from the Slade or the Royal College or from the Academy Schools put their work on the walls. Professional artists went up there too, because there just were not the galleries to show in then and this would be one way in which you could make a little bit of money from your work. There was even a hierarchy, with better painters getting better positions at the top of the exhibition. Some of the screens that were actually covered were placed there, whereas further down the hill there was no cover on the wall so you had to take your work down fairly quickly if it rained. As time went by you gradually worked your way up the hill until the committee knew your work, and if they respected or liked it you got a covered position at the top. I shouldn't exaggerate this – there was no selection process as such, so there was also some very amateurish work on display. The only element of selection was that the organising committee could give better places to the more 'serious' or 'better' painters, whatever that may mean.

My grant of £1.40 per week (plus what I could earn at the butcher's shop) could thus be supplemented by the Hampstead Open Air Exhibition. If I was lucky I could sell a drawing or a small painting for one or two pounds, although you weren't really supposed to do this as the work you were doing was meant to be only for the art school. In fact, at the Royal College they were quite severe about students exhibiting work that they had done at the college. But at Hornsey no one seemed to realise that we were doing this, so I went up there each weekend to try and increase my income a little bit.

I remember one weekend quite clearly. It must have been in 1952, and an old man came up with a raincoat on. I know when you are young everybody seems old, but this man must have been in his seventies or eighties. He examined one of the little paintings I had done, showing the terraced houses on the street next to mine, at the bottom of the garden, from the back bedroom window at home. Then he said, 'I like your picture, sonny. You want £3 for it – I'll give you £2.' Two pounds was nearly double my grant for the week, so I agreed. Then he asked if I could deliver it to him. I thought that was a little bit off, but when I asked where he lived and he replied Highgate, I said, 'Funnily enough I cycle through Highgate every morning on my way to Hornsey'. This was not necessarily true, as sometimes I did the North Circular Road and other times I went over the top at Hampstead and along by the Spaniards Inn through Highgate, then down to Hornsey School of Art that way. But I said I could come through Highgate the next day and he gave me his address. The next morning I took the little painting in a bag on my back and cycled up to Highgate. I arrived at the door a little bit early, I suppose about nine o'clock, and the old man said, 'Would you like to come in and see my other paintings?' I entered this Aladdin's cave – I won't forget it until my dying day. When I went through the door my eye was caught by ten of the best early Sickerts I had ever seen, the music hall pictures. I then saw a Degas, followed by a Henry Moore underground drawing, a Bonnard print and a Vuillard print. The whole place was full of wonderful paintings and prints and drawings. I looked at this old man and said in wonder, 'Good Lord, how did you possibly get this collection together?' 'I've had only one passion all my life,' he replied, 'and that is collecting paintings. I've never had a big house.' He just lived in the flat in Highgate. 'I've never had a car, I've never been married, but I have a passion for paintings.' He looked at me and added, 'I've never paid more than £25 for a painting in my life.' Well, of course, when he was going round the Paris studios at the turn of the century, which he obviously had done, £25 would have been quite a reasonable sum of money, but even by 1952 it seemed an impossible sum for the quality of work he owned.

I remember I cycled down to the art school and couldn't wait to tell my friends this story of this old man who had bought my painting at Hampstead the day before and who had this incredible collection. Of course, typical of youth, I didn't make a note of his name or where he lived. Three years later I decided to have another look at his paintings and cycled into Highgate village to where I thought he lived, but he wasn't living there and I couldn't trace him through anybody. Whether he had died or gone abroad, I don't know. Nor do I know what happened to the collection. I certainly never saw my painting come up in the sale room again, although others, of course, have come up regularly over the years. It was a wonderful collection that quite possibly arrived in a sale when the man died – probably selling for quite a reasonable sum. I remember there was a Boudin, there was Degas, there was everybody in that collection. I only wish I had known the man's name.

There was also the opportunity, even at that young age, to submit to exhibitions. I remember that in my second year at Hornsey I submitted for the Royal Academy and was rejected. Of course I was quite hurt and upset because I was beginning to see my strengths and thought, 'Aha, I'll get it in'. When I went to the Royal Academy exhibition – as everybody does who has been kicked out – I couldn't understand why I had been rejected when so many boring portraits and pictures had got in. The following year I submitted again, but I was a little bit cleverer. The first year I sent a still-life, which of course was judged purely on its craft and its academic ability, if you like – still fairly poor at this stage. The second time I boldly sent in to the Academy a painting of a gentlemen's toilet at St Paul's underground station.

In those days toilets at underground stations were wonderful. Little bits of mosaic tile covered the walls: visually they were incredible. I remember going down there one day on outdoor drawing and thinking, 'Good Lord, I've got to paint this, but how can I get the studies?' I took a sketchbook down and stood as if I was washing my hands. Every time anyone came in for a pee the urinals were reflected in the mirror in front of me and I would draw someone standing at them. Luckily I never got arrested, and in the end I made this painting which I sent in to the Royal Academy. It was a self-portrait of me washing my hands and the backs of three men behind me, obviously peeing – and all these mosaic tiles. And that one got in and I was so pleased. I believe it was hung in Gallery 10, the last gallery in the exhibition, now a shop, but that didn't bother me. I don't remember whether I sold that picture or not – I certainly haven't got it any more. Maybe with the folly of youth I painted it over when I got it back; canvases and boards were obviously in short supply. I don't think so, however, as it had been shown at the Academy. Maybe I did manage to sell it.

The other opportunity was called Young Contemporaries. It was an exhibition organised by students all over the country, mainly headed up by those from the Royal College, the Royal Academy and the Slade. They more or less became the organisers, but anybody from any art school in the country could send work in. The exhibitions were held on Suffolk Street in London, and as I recall (though one doesn't always remember very clearly, of course) the quality of these exhibitions was very high. Younger students used to go along and be inspired by what final-year students of the Academy or the Royal College or the Slade were doing and the work they had submitted. Eventually, I finished up on the organising committee of Young Contemporaries, and I remember that year there was a young painter called Alan Reynolds who was doing his National Service in Germany; he sent in a watercolour from Germany. I remember how impressed we all were with his work, and to the best of my recollection he won the main prize for that year. The committee was always very good – I remember the judges that year included people such as Carel Weight and Keith Vaughan, and I think Johnny Minton. Each of the committee was given one of the judges to look after over lunch – giving them lunch was the one thing we could afford to do for them – and I think I looked after Keith Vaughan. I don't remember it clearly, but I know that I was in awe of him. He was a rather shy, quiet man who didn't say much to me over lunch.

There was also the possibility of getting the odd commission. When I was at Hampstead I learned what I suppose was my first bad lesson, from a woman who bought a watercolour of Hampstead from me for 30 shillings. When she bought it she said, 'I'm leaving the country now and I've lived in Hampstead for a

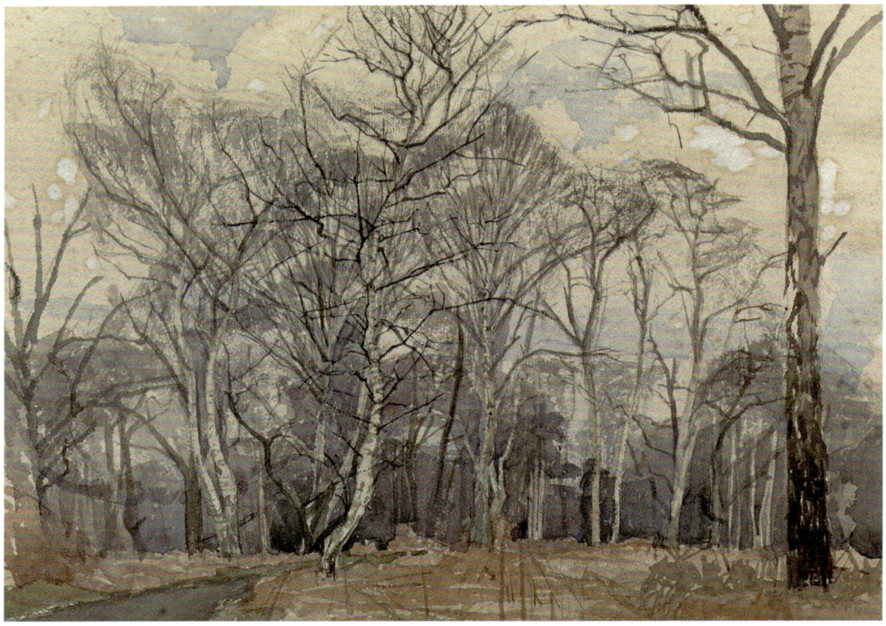

lot of my life; I would like to commission you to do five more watercolours of Hampstead.' To me a fee of seven pounds ten shillings was quite a lot of money. I took on the commission with great glee, and as far as I remember I worked hard on the watercolours. There was Keats's House and Whitestone Pond, along with other well-known sites in Hampstead. When I'd finished them I rang the number she gave me and she said, 'Oh, yes. I'm staying at the hotel by Victoria station. Bring them there.' I took them in and when I arrived she wasn't there, so I left them with the concierge. I asked him to give her the paintings and put in a little invoice, one of my first, for the £7.50, then went home. I never saw the woman again, I never heard from the woman again and I never saw my watercolours again. She left the country, and when finally I managed to track her down I discovered she had come from Richmond in Yorkshire. The solicitors wrote to me and said that she had such heavy debts that if I got anything it would be only twenty per cent of what she owed me. Of course, I never got anything. It was a hard lesson to learn, but fortunately I didn't let it prey on me. In fact, I did get caught again once or twice in my life, but so what, in the scale of things? I have also had some very happy outcomes from doing commission work.

These little bits and pieces on top of the £1.40 a week grant allowed me to have not only a working life, but also to do a few social things. Life wasn't only work – though it must sound like that from what I have been saying. Before going to art school I had become quite a regular cyclist with the Willesden Cycling Club, and I enjoyed my Sunday runs. I eventually had to give them up because there was always homework to do when I was at Hornsey, but nevertheless my bike remained a great source of pride. I even did a little bit of racing. It all really arose because my sister's boyfriend was in the 1948 Olympics, which were held in London, and so I had become interested in cycling even when I was at grammar school.

As well as cycling, I loved jazz. Sometimes on a Saturday night, drawing on my other little bits of earnings, I could afford to go to 100 Oxford Street where there was traditional jazz playing. In those days there was no drink whatsoever in the club itself. You had to go round the corner to a pub – I can't remember the name of it any more – if you wanted a drink, but the experience of the jazz club was great. In the breaks there used to be good musicians who would get up and play for nothing. I remember there was a good guitarist, Big Bill Broonzy, in from America.

The first exam we had to take at Hornsey was after three years. It was known as the Intermediate Diploma, and you were examined in drawing and painting, in the craft you had undertaken – in my case lithography, and in perspective and anatomy. It was a demanding and very thorough examination of the work that one had been doing for the previous two years. After Intermediate we were meant to go on and do the National Diploma in Design (NDD), but by this time I knew that I wanted to apply to the Royal College of Art. My parents had made it clear to me that although I was paying a small amount to stay at home, I certainly wasn't paying my keep. I would have to apply for the Royal College as soon as possible to keep student time to a minimum. I went off to see John Platt, the head of the school, to ask him if I could apply to the College during my first year of National Diploma studies. He said no, I could not; the usual form was to apply when you had taken the NDD, and that was the way that you had to do it.

I went home and relayed this to my parents. They were a bit upset by it all, so the next day I went back to see John Platt again to try another tack. Couldn't I have a try at the Royal College because even though I might fail, the experience of it would stand me in good stead? Finally, very reluctantly, he agreed that I could have a try that year. I had been working quite hard so I had a big portfolio of work, typical of me – probably more quantity and less quality. The pictures were largely of Neasden and Cricklewood, the railway sidings – the working-class, industrial environment in which I lived. Looking back, it wasn't a bad set of work, and of course it did fit in well with the social realism of the time. I also had a portfolio of drawings that I had made in the life class and in my own spare time, as well as a mass of sketchbooks, which in those days were very important. If you applied for anything, people always wanted to see your sketchbooks; they wanted to see your 'early stage' ideas.

I submitted all this material to the Royal College and was eventually informed that I had got through the initial stage and was asked to go to the College for an interview. As far as I remember it, I turned up with possibly another 100 to 200 students – all of us after 30 places. The entrance exam went on for three or four

Roehampton, *c.* 1953
Watercolour, 30 x 46 cm

This early watercolour was made at Roehampton during the winter. The drawing of the winter trees is quite tight; it was only later, after much practice, that my watercolour technique became more selective.

days, during which time you had an interview with members of staff, and while you were waiting for that interview or afterwards you did two tests. First you had to do a life drawing. When I was doing mine I could hear the person behind me drawing furiously and out of the corner of my eye I glimpsed a big build-up of black charcoal falling on the floor just behind me. During the break I went back to have a look at his work and saw a wad of paper on a big drawing board which the student had gone right through. I looked at the drawings and I couldn't understand them at all.

We then had to do a composition. We were actually given a subject and ours was 'The Expulsion from the Garden of Eden'. I did a rather boring painting of some children being thrown off Neasden railway sidings – these being my equivalent of the Garden of Eden. The student who had been doing the big black drawings had a table, I remember, with a big sheet of paper on it and some tins of powder colour. He seemed to scatter these over the paper, mix them with water and, it seemed to me at the time, stir the colour together. When I had a look at his work I didn't understand it at all and thought, 'Well, maybe I've got a chance of getting in.' Little did I realise at the time that this particular student was Leon Kossoff, who would, of course, go on to have a massive reputation in London.

When I went in for my interview the staff were all sitting in front of me. Carel Weight, Roger de Grey and Robert Buhler were there, as were Colin Hayes, Ruskin Spear, John Minton and some others who I can't remember now. They didn't seem to ask me anything about my painting, and eventually Robin Darwin came in to join in with the interview. The first thing he asked me was what I had been reading. Of course, in those days you would talk to other students about these interviews and you knew that one of the main questions was about what you had been reading. I actually didn't read very much; I suppose I didn't have much time, and I was obsessed with my work and the art school. However, I had read a book specifically for this interview: *The Little Misery* by François Mauriac, so I told Darwin this. He obviously knew the book inside out, and he gave me real grilling on it. I was very nervous and Darwin was a very tough interviewer; in fact his first question about reading had been: 'Do you read very much, Mr Howard, or do you talk all the time?' I suppose I had been gabbling on in my nervousness.

Carel Weight and Ruskin Spear appeared to have some sympathy with me, however, and seemed to help me through the interview. Ruskin asked, 'Do you normally paint sitting in the middle of a railway line, Mr Howard?' and I replied that I normally sat at the side of it. 'It's very dangerous, you know,' he admonished.

'You could get killed by a railway.' And Carel asked me some amusing questions and then said I could go. I seemed to have been in the interview for maybe five minutes and they didn't seem to have discussed my work at all. I was so anxious that I even objected, 'But you've asked me nothing about my work.' Rodrigo Moynihan said again, 'You can go now, Mr Howard,' and I got up rather disconsolately to leave. Then I couldn't find the door because the wall looked to be all windows and the door was part of them. I finished up almost a sort of gibbering idiot and eventually got out into the hallway.

I then met one of the students who had gone in before me (I had been waiting outside while he was inside) and whom I'd got to know. He had been in for almost three quarters of an hour and he asked me how my interview had gone. 'Dreadfully,' I groaned. 'They didn't ask me anything about my work. They didn't ask me anything, they just seemed to joke with me.' 'Oh,' he said, 'they asked me all about my work. They asked me where I would live when I came down to London and all sorts of questions, and the interview went on for three quarters of an hour. I feel quite confident.' In fact he didn't get accepted. I went home and my mother said, 'How did you get on?' I replied, 'Absolutely dreadfully. I'll have to try again next year.' But a few weeks later the results came through and I found, to my great joy, that I had been accepted.

It was another milestone in my life. The first had been getting into Hornsey, and now I felt that by getting into the College doors were beginning to open. I could start to think that it might be possible eventually to realise my ambition and make a living from painting. By the time I left Hornsey I suppose I was one of the best students in the school, if not the best. A few years after I left and was doing my National Service, in 1954, I remember there was an exhibition at the school. The head asked me if I would let them have some work I'd done while I was in the Royal Marines on my National Service (which I had to do before going to the Royal College). Naturally I was pleased, and gave them some work. Apparently when the chief inspector for art schools visited the exhibition and saw my paintings for the first time, he said to the principal of the school, 'That man will become a Royal Academician.' He was to be proved right, but that was still many years away.

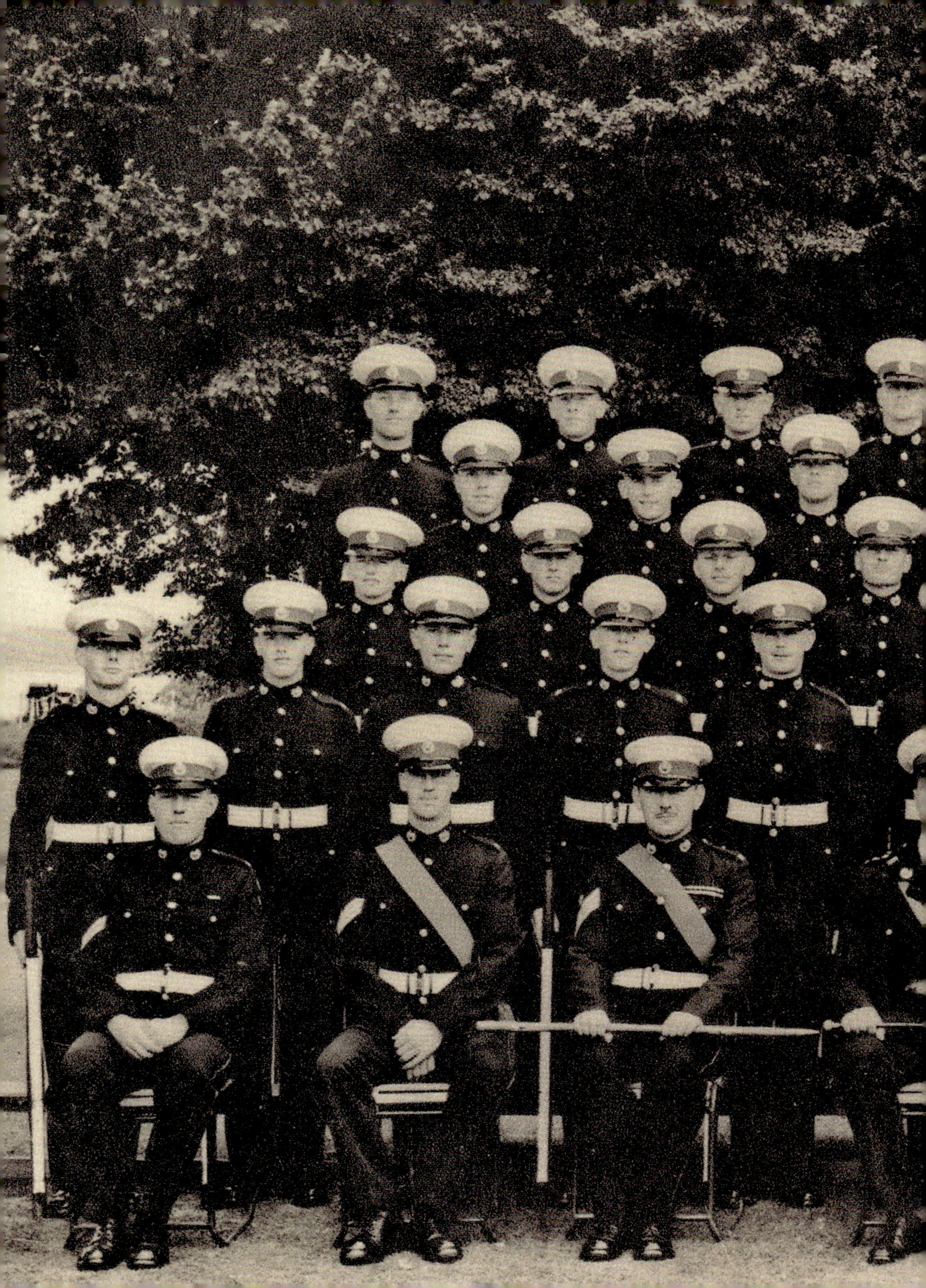

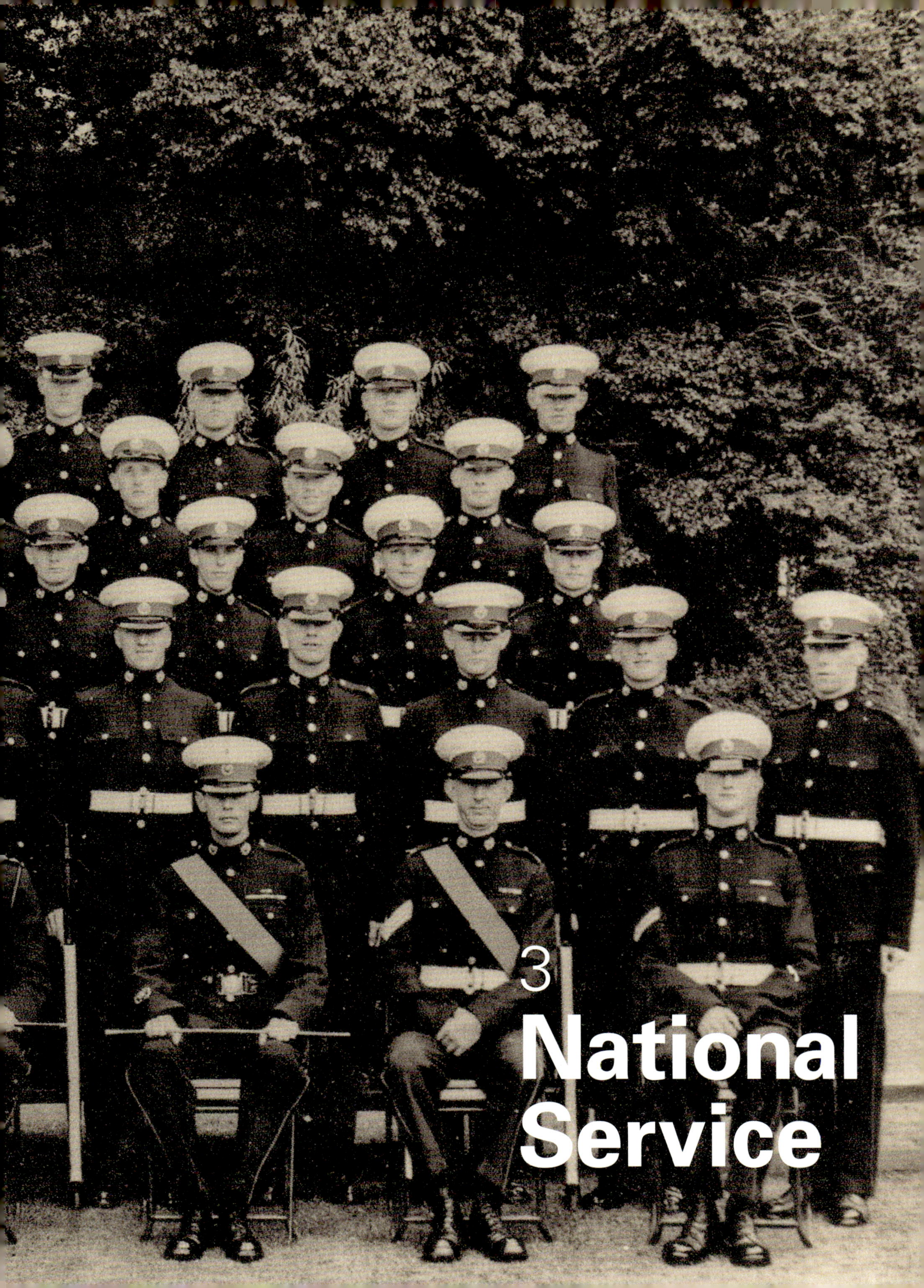

3
National Service

Before I could go to the Royal College of Art, however, I had to do my National Service. This involved serving in the armed forces for two years and I wasn't particularly looking forward to it. I applied for the Navy because I thought the best thing about National Service was being able to travel, and I got accepted as something called a 'Coder'. Then about three weeks before I was due to go in I got a letter to say that the Navy was in fact full, but that they had one vacancy for that month's intake in the Royal Marines. Now I knew nothing about the Marines; I thought it was just soldiers on ships, and because I wanted to get in – and out – as soon as possible, to have some time to recover and get ready for the Royal College of Art, I agreed to do my National Service in the Royal Marines. So I was told to report to the Royal Marine Infantry Training Camp at Lympstone in Devon.

On arrival at Lympstone we were all lined up by a sergeant in the Royal Marine Commandos who looked at us with great disdain and said, 'I suppose you all think you're going to sea.' Of course, we all did. Most of us had agreed to go into the Royal Marines because we didn't think it was any different from going into the Navy. We had visions of eventually serving as soldiers on a ship, still sailing around the world and spending our two years of National Service having a great experience. The sergeant immediately disillusioned us and said that we were not going to do any such thing. We were going to be Royal Marine Commandos. When I'd said I would go into the Royal Marines it hadn't even crossed my mind that this was a possibility. I must admit that the idea struck terror into my soul because I knew that I was not a very fit or physical sort of person.

He lined us up in a long line. Strangely enough, you didn't have to be of any set height or weight or any particular physique to be in the Royal Marines, so there were tall boys and short boys. I arrived towards the end of the shorter ones. The sergeant came down the line, being thoroughly rude to everyone he stopped at. 'And what did you do in civvy street?' he would ask. The boy would reply that he was a student, and the sergeant would reply, 'What you mean is you're a layabout.' He asked several boys what they did, and of course a vast range of jobs emerged. Luckily he didn't ask me because as he approached I thought, 'God, if he asks me what I do and I say I'm an art student, well, that'll be the end.' He passed me and when he got to the shortest boy at the end of the line he looked down at him, almost in disgust, and asked, 'So what did you do in civvy street, lad?' The boy looked up and said that he had been a bank clerk. The sergeant sneered, 'A bank clerk! What you mean is that you took the bank manager a cup of tea in the morning at ten o'clock.' And the boy looked at the sergeant in complete innocence and said, 'Oh no, we had a retired Marine Sergeant that did that job!' He actually meant it. The sergeant almost took off from the floor. 'Are you trying to be f—ing funny?' he raged. He never really forgave that poor boy, who was to suffer quite a little bit for his genuinely honest answer.

We were then marched into the camp, where the first thing we had to do was go and have our hair cut. When I walked in the barber took one look at me and said, 'Gawd! It's my birthday today.' He sat me down, took a pair of clippers and just went right across my hair, which was quite long and in this sort of DA (short for 'duck's arse') style. He made such a mess of it that when I looked in the mirror I just told him to take the lot off. So he went over my hair with clippers, shaving right down to my skull. In those days, of course, to be bald or have a bald head wasn't fashionable – in fact it was considered very strange. Everybody who had seen me first arrive at the camp howled with laughter when I went into the mess in the evening for a drink and a meal. They looked up and chortled, and some wit shouted, 'Go and get your hair cut!'

We National Service recruits were a mixed bag, from all walks of life. There were boys from public school who had just come in to do their infantry training on the way to a WOSB (War Office Selection Board). There were tough, working-class boys from the north – Liverpool, Newcastle, Manchester – many of whom had been Royal Marine reservists as young boys. They seemed pretty hard, and reckoned they knew what it was all about. Some of them even had their green berets, which meant they had been through a form of commando training.

I was just about the worst recruit in the squad. I was very untidy and proved fairly incapable of keeping my bed space, as we called it, in order. This was inspected every day, and I wasn't the most popular among us because if one person did something wrong then the whole squad had to suffer. I remember an incident on the parade ground with our colour sergeant, a man called Colour Sergeant Sowdon, who was responsible for our training. He had been in Korea, and the story was that he had been in so many battles he had finally had a nervous breakdown, so was put on the training staff at Lympstone. I don't know if that was true, but he was certainly a very tough man. One day he was drilling us and he gave an order: the whole squad turned one way and I turned the other. There was the usual joke about the man with the two left legs or the man with the two left hands. But when he got us together again he said, 'Right. Tonight we will have extra drill for an hour so that when we are told to turn right, we will all know which way to turn.' Of course, that didn't endear me to the rest of the squad, but in a way we all accepted it as part of the ritual of infantry training in the Royal Marines.

Our uniforms were rather smart in comparison with normal soldiers. We had a dress uniform consisting of a white cap, a white belt, trousers with a broad red stripe, a high-necked jacket and a lot of brass that had to be cleaned. When we went in we were all fairly unfit, and these high-necked jackets didn't look right unless your neck really filled the collar. So every day we did exercises to pump up the muscles in our necks and we all finished up looking like rugby players or wrestlers. I remember the first time I went on leave my mother was terribly upset to see that her boy had changed so much in about six weeks of hard physical training.

We did all the usual rituals of keeping the barrack room clean and having to whitewash the coal bucket and other ridiculous things that you were meant to do as a form of discipline. In a way we all accepted it as a game, I suppose. I was so bad that in the end I was pulled up in front of the officer who commanded our squad. The squad also had a colour sergeant who was our main commander, if you like, and then a major who was the squad officer and had ultimate control over us. Eventually I was summoned into the major's office. The poor man had a stutter, quite unusual for a Royal Marine, and when I walked in he said, 'H–H–Howard, you are the most m–m–m–manky Marine I have ever seen in my life. Your k–k–k–kit inspections are t–t–t–terrible and your drilling is equally terrible. Haven't you r–r–r–realised that a–a–a–at all times Marines must be s–s–s–spick and s–s–s–s... tidy.' It took me all my effort not to laugh. I'm sure I must have smiled, and yet I felt almost humiliated to have been singled out for this interview. A strange thing happened to me that day. I knew I wasn't stupid and I didn't believe I was that bad. I determined to prove it to them.

From that day on I started to work a bit. Up until then, I suppose, I had resented it and hadn't concentrated on anything. I'd still been trying to get some work done; I had a sketchbook with me and tried to go out and draw in the evenings. I suppose one of the reasons why I turned the wrong way when I was on parade was that I was usually looking over the Exe estuary and admiring the landscape on the other side. After my dressing down I decided to concentrate on the job in hand, which was to become a reasonably efficient National Service Royal Marine. As soon as I did this, I started to enjoy it a lot more. I began to enjoy the physical aspect of it, the exercise part. I realised that being thin and not very muscular could actually be an advantage. In a lot of the things we had to do, such as speed marching and climbing and doing what they called a Tarzan course, it was a great benefit to be light, and I began to do quite well. It was rather strange really because the bigger boys in the squad, who one would have expected to do very well, laboured under some of these tasks. I also found it quite amusing that when we queued up for the various injections that we had to have from time to time, those who passed out were always the big boys, not the thin, weedy ones.

Another thing happened to me at that time that changed my attitude completely. A very sympathetic priest on the camp saw how unhappy I was, and how bad in my training, and he took me under his wing. I began to attend his services, in fact deciding to become confirmed into the Church of England at that time. We became very good friends and he helped me through this very difficult period. The priest had a painter friend who turned out to be John Piper, and he must have told Piper about this young Royal Marine Commando art student who was very unhappy at the camp. Piper then wrote me an encouraging letter to help me through what had been up until then a very miserable few months.

The strange thing was that eventually I became not the worst recruit in the squad, but officially the best. For some reason once I smartened up and started to work at the physical side of it, I began, strangely enough, to excel at it. Halfway through the training they picked out four recruits to become what they called Section Commanders. There were four sections in each squad and each had to have a commander. I was selected to become one of them and was really keen to do it because life became much easier. The Section Commander never carried a Bren gun or ammunition, he only had a Sten gun which was very light. He had to do the map reading and lead the section to exercises, so he could make decisions – all in all, much more enjoyable. Then I very much wanted to become the No. 1 Section Commander, which was a highly privileged position, and eventually managed to attain that.

It wasn't achieved without cost, mind you. I remember going in to the Mess just before the tests that the various recruits standing for Section Commander had to take. I put my things down at a place at the table before I went to get my food and when I came back one of the squad members – a particularly tough fellow from Liverpool who had been a Marine Volunteer before he came into National Service – had taken my seat. 'Hey,' I said, 'that's my place.' 'Why don't you f— off?' he retorted. I looked at him and replied, 'Oh! Don't be a stupid bastard.' Little did I know that the man was in fact illegitimate, and he got up and punched me straight in the middle of the face. I hit the floor and was about to leap up, because by that time one was trained quite naturally to retaliate. Then I realised that if I had got into a brawl in the middle of the Mess we would be separated, and without any doubt at all I would lose any chance I would ever have of becoming a Section Commander, which I wanted to make my life easier. So I got to my feet and I told him, 'I'm not going to brawl with you here. I'll see you in the gym tonight.' It was the last thing I wanted to do because he was tough and I'd seen how good he was when we did milling and boxing. Still, I saved face and had my meal, and that evening I met him in the gym.

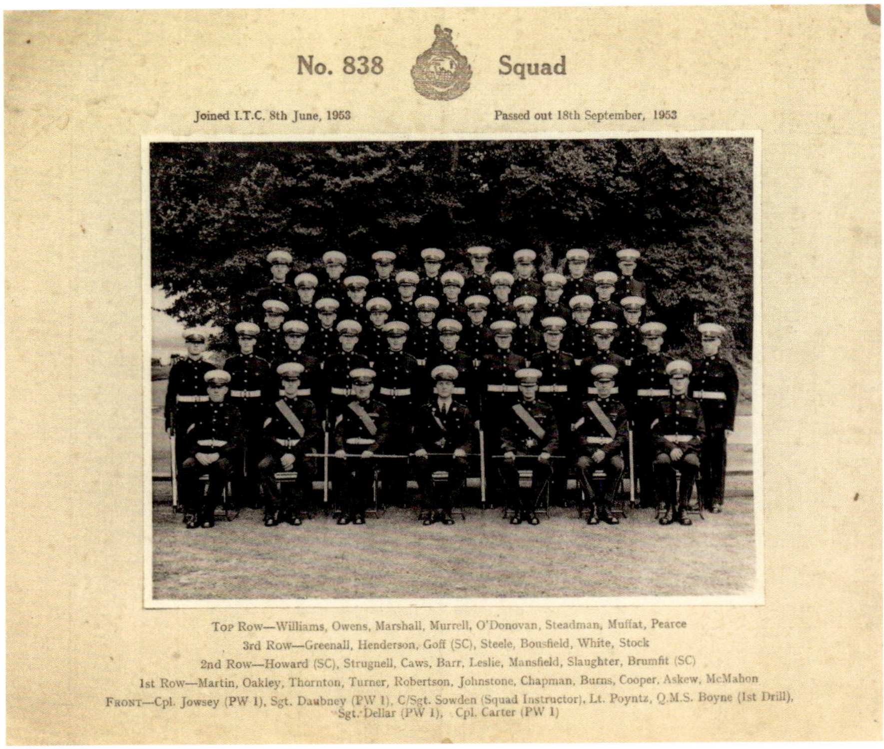

We fought together and he gave me a good pasting, but from that day on, oddly enough, we were good friends, and he never tried his luck in that way again.

In the end I would say that I enjoyed the training. For the first time in my life I was conscious of being fit, and I became even fitter and felt even better as the weeks went by (training lasted for ten weeks). At the very end of training an award called a Certificate of Merit was given to the best recruit in the squad. I managed to win this so-called Certificate of Merit and got an emblem to wear for the rest of my time in the Royal Marines. My mother came down for the 'pass out' parade, and after I had marched up and collected my award the Colour Sergeant took my mother out to lunch. She told me afterwards that he said he had never been so surprised in his life that her son, who had come in as possibly the worst recruit he had ever seen, had finished up that day winning the Certificate of Merit. I must confess that it gave me a lot of confidence.

I was certainly fit. I remember when I went home on leave I would never think twice if there was a bus coming and the bus stop was 300 yards away. I just started running because I knew very well that I could reach the bus before it started moving away again. I had a girlfriend who lived at Hendon, and her house was about four miles away from mine. Whenever I was on leave and took her out and home again in the evening, I would never think of getting transport home. I just ran the four miles home without even thinking about it. It was the only time in my life that I was ever fit. It was a wonderful experience and I greatly regret that I never did it again. But when in one's life do you find time to spend all your waking hours working at physical things and not having to think too much about anything else?

This photograph of 838 Squad Royal Marines was taken at our 'pass out' parade at Lympstone, Devon, in September 1953. The initials S.C. by my name indicate that I was a Section Commander.

After our initial training we decamped and went down to a place called Bickleigh, just north of Plymouth. This was to be the tough bit. I remember the Commanding Officer got us all together when we arrived and told us that while we were at this commando camp we would start off with confidence, but would gradually be broken down until in the end we knew the limits of our endurance. I don't know whether they still do it these days but they certainly did then, although I don't think we found it a terrible thought. They were going to drive us and drive us until we broke. They said they would know when we broke and, of course, they did, because at the beginning of training we would sing when we came back from exercises, trying to prove to them that we were still very much on top of it. But by the time training ended there was no singing. All one could do was to try to endure the physical effort, and in many cases there was pain in the whole training process.

The discipline was rigorous. We started at six every morning, going out on parade, exercising and doing the Commando course. This was made up of all kinds of courses, including exercise up in trees and in rivers, long marches, speed marches, a lot of cliff climbing and even sea landings. This went on day in, day out, seven days a week, for a course that was, I believe, six weeks long. Because I had arrived there with the Certificate of Merit and was a Section Commander, I was immediately made No. 1 Section Commander at the Commando School. Again, this made life much easier for me because I was more or less in charge of the section and didn't have to do much of the heavy work. I suppose I have always been rather adept at avoiding things that I didn't particularly enjoy and that were especially demanding physically.

The training was intense. In fact one boy in our squad died of heart failure on a speed march, which really brought home to us just how intense the training was. On another exercise, not just involving our squad, we were doing a big exercise of sea landings and cliff climbing, with a boat carrying some recruits. The boat went down on a dark night and, instead of swimming towards the coast, the men in the boat swam out to sea and two of them were drowned. I don't know what the reaction would be today if this happened on a training course, but then, in a funny sort of way, one accepted it.

The sort of things that went on certainly wouldn't be tolerated today if they were known. I remember that when we did our cliff climbing, in order to stimulate us to climb the cliff as fast as we possibly could, the last one to get up the cliff always had to run the gauntlet between everyone else. The squad had to line up each side of a passage, down which the last one up the cliff had to run. Each man had to take off his belt and hit the man as he went through, and if you refused to do it you were made to run the gauntlet as well, and the others hit you. So gradually they taught us a certain sort of discipline, which I don't think particularly damaged us. I don't think we became especially violent or dangerous human beings, but we did learn discipline.

There was one particularly bad corporal, I remember, a Corporal Carter. I used to do little cartoons of him in a small sketchbook – this was about the only work I ever did during training, after my decision to concentrate on the task in hand. One day I was up in a tree, crawling along a rope upside down (part of the Tarzan course) when my sketchbook dropped out of my jacket pocket and fell to the floor. It landed at the feet of Carter, who picked it up and opened it, and realised without any doubt that the drawings were of him. He summoned me down from this tree straightaway. He gave me an earful and made sure I had a very difficult time from then on. He was the sort of man who on speed marches, when there was someone at the back who couldn't keep up, would take the bayonet out of the boy's belt (we had to wear normal sort of weapons when we were doing training) and put it into the small of his back. 'Right, run!' he would say, and of course the boy would run until he collapsed.

Carter was a particularly unpleasant man. He had been in Malaya during the troubles, and delighted in showing a photograph of himself holding the heads of two Malayan insurgents – terrorists, I suppose he would call them, although other people might have used other names. Of course, that's why the Marines had been sent there, to stop the insurgents coming into Malaya, but Carter got real pleasure from these photographs of himself holding the two heads. Eventually he overstepped the mark, quite naturally, and was reduced to the ranks. Then the authorities had to get him out of the camp quickly. They knew that once he was the same as the other Marines we would even the score if we had half a chance, after the way that he had treated us during training.

The Tarzan course was particularly rigorous at the Commando School. We would go up the trees by various ropes, hanging underneath, climbing on top, swinging from tree to tree and so forth until you got to a river where there was a rope across. You went to the middle of the rope, where you were told to hang underneath by your hands. We then had to perform what was called a full regain, which involved pulling yourself back up onto the rope – this was quite difficult because your kit got caught up and forced you down again. Eventually you ran out of strength, dropped the rope and fell into the river. Of course your kit was then totally sodden, but it had to be completely fresh and dry by the following morning. It was a night's work to dry everything out and then re-polish all your webbing, which at Commando School was cleaned with black polish. If your kit dropped in the river all the black polish would be dimmed, and you had to re-polish the whole lot. It was an expensive business. At Commando School we spent all our wages,

28 shillings a week in those days, on buying black polish to feed all our webbing, which included belt, pouches and so on.

So it was a very rigorous training, reminding me of when I was at grammar school and feared the French lessons because I knew I wasn't any good at French. There were bad days when you knew you were going down to Bickleigh Vale to do the Tarzan course. I used to dread reaching the middle of the river in case I fell off and my rifle dropped in. Yet I managed to get through it all. One thing we did learn from the course, for the first time in our lives, was that if you had to do something and really wanted to do something, you were capable of it. And this belief has stayed with me for the rest of my life. There was nothing that I thought impossible after having done the training at Bickleigh.

It was a strange life, the more so because one never saw what we were supposed to be training for. At Commando School they taught us efficient ways of killing people with a knife and techniques to overcome people in the dark. We also had to do a lot of unarmed combat. Our training instructors showed us no quarter when we were made to fight them, and if you tried to cheat and overcome them in that way you were in for a very hard time.

By this time, of course, it was autumn – October or November. It was getting bitterly cold on the nights when we were out on the moor and Dartmoor was always very wet. I learned later that it was probably the wettest place in England, in terms of average rainfall, and we would lie all night in cold wet puddles at the bottom of trenches. On other nights you would be dropped from lorries on the middle of the moor at night, and told to get back to camp by breakfast in the morning. You were dropped off separately so you had to wander across Dartmoor alone in the mist, fog and dark. Your imagination would run riot – it was easy to believe that bushes and rocks were people on the moor. I must admit that it was quite scary. We used to try and meet up so that there'd be at least two or three of us walking together rather than one on his own.

At the end of training we were beginning to break down, but the rules were that if you didn't finish the full six weeks of training, you had to do all of it again. I eventually got a very bad Achilles heel during the last week of training, but there was no way that I was going to drop out of the course. I couldn't wear a boot on that foot any more because of the Achilles tendon, so I started doing all the exercises with one boot and one canvas 'slipper' – our name for the canvas shoes we used to wear. The final exercise was to walk from Bickleigh on the south of Dartmoor to Okehampton on the north. As far as I remember it was about 32 miles and we had to go across the moor, not take roads. If you didn't get there in the requisite time, which I believe was eight hours, you were immediately put on a lorry and taken back to Bickleigh, where you had to begin the whole thing again. This, of course, was a great incentive to complete the exercise on time.

We crossed one road at Two Bridges, and in order to make things realistic we were given our mail and some food before we set off again. I was so determined not to have to repeat these six weeks that I actually did the whole 32 miles in one canvas shoe and one boot, and so completed the course.

Anyway, at the end of training there was an award given, the Commando Medal, for the fittest recruit in the squad. Because I had managed in the last week to do all the final exercises – not very easy and including the speed marches – in one canvas shoe and one boot, I was awarded the much-coveted Commando Medal. I received this at the end of training, along with my green beret. As a result I was offered the chance to go to an Officer Training School at a place called Eaton Hall. Although by this time I had changed a bit psychologically from the boy who had commenced his training, becoming in many ways a different person, I still knew that the one thing I wanted to do was paint. I didn't want my two years just to be spent doing soldiering, so I turned down this possibility. Then the authorities said that if I didn't want to go to Eaton Hall, I could become a Marine Educational.

To begin with I was posted with the squad to Stonehouse Barracks, the headquarters of the Royal Marine Commandos in Plymouth. Then the squad was kitted out and sent off to Cyprus, while I was dispatched to Portsmouth to train as a Marine Educational. There I was taught the basics of teaching. I remember we were made to record lessons and to hear our own voices, and what a shock it was to hear my cockney voice. Staying in Plymouth was the last thing I wanted to do, however, and I immediately said in that case I don't want to be a Marine Educational; I wanted to go back to general service and go out to the squad in Cyprus. They said this wasn't possible now they had trained me to be a Marine Educational, and that I would have to stay in Plymouth for the remainder of my two years.

What I, and most of my contemporaries, wanted to do above all else during one's National Service was to see a bit of the world. At the age of 21, apart from one trip to Spain, I had hardly travelled at all.

In fact, it turned out very well because in National Service, if you had any skills, they used you. You were never going to be a really efficient soldier or marine in that short time – the professional army was far too well-trained for you to catch up. However, if you could do anything, such as play rugby, they used it. When I was at Stonehouse in Plymouth I remember that there was a Welshman, inevitably called Terry Davis, who had played rugby for Wales as fullback. After his training was over he played rugby for the Royal Marines, and the Royal Marines won everything in rugby at that time. It wasn't only sport. If you could play the piano, they used you to do that. Eventually they realised that I painted, so for the remainder of my eighteen months in the service I spent a lot of my time painting. I produced decorations for Mess Balls or Sergeants' Mess Balls and eventually did many, many portraits, so the time for me wasn't completely wasted.

When I was first drafted to Plymouth and became a Marine Educational, the existing Marine Educational was just leaving. On our meeting he said, 'Oh, you just have to sign for a few things. You are now the Librarian for the Barracks, so will you sign for the library?' and I, in my innocence, duly signed for the library, which I think was supposed to contain about 500 books. At the end of the first week I was asked to do an inventory of the library I had signed for by the Naval Commander (the educational side came under the Navy). When it came to it there weren't 500 books at all – there were about 50, and the rest were magazines and newspapers. I didn't know what to do, so I went to see the Commander and confessed that I'd signed for a library that wasn't there. He seemed very unperturbed, but asked me to pack it up and send it back to Chatham as a used library, so that they could send us a new one. This they duly did, and we got an entire new library. I was astonished at this and questioned the commander as best I could, being only a Lance Corporal Royal Marine, but he replied, 'Don't worry, Howard, I've lost more than a library in my time. In fact once I lost a lorry and a Royal Marine.' I never really understood what had happened in that case, but he was a very laid-back and agreeable man to work for.

By this time, as I say, I had arrived at the dizzy heights of Lance Corporal. We always used to joke that this was one rank below a normal Marine. It wasn't strictly speaking true, but it was decided I had to have a stripe so that I had some form of authority when teaching. In the services everything works by rank, and therefore I had to have one rank above that of the men I was teaching. Not that I did much teaching – mainly I was giving instruction in simple literacy and signing names etcetera, because Marines at that time were fairly illiterate.

I was the only National Serviceman in the Stonehouse Barracks. All the others were usually drafted to Cyprus or to whatever part of the world was giving trouble at that time, but because I had been given the post of Marine Educational I was stuck in the barracks. I was in a room with fourteen hardened soldiers, many of them three-badged Marine Commandos (three badges meant that they had served for quite a long time). Because I was a Lance Corporal I was put in charge of the room, which all the old hands found quite strange, but they tolerated me.

It wasn't always easy, though. On the first day I was in charge of the room, because I had been in training for six months, so when the bugle sounded at six in

Marine, 1954
Oil on hardboard,
41 x 30 cm

This study of a regular marine was one of the many I made of my roommates in Stonehouse Barracks, Plymouth. I had to work quite quickly as they weren't willing sitters. At this stage I was using commercial white undercoat for my whites as it dried quckly and was cheap.

the morning I jumped out of bed and said to everybody, 'Right! Six o'clock. Time to get up.' Of course, the reaction I got was, 'Why don't you f— off?' Unfortunately that morning the Duty Officer came round with the Regimental Sergeant Major – and the RSMs in Commando barracks were fairly terrifying characters. They burst into the room and looked around and saw everybody still in bed except me, the National Service Lance Corporal. The RSM walked up to the first bed, as I had done originally, and shook the man by the shoulder. Thinking it was still me, the man didn't even open his eyes, but repeated, 'Why don't you f— off?' I've never seen a man get out of bed as quickly in my life as he did when he realised he had told the RSM to 'f— off'. The men in the room eventually accepted me and I became a sort of mascot for them. I was nicknamed 'Skin', which I suppose was a reference to homosexuality. I was pretty young, and although none of them ever made any approaches to me there was, as in the Navy, always a certain undercurrent or talk of homosexuality. Anyway, I quite naturally became 'Skin'.

I used to draw every evening in the barracks, eventually getting the men to sit for me and beginning to work on big compositions at the weekends or in the evenings. Of course, these were always free times for me. Training was over, there was no cleaning to do and there was a thriving arts centre in Plymouth where I would go to paint or draw from the figure two or three times a week. After a few weeks the art centre organisers saw I had a certain talent and offered me my first ever show. I naturally grasped the opportunity. I had the time to do the work and I produced a whole series of paintings featuring Marine barracks, Marines writing letters, cook-houses and general life in the barracks. Not having painted for six months, and indeed having hardly thought about it in that time, my mind was incredibly clear. During my four years at art school I had collected a lot of dross that didn't matter, but I didn't know this – rather like when you are working on a painting, you can lose sight of what you are actually working on. But those six months had cleared my brain out; what didn't matter, or wasn't relevant to me, disappeared, and what I was left with was what did matter. I also had an incredible energy and desire to paint, after six months without doing so. My productivity was even greater than normal and in a few months I had 30 paintings ready for the exhibition at Plymouth Arts Centre.

We asked the Major General of the Royal Marines to open the exhibition, which he agreed to do. Someone leaked it to the newspapers and, as a painter-Royal Marine Commando was naturally something of an oddball, some papers got interested in it. Only the best ones, of course! Sensing a good story, I remember the *News of the World*, the *People* and the *Sunday Pictorial* all came to my exhibition – but the *Sunday Telegraph*, the *Sunday Times* and the *Observer* did not. The papers that came obviously wanted

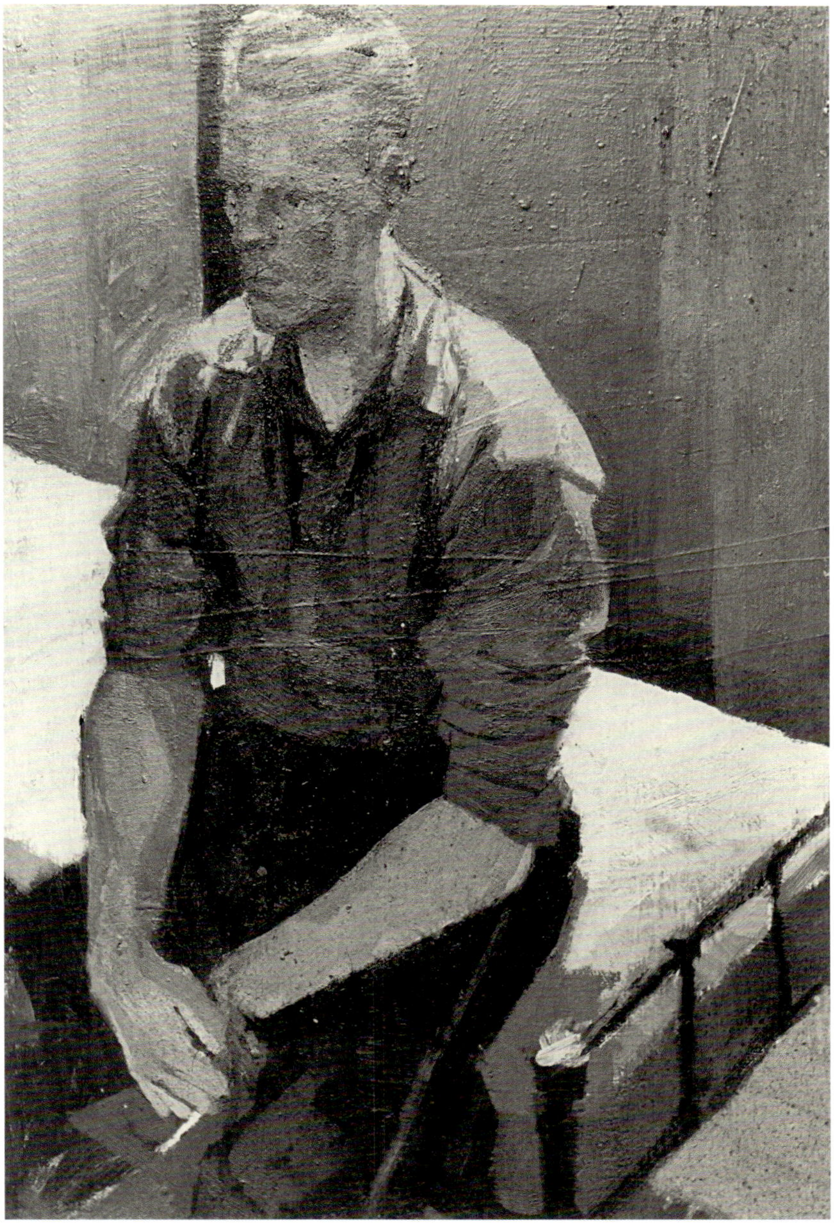

some sort of scandal and they kept quizzing me, saying it must have been very difficult being a painter in a Royal Marine barracks. Since I had been painting after training I had been treated very well, so I said no, nothing of the sort. But they just kept on trying to get me to say something negative about the Royal Marines. In the end I turned on them and said, 'You're not interested in my paintings at all, are you?' They admitted that they weren't really, but that they wanted a story. I glared at them and said, 'If you're not interested in my paintings, I'm not interested in your f—ing papers.' 'There's no need to be like that,' they said, whereupon two of my barrack roommates, who had attended the private view in their full uniforms, got hold of one of the reporters. Saying, 'Mr Howard isn't interested in your f—ing paper,' they threw him out of the door on to the pavement. I don't imagine that made the press particularly sympathetic to my situation.

Because of all the publicity, I was commissioned by the Royal Marine barracks at Plymouth to paint a portrait of General Cornwall's wife, to be presented to him on his retirement later on in the year. Although I hadn't yet been to the Royal College and had only done four years at the Hornsey School of Art, I had become quite a dab hand as a draughtsman and could get a very good likeness in a portrait. I did a painting of this good lady and it was presented on the Saturday night. Before it was presented, however, someone had leaked the story to the national papers and once again the press arrived en masse. I asked Lady Cornwall if she wanted anything in the newspapers and, being a very shy woman, she said no, she would rather not. So when the newspapers came I said there was no story. They were all quite good except the *Sunday Express*, whose reporter said. 'If you don't give me a story, I'll just write one.' 'You can write what you like,' I replied, 'but just remember one thing: I haven't said anything.'

When the painting was unveiled it was a great success. The General liked it, as did the audience at the unveiling. However, the following day a story appeared in the *Sunday Express* under the headline 'Corporal meets General's wife in secret'. Unbeknown to General Cornwall, the story ran, I was meeting his wife three times a week in the Commanding Officer's residence at the barracks. This was quite true, of course: the commission was a secret, so I had met her there to paint without the General knowing. But the innuendo was, of course, that it was nothing to do with painting a portrait, and that everyone thought they knew, nudge nudge wink wink, what Corporal Howard was up to. On Monday morning I was marched in to the General's office and the paper was on his desk. 'I don't think much of this, Howard,' he said. 'I'm sorry, sir,' I answered, 'I didn't say a word. They just wrote what they wanted to.'

After the publicity, however, I began to get letters from all over the country asking me to do portraits. By the time I had left the Marines in 1955 I had about 30 portrait commissions lined up waiting to be done. I worked on them that summer and they made an enormous difference to the money that I had to start off my time at the Royal College of Art, when I was back on a grant of £1.40 a week.

As well as getting requests to do portraits, the publicity had brought me to the attention of the other officers in the barracks. Soon I was spending all my weekends at various officers' houses, painting their wives and children. I enjoyed this work very much – it was good practice and it was encouraging for me, because I could always get a likeness. Maybe they weren't the greatest paintings ever done, and I don't know how many have survived. I've always believed in portraiture that it is better to have a good painting that is a bad likeness than to have a bad painting that is a good likeness. This is because a bad painting will only be binned after the sitter dies, whereas a good painting, even if considered a bad likeness, will always be kept. Of course memories also fade with time, and people in time would come to believe that the person actually looked like that.

The exhibition at the Plymouth Arts Centre did very well, and I think I sold 20 out of the 30 paintings. All were admittedly sold at modest prices, £5 and £10, although in those days this was quite a lot. The Director of the Plymouth Art Gallery came to the exhibition and bought ten pictures for his Pictures for Schools Collection. Naturally I was very flattered.

While the exhibition was on someone came from the Arts Council in London, and I was told to meet him at the exhibition. The man concerned was a highly placed official in the Arts Council, and he eulogised about the work. I suppose in a way it was fairly tough and it wasn't a bad exhibition, though I say it myself. Anyway, the man told me that he could get me an exhibition in London – which, of course, was unheard of at that time. Students didn't get exhibitions. I was 21 years old, and I felt that already things were beginning to happen. The second day he was in Plymouth he took me out to dinner and we discussed the details of what we were going to do. I was on cloud nine, and he invited me back to his flat for coffee to discuss the final details. When we got there he offered me a drink and I noticed that he poured rather a lot of gin into it. I was very unsophisticated, but I realised that there was something rather odd about it and I just sipped the gin. He then began to ask me about my girlfriends, and as I didn't have a girlfriend at that time I foolishly told him so. I suppose this was a little bit of a 'come on'.

I have to say at this time I was extremely fit, very young and I suppose quite an attractive boy, if you can put it that way. He asked, 'If I'm going to do all this for you, what are you going to do for me?' 'What can I possibly do for you?' I asked, and he replied that I could stay the night. I had really not seen this coming, and I was hurt and furious. He began to cry and begged me not to tell anyone what had happened – homosexuality was still illegal then, of course, and I believe you could go to jail if convicted. I told him that I would never, ever say anything about it to anybody, but that he should not approach me again. Then I went off to the barracks. It all seems very strange in the light of how we live now, but at the time it was very shocking to me. I suppose I was still quite an innocent.

My life in Plymouth was very productive and very enjoyable. In addition to the portraits I did in the barracks, I received commissions for portraits from other people in the area. One commission was to paint the wife of a well-known writer, Eric Williams. He had written a very good book called *The Wooden Horse* –

the first book about escaping from German prisoner-of-war camps. I remember Eric telling me the story of how it came about. When he returned after the war he wrote this story down and tried to get it published; no one would accept it and finally he took up work as a sales representative for a publisher. One day he was having lunch with another sales representative who said, 'I hear you had quite an interesting time during the war. Tell me about it.' 'I've written it down,' Eric replied, 'I'll send you a copy.' By then he had been rejected by most of the main publishers, but he sent it on. This time the publisher wrote back, 'I think it is a good book. If you can cut it to, say, 60–80,000 words, I think we can publish it.'

Eric did cut it and the book was published. He said he could never forget the weekend when the book came out – reviews appeared in the Sunday papers, and they were all brilliant. Overnight the book became a bestseller, and eventually films and television programmes were made. Suddenly Eric was a success. He had a wonderful Rolls-Bentley which he brought, with the number plate RB1, and he and Sybil, his wife, had a wonderful house at Street, close to Slapton Sands in Devon. I used to go there each weekend to paint Sybil. Eric was a very organised writer – something with which I could identify – who used to write from early in the morning to midday. Once he had finished at midday, the rest of the day was spent with Sybil – either working in the garden, or sailing, or doing other things. He had a very good life.

While I was painting Sybil, Eric commissioned Stanley Spencer to come and paint him. He told me a wonderful story about how, when he went down to Kingsbridge Ferry to pick up Stanley off the boat, he was puzzled by his lack of luggage, as the artist was coming to stay for a week. All Stanley had with him was a small straw bag, containing an easel, a small canvas, his brushes and paints – and nothing else. When they got back to the house, Sybil offered Stanley a cup of tea; he accepted and went to sit on the sofa. He pulled his trouser legs up, as one does when one sits down, and there were his pyjamas – sticking out from beneath his trousers. He was obviously a very original man.

Although I didn't actually paint with Stanley, Eric took photographs while the painting was going on. Of course, I also saw the picture at the very end, when it was finished. It was a wonderful portrait, one of those realist portraits that Stanley did so well; the photographs showed me the way it had developed, and to me it was a complete revelation. At art school we had already been taught that you worked a painting as a whole, laying it in and developing it as a single composition. Stanley ignored the rules, as good painters do, and I saw from the photographs how the painting had developed. On the first day he drew an egg shape to begin with, in the middle of the canvas where the head was to be, and that was the drawing. He had done a drawn study beforehand, but that was not on the canvas.

Instead, Stanley took the egg shape and started to paint within it. At the end of the sitting there were two eyes and a bridge of the nose – and the rest of it was still a white canvas with the egg shape in the centre. By the end of the second day, he'd worked down the nose and round the mouth – not easy, as Eric had a wonderful beard. The portrait base itself was now complete, but the rest of the canvas was still completely white. On the third day Stanley painted in the background and the heavy, knitted sweater that Eric was wearing. The last things he painted in were the rigid stitches in the corners of the canvas. This was the complete opposite to what we had been taught at art school, and yet the result that emerged at the end was brilliant.

I came across Stanley again later on, during my time at the Royal College, when he was commissioned to paint a picture for the City of Plymouth. He stayed at the Plymouth Arts Centre with some old friends of mine, Margaret and David Thompson, who ran it. They said that after the first day he disappeared and nobody knew where he had gone.

Stanley disappeared for several days and showed nothing of what he was doing in that time. At the end of three or four days, however, he said he had completed the painting and the City Fathers came to the Arts Centre to see the finished work. True to tradition, he had included Sir Francis Drake in the picture. But, typical of Stanley, it wasn't a grand painting of the Hoe with Sir Francis's statue in the middle. At the end of the Hoe there was a gentlemen's loo, behind which was a small piece of ground; I think it was a sort of allotment, with flower pots set against the back of the loo. This is what Stanley had chosen to paint: the gentlemen's loo at the end of the allotment and the flower pots. And sticking up behind the loo was the statue of Sir Francis Drake. It wasn't exactly what the City Fathers had expected, and I heard at the time that they weren't particularly delighted.

Later on, during my time at the Royal College, I remember going down to Cookham to Stanley Spencer's studio and asking him if he would come down to the chapel at Burghclere with the students from the college (I was then secretary of the sketch club). He spent a magical day with us, describing how the murals had evolved.

Eric and Sybil became minor patrons to me at the time, as did several other people in Plymouth after my first exhibition. They had bought a small painting of mine at the exhibition, showing some cranes at the back of the Stonehouse Barracks by Millbay dock. It wasn't a bad little painting, but nor was it particularly astonishing as far as I remember it. They both went off travelling quite a lot, driving

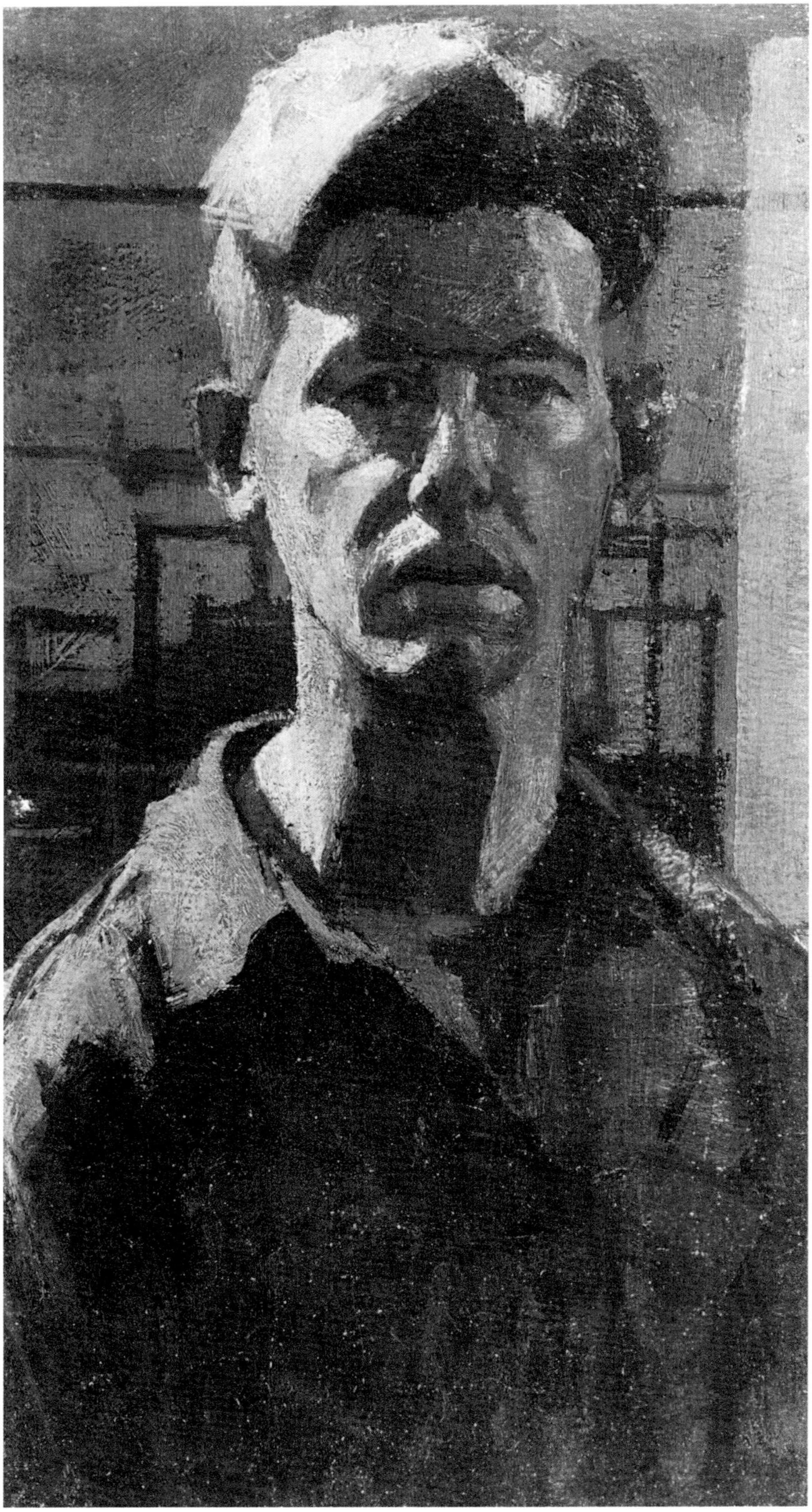

across Russia in a jeep, I believe, looking for another tale to tell. Eric was a storyteller as well as a writer. He had told his first good story very well and achieved great success, and had followed it up with another book, *Goon in the Block*, which had also sold reasonably well, buoyed by the success of *The Wooden Horse*. He needed another story and they travelled in search of one, but I don't know whether they ever found it.

When Eric and Sybil were away, however, they left their paintings with Plymouth City Art Gallery. One day I went in there and saw my little painting of Millbay dock alongside a Stanley Spencer and another very good painting by Philip Wilson Steer. My painting was not particularly good, but in that company it looked as good as it possibly could. Had the painting been hung with a couple of bad paintings, it would have looked less good. So through Sybil and Eric I learned that paintings, like anything else, are only as good as the company they keep.

I was reminded of this lesson some years later when I had a patron in London called Barney Shine. He was a millionaire property developer with some big offices in Berkeley Square and he bought twelve pictures from my first one-man exhibition in London. Barney went on to become my patron, buying work regularly. One day he bought a fairly indifferent painting of the river from me – not bad, but not particularly good. He then rang me up and said, 'Boy, I want you to come and see where I've hung your new painting' (Barney was a Jewish businessman and always called me 'boy'). So that afternoon I went into his office to see this painting that I wasn't particularly excited about. When I walked in there it was on the wall, hanging between paintings by Marquet and Degas – and, believe it or not, my picture looked good. It is against everything one would believe, but if you get hung with good work, you look good. If you get hung with bad work, you look bad. I've always believed that this is one reason why many painters don't submit work to big open exhibitions. At the Academy, for instance, if you are hung next to a good painting it does you a lot of good. In the Summer Exhibition there are some poorer quality paintings, however, and if you are hung with those it brings the worst out of the work that you do.

One of the best paintings in my exhibition was of a man called Marine Broadly (see page 86). I had made many, many drawings of him and finally did a quick, vivid portrait, which was bought by Harry Cooper, a Plymouth builder. Harry and I became great friends and he began to buy more work off me, eventually commissioning me to paint his daughter Christine. We stayed friends for many years and he bought many of my paintings and introduced me to other patrons in the Plymouth area.

By this time, towards the end of my National Service, my position in the Royal Marines had naturally become somewhat ambiguous. I was obviously seen

Self-portrait, 1954
Oil on canvas,
42.5 x 22.5 cm

This self-portrait was greatly influenced by a life-sized self-portrait by Stanley Spencer, a painter who influenced many of us during my early years at Hornsey School of Art.

as a friend of the General, the Commanding Officer and the other officers as I visited them at the weekend and painted their families. Yet I was only a Lance Corporal and within the structure of the Royal Marines I had to fit in to that life. It was not an easy balance. We had a very special Regimental Sergeant Major at that time, RSM Franks, and the poor man couldn't quite work out what to make of Lance Corporal Howard. On the other hand, if RSM Franks wanted his Sergeants' Mess decorated for a ball, which he did from time to time, he was quite happy to have me go in and do the decoration. But I disturbed him, I think, because he was used to everybody being in his right slot.

One day I entered the barracks and had to cross the square, a piece of almost sacred ground. Half way across the square a window flew up at the side and I realised that my squad had come back from Cyprus – at the window was a boy whom we had christened Nonesuch, who called out, 'Hey, Ken'. Then I suddenly realised that Franks was striding across the barracks square in front of me and thought, 'Oh no, now I'm in trouble.' I got my arm up to shoulder height in the salute, hoping that would help and he would pass me by. No such luck. 'Corporal Howard!' he said as we grew level with each other, in such a way that it was an order to stop. So I stopped and we turned and faced each other in very military fashion. 'Corporal Howard,' he demanded, 'who was that man calling you Ken?' I looked at him and said, 'Oh, sir,' (you always called the RSM 'sir') 'he's my oppo' (slang for friend). 'Your oppo?' repeated the RSM. He looked down at me and said, 'Sergeant Light in the cook-house was my oppo. Sergeant Swift in the guardroom was my oppo.' He pulled himself up to his full height and came to the point. 'And they call me "sir". Never let me hear a Marine calling a Corporal "Ken" again.' Such was the protocol and once again, I must admit, I found it quite humorous.

Meanwhile, Nonesuch was still at the window, watching all that went on. Of course this was a nickname, acquired early on in the Royal Marines, when we were given a piece of paper to write home with an example of the address that you should give to your parents. It began 'You are RM 10,000', indicating that you should there write your own number, in my case RM 130209. The paper continued 'Marine Nonesuch, 999 squad' – you were supposed to put your name and squad, for example Marine Howard, 838 Squad Lympstone, Exeter. Then we dispatched them off home. Two or three days later the Sergeant came into the barrack room. He looked round and began, 'Who is the f—ing idiot…' so we all looked at him. In his hand was a letter. 'Who is the f—ing idiot who's got a f—ing idiot as a mother?' he demanded. On the envelope of course was written RM 10,000 Nonesuch,

999 Squad; poor Nonesuch had just written that as his address and his mother answered without questioning it. He remained, inevitably, Marine Nonesuch for the rest of his two years. And what I remember most clearly about him was that he was the only man in the squad who caught the clap when they went to Egypt from Cyprus for R&R.

By this time, of course, I had become a sort of minor celebrity. Local papers such as the *Exeter Morning News* followed my career, as did the national press and radio programmes. I remember Charles Causley did a piece on the radio about the Royal Marine Commando who painted. Offers of work flowed in, and when I finally finished my National Service in 1955 and returned to London I had saved £350 – a fairly large amount of money, though not a fortune. It was quite an achievement, as although I had been earning 28 shillings a week on National Service, every penny of that had gone in polish and so forth. So the £350 was very welcome and, spread over my three years at the Royal College, made a reasonable addition to my grant.

I also had a summer to enjoy before I went to the Royal College. I travelled round the country painting the various portrait commissions that I had been asked to do while in the services. One funny incident happened in the final month of my time in Stonehouse Barracks. In my very last week a notice went up on the noticeboard to say that the Wimbledon Championships were looking for seating stewards, and it so happened that the tournament was to begin on 8 June, the week that I was due to be demobbed. I put in for a recommendation from my commanding officer, but an event a couple of weeks earlier made me believe it was highly unlikely that I would ever get to Wimbledon.

This was because a new CO, Colonel Eustace, had just arrived at Lympstone. He soon summoned me to his office. 'I understand you paint, Howard,' he said. 'I have always wanted a set of watercolours of Corps uniforms. Would you be willing to do them for me? Of course, I'll pay you for them.' I agreed, of course, and thanked him. I went away and gathered all the necessary references to these Marine Corps uniforms over a period of time. In the end I painted twenty small watercolours of Corps uniforms, actually not at all bad. I delivered the finished works to the Adjutant, Captain Potts, who took them into the Colonel. The next day I was told that the Colonel wanted to see me, so I spruced myself up as best I could and went to his office. The watercolours were strewn across his desk. 'I'm delighted with these, Howard,' he said. 'Thank you very much.' 'Oh, good, sir,' I replied, 'I'm very pleased.' 'And how much do I owe you?' Now I had spent quite a lot of time on these watercolours, so

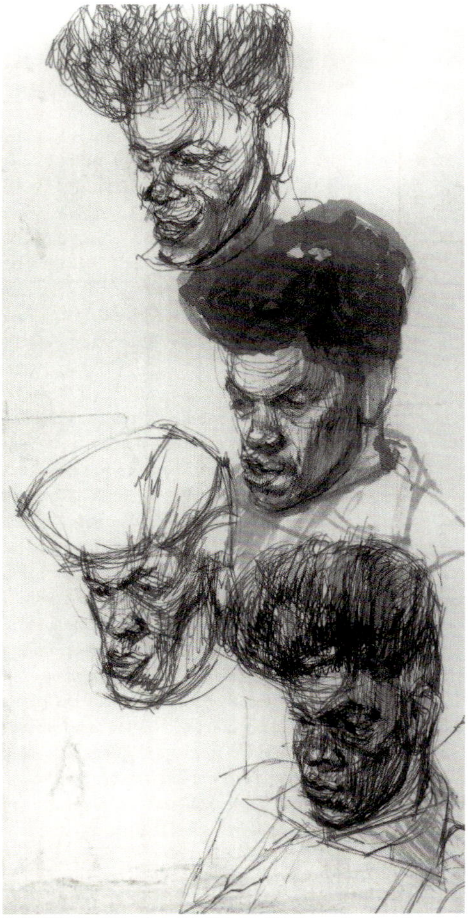

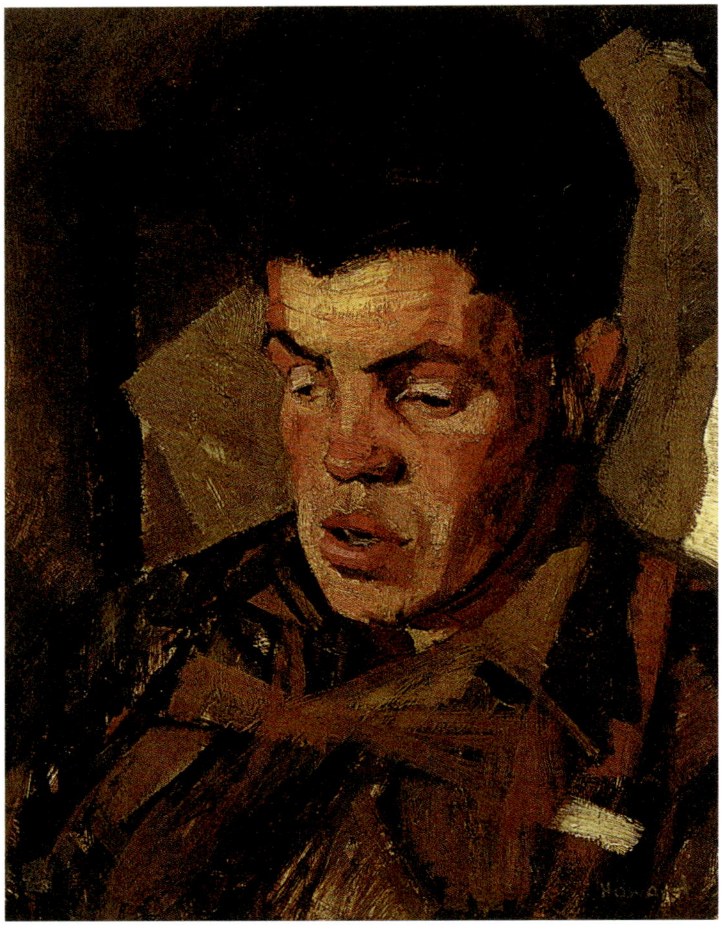

I thought that 30 shillings (£1.50) wasn't too bad. When I said '30 shillings' his face lit up – until I added 'each', when it abruptly fell. 'I think that adds up to £30, sir,' I concluded. By this time the Colonel was purple. He didn't know what to say, but he had to agree. 'I will leave a cheque with the Adjutant.' I threw up a salute and, as I reached the door, I thought I had better give him another. So I turned and saluted again, and this time he was almost frothing at the mouth. He looked at me in fury and the only thing he could say was, 'Howard, the next time you come to see me, make sure your bloody belt's clean.' It was the only way he could get back at me, but I naturally wondered whether he would give me a recommendation. To his credit, however, he did.

I remember that summer well. I left the Marines, came up to London and went off to Wimbledon on the first morning, when the organisers were meeting all the various people who were going to work there. Because I had a rather nice dress uniform, and was reasonably smart by normal standards, I was given the job of seating the press on Centre and No. 1 Courts. I had an idyllic fortnight. There was nothing to do because the press all knew where they were going, so I could cross between No. 1 and Centre Court to watch the matches I wanted – and, into the bargain, I got paid for it. I remember that year there were great players such as Lew Hoad and Ken Rosewall, and to my best memory Tony Trabert won the Men's Singles. For the first time I saw film stars like Ava Gardner and James Stewart, and everything was romantic.

Life was once again moving along on a very positive note. I had the summer to fill and a little bit of money, so first of all I decided to go back to Spain. I hitchhiked to Spain, renewed my love of Velázquez and Goya and painted a bit down there. On returning to England I decided to paint an epic piece before I went to the Royal College and chose as my subject the fishermen of England. I hitchhiked down to Devon, where I met my future brother-in-law in Plymouth. Then I continued on to Penzance, in search of a boat to take me out. I asked a trawler captain if he would take me out on a trawler trip in exchange for cooking and general work on the boat; all I needed was a bit of time to paint. He looked at me and asked, 'Have you ever been on a trawler before?' I said no, but I had just come out of the Royal Marines – I didn't mention that I had never been on a ship. 'Well, if I were you, my lover,' he said, 'I would go on a liner first.' He didn't mean a big liner – it was a fishing boat that put out lines and only went out for a couple of nights. They caught big fish on these lines. The captain told me, 'If I were you, I'd go out on a liner first and when you get back, if you still want to come with me, I'll take you out on a trip.' I couldn't really see the point of this at the time, but I agreed. So I arranged with a liner captain that he would take me out for a couple of days.

We went out off Land's End and then laid up once the lines were out, as liners do, to wait for the fish to bite. It was summer, July or August, but I can only describe the weather that followed as a heavy storm (the fishermen said it was a slight swell). All I know is that I was diabolically sick. I lay groaning on the deck the whole night long, and when they started to pull the fish in, gut them and throw the guts overboard, I was feeling so ill that I just wanted them to do the same to me. Meanwhile, all my drawing equipment, my sketchbook, my paints, had gone overboard. I didn't care. I only wanted to die. Finally I managed to get below and into a hammock. Once I was horizontal, life was at least endurable, and I stayed down there until the boat got back to Newlyn. When we docked at Newlyn a couple of days later it was dawn. The captain called me to come up and see the sun rise, but I wouldn't move out of that bunk until I felt the ship hit the side of Newlyn Pier. I swore I would never go to sea again. In fact I did use ferries from time to time, but I think that liner trip was just about the most miserable experience of my life until that date. I still remember it vividly – I truly wanted to die.

Marine Broadley, 1954
Far left: pen and ink,
30 x 16.25 cm
Left: oil on board,
50 x 40 cm

These are from a whole series of preparatory drawings I made of one of the regular Marines in my room. I probably drew him quickly as many as fifty times before painting the portrait in one sitting of two hours.

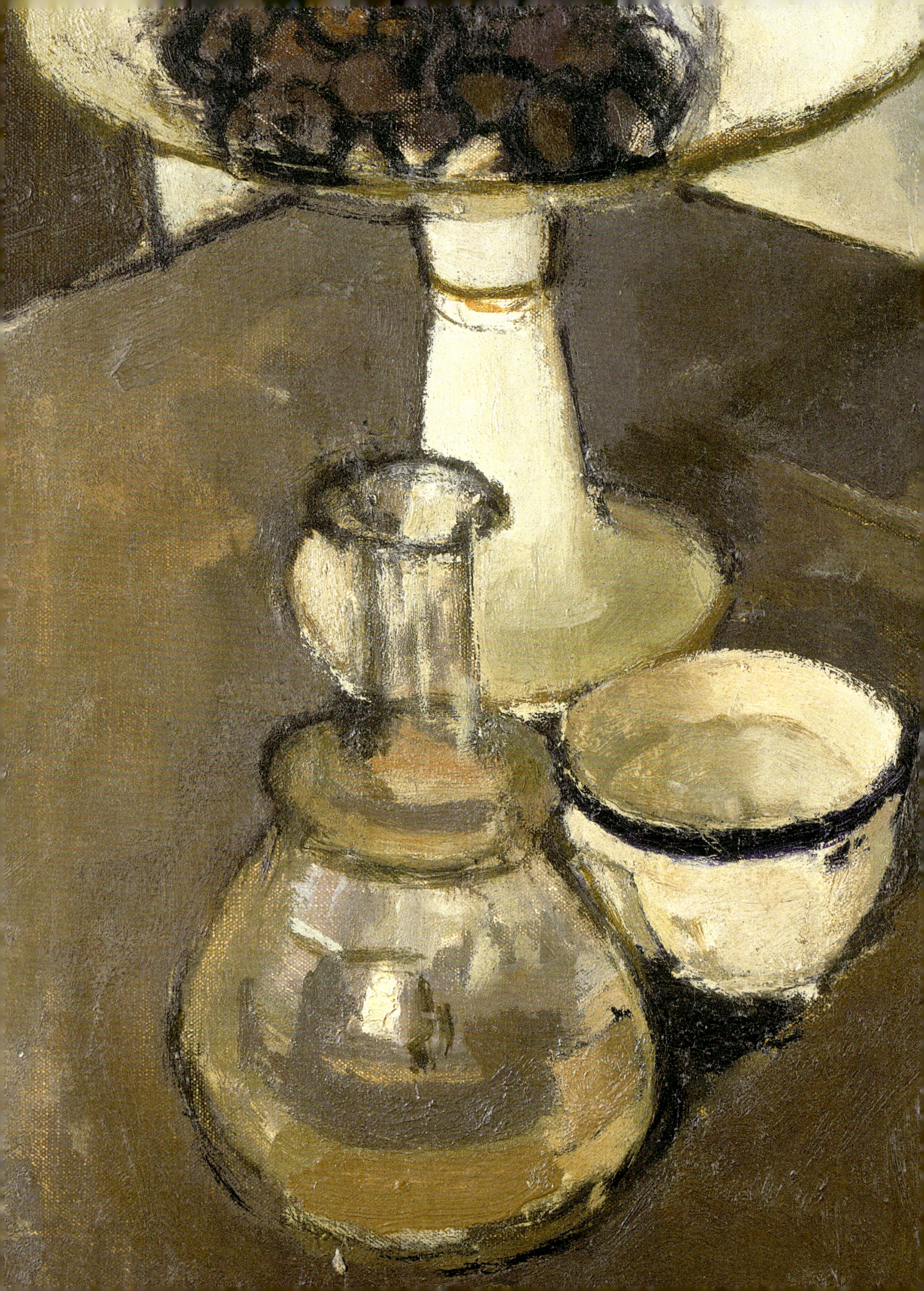

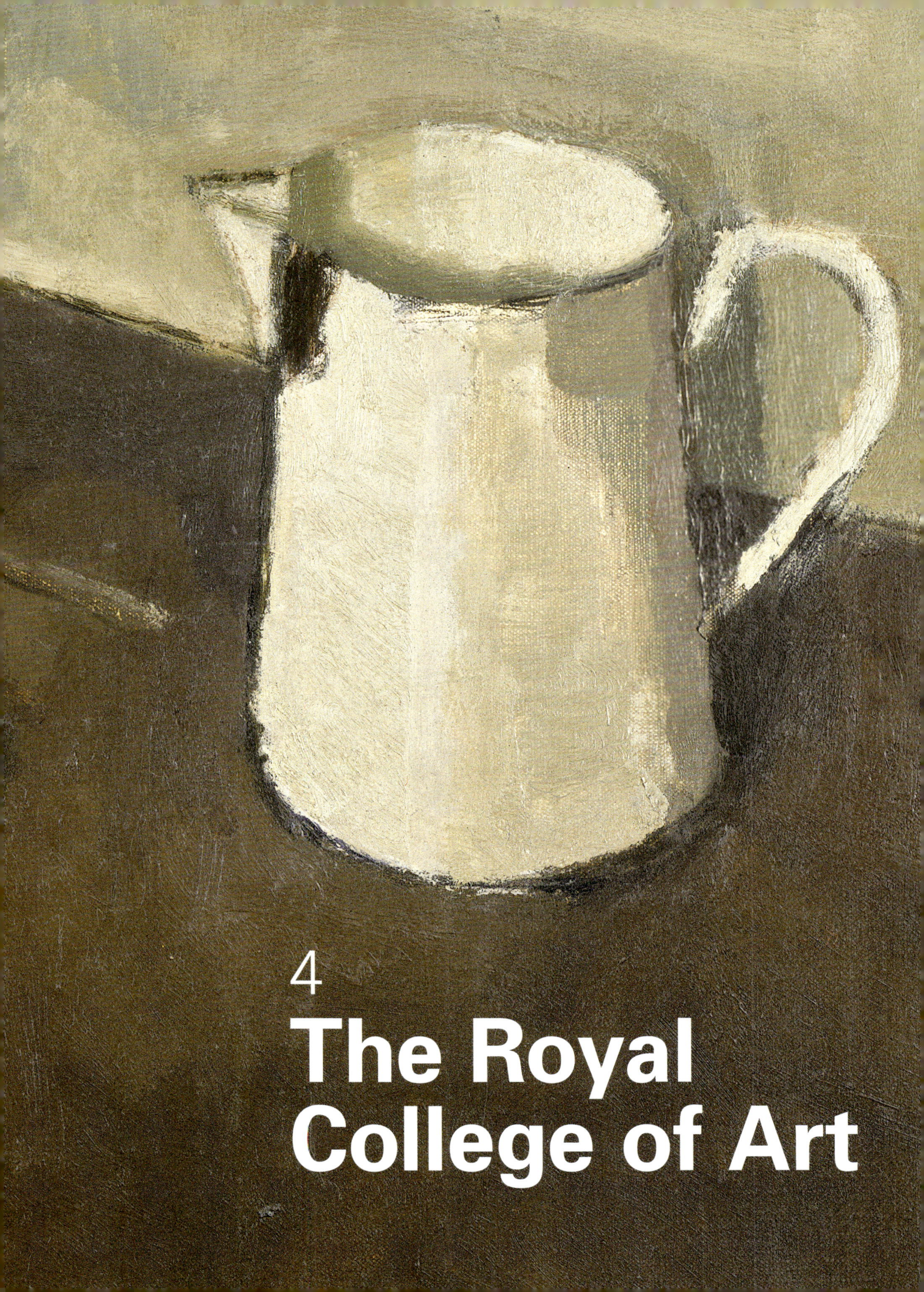

4

The Royal College of Art

The summer was over. In September 1955 I started at the Royal College for what I, a different person from the boy who had originally applied to go there, thought was going to be one of the three most eventful years of my life. As it turned out, they were some of the most difficult. I suppose I arrived at the College with a certain reputation due to the national press coverage etcetera, and perhaps this was the reason the staff, quite rightly, wanted to bring me down to earth. So although the Royal College certainly wasn't a totally negative experience for me, it was a very difficult one. I suppose I had received an unwarranted amount of attention and success for a few years, then suddenly found myself back in the deep end again. I was by no means the best student in the year, nor was I confident about the road I was going down.

I remember the first criticism we had, which was again at the sketch club. Even the Royal College had a sketch club, and when we came back after the summer everybody, even the new, first-year students, was invited to put into its exhibition. I put in some of the work that I'd done in the barrack rooms at Plymouth – pictures that had been well received and that I thought were quite good. When Rodrigo Moynihan came in to give the first criticism he picked up on my work. My spirits rose. The professor thinks my work is good, I thought. Then he started gradually to destroy it – with justification as I realise in retrospect. The crit got worse and worse, in front of all the students at the Royal College, and Rodrigo finished up by saying, 'This man should go away and consider becoming an illustrator on *Woman's Own*.'

I was completely shattered. For several years things had got better and better for me; I had begun to feel that maybe I did have a certain talent, but in this criticism Rodrigo completely destroyed me. The rest of the year was no less painful, and by its end I was really beginning to wonder whether I would be kicked out. In fact I wasn't, nor did they give me a 'provisional' pass – meaning that you had to produce a set of work over the summer which would then determine whether you could stay at the college or not. I did get a pass, but my confidence was so shaken that I began to wonder for the first time since a very early age whether I was capable of going on and earning a living by painting.

In my first year summer I hadn't technically left college as such, although in my mind I had. I went up to Elstree and tried to get a job at a film studio there, thinking that my style of painting could perhaps get me into films, so I could at least do something visual and creative. But in those days there was no way you were even going to get through the gates without a union ticket, never mind get a job in the film business. So I went up into Hertfordshire instead and worked on a farm for six weeks. At the end of this time my mind was clear. I knew that however bad I was, there was only one thing that I really wanted to do, and that was to try and paint pictures. I decided to go back to the Royal College in September and try again.

The early criticism in my first year made me re-group in the second. I began to question what I was doing far more, and in fact started to destroy everything that I produced. At the end of the second year I had only two paintings left that I felt reasonably happy with, a still-life and a painting of a model. The disturbing thing about the Royal College was that the rest of the students were all extremely bright, and I had really gone there a year earlier than I should have done. Most of the others had already completed their National Diploma in Design (NDD) or four or five years' study before they went to the Royal College. I hadn't done my NDD, and although I was pleased to get in early I realised once I was there that this extra year was an enormous time when you compared it with a period of only four years before. And so I always felt rather on the back foot and slightly inferior to the other students.

I didn't have a happy time at the Royal College. Interest in painting was shifting away from the Kitchen Sink and Romantic schools that had been so strong after the war. The focus was moving off social realism, and the sort of work that I was obsessed with doing and hoped wouldn't change was fast becoming seen as passé. All the best and brightest students were becoming interested in Abstract Expressionism in America, following the influence of the New York school. I remember Richard Smith, who spent many years teaching and painting in America and later brought painting close to a form of sculpture, was in the year above me. So was Robyn Denny, who went on to teach at the Slade and exhibit widely in Britain and abroad. Peter Blake was in the year above me, too, but he was doing his own thing, sitting in the corner of the studio painting on what looked like pieces of old driftwood – and yet one recognised that this was a unique talent. This movement towards America and Abstract Expressionism made me feel even more isolated. I still believed in what I was doing, but I was certainly made to question the whole process.

The best thing about the Royal College was the other students, most of whom I found easy to work with. There were many very talented people in my year – as I realised when I applied, it was the best talent from all over the country. My year included people such as Charles Hardaker, a member of the New English Art Club with whom I have kept in touch ever since, and Ian Simpson, a very good painter who went down the teaching line and eventually became principal of St Martin's School of Art. There were artists such as Olwyn Bowey and Sonia Lawson, both of whom have since become Royal Academicians. I think our year at the Royal College must be one of the very few years, if not the only one, in which three of the students ultimately became RAs. Certainly it didn't make me feel very confident, knowing that I had got there early and receiving the strong criticism from the staff in the way that I did. Not all the staff hammered me, of course – Ruskin Spear was extremely sympathetic and Robert Buhler, when he was in the right sort of mood, helped me a lot. Carel Weight also was very helpful, and over the years was very supportive in many, many ways.

Another student in our year, Bill Green, got a provisional pass at the end of his first year because he was a rather poor figurative painter. He went off to New York over the summer where, of course, although it wasn't completely new, he saw at first hand the work of the great Abstract Expressionist painters, including Jackson Pollock. Bill came back a totally changed man. No longer a rather poor figurative painter, he started putting sheets of board on the floor and pouring bitumen over them. Then he rode a fixed-wheel bike over the pieces of hardboard and the wet bitumen, producing, I suppose, a sort of equivalent to the Jackson Pollock pictures. It also earned him the student nickname of 'Bicycle' Bill Green. From there he progressed to setting them alight, which got him into quite hot water because of fire regulations, but by now he was a complete original and no one knew what to make of him.

When Bill got to the end of the third year, I think the Royal College staff were somewhat perplexed. They called in a well-known critic, Lawrence Alloway, who eventually went to America as curator of the Guggenheim. Alloway looked at Green's work and declared that he was going to be a very great painter and must be given a first-class degree. So Bill was duly awarded his first-class degree, but I don't think he ever really painted again. I met him some years later in Tottenham Court Road and he told me he was mainly interested in cinema.

While I was at the Royal College one of the most influential painters was Francis Bacon. Although not particularly influenced by him, I admired his work enormously. In 1956 he had an exhibition coming up at the Hanover Galleries, so he came in to the Royal College and they gave him a studio to work in. Apparently he had just come back from the south of France and had been gambling – he had an obsession for gambling, and for champagne. I remember well that he was in there every day – typical of all serious painters, he was very disciplined. He didn't mix with the students, and we saw nothing of him; only after he'd left did we go into the room where the great man had been working and see the terrible condition it was in. Bacon had wiped his palette knife on the walls and his brushes on the curtains – the whole place had to be re-decorated. Some months later I went in to the Hanover Galleries and saw the paintings that he had created during that time – some wonderful paintings of dogs, I remember, and also the series of Cézanne, or was it Van Gogh, going to work.

I also remember Peter Blake, who was in the year above me. He was a very retiring sort of person, quiet and shy, and worked away in a corner of one of the studios. I remember seeing him working on some paintings of tattooed ladies. If I remember rightly they were strippers or circus performers. They were beautiful paintings. Peter was completely untouched by what was going on at the time – everyone was becoming obsessed with Abstract Expressionism while he, of course, was laying the foundations for British Pop Art. Eventually Peter became the grand old man of British Pop Art, and one of the high points of his early career was the 1967 cover of the Beatles' album *Sgt Pepper's Lonely Hearts Club Band*.

I well remember chatting to him in the staff room at Walthamstow School of Art, where we were both teaching in 1961. Peter had been up to Liverpool to collect First Prize in the Junior Section at the John Moores Liverpool Exhibition, which he had won with an incredible portrait of himself with badges pinned all over him (*Self-portrait with Badges*). As we sat talking he told me about the new group called the Beatles. I remember thinking what a silly name for musicians, the Beatles – we weren't sure then whether it was 'beat' in terms of music or 'beetles' like the insect. Some weeks later I was driving home with my radio tuned to one of the pop radio shows. The DJ said, 'Now I've got a record from a new group in Liverpool, the Beatles.' And I thought, 'Oh, that was the group that Peter told me about.' Little did we know at that time, although it happened very quickly, that the Beatles would become the key group in the 1960s and have such a huge influence on the decade's music. Peter first met them in the early '60s when he went to watch the rehearsals for a television programme at Twickenham where Billy Fury was the lead act and the Beatles played the opening song.

After Peter graduated from the Royal College in 1956, it was me really who was influential in him getting a teaching job at the Walthamstow School of Art. The principal was Stuart Ray, a very keen member of the New English Art Club, with which I was also involved. He knew Peter's painting and, although Peter had nothing to do with new English painting, Stuart mentioned to me that he had some teaching work going and that he had received a letter from a Peter Blake, who had left the Royal College a few years before. 'You should employ him,' I told Stuart. 'He was one of the best students while I was there.'

Art schools during my time of training insisted, or mainly insisted, that those who were teaching also continued with their own work. There were a few full-time tutors – probably one in each department – but the rest were all part-timers who did no more than two days a week. J. G. Platt at Hornsey School of Art, for example, insisted that most of his staff were practising artists. If you taught for more than two days a week, he didn't want you on his staff. This was a very healthy situation as it stopped anyone getting bogged down, as often happens when people go straight from art school to teach full-time: their creative progress tends to stop and they don't develop any further. At Hornsey, however, and certainly at the Royal College of Art when I went there, the majority of the staff who most influenced me were relatively young artists, painting most of the time and teaching two days a week. I also carried on in that system, of course, and after the first year never taught more than two days a week.

I've often thought that the majority of people who go to art school reach their high point, as far as the painting goes, just after they finish. It is certainly very true of those who go straight into teaching very young. Practising artists, by contrast, reach their high point maybe ten or fifteen years later, or even thirty in special cases. As for geniuses, they reach their high point the day they die; right up to then they could have gone on and developed further in their art.

Such people, however, are very, very rare. I remember that when I started teaching, one of the first things I said to students was that they were going to have to work very hard in this school. They could forget about being geniuses because one of those was born about once in every 50 years, or even less. 'So it is very unlikely than any of you lot are going to be one!'

The teaching I encountered at the Royal College was in a sense indirect. A good example of how the teaching worked is shown in the case of a painting of a nude which hangs in my studio to this day (see page 96). I remember that it was in a particular state at lunchtime, and Roger de Grey, senior lecturer in painting at the Royal College, came along and looked at it. 'That's very good,' he said. 'Don't touch it', which was quite unusual for him. But after lunch I carried on because I wasn't satisfied with the work myself. Later he came back into the room and said, 'You have touched it, haven't you? You've ruined it.'

The person I met at the college who most affected my life, I suppose, was Carel Weight. When I started there he was a painting tutor, and in my second year, when Rodrigo Moynihan went abroad, Carel became professor. He was very good and could teach by inspiration, and in a very indirect way. During his time as professor he produced a continuous stream of people who would make their mark on the visual arts. David Hockney flourished at the Royal College, as did Peter Phillips and Derek Boshier. The whole of the Pop Art movement burgeoned, and yet in his own work Carel was not about any of that. He obviously wasn't a teacher who taught people to work like himself. Instead, he stimulated them to find their own language from the beginning. Carel was above all a generous man who gave his time generously to everybody. He did not have to think that you were particularly good. The only thing you had to be was serious about it, and committed.

I remember many years later, when I was elected to the Royal Academy, Carel came up to welcome me, saying, 'Oh, we're so pleased to have you as a member.' I replied, I suppose rather meanly, but I knew him so well by that time, 'Come on, Carel, I'm a rather nice painter by your standards. You like painting to have a bit of an edge to it.' I knew this was true, but he smiled and denied it. Throughout my life Carel helped me because he saw that I was committed to what I was doing.

Carel had a habit, as many teachers do, and like most students we quickly picked up on it. His was the habit of saying, 'Don't you think you've got the head too big?' I remember a model once asking us about the members of staff and whether they had comments they tended to repeat, and I said that if Carel came in now he would come up and tell me that I had got the head too big. Anyway, the model started posing and the door opened and, lo and behold, Carel entered. He went up to the first student, stood back for a little while and then enquired, 'Don't you think you've got the head too big?' I saw the model smile. Carel carried on with his criticism for the student and then moved on to the next one. There he stood back for a while, took a hard look at the painting, walked forward and remarked, 'Don't you think you've got the head too big?' The model almost giggled, and by this time I was smiling and praying that he wouldn't do the same thing with me. Then it was my turn. I could feel Carel behind me as I painted, then he came up and said, 'Don't you think you've got the head too big, Howard?' At this point the model collapsed in laughter. I was convinced that Carel knew why, but, typical of this kind, generous man, he never held it against me – or maybe he really didn't guess, I don't know.

I remember one day soon after I left the College standing on the waterfront at Chelsea. I was painting a landscape, looking across the river – I suppose it was rather 'Whistlerian' really, with the factory, called Morgan Crucible, on the other side. Carel came along and looked at the painting. 'Ah Howard,' he said, 'I like that painting you're doing.' 'Thank you very much, sir,' I replied (in those days I didn't call him Carel and he didn't call me Ken). Carel offered to write to the factory owners and get them to buy the work, then off he went. I thought, I suppose rather cynically, that I'd heard that before, but two days later I received a letter from Morgan Crucible. It said that Professor Weight had given them my name and they would like to see the painting I was doing of their factory. I took it across a couple

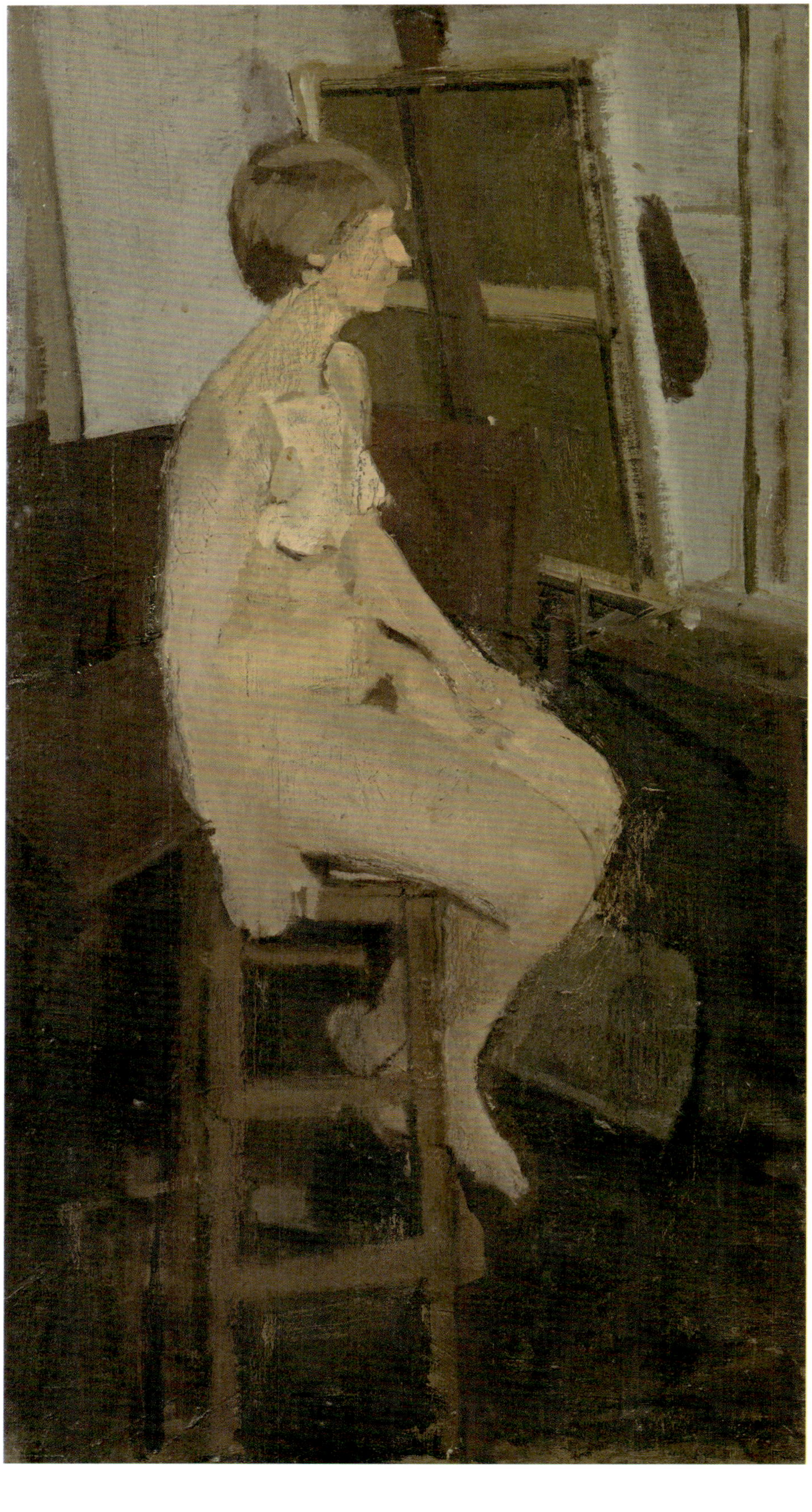

of days later, and they bought it for I think ten pounds. This was in 1960, and it seemed a lot of money.

Later on, after I'd been away from the College for fourteen years, Carel was still teaching there. He received a letter from the Imperial War Museum asking if he could recommend someone who might be suitable to go to Northern Ireland as an official war artist. Carel wrote back and kindly put my name forward – even though I was no longer a student, hadn't been a student for many years and hadn't particularly excelled when I was. He had seen some drawings that I'd done of wards and operating theatres at Charing Cross Hospital. I think this work, which I had made for the Friends of Charing Cross, had impressed him. I got the job and it was to prove one of the turning points in my life.

Carel was a very good man who, like all of us, was attacked very often by the critics. Brian Sewell, who seemed to have a blind spot when it came to Carel, could be particularly scathing. I think a lot of Brian's work is very well written and I think it is very well considered. However, he can sometimes be cruel for the sake of being cruel, and sometimes he can be savage about people that he should not. Carel had sacrificed a lot of the time that he should have given to his own work to help young painters and students, and he should be very well respected for that, as well as for the fact that he was a very good painter. No one should let personal opinions cloud the many other positive things that the man has done. When Carel died he left me his easel. I still work at it and think of the great man.

I had a very good tutor in drawing at the Royal College, a man called Rodney Burn. Probably nobody reading this will know his work, but he was a very good painter, an excellent teacher and a fine draughtsman. I can well remember how Rodney would come up and watch you draw for a while. Then he would move you over, sit down at your board and start drawing your figure. He might start off with one of the feet and work his way up the leg, round the figure and down the arm, then go over the head, down the other arm and down to the other foot, and so through the other side of the leg to where he had started. And it would be right. It was a remarkable way of drawing, as he followed the line of the drawing all the time.

And I remember Rodney telling me something once, which I think to a great extent is true, even if it doesn't really sound very fashionable. 'What you have to do first of all,' he said, 'is to recognise your limitations. When you have recognised your limitations, work as far as possible within them.' Geniuses don't have limitations but most men do, and many painters fail because they try to do things that are not part of their natural language, that are beyond their capabilities. I have seen many students in my time who were as good figurative painters as I am – sometimes

Life Model, *c.* 1965
Oil on canvas, 91 x 56 cm

This nude is one of only two paintings I kept from my second year at the Royal College – all the other work I painted over. I remember that Roger de Grey, my tutor (later President of the Royal Academy), told me I had overworked it.

even better – but who very often felt that they should be doing something more innovative, more avant-garde or whatever you want to call it. So they gave up figurative painting, but none of the ones I can think of ever earned a living by painting after that. Many of them ended up being very dissatisfied. In other words, they hadn't recognised what their language was, or they had chosen to disregard it. I suppose when Burn urged me to recognise my limitations, he could also have said, 'Recognise your languages, and work as much as you can within them.'

Of course it didn't necessarily mean that if you did very well as a student at the Royal College, or I suppose at the Slade, that you would necessarily go on and make a reputation later on. Many, many are those I could cite who were extremely bright students at the Royal College or the Slade but were never heard of afterwards. It often strikes me as strange how few of all the students who go to art school carry on doing what they have chosen in the fine arts. It is undoubtedly a difficult profession to make one's living in – one in which it is not just talent that's important, but persistence. One of the things that Carel Weight told me at the Royal College, and which I'll always remember, was, 'Howard, those who make their living painting are those who go on longest.' I didn't appreciate what he meant at the time, but years later I did. Carel also remarked that, 'Painting isn't that different from playing the piano: you've got to practise it and practise it every day.' That observation also affected my approach to painting.

Rodrigo Moynihan was a very hard critic who could sometimes be devastating. He was a good painter in the figurative, realist sense, and he did some wonderful paintings during the war: I remember an ATS girl and a wonderful still-life of a skull. Just before I got to the Royal College of Art he painted a remarkable portrait of the staff at the college. I think he finished it during my first year. Moynihan later went to France and became an abstract painter. I used to be cruel to him as he had been so cruel to me, making smart remarks like, 'Rodrigo's had an art attack and it's left him blind.' I'm sure he wouldn't have been very pleased if he'd heard that, and of course it was the comment of an arrogant young man who was in a sense covering his own position and feeling a sense of injustice. When Rodrigo returned to England he started painting portraits again, but they were nowhere near as strong as his early realist paintings. One of my nastier observations was that some of them looked as though they had been filleted – the whole bone structure seemed to have gone.

Not all the teachers who inspired us were permanent fixtures, of course. Some very interesting people also came and lectured to us at the College. One particular man who had influenced me while I was at Hornsey was Ben Shahn. He was an

American painter and illustrator who flourished at the time of the New Deal, producing large murals and painting political themes such as the Sacco and Vanzetti case in America. Nicola Sacco and Bartolomeo Vanzetti were Italian anarchists who were active in workers' strikes and demonstrations in the United States after the First World War. They were arrested in 1920 by the American authorities, anxious to clamp down on workers' unrest and to eradicate communist and anarchist beliefs. Both were accused of committing a payroll robbery the previous April, during which two security guards were killed. They were convicted despite the lack of evidence to support the charge (there was even a confession by another party, who declared that they had nothing to do with it). Sacco and Vanzetti spent six years in prison, with appeal after appeal being rejected, before they were finally executed in August 1927.

Shahn affected us all because he was very much to do with social realism. He came to the Royal College to give a lecture, and during the course of this he said something which made a real impact on me – I will remember it for the rest of my days. He was talking about drawing, emphasising that drawing was about the particular, not about the general. To illustrate the point he said, 'When I draw a pair of trousers, I want people to know whether they are a $50 pair of trousers or a $30 pair of trousers.' That hit home with me, and I thought that in future I will make sure that my drawings are particular.

In a similar way I read that Sickert, when he was teaching drawing, told a student to 'indicate that you have noticed the particular thing'. That again is, I feel, a truth about drawing, but Shahn's example was very succinct. This has nothing to do with detail. Shahn's drawings were not detailed academic drawings, but very simplified pieces of art. The simplification and abstraction got down to the actual essence of what the drawing was about. And in all Shahn's drawings that I looked at, I realised that there was this truth in what he had said.

Another man who lectured to us was an architect called Sergei Kadleigh. Strangely enough, his themes were very big at certain times of his life and then they seemed to disappear. When you spoke later to people about them, they had never heard of Kadleigh unless they were particularly involved in that field. Sergei came to lecture us about architecture, art and the creative process in general. One day he told us that 'the artist should think of himself as a musical instrument. He spends his life tuning that instrument in order to be able to express the beauty of nature.' It may sound very strange now, but when he said it I was at a very impressionable age. I was full of life and hope about the whole creative process, and I remember that his words immediately rang true to me. They weren't referring to art having to be innovative, having to be new. They were referring to the simple process, the gradual honing of one's sensibility in order to be able to express oneself better.

Artists are people who develop their own particular interests or ability. Critics and writers create the movements or 'isms'. I always knew when I was young that the Impressionists didn't give themselves the term. It was critics who created the word 'Impressionism', and no doubt created all the many other 'isms' that happened during the twentieth century through which I have lived. As a student I was conscious of how many 'isms' there had been – Impressionism and then Post-Impressionism, Cubism and Surrealism, Realism and Futurism, as well as Fauvism. During my time there has been the art of the Kitchen Sink school, Abstract Expressionism, Pop Art and Hard Edge, not to mention Minimalism, Op Art and Action Painting. Later on, after Minimalism, there has been Conceptual Art. However, painters and sculptors don't really concern themselves with whether they have been part of this or part of that. They do their work and other people fit them into these 'isms' and if they can't fit them in, if they don't belong to an 'ism', some critics believe these artists are not worth being considered. They are not new. Yet in reality nothing is new, everything has been done before.

Most of the things that have been done in Conceptual Art were first created by Marcel Duchamp at the time of Dada – another 'ism' of the early twentieth century. When people say there is no point in painting representational art any more because it has all been done by Cézanne, that is all nonsense. As long as you are expressing your own feelings, what you are doing will be new, you will find a new language which will be your own. Generally speaking it might be like Impressionism or Realism, or some other 'ism', but if it is of yourself, it will be like nothing else that has ever been done. It will be your language and people will recognise it.

As well as Ben Shahn, I remember that I had a tutorial with Claude Rogers, a very good painter who had been a member of the Euston Road school. They believed in painting traditional subjects in a realistic manner, reacting against avant-garde styles. Rogers was a greatly respected man when I was a young painter. He came to the College while Carel Weight was professor, and gave tutorials to a few students. I was lucky enough to be one of them.

It is my belief that people who go into the arts are usually born with one talent and they have to develop others. Probably the really great people in any field have a great many talents, but I think that most people go to art school with one particular talent. Mine to begin with was certainly drawing. I could draw naturally – drawing came to me as easily as speaking.

And along with drawing I had a very good understanding of tone. Right from the beginning I could see what tone was about and grasped the whole business of tonal relation to drawing. The one thing I had no clue about was colour – something that I don't think you can teach. I think that colour is something intuitive; you cannot teach someone to paint in the way the colourists such as Bonnard did. If you were to give Bonnard 50 colours and say you can't mix any of them and make the painting with all of them, he would do it – they would harmonise and go together. If you were to give me 50 colours and say 'don't mix any of them', I would just make a mess.

When I had a tutorial with Claude Rogers he did teach me something about colour, however. One very true observation he made was that when you are trying to make colour or see a colour or mix a colour, never look at the colour itself but always look at the one next to it. Glimpse the colour that you are trying to assess out of the corner of your eye, and then you will really see it. What he meant, of course, is that there is no such thing as a colour in itself – it exists only in relation to other colours around it. This is true of everything in the arts, whether it is line, shape, tone, colour or something else, but it was Rogers who brought this home to me. He had a considerable reputation at the time and produced very beautiful paintings, I remember, including some to do with hospital interiors.

One amusing story from my time at the Royal College concerns one of these criticisms which I have mentioned. Robert Colquhoun was scheduled to be the critic that day, and it was due to start at 2 pm. We gathered in the main studio, all the students and staff, including the principal, Robin Darwin. He wasn't the most patient man or the nicest character I'd ever met, I must admit, but he was a very good head and he made the college very much the leading art school of the time. Anyway, Darwin had attended for this criticism, but of course at 2 pm there was no sign of the critic. So Robin spoke to Johnny Minton and asked him where Robert was. I think Johnny knew very well where he was, and he promised to go and find him. He went down to the Hoop and Toy public house at South Kensington to dig Colquhoun, a notoriously heavy drinker, out of there. We all sat waiting for him to come back. Half past two came and went, and Darwin was beginning to twitch. All of a sudden the door opened and in came Johnny with Colquhoun. The critic staggered to the middle of the room and we all fell silent, waiting for his utterances. He swayed somewhat and then looked directly at Robin Darwin. In his strong Scottish voice he said, 'Och! I cannie do it' – and just walked out of the door and disappeared. I have often thought of that and been tempted to do it myself, but have never actually managed to do so.

Cricklewood, ***c.*** **1952**
Oil on board, 25 x 43 cm

This painting of Cricklewood sidings was made when I was a student. Hard up at the time, I painted it on a piece of hardboard using commercial white undercoat. I saw the work many years later, after it had been bought by the Plymouth City Art Gallery. Despite the primitive materials, it was in perfect condition.

Johnny Minton was himself a fearless critic. Of course by the time students got to the Royal College of Art they were fairly confident about themselves, even in our time, and unlikely to be intimidated by the staff. This wasn't the case with Johnny, however. I remember that he gave one of these criticisms, for which all the students had put up their work. By this time Abstract Expressionism was very much coming in; some of 'Bicycle' Bill Green's paintings hung on the wall at the time when people were beginning to look at him somewhat in awe. Johnny walked in and looked along the paintings. He went straight up to 'Bicycle' Bill Green's painting and said, 'This student looks as though he has taken a piece of the floor and put it up on the wall as a picture' – fairly near the truth, I suppose, as Bill had poured bitumen over the flat hardboard on the floor and ridden his bike over it.

Not caring what sort of reputation people were beginning to have, Johnny said exactly what he thought. When he committed suicide during my time at the Royal College it was an incredible loss to the art world. I have no idea why he did it. It has been suggested that he wasn't accepted by the Royal Academy because of his homosexuality; his friends had all become members and he felt somewhat outside it. I suppose he was a bit of an outsider. Johnny drank heavily and was seen to be a sad man, although he was very often so full of vibrancy. He seemed so alive that I can remember what a terrible shock it was on the day that we heard that he had died. To us students it was the equivalent of hearing about John F. Kennedy's assassination – although I must confess that I can't remember the exact day, as we all can in that case.

In many ways the staff were great people who have helped me and influenced me all my life, not only at the Royal College. They were a remarkable group: Ruskin Spear; Carel Weight, who helped all the students, particularly when they first left college; Colin Hayes; Roger de Grey – all these artists, who later I'd know professionally, were my tutors at the Royal College. When you're young you simply meet these people and their stature doesn't really dawn on you.

Many of the teachers at the college favoured the subtle approach. I remember one day particularly, when I'd been working on a painting for about three weeks. It was a Friday afternoon, and there was only me and the model left in the room. Suddenly I heard the door open and Ruskin came in – he had a gammy leg so when he came in, although you couldn't see him, you knew who it must be. I heard him stop behind me and watch me paint. By this time the painting had been dead for at least a week and should have been abandoned, but I was doggedly carrying on with it. All of a sudden Ruskin came and tapped me on the shoulder. 'Howard,' he said, 'I'm just off down to the staff room. If you make a mistake while I'm away, will you

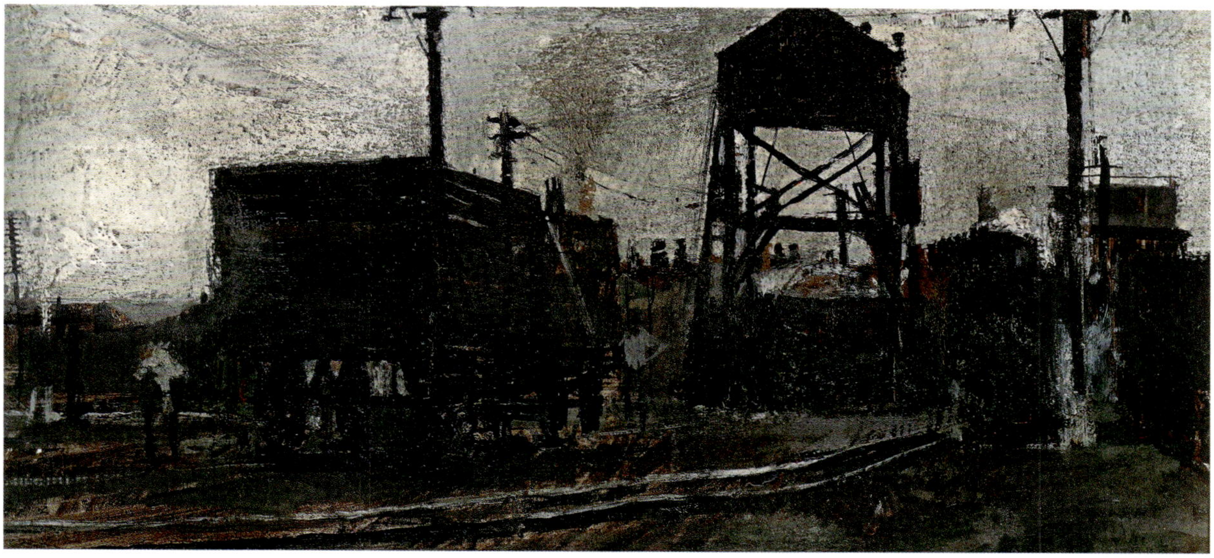

come down and let me know?' That was typical of the indirect way they knew how to teach. It said it all. I ditched the painting and started something else.

Another important aspect of Hornsey and the Royal College were the models. They were, of course, very much part of our lives, and in those days they were very professional and took a delight in posing well. I particularly remember Quentin Crisp when I was at Hornsey in the very early 1950s. Quentin delighted in being able to hold difficult poses. He loved to hold a pose of the crucifixion, for example, where he would hold his arms up and stand there for a long time, never complaining. He had a long pole that he used to make his particular poses. They were always full of life and movement, and one felt that he was as involved in the process as the students who were trying to draw him. Quentin later went on to become the Naked Civil Servant, of course, and moved to America to live. Many years later I went to hear him speaking at a Chelsea Arts Club lunch. By this time he had become a great entertainer and raconteur, but in the early days he was a very fine and professional model.

Quentin was at first a great shock to us because he was the first man that I had ever observed wearing lipstick. When it came to the break he would say, 'Where is my Dorothy bag?', pick it up and mince off with it to the loo to preen himself, or do whatever he did there. But he was a marvellous model and a marvellous character. Most models were not of his quality, but they were as serious and professional about their job as Quentin was.

We had one wonderful model at Hornsey. She was very large and the first model I ever painted. I had never seen a woman without her clothes on before and was rather nervous when I went to my first life class. I had almost sharpened away a pencil before I looked up, and there she was in all her glory. Not the prettiest of sights, I must admit, but she took it upon herself to break us in, as students, and would tell us jokes while she was posing. I remember when the first break came she slipped on a pair of very high-heeled shoes and stepped down from the podium.

She came over and stood immediately in front of me, talking to me as I sat on the donkey (a low seat that you drew on). When I looked ahead the top of my head was exactly level with her crotch. She stood in front of me and there was nowhere else I could look. She knew exactly what she was doing, and I was so embarrassed it was unbelievable. She was large and she was soft, and we students christened her 'Velvita' because she spread easily.

Some of the models in those days were obviously 'on the game', as they say. We had one particularly beautiful model who was very large but very shapely. Her hair colour changed every time she sat for us, and I remember a number of years later driving down the Edgware Road in my first car and seeing her at the lights. Instinctively I stopped and offered her a lift and she dived into the car. She was on her way to the West End and every time we stopped at the lights people looked into the car. They looked askance, obviously wondering what this young man was doing with that rather dubious lady sitting by his side.

On another memorable occasion she was posing for us at the Royal College of Art. We were queuing up with her for our tea, served up by a Mrs Bucket in the morning break, and this model was standing chatting to us when the staff went past. They walked along the corridor and the last one was Ruskin, limping along. As he went past she turned to him and said, 'Morning, Ruskin', and he looked ahead and walked on without responding. Whereupon, in front of all us students, she called along the corridor in her very loud voice, 'You'd have recognised me a fortnight ago at that weekend school when you were sleeping with me, wouldn't you?' We saw Ruskin's hair rise on the back of his neck and we all laughed.

They were wonderful times, terrific times, full of beautiful things and unexpected events. I only wish I had written more down at the time, but there would probably have been far too much to record. At least now I am setting them down before I forget them completely. One of the most memorable moments occurred when I was working at the Working Men's College in Camden Town, near to Mornington Crescent in north London. (It was a way of getting experience for teaching, because you knew already that when you finished you would have to teach part-time in order to survive.) That evening, as I came down from the drawing-school studio where I had been teaching, I heard this magical music coming from the basement. It was Vaughan Williams's *Lark Ascending*. 'I must go down and listen to the college orchestra practising,' I thought, and I went down to the basement. When I got there I saw Vaughan Williams himself, by this time quite old and heavy. He was slumped in the chair with the orchestra in front of him and he was directing them on practically every note of the music. It was a truly magical experience.

I was glad to have this unpaid teaching from the Working Men's College in my last year at the Royal College of Art. At that time the degree you got from the Royal College, the ARCA, was a teaching qualification without doing an art teacher's diploma, but of course when applying for a job it helped if you could show some experience. Voluntary teaching like that at the Working Men's College was to prove invaluable.

One evening Maurice Cox approached me and asked if I would teach him to draw. I asked to see a portfolio and realised he was quite talented, but his history, unlike mine, was a sad one. As a young man he wanted to paint, but his Victorian father wouldn't hear of it and he had to leave home. He couldn't survive alone, so he returned home and became a surveyor with the London County Council. He continued to paint in his spare time and started to attend Sickert's life classes, whereupon Sickert said he had no talent. Eventually, after retirement, he pursued his passion and we met at the Working Men's College when he was 70 and I was 25. Once a week we would meet, play chess, smoke our pipes and drink a bottle of cheap wine. I learned more about life from that wise man than from anybody. I was sitting by his bed on the night he died, aged 82, and the last words he said before he went to sleep for the last time were, 'Isn't life good, Ken?' What a way to go. During his last 20 years Maurice went to the Wallace collection every week to look at the Velázquez painting *Woman with a Fan*. I asked him why always that one painting. Maurice replied that, to him, 'every week she is different' – the epitome of a great portrait painting.

Not everything was ideal of course. By the time I had finished at the Royal College I was still living at home. It wasn't possible in those days, even after doing National Service and going to university, to apply for a living-out grant. If you were studying in the same city as your parents were living, you were obliged to remain at home. I was still on my grant of £1.40 per week, although this had been boosted by the various commissions I had received. I was also exhibiting regularly, and the staff at the Royal College gave me one or two more commissions. So I had a little bit of money and no longer had to rely purely on my pedal bike for transport and freedom.

By this time I owned a Lambretta. This was towards the end of the 1950s; scooters were coming in, and Lambrettas and Vespas were the ones to have. I had bought one – I can still remember it – in Venetian red and beige, with imitation tiger-skin covers on the seats. I thought this scooter was rather posh, and naturally it helped me to pull the girls. I fell in love with a girl who was working at an art shop in South Kensington. She was quite large and very beautiful, and for some reason she seemed to take a shine to me – I really do believe it was because of my

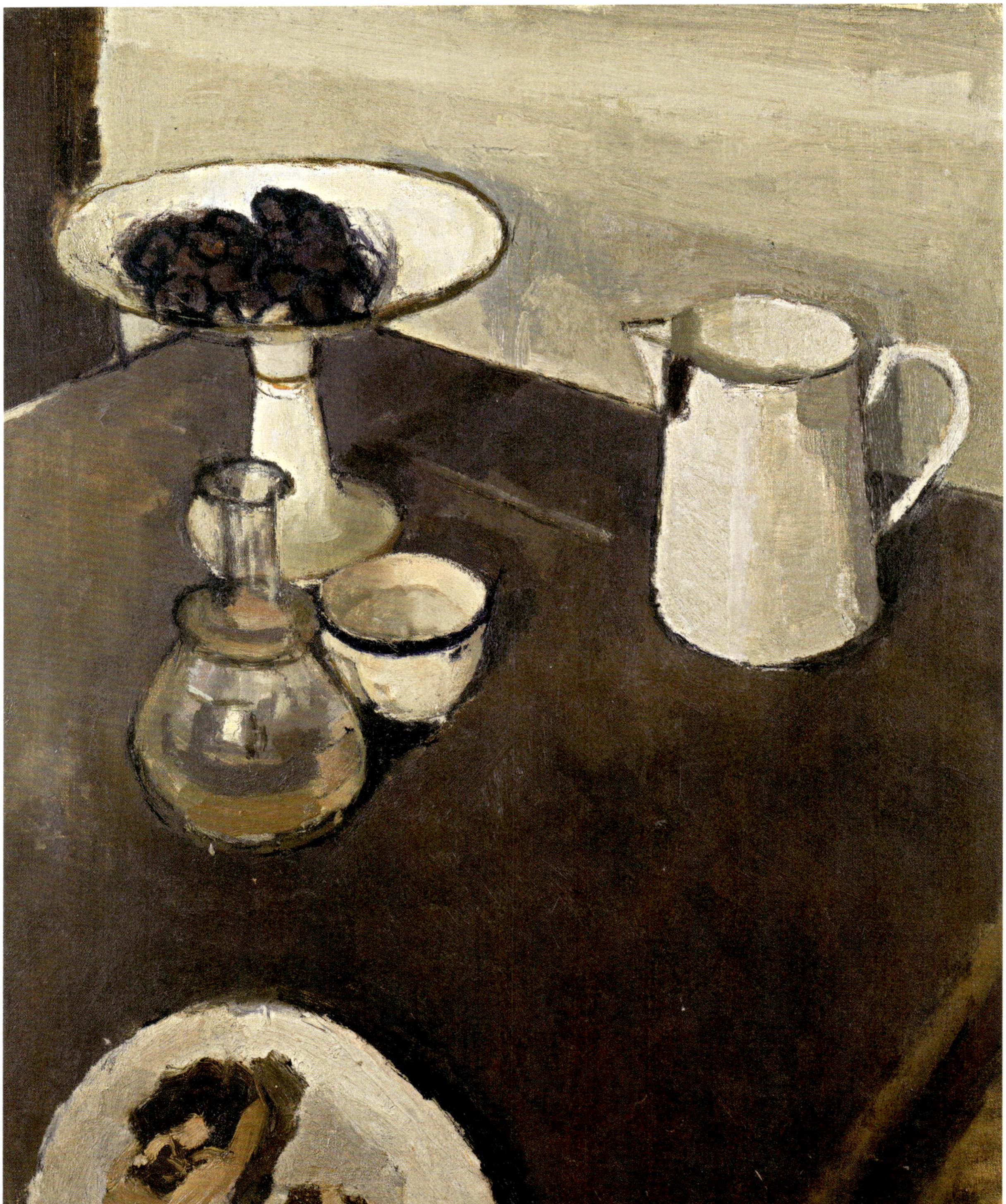

scooter. I remember taking her down to Brighton riding pillion and feeling very proud that she was on my bike.

Eventually I heard that a member of the Bonzo Dog Dooda band – one of our Royal College bands – had also fallen in love with her. Together with The Temperance Seven, another college band, they were made up of very young musicians. This was before the time of the Beatles and the success of a long stream of pop groups, and the Bonzo Dog was a very original group. I remember that they used to go round in an old refuse-collecting truck. My rival proved far more imaginative than me, leaving a rose on the step of the art shop each morning. It had its effect and eventually she deserted me for him.

Despite this, not all was bad by 1958. At the end of the third year at the college I had recovered from my horrendous first year and gained an Upper Second in the final assessment. I applied for a British Council scholarship to Paris, which I failed to get, but I did manage to be awarded an Italian government scholarship instead. This came through the British Council and would allow me to study in Florence for up to a year. It was, quite simply, to change my life.

RCA Still-life, *c.* 1957
Oil on canvas, 60 x 50 cm

This is the other painting I kept from my second year at the Royal College of Art. I gave it away and later it was sold by Agnew's for £5,000. I often wonder about the value of the work I destroyed. The painting was made with a limited palette of raw umber, blue-black, light red, yellow ochre and white. By limiting the palette in this way, I hoped to improve my colour sense.

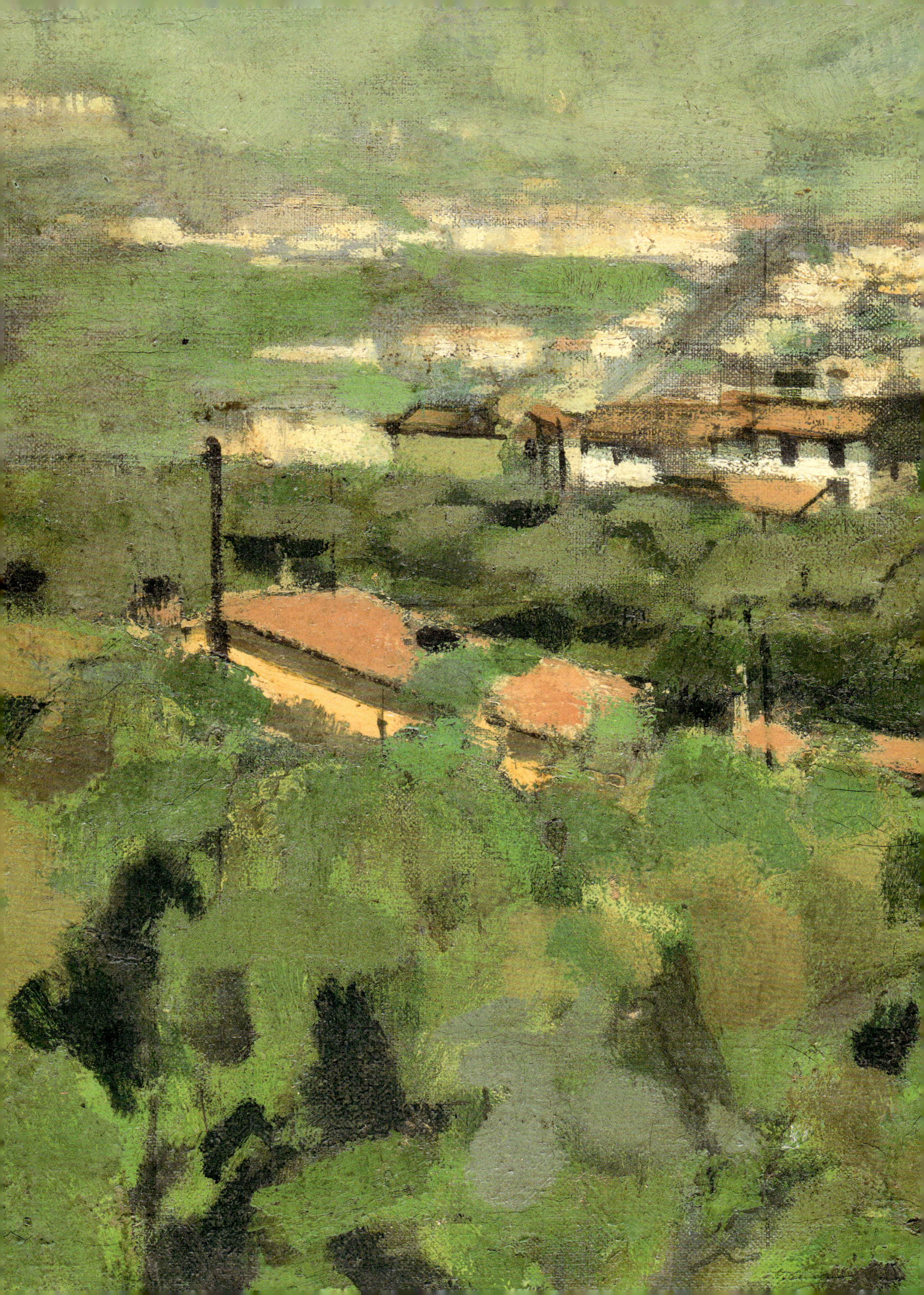

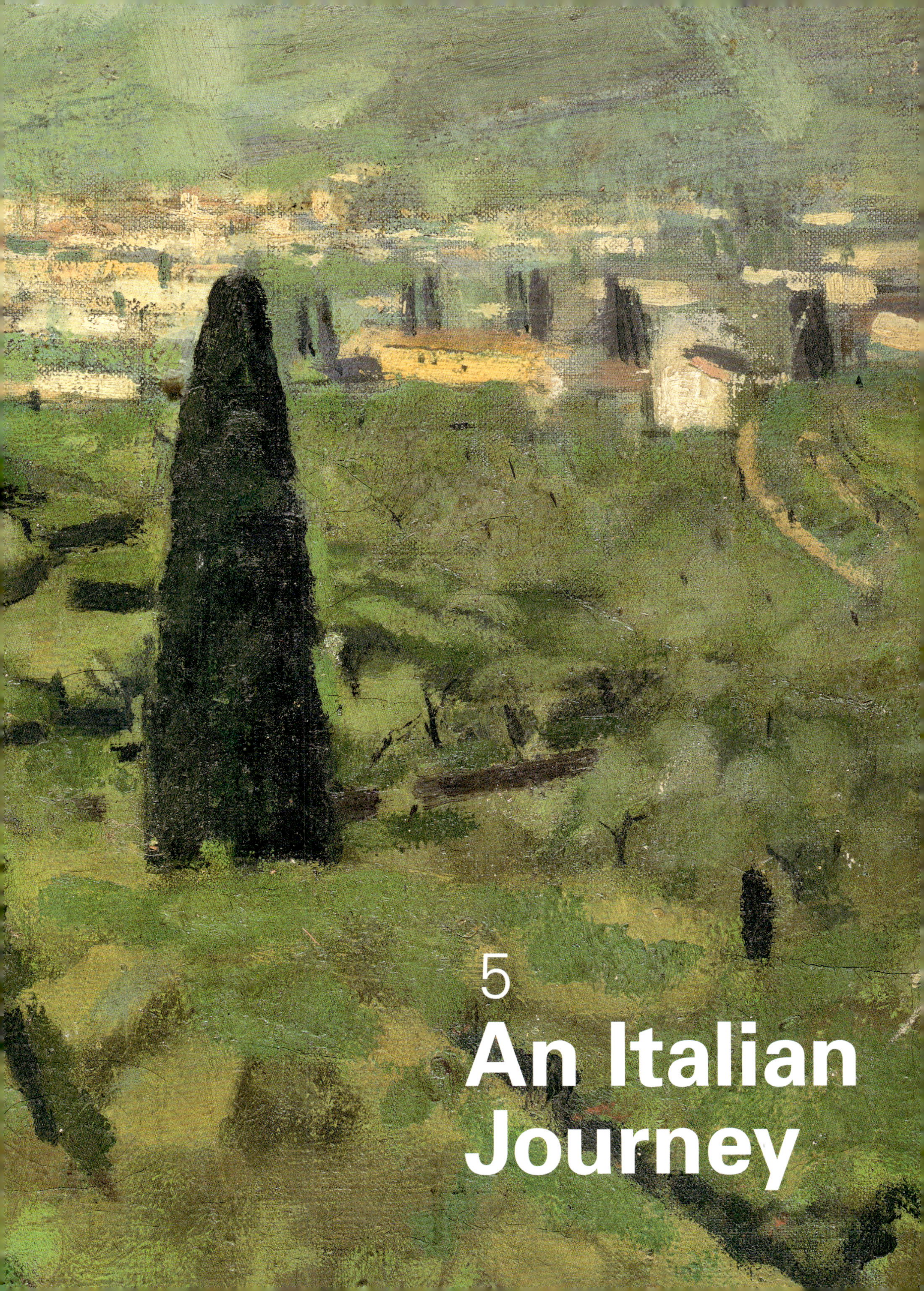

5 An Italian Journey

My scooter was in those days rather the pride of my life, and the only way that I wanted to get down to Italy to take up my scholarship. So I set off from London to drive through France without really knowing what I was doing. My mother insisted that I put on a crash helmet – they weren't obligatory in those days, but it seemed sensible. As things turned out, I had a whole series of crashes during the journey, so it was a very good thing to have done. The problem was luggage. I had intended to stay in Italy for a year, so the scooter had to carry most of the things that I would need. I didn't have many clothes or canvases, which I thought I would buy there, but I did have to carry my materials. In the end the back of the bike was extremely heavy and the front was extremely light – a very dangerous combination. When I set off I soon realised this, but, buoyed by the optimism of youth, I still thought that I would get to Florence all right.

I did manage to get to the coast and down to Paris safely. Here, I stayed with Mike Brown, a New Zealander who was an old friend of mine from the Royal College. He was on a travelling scholarship that New Zealand awarded to one student a year to go to the Royal College. Mike had married while he was at the college, and I stayed with him and his wife for two or three days in Paris. It was idyllic, apart from the fact that I was beginning to suffer quite a lot from the stomach ulcers that had developed while I was in the Royal Marines. (When I left I had a small disability pension because I had gone in A1, as they called it, and came out with a disability. I can't remember how much this was – about 1s 9d a week, I think, which wasn't particularly worth worrying about.)

Anyway, I left Paris and set off for Italy. I had been driving for about half an hour, along roads that in those days didn't seem to have kerbs at the side. Then a lorry went past very, very close to me. I swung over and skidded on some loose gravel – the scooter was already fairly uncontrollable, and it then spun quite out of control. I ended up in a ditch, luckily not injured, but the bike was very badly damaged. I managed to get a local garage to pick up the bike to repair it. I didn't have any money, but they were willing to take my insurance details. My ulcer was playing up very badly by this time, so I put up in a small bed and breakfast for five nights while my scooter was repaired. I didn't go back to Paris, nor did I let my parents know what had happened.

Once the scooter was repaired, I began to drive south again. Eventually I reached Switzerland and travelled over the passes and down the other side to Italy. I remember in Switzerland it rained a lot. I had a tent with me that I could sleep in because, other than staying with friends, I couldn't really afford very much. I slept in the tent by the side of Lake Lucerne, where it poured with rain and everything got absolutely sodden, including my clothes. They were in the various containers littered around the back of the scooter.

Just as I reached Milan I got pushed off the road again, by another lorry. Once again the bike arrived in a workshop, to be completely rebuilt at the front end, while I managed to get a room at the university that had been vacated by students. When the scooter was ready I set off for Florence again, undeterred by the misadventures. On arriving at Bologna I saw a very fine landscape just at the side of the road. I was musing about this landscape when I failed to notice a Vespa in front of me. I drove into it and slid off the side of the road, whereupon the whole village seemed to descend on me because the rider was a local boy. '*Pagare, pagare*', they shouted. I knew very little Italian, but I knew they were demanding that I should pay. One word I had learned from my first two accidents, of course, was *assicurazione* (insurance), and so I called this back, but they simply repeated '*pagare, pagare!*' I repeated '*assicurazione*', and at last they said, '*Basta, basta!*' With my lack of Italian I assumed they were calling me a bastard, of course, and I was rather offended by this as I was only trying to put things right. Eventually both bikes were taken off to a repair place, mine for the third time, and I went and stayed at the local youth hostel.

I had very limited funds as I couldn't draw any money until I actually got to Florence, where my grant would start. Having not very much to eat, I asked myself what Italians ate, coming to the conclusion it was spaghetti with orange stuff on it. So I went out and bought some spaghetti and a tube of tomato purée, then began to make a meal back at the youth hostel. Of course I didn't read the instructions on the packet – whether I would have known what *cottura otto minuti* meant is uncertain anyway – but, having no clue I cooked it for about 20 minutes. By this time it was becoming a purée, which I piled onto my plate and squeezed some tomato purée on top. It was an absolute mess, and just at this moment the woman who ran the youth hostel came through the door. She took one look at what I was going to eat, picked it up and threw it in the bin, muttering, '*Mamma mia, gli spaghetti.*' Then she set about teaching me how to make a proper spaghetti meal.

I stayed in Bologna for three or four days, and as a result the one thing I have really learned to cook in my life is a proper spaghetti bolognese. First the signora told me that the most important ingredient was *spezzatino di vitello* (pieces of veal), which, as I now appreciate, had to be minced. Basil was another main ingredient. Then she taught me how to make the base of celery, onion and carrot. There was no automatic mincer or anything; all had to be chopped extremely finely with one of those Italian chopping knives with a handle at each end. The mixture was then cooked with olive oil. Next, she cooked minced *spezzatino di vitello* in a separate frying pan until the meat went a light colour, whereupon it was added to the celery, onion and carrot mix, and it was all cooked together for some time. Various things were added after the basil, including some red wine (very cheap at the time), a pinch of sugar and some salt. Strangely enough, I remember that she added a dash of milk, which I still do to this day when I am making a spaghetti bolognese, without really understanding why.

Inevitably, the final thing was a tube of the famous tomato purée. This gave the mixture colour, then it had to be cooked – and cooked and cooked. The signora at the youth hostel said you can eat it this evening, but it would be better tomorrow when you've cooked it for some hours. You could eat some tomorrow, but it would be even better the next day after it had cooked for still longer. And with a good bolognese sauce, of course, the longer you cook it the better – always on a very low heat and always with a lid on the saucepan to keep the goodness in the sauce. When the sauce was complete it was a feast. I realised just why Bologna is renowned as the centre for Italian food, and also why spaghetti al ragu (bolognese) has such an important role in Italian tradition and cooking.

Some time later I went up to Bologna again to see the Italian painter and etcher Giorgio Morandi, who had long been one of my heroes. We spent the evening together in his studio, which I later saw, after he died, in a museum in Bologna where it had been reconstructed. He spoke very little English and I spoke very poor Italian, but we managed to communicate and during the evening I asked him if he travelled very much. He replied that he never left Italy, but that every week he went to Milan. His dealer sent a car for him and he went to examine all the 'Morandis' that had come on the market and say which ones were his own works and which were fakes. With a little twinkle in his eye he said that he was certain about the early ones, but not always sure of the later ones. At the end of the evening he took out a very beautiful still-life and asked would I like it. I said that I couldn't possibly afford it and he offered it to me for 50 pounds. This was a lot of money in 1958 and, as I was only on eight pounds per week from the Italian government, I decided to have my last few weeks in Italy rather than the Morandi. In later years, as I saw the prices rocket, I wondered whether my decision was right. However, if I had owned it I would have been nervous about hanging it on the wall, so it would probably have had to be kept in a bank vault.

After a few days my scooter was ready again, and when I had made sure that all was well with the poor boy who had fallen off his Vespa I got on the road and went down to Florence. I must admit that when I got there I never wanted to look at a scooter again. After a few days I received a letter from my insurance company. 'Dear Sir,' it ran, 'we understand that you have had an accident. Unfortunately we have three different dates for your accident. Would you please write and confirm which of them is right.' So I wrote back that, unfortunately, all three were right, whereupon I got another letter from my insurance company telling me that my insurance for next year was not invited! Fortunately at that time a scooter in Italy was not considered as a motorised vehicle and so I was able to ride it for the whole year I lived there with no insurance. I did wonder what would I do if I knocked down Sophia Loren, but my friends told me to worry about that when it happened. And, of course, I never knocked anybody down, things proving uneventful, at least in that way, as the year progressed.

When I got to Florence I went to the student *mensa* (canteen) on via 27 Aprile for a meal. Standing in the queue I got chatting to a young Italian medical student, Silvano Pei. He was also looking for somewhere to live, so we decided to share a place for a while. We found a note on a noticeboard saying that two Americans who were staying in Florence temporarily had a room to let and we went to see them. They were called Hans and Wilma Dresner, and we became good friends, keeping in touch for many years. Wilma was a teacher, but I'm not sure whether Hans particularly did anything. He was very worried about whether he would be allowed back into America because he had subscribed to a left-wing weekly magazine. There was a lot of anti-Communism and McCarthyism going on at the time and Hans had been questioned about this magazine. However, all that was to be in the future.

Silvano and I lived with them quite happily and we spent our first, very memorable Christmas with them in the hills. When I came back after Christmas I met another American called Hector who had come to Italy on the GI Bill – a type of scholarship given to any American serviceman who had served at the time of the Korean War, which had just finished. They didn't have to have served in that war, just to have served during the period in which it was fought. When they were demobilised, the servicemen were given a certain sum of money under the GI Bill to study any subject that they wanted – except, I may say, painting. Many of them came to Italy with a romantic idea about being a painter, and as they weren't allowed to study painting they took up Italian instead. In reality they painted and frantically learned a bit of Italian when the inspection was due. Needless to say, their Italian wasn't very good at all.

As usual, I was a bit of an oddball and the American students used to say to me, 'Why do you go into Florence and into the country to paint? There's no need to do that any more, it's old-fashioned. All you have to do is to smell the country, feel the country, see the country and then go away and express the country.' I, of course, having had a thorough grounding in painting, thought that this was all pie in the sky. Many of the young Americans were trying to paint in an Abstract Expressionist manner, although they hadn't had any training and they didn't know much about what they were doing. I don't believe any of them finished up actually making a reputation as a painter. In a funny sort of way I think they appreciated that I had something that they couldn't fully understand and knew that they certainly couldn't get themselves without a lot of time and practice.

The American students found studios all around Florence, for instance in Fiesole. One day Hector told me that there was a studio up for rent at Pian dei Giullari and asked, 'Would you be interested in coming up and sharing it with me? There are two students there already, but there are four units and they need two people to join them.' The Pian dei Giullari is a village just to the south of Florence. When you came out of Florence you went round the Viale Michelangelo and turned and went up towards the Viale San Miniato. There, up in the hills, was an idyllic little village with one of the best trattorias in Florence at that time – which, of course, none of us students could afford to eat at. Beyond the village was a small track which wound up to the top of the hill called the Viuzzo di Monteripaldi. There was a story that D. H. Lawrence had been seen sitting there on the wall, writing *Lady Chatterley's Lover*. How true that is I haven't a clue, but it was a nice romantic idea about the place.

By this time I had regained the confidence to drive my scooter. Hector had also bought himself a Vespa, so we drove up to the Viuzzo di Monteripaldi to have a look at the studio, as it was called. The actual address was Sei bis [6½], Viuzzo di Monteripaldi. It was actually a small gathering of studios set in a small garden. We walked down the path, accompanied by the *contadini* who worked the grounds for the owner, and there they were. One stood by itself, another was part of a complex and a third had a long room in the complex and was suitable for two people. Two Americans were already living there, but they needed to rent the other two to spread the cost between the whole lot. The actual complex belonged to a Swiss hotel owner who inhabited a large house above Viuzzo di Monteripaldi, with the *contadini* living just inside the gate.

I managed to get the single studio by itself. Hector wasn't particularly attracted to it as it had no curtains on the windows nor any amenities, whereas the second one was part of the complex and had a small kitchen. Nonetheless, I was quite pleased to be by myself, in the garden, in the separate studio. And in front of the studio there was a swimming pool – not very effective as its filter system wasn't particularly good and so it was never exactly ideal for swimming in. However, it was nice to sit by in the evening with a glass of cheap Chianti – you really felt as though you were living. All in all it cost us each £6.50 per month for a studio with an unusable swimming pool overlooking a wonderful olive grove.

The Italian government grant was eight pounds per week, which you could live on very well in Florence in 1958. I had never had as much money in my life. We used to eat very cheaply at the *mensa della ferrovia*, a railway canteen down in the city, or at the *mensa degli studenti*, which was also very cheap. A lot of the time we cooked and ate at the studio – very simply, but I remember that we ate very well. I know that we used to cook an enormous pan of rice and live on it for ages, either eating it sweet or adding vegetables.

For the first time in a long while I found myself becoming more relaxed. I didn't feel under enormous pressure. The Italian government didn't demand anything once they had given you the student scholarship, or at least the British Council did not. Getting the scholarship had been quite difficult, but once you had it you didn't have to study at a particular school. The only thing you were obliged to do was to stay in Italy. I worked each day, starting to paint the vineyards and the Florentine landscape. I still had my vision of what I wanted to do, but my work, previously reflecting the strong influence of social realism, began to evolve. As always a painter paints his life, what he is, and I had moved away from the city and industrial north London. Now I was living in an idyllic landscape outside Florence. I suppose in a strange way I had moved forward, and now I was influenced not by Corot, whose little book of Italian landscapes I had taken with me, but by Cézanne.

The other two members of our little quartet up at Sei bis, Viuzzo di Monteripaldi, comprised another American and a very attractive young Australian man. The latter always 'pulled the birds', frustrating us by bringing girls home and spending the night with them, even in those days. We would go to the bathroom in the morning and sense this feminine presence there, which, young as we were, was incredibly frustrating. The American drank a bit too much, sometimes losing his marbles as a result. On such occasions we had to lock him in his room as he would throw bottles around. He eventually committed suicide when he returned to America.

The social life at Sei bis, Viuzzo di Monteripaldi, was very good. The studios were a very romantic setting and the whole area, complete with swimming pool, was really attractive. Every weekend a group of students from Florence used to wind their way up the hill carrying carafes of cheap Chianti, often drinking them before they ever reached the studio. We would start a party and it would go on and

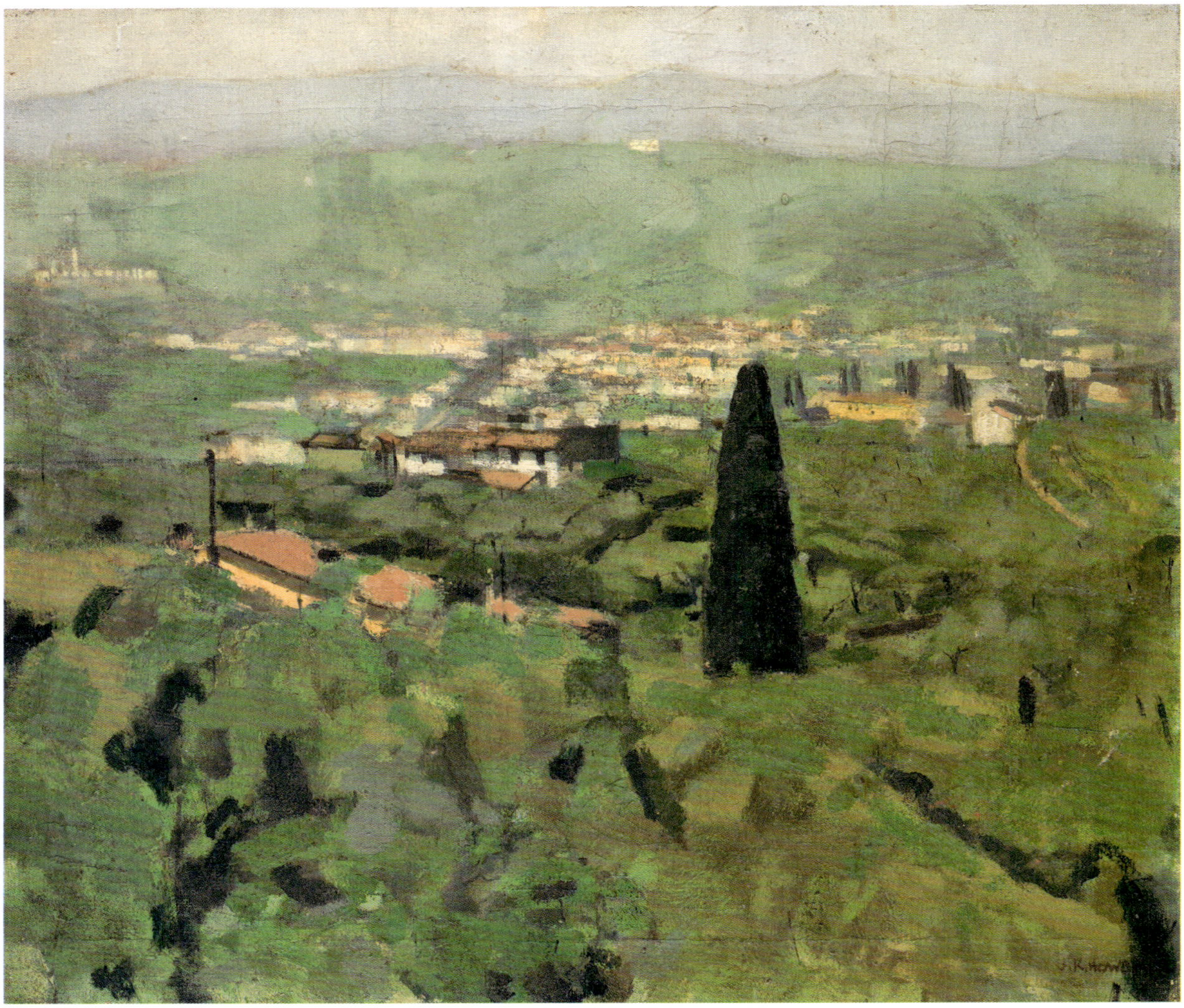

on all through the night, probably lasting into Sunday. We sang songs from our own countries and I remember I had a particular party piece. There was a whole mixture of nationalities. I remember there were Israeli students, as well as Germans and Americans, although I was the only British one. But it didn't make any difference where you had come from or what your background was. We always felt a great sense of togetherness, and these weekend parties were memorable – I only wish I had been able to record some of them. At one of these parties my life was literally to change, with an event that affected the next 33 years of my life.

It was a typical Saturday evening at the studio. The rooms were full of people dancing and singing when suddenly, across the far side of the room, I saw a friend come in with a young girl. By this time I was 26 years old. I had had several girlfriends, but had never taken anything seriously and it was certainly never my intention to marry. In fact, I had already settled in my mind that if I wanted to paint I had to dedicate myself to it, and that a room and an easel were all that I needed. Obviously it was a silly thing to think. I had enjoyed girlfriends, but when I realised I was getting serious I usually dropped them – or, if they realised that I was too committed to what I was doing, they dropped me. Anyway, until that time I had never thought of getting married.

Suddenly this girl came in on the other side of the room, with this friend of mine, Tista. And as I looked across the room I knew, stupid and romantic as it may sound, that I was going to marry that girl. It was just like that. Tista and this girl, Christa, had decided between them that at the party Tista would introduce Christa as his niece, although in fact she was his girlfriend. Christa loved walking and Tista loved hunting early in the morning. They used to go out, she to enjoy the countryside and he to shoot the little birds as they did in Italy at that time. So Tista introduced her to me as his niece. If he had introduced her to me as his girlfriend life might well have been different. Being English, maybe I wouldn't have tried to cut him out that evening, but as she was his niece I concentrated on this lovely girl.

Christa – Chrissie – was then aged twenty and I was six years older. She was German; she came from Cologne and was studying art history in Florence on what I used irreverently to call a 'daddyship'. In other words, her family was rich enough to allow her to come down to Florence to study. She was engaged at the time to Hartmut, the son of a wealthy Cologne businessman. They had been friends for several years, in fact since they were very young. Chrissie's brother was the apple of her parents' eye and she had always felt slightly 'left out', but Hartmut had made her feel that she really mattered. He taught her tennis, which he was good at, and Chrissie in fact became a very good tennis player. She was among the best junior

From the Viuzzo di Monteripaldi, 1959
Oil on canvas, 50 x 60 cm

This picture was made in my studio at Viuzzo di Monteripaldi; the outskirts of Florence can be seen in the middle distance. This and several other paintings of that landscape were included in my first mixed show at the Wildenstein Gallery in Bond Street. During this period I reacted to my environment and became, for the first time, influenced by Cézanne.

Florentine Farmhouse, 1959
Watercolour, 30 x 46 cm

I painted this near my studio in Florence in the garden of an old farmhouse where I first proposed to Chrissie.

players at that time in Westphalia, and her friend, who later got leukaemia, became a junior champion of Germany. So Hartmut and Chrissie had been very close friends for a long time, but nothing else had developed between them. I think Chrissie was beginning to realise this, and to recognise that there was probably something more in life. And that something more, I suppose, was love.

When I met her, Chrissie had been on her own in Florence studying – Hartmut was already in his father's business in Cologne. Tista was a graphic designer, a very original one in fact, but he really wanted to be a painter and had become one of the Florentine group of young artists. I knew him quite well, which is why he had come to the party, bringing Chrissie, whom he had met in Florence. Many years later we went to visit him in Lucca, where he was making a living by painting.

I spent the whole of that evening with Chrissie. I danced with her and talked with her – immediately we discovered that we could really talk about anything and everything. At around 2 am she disappeared and went back with Tista down to Florence. That particular party petered out at about 5 am and I withdrew to my studio. I got up at about 11, I suppose, emerging to a hot, late spring morning in Florence. I lay on a little veranda outside my studio, and I remember that I was reading *Tropic of Cancer*. In those days there were certain books that you had to read, such as those by Aldous Huxley and Henry Miller's *Tropic of Cancer* and *Tropic of Capricorn*. There I lay, reading. All of a sudden I heard a voice calling 'Ken!' I looked up and there was Chrissie, standing above the veranda in the road that went down to the main gate. I remember she had a beautiful sheepdog with her, and she said, 'I've just come to see you.' She came down and we had coffee and went for a walk across the fields. And again we talked and talked, feeling a great kinship growing between us.

Another person at the party, with whom I became very friendly, was Giordano Manfredi. He was about our age but already an agricultural doctor, and the only one of us who had a car because he was already working. I can't remember exactly, but Giordano probably came to the studio again that evening. He had also taken a shine to Chrissie and in the following few days he took her to various farms where he was working. Then she disappeared because she had gone off to see Hartmut, who had come down to Italy to visit her. So it was probably about a week before I saw her again, and I couldn't help thinking about her and hoping that maybe she would come to the studio. Sure enough, as soon as she returned to Florence she arrived at the studio again with the dog.

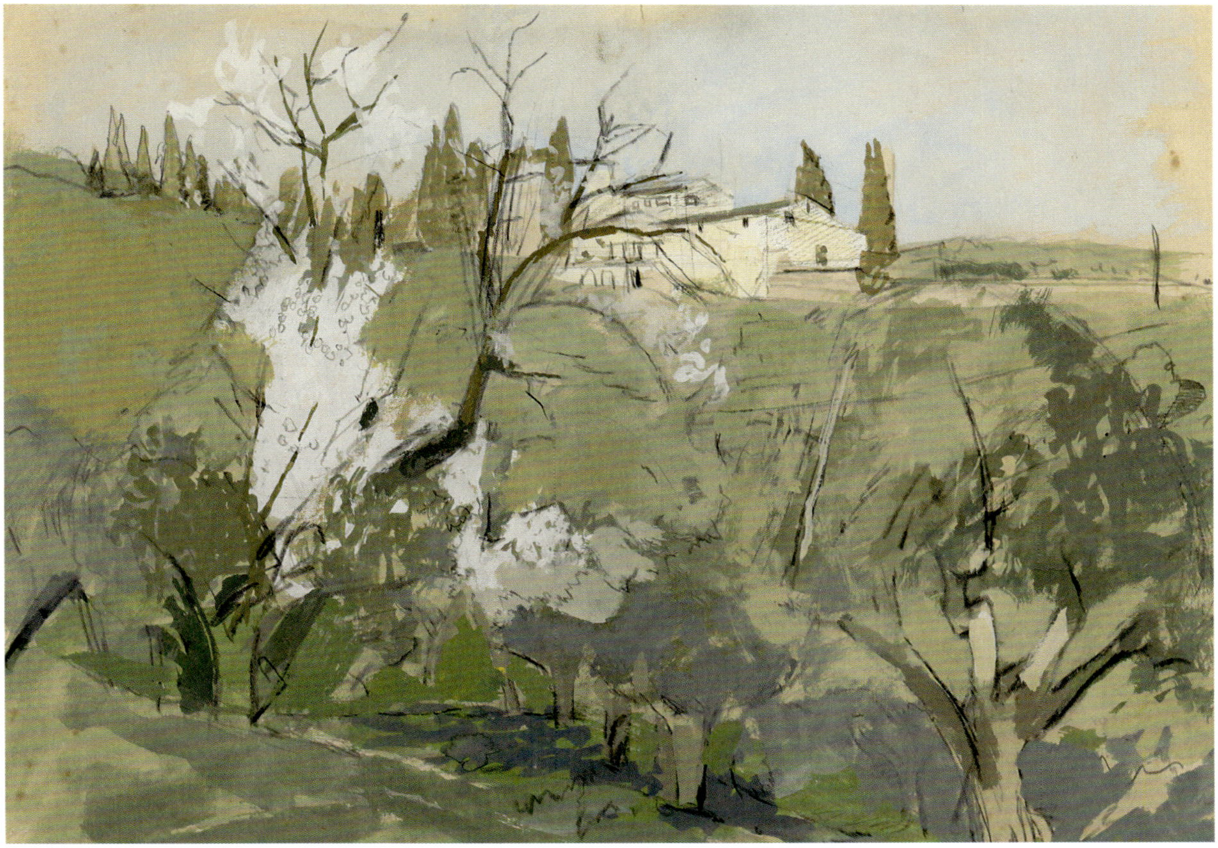

It was a Saturday evening. Another large gathering had come up to the studio and there was a big party in flow. It went on all night and we danced and we talked. Just before dawn, we walked over the fields and stood above Florence. It was one of those idyllic nights when you could hear the soft sounds of nature and birds chirping. The light was just coming up and Florence was silent. Then we heard the first scooter down in the town, and then a car, and then gradually a little buzz began to build up in the dawn down in Florence. And I asked Chrissie to marry me, there and then. I hardly knew her, I had hardly seen her in that week, but I just knew completely that I had to marry this girl – and surprisingly, she turned to me and said yes. She stayed on at the studio and we spent an idyllic week together. During the day she would sit for me and I would paint her, or we would walk through the landscape and talk. Talking was an enormous bond between us. I wasn't a very romantic character, but suddenly I felt full of romance. We read poetry and sat in the olive groves, talking about socialist politics as young people always did in those days. We were very idealistic and I was full of optimism for the future. I never for a moment questioned whether it could work or not.

At the end of the week, I told Chrissie in all innocence that I thought she should go back and tell her parents and Hartmut what we were going to do. And she said, yes, she thought it would be a good idea, but we never thought for a minute that they would question our decision. For us it was so right that we

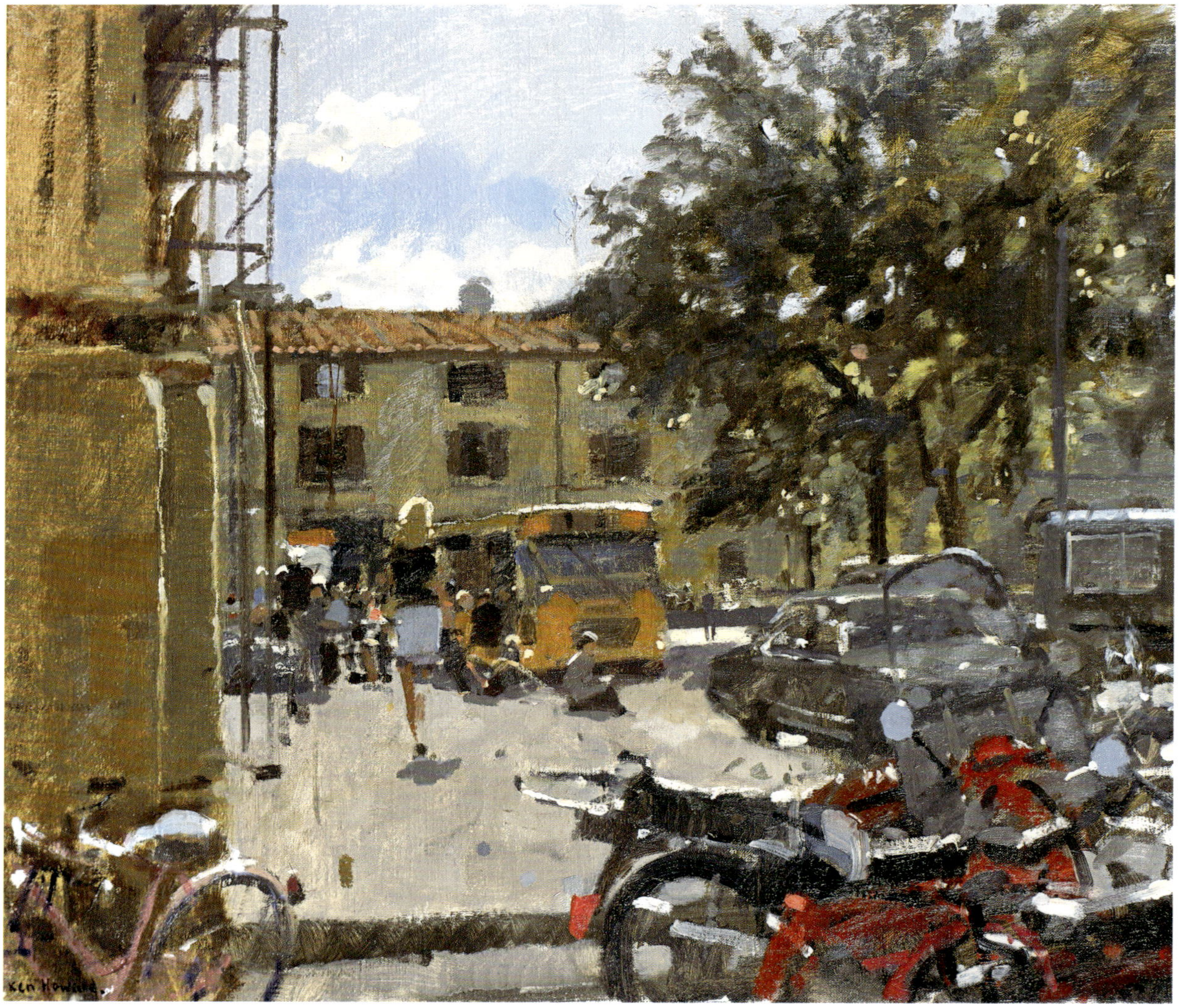

couldn't imagine anyone for a moment questioning it. And this was the 1950s – a time when you 'saved yourselves', if you like, for when you were married, and when you fell in love with someone you put them on a pedestal. So during that week, although we had slept together, we had never made love. As it turned out, that was ridiculous – we should have gone to bed and made love, and Chrissie should have become pregnant in that week. But it didn't happen: we had this pure, idyllic, romantic relationship and we were completely in love with one another. She never went down to the university during that week and I painted very little, and when I did it was of her. I remember going into the villages where there were little birds caged to attract other birds, which the hunters could shoot when they came in. We used to creep up and try to release the little birds into the air, recognising that they needed their freedom as we need ours.

Chrissie and I agreed that she should go back and speak to her parents and Hartmut. Just before the weekend when she left we went down to the little church in Monteripaldi. It was no longer used for services as far as we could see, but it was still a perfect little church. So we went in and knelt by the altar and we married ourselves. There was nobody there, no priest or witnesses, but we swore to love one another for as long as we lived and that nothing would ever come between us. After that we felt as married as anyone could ever feel. We told the other students, and soon after that presents started arriving at the studio: a little painting here, a small piece of pottery there, a letter here. Everybody was completely fascinated by our situation; they were all in love with love, and I suppose the other students began to see us as a sort of Romeo and Juliet. Word had spread, we had been seen around constantly together and we had become a sort of romantic story within Florence. I remember the week before Chrissie left for Germany we went to the Maggio Musicale, where the Modern Jazz Quartet was playing. It was a magical evening in a magical theatre, and as far as we were concerned there were only two people there.

Eventually it was time for Chrissie to go back to Germany. I went down to the station with her and put her on the train, telling her to 'write to me as soon as you can' as we didn't have a phone at the studio. I didn't expect a letter immediately, but after two or three days I began to look for the postman. Where was the first letter? Another day went by and I began to miss her more and more. When Chrissie had first left I had thrown myself back into my work as hard as I could go. I was stimulated and happy; I could see a bright future. All I wanted to do was work, but as the days went by and no letter came I began to get distracted. In the end I couldn't work and just sat and waited for the postman. He never came, at least not with a letter from Chrissie.

Piazza San Marco, Florence, 1958
Oil on canvas, 50 x 60 cm

Someone stole a leather strap from my scooter, which was parked in front of me while I was painting this canvas. I was concentrating so hard on the painting that I didn't even notice it happen.

After about a week I decided to try and ring her number because Chrissie had given me her telephone number in Cologne. I got no answer, and days went by with no letter. In the end I managed to make contact by phone. The Swiss hotel owner up at the house knew the story, and when I went and asked him if I could ring Cologne he immediately agreed. This time I got through and as soon as I heard Chrissie's voice I knew there was something radically wrong. I had been writing to Chrissie every day since she left. I suppose they were passionate letters, certainly they spoke about love and how I envisaged our future together. The first thing she said to me was, 'Why haven't I heard from you?' I told her that I had written every day, and it immediately became apparent that her parents were destroying anything of mine that came from Florence.

I was so disturbed by the sound of her voice that I said, 'I'm coming to Cologne straight away' and put the phone down. I immediately packed and Hector ran me down to the station on the scooter. Soon I was on a train going north, not carrying a lot of money but with enough to see me through. I arrived at Cologne, which I had never been to before, after many hours on the train. It was still a city of devastation, with many buildings destroyed by the war. Some new buildings were going up by this time, but all round the cathedral it was still flattened. I got off the train and went straight away to a hotel booking office to look for a room. The man said he had a room and gave me an address quite near the station. I went round there, dropped my bags, cleaned myself up a bit and decided to go and find Chrissie's house. I had her address, but no idea where in Cologne it was. She lived in a street called Geilenkirchener Strasse, and eventually, by asking questions, I managed to find the street.

By this time, of course, I was getting pretty canny. I had guessed what had happened – that the family had completely refused even to listen to Chrissie's story. I decided not to go and knock at the door because I knew if I did they would know that I was in Cologne, and I wondered what would happen then. So I went to the end of the street and hovered there. I should explain that at the time I wasn't dressed in a particularly elegant way. As it was still a northern winter I had an anorak on, and I was growing a rather bad beard. I never could grow a beard properly, but I was trying to; it was a sort of sprout along the line of my chin. I suppose I resembled a rather 'Frenchified' artist. I suppose I also had fairly long hair, although at that time we didn't wear it very long. Very simply, I had what would have been called a Roman haircut, or later a Beatles haircut. Altogether, I must have looked somewhat original, especially on a smart German street.

As I stood there watching the house, halfway down the road, a large Mercedes drove round the corner. It seemed to hover for a minute, then it went down the street and stopped in front of Chrissie's door. I saw a woman get out and realised it must be Chrissie's mother. But how could she know that the man standing at the end of the street had anything to do with her daughter's latest adventure? So I carried on waiting for a while and eventually, to my delight, Chrissie came round the corner. She was dressed in tennis gear and she was walking with Hartmut; obviously they had just been playing tennis together. She was surprised, even shocked to see me – and Hartmut, as he was to do throughout the rest of our history, realised the situation and said straight away, 'I'll leave you two together.'

We began to walk and she began to tell me all that had happened since she left Florence. She had first gone to Hamburg to see her father and had expected him to be very understanding. But instead, when her father heard the story, he immediately rang her mother. She had quickly got into the car and driven to Hamburg to pick Chrissie up. Years later I could understand what they must have thought. Here was their daughter, engaged to a very nice, eligible, rich young man with the right sort of background, from the right sort of society in Cologne. They wanted her settled and married and, I suppose, off their hands. They thought that was all going to happen, and suddenly their daughter had returned from Florence saying that she wasn't staying engaged to Hartmut, but was going to marry a penniless English (a bad start as her father had been a General in the German army) art student, of all things. She couldn't even say an English painter – I was still an art student, without a job, from a working-class background in London. As a son-in-law's CV, of course, it wasn't very impressive, and naïvely I hadn't even considered this. Nor had Chrissie. She had a very simple attitude to love, and I remember when we were talking, many years later, she said to me, 'You know, when I met you in Florence, you were painting like an Impressionist. I couldn't believe that anyone ever painted like that, or could be painting like that at that time.' I was surprised by this and replied, 'But, Chrissie, you hardly knew me. You didn't really understand what I was doing, or even sort of approve of it, but when I asked you to marry me within a week of our meeting, you said yes.' She just looked at me and said, 'What's that got to do with loving someone?'

So her mother had driven Chrissie back to Cologne and all the way told her how ridiculous the situation was. If she married me she would go to London and would have to live in a poor part, in an environment that she wasn't used to. She would have no money and I would have no job. We would have children fairly quickly and the whole of her life would become a struggle. First of all, naturally,

Chrissie protested, but her mother was a very persuasive person. She worked and worked on it, and by destroying any letter that came and refusing to take any phone calls, she gradually broke down Chrissie's resistance. Chrissie had, after all, really only known me for about two weeks. There had been no physical bonding between us, just bonding of the mind, I suppose. And gradually her mother got her to believe the things that she said.

Hartmut, of course, did exactly the right thing, in a genuine and not calculating way – that was his nature. When he heard the story he said, 'I will give you the fare and you must go back to Florence and live with this man for some time and find out whether your feelings are serious and whether they will last.' This was, of course, the best thing he could have done, although he didn't do it consciously: his kindness only made Chrissie doubt her feelings even more. And after days of this kind of bombardment, I suppose, with no new word from me or anything really to give her strength again, she was gradually worn down. By the time we met that day, she was in a condition where she didn't really know what to think.

This, of course, hadn't happened to me, and I still had a very clear vision of everything I believed in for the future. I talked to her and talked to her; gradually I began to win her back, and I realised this was happening. In the house, of course, her mother guessed what was going on when her daughter didn't come back with Hartmut and the strange man at the end of the street disappeared. With due efficiency she rang the various hotel agencies, eventually getting on to the one that I booked into. Then she called the hotel owner and offered to pay him a sum of money to report whenever I went in or went out of the hotel. Next she rang the police and explained the situation, being a person of considerable influence in Cologne as her husband was an important businessman. She told the police that she believed her daughter was going to be abducted from Cologne that night. Immediately the police went to the station and began to check every train going to Florence. By this time it was dark. Chrissie and I were still walking through the streets of Cologne, but Chrissie knew her mother very well and said, 'I'm sure my mother will have done something to try and trace us.' We went to the local church and sat talking for quite a while, but eventually we had to go back onto the street again. I can remember clearly leaning back against walls while police cars were going around with headlights, searching for this couple who were supposed to be trying to run away from Cologne. It was bizarre – cinematic in a way. I had never come across anything like it in my life. Now I realised that it had been in complete innocence in Florence that we believed her parents would ever agree to our marriage.

We stayed out the whole night. In the morning she went home and I knew that from then on I wouldn't be able to see her because they would just keep her in the house and wouldn't allow any phone calls. But by the time the morning came I had convinced Chrissie that what we had decided, and the fact that she had decided not to marry Hartmut, was right. I had emphasised to her that if she wanted a full life she had to have the courage to go ahead with what she believed. We agreed that when my scholarship ended in six weeks' time I would run up to Cologne on my scooter, on my way home, and that Chrissie would come back to London with me. I would then find a flat for her in London – I wouldn't try and convince her to marry me straightaway as I realised that her confidence had already been somewhat dented by her parents' arguments. Instead I told her that if she would come to live in London I thought it would be highly likely that I could get her some teaching in a London art school. I said I was sure that she was a very good art historian. And when she was ready, and not before, we could get married. Chrissie was in complete agreement and encouraged by this idea.

Then I got on the train and went back to Florence. On the train I wrote a long, long letter which I posted when I got back; we had agreed to have a *poste restante* so that she would get my letters and they wouldn't be destroyed any more. Strangely enough, I was to be proved right. I spelled out exactly what our lives would have been if she had then, or six weeks later, come to England. I told her that I would teach, and that this would give us an income. I told her that eventually I would get a gallery and a studio in London, and that we would find a nice place in the country. It was all very romantic, but I truly believed it was possible. By that time I believed that if you wanted something badly and you worked at it enough, eventually you would get it. So during the following six weeks I worked hard, feeling full of hope and confidence. When my time in Florence finally ended I put all my things – not as many as I had brought with me, naturally – back on my Lambretta. Then my scooter and I headed for Cologne.

I had noticed over my last weeks in Florence that although the letters I wrote were very passionate and full of hope for the future, Chrissie's letters, even though there were plenty of them, became shorter and less positive and less focused on what was going to happen. I didn't let that thought worry me too much – at least I was getting letters most days. I was also sending letters most days, and I believed that they were bound to be having the effect that I wanted them to have.

When I got to Cologne I obviously couldn't go to the house and let them know that I was back. I got a room again and got in touch with Chrissie. I can't now remember clearly how, but I know that eventually she came to the hotel where I was staying. As soon as we were together I saw that they had worked their arguments on her as before and she was full of doubt again. However, she said that she had arranged with her parents that she was going to stay with some friends for the weekend. They wouldn't worry where she was and we could spend the weekend together.

Near to Cologne was a very open area of country; it lay to the west of the Rhine between Cologne and Aachen on a road that I have used many, many times since. Whenever I travel along that road I always remember that weekend, which in many ways, I suppose, was a disaster. I had my tent with me – I couldn't really afford a hotel, and anyway Chrissie wanted to camp. We found a lake nearby and that evening we pitched the tent in a field close to it. Then we sat and talked about everything. By this time, of course, I realised that I was losing the argument and that unless something radical happened, her parents were going to win. I suppose I then began to think more logically about the situation.

So that night, as we came together in the tent, I tried to make love to Chrissie. By this time, however, her whole belief in our life together had become so distorted by her parents' arguments that she could no longer give herself to me. Had I done this in Florence I know that we would have become lovers straightaway – and in retrospect I know that Chrissie would probably have got pregnant straightaway. And then, without doubt, her parents would have said that she must go to London and live with this man because they wouldn't have wanted the shame in Cologne society of a daughter being pregnant and not married. They would have probably tried to talk her into having an abortion, which of course Chrissie would never have agreed to. But now it was too late, and I realised that. The following day we walked and we talked, and I still tried to win her over to my way of thinking. And on the Sunday evening we realised that we had to return to Cologne.

We piled everything onto the scooter and began to drive out of the field. On the edge of the field was a slight bank and I tried to get up it but slipped down. Little did I know that the exhaust pipe had dug into the earth and had blocked. When we finally got the scooter out of the field it wouldn't function any more. We tried everything, but the engine just wouldn't turn over. As I wasn't mechanically minded it didn't dawn on me that the exhaust was plugged and therefore the machine wouldn't go. In the end we had to abandon it because

Chrissie was desperate to get back: her parents were expecting her home that evening. We began to hitchhike, but didn't do very well. Eventually it grew very dark and we crawled into a barn by the side of the road where, exhausted, we both fell asleep in the hay. Very early the next morning we left and got to the nearest town, where Chrissie caught a bus back into Cologne. She explained to her parents that she had stayed an extra night. Meanwhile, her friends had known the situation, so had her parents rung the evening before they would have made some sort of excuse.

I myself went back for the scooter and got it into a garage. As soon as the mechanics looked at it they knew what was wrong; with the exhaust cleaned out, the machine worked perfectly. I drove back into Cologne to my hotel. Chrissie knew where I was so she came to the hotel to say goodbye. We talked and decided that we would continue to write, agreeing that when Chrissie was stronger in herself again she would come to London and we would follow our plan. At that moment, however, she didn't feel strong enough. I remember we lay together and I tried very hard to make love to her, but by this time there was no way it was possible. As she explained to me some years later, it was a completely ridiculous thing to do. She had brought me a wonderful book on Cézanne which she gave to me as I left, and when I got home we would continue to write via the *poste restante*. I was completely determined that our relationship was going to work. As I left Cologne I was depressed by what had happened but still believing, though I suppose with not quite such a bright flame.

My friends in London were all expecting to meet Chrissie as I had been writing to them about her, explaining what we were going to do and what our plans were. My mother had agreed that when we first arrived we could have a flat on the first floor of the house. My sister had left home by this time and it was possible to make the rooms upstairs into a flat. In the end, of course, I arrived by myself. My mother tried to cheer me up by saying, 'Ah well, perhaps it wasn't such a good idea' (in her wisdom she could see what was going to happen). I, however, in my blind love, couldn't countenance for a minute the fact that we weren't going to be together. I still thought that when Chrissie arrived we would have to get a flat, and I had to be able to keep her when she was in London. So the first thing I did on my return was to try and get some work. The Italian adventure was definitely over.

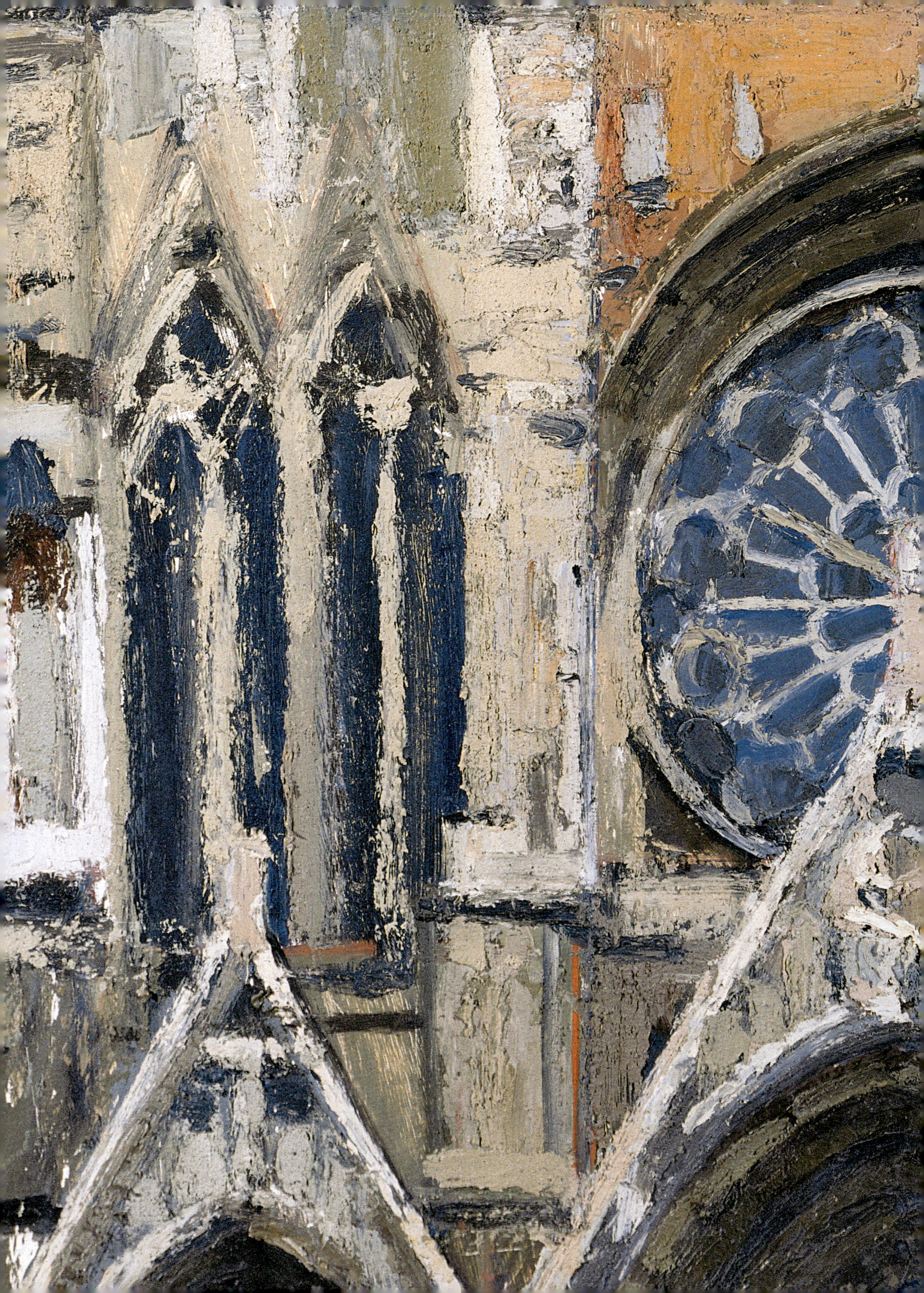

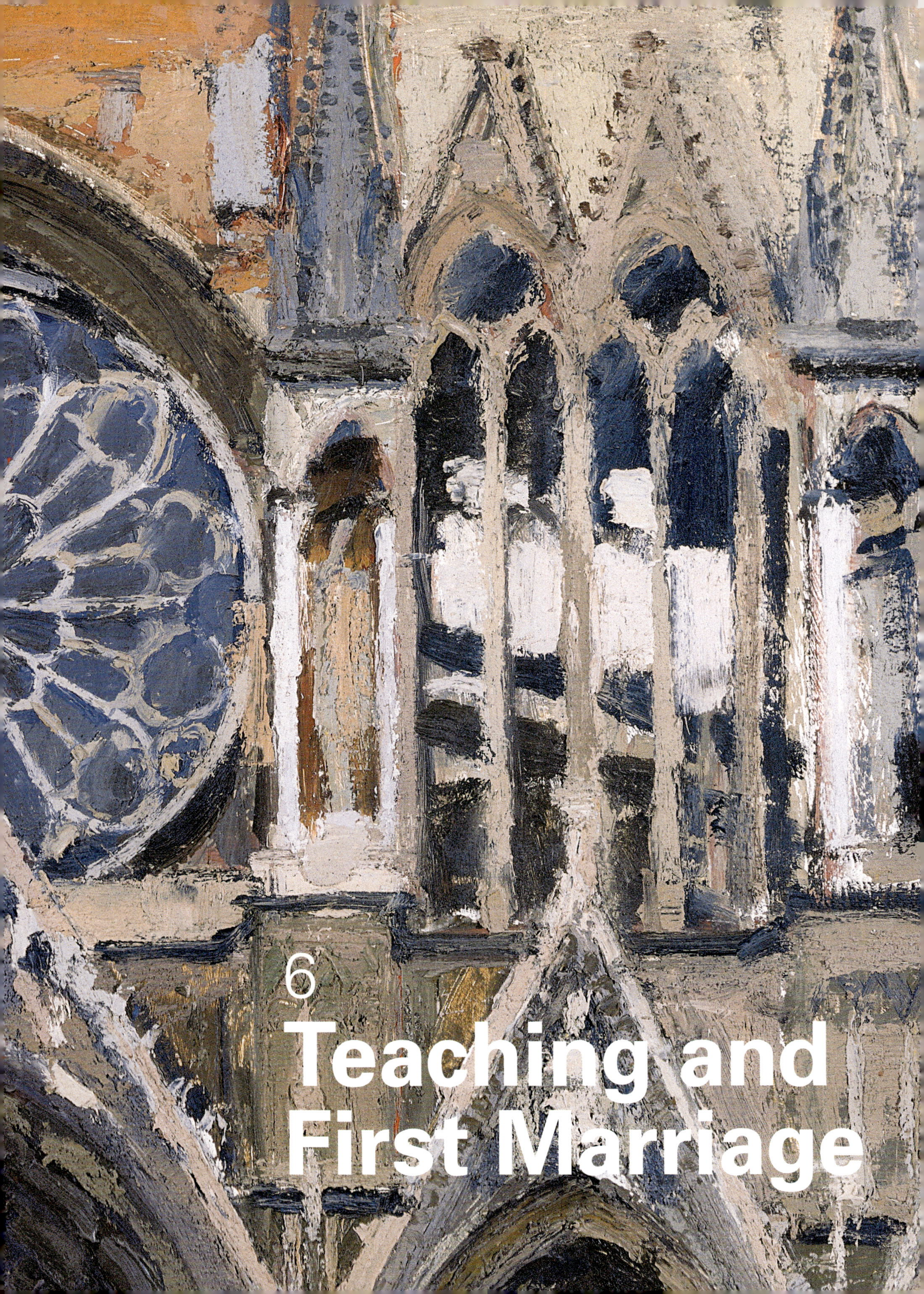

6
Teaching and First Marriage

At that time things were very positive in the art world, and I approached the search for teaching with confidence. The head of Hornsey School of Art, J . G. Platt, had followed my career over the years; he knew of my work at the Royal College and my time in Italy – in fact he had written a letter of recommendation for the Italian scholarship. Before I had left Hornsey, J. G. had told me that if I came back there when I finished at the Royal College of Art, he would give me a couple of days' teaching. Unfortunately he had retired by the time I got back, although I was still quite well-known in the school because of my time there. I showed my portfolio to Maurice de Sausmarez, a very good teacher who was in charge of drawing there. Maurice looked through my portfolio, liked what I had done and offered me two days' teaching a week.

This to me was marvellous as it was worth a considerable amount of money in those days – I think it worked out at about £16, but I can't remember clearly. Anyway, my hopes were dashed. When I reached the front entrance to the school, the new head came out. He took one look at me and said, 'You're Howard, aren't you?' I said yes, and that I'd just been given two days' teaching at the school. Shelton just said, 'We don't employ ex-students,' and walked away. That was it, and there was nothing that Maurice could do.

Before I'd gone to Italy the art school at Kingston had offered me a full-time position. When I won the scholarship, however, they advised me to take it, and said they would give me some part-time teaching on my return. I had written to them from Florence and realised that something wasn't right. When I got back and went to see them, although they didn't tell me explicitly I realised that somebody there had undermined me, and the two days' teaching had evaporated. So I was left with nothing, but was still determined.

The first thing I did was to go to my local art school, which was Willesden. I went along and asked to see the head, who had interviewed me years before when I was still at grammar school – without an appointment I may add. Little did I know that Willesden was just about to close and he was about to take over the Ealing School of Art. When I went in he said how pleased he was to see me and asked how had I got on in Italy. After we had chatted a while, I asked whether by chance he had any teaching for me next term. The head went ballistic – he was quite a strange man in some ways – demanding, 'How dare you come and see me and ask for teaching, without an appointment?' I backed out and hastily left. The next day I received a letter from him, obviously somewhat embarrassed and apologising for his behaviour. He told me that he was about to become the head at Ealing and that he would offer me one day a week there. So at least I had a start.

The next port of call was Harrow, a leading art school in west London, where again I struck lucky. They were looking for staff, partly for the junior art school and partly to teach drawing to intermediates, which was right up my street. So I had then picked up two days' teaching, plus two evening classes on the same days. Finally, I managed to get some teaching at Walthamstow School of Art, which was a very high-profile school at that time; I was very pleased to be given an evening class there too.

One problem, of course, was that the classes were spread across London – Walthamstow, Ealing and Harrow are hardly next door to each other and I had returned from Italy without a licence for my scooter. I had to get a car. I rang the insurance company and asked if they would insure me if I got a car, and thankfully they agreed that what happened on two wheels didn't concern them – they would insure me for four. To get a car was quite a monumental task, however, as I had no money. So I thought about what I could do and went to work on a road-construction site at the end of the M4 – on the large overhead part from Chiswick to Heathrow. Road construction was quite well paid and naturally a six-days-a-week job, which was possible for me as term had not yet commenced. I can't now remember exactly what I got paid, but it was probably about £12 a week, for a period of approximately six weeks. I worked with a gang of navvies – all Irish except for me and the foreman, who was a fairly heavyweight Cockney. It was hard work, but the Irish navvies were wonderful and they treated me as a sort of mascot, I suppose. Although I worked as hard as I could, I wasn't up to their strength.

I remember one day we were removing some heavy wooden blocks from under the motorway; they had been supporting this prestressed concrete until it was in place. These were enormous pieces of timber and had to be loaded by hand on to a low loader. We all gathered around it and the Irishmen looked at me. One of them said, 'I tell you what, Ken, we'll lift and you grunt!' That was typical of their attitude, and they were a marvellous crew to work with, although I remember the Cockney foreman was not quite so understanding. Each of us spent one day crane directing – an easy day as it wasn't heavy work. You sat on the edge of the flyover to direct the crane operator below, showing him where to lift the concrete for the bed of the road. He started to raise the container and then came across the road, whereupon we indicated to him how far down it should come – by that time the operator could no longer see where it was to go. I wasn't really very good at that. I managed to get the first one up and across, but didn't signal quickly enough when it began to drop towards the road. As a result, the container

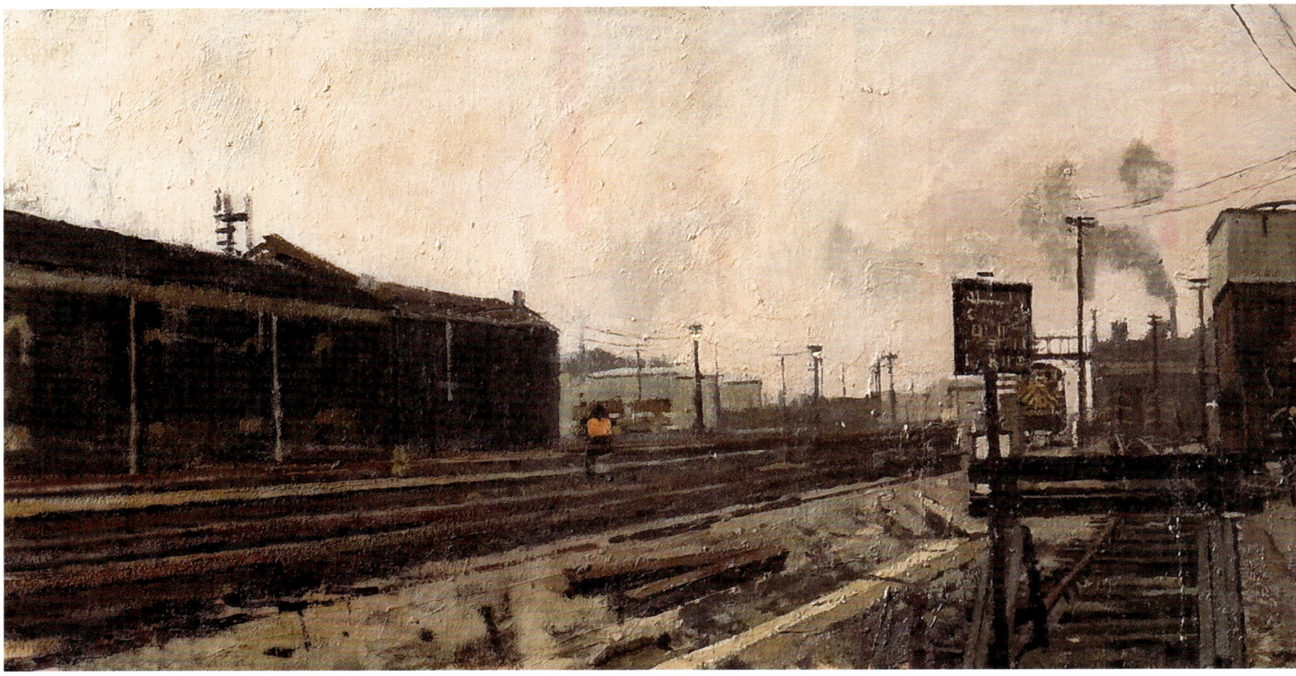

Southall Sidings, *c.* 1965
Oil on canvas, 60 x 180 cm

This painting celebrated the beauty of industrial north London, a landscape that I loved. The starting point of all painting is the idea, or concept; one must love this or it is not worth picking up a brush.

hit the road, spilled wet concrete all over the place and bent the various iron pieces that were the stressing for this particular section of road. As you can imagine the foreman wasn't very pleased, and I never got that easy job again.

There were lunch breaks while I was there, of course. I used to draw in these and begin to get ideas for paintings, which I would work up on Sundays. One day a director of Stelmo, one of the construction companies working on the project, came along and saw me drawing. He asked if I was an artist and said he would like a painting of this site, an important contract for the firm. So I did him a painting – quite a large one, as I remember it, about 90 by 75 cm I would think, maybe a little less. I did the painting and took it along to the director. He liked it very much and agreed to pay me £20, I believe, for the painting. He also showed it to the other contractors, as the road was being built by a consortium called Marples, Ridgeway, Keir, Christiani & Nielsen. When the various contractors saw this painting they wanted one too, and I got another five commissions. So with the combination of my job – which I kept, despite my crane-directing mishap – and the commissions, I had earned enough money in about six weeks to buy a car.

Many years later, when I was better known and exhibiting regularly in the Academy, I received a letter from Stelmo, asking if I was the Ken Howard who sold them a picture of the road works in Chiswick in 1959. They were pleased when I said yes – I think they realised that they had got quite a reasonable deal out of it.

Once I'd earned the money I had to find a car. A friend of mine had a garage on the North Circular Road just beyond Neasden, and he had a wonderful car there, a Triumph Mayflower. It was beautiful and quite unique – one of the first cars that didn't have mudguards. They called it the 'poor man's Rolls Royce' because it had these sharp edges. It cost me around about £100, horrifying my mother who

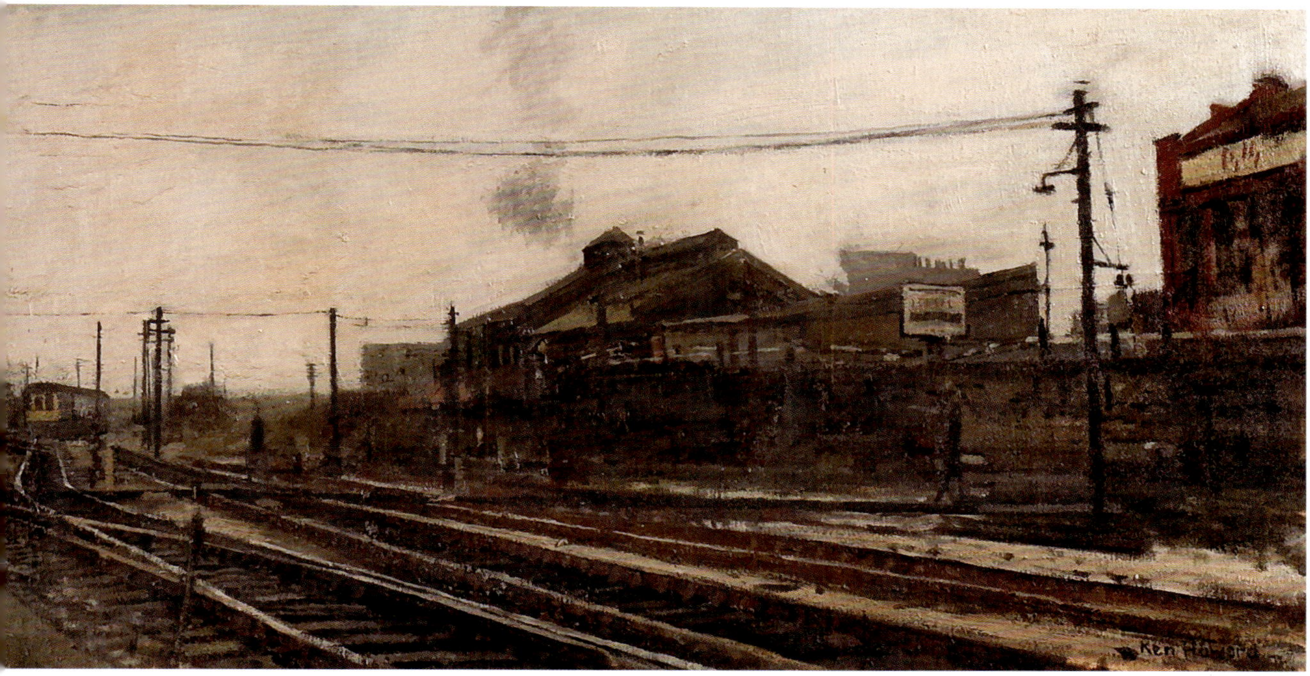

thought I could never afford it, what with the insurance premiums and petrol (in those days actually very cheap) as well. 'I have to have it, I'm afraid,' I told her. 'Otherwise I can't earn my living.'

A man in our street ran a little repair place and he agreed to come to the garage and pick up the car with me. When we got there he told me to get into the driving seat. I protested that I'd never driven, although by this time I had a provisional licence, but he said to me, 'Well, this is the time to start.' He had an L-plate with him, which he put in the back window. So he showed me which pedal was the accelerator, which the clutch and which the brake, and how to work the gear lever, and I drove us home. Never will I forget that first drive on the North Circular Road. I had never driven a car in my life, I had only driven a scooter, and I must confess that I was scared stiff and sweated – but I drove the two miles back home. I often wondered afterwards how he was feeling, sitting next to somebody who he knew full well had never driven a car before. But I think he was a man with great insight because in those days, with less aggressive traffic, it was the easiest and the best way to teach somebody quickly to drive. You will never believe it, but on that evening I felt so confident that I drove into town by myself in the car. It was a ridiculous thing to do because I only had a provisional driving licence and so should have had somebody with me.

I then started to go to my teaching work by car, and by the time I got round to booking my driving test I had driven some 6,000 miles. I booked the test some time in advance, but decided to have one formal driving lesson before I took it, just to brush up on the ropes. The driving instructor asked me how many driving lessons I had had before, so I explained this was my first, but that I had my test tomorrow. He looked at me rather critically and said, 'Drive me then, and show

Southall Sidings II, *c.* 1965
Oil on canvas, 50 x 60 cm

For several years before I made this I had been interested in patterns of dark lines against light skies, such as trolley-bus wires and telegraph wires. This work reflects my interest in the opposite effect, of light railway lines against the dark earth.

me what you can do!' By this time I was totally confident with the car, so I drove him up the road. After a mile or two he turned to me and asked, 'Just how many miles have you driven before this lesson?' I told him about 6,000 and he said, 'You will pass your test easily tomorrow.' And indeed I did. A few days later I was driving down the Mall when a policeman stepped out and pulled me up, asking to see my driving licence and papers. I took them out and showed them to him. 'Yes, that's all right,' he said, and I asked why they were looking. He answered that they were just checking up on cars to see whether they were stolen or not. If that had happened a week earlier I would certainly have lost my driving licence, and with it my ability to fulfil my teaching jobs. Luck had smiled on me again.

So I had started my professional career. I was teaching far more than I wanted to – indeed in that first year I got another day's teaching, which made four days and three evenings. In actual fact I taught four days, three evenings and Saturday mornings, as a friend of mine, the head of art at Berkhamsted School, had offered me a day and Saturday morning. I willingly took it, as the more I could earn that year, the more capable I thought I would be of supporting Chrissie when she came to London.

My mind was still totally set on that goal. As the weeks went by and I got more involved in my teaching, I realised that Chrissie's letters were getting increasingly less personal and less involved. And having gone through so much already, I could well imagine what was going to happen. Finally, I got a letter from Chrissie saying that her parents were sending her away to a family in France who took girls from German families. It wasn't as grand as a finishing school, but it was that kind of idea, and obviously she would be living in fairly luxurious surrounding for several weeks. I saw that her parents were working at this very logically, and believed that this experience would show her that she was not cut out to go and live with a penniless painter in London.

Then, of course, I made another mistake. I wrote to Chrissie and said to her that I thought I could understand what was happening and I wasn't a person who could go on waiting and waiting and finally losing. She had to make the decision and either come to London now and live with me, or stay in a flat that I would find while we got to know each other well. If she couldn't do that, I didn't see that there was any point in going on. In retrospect it was a silly ultimatum to issue, but I suppose it was the way I have done things all my life. Once I have decided to do something, I have to do it. I never got a reply to that letter.

For weeks the bottom seemed to have dropped out of my world. I already wasn't painting a lot because I was teaching far too much. As the weeks went

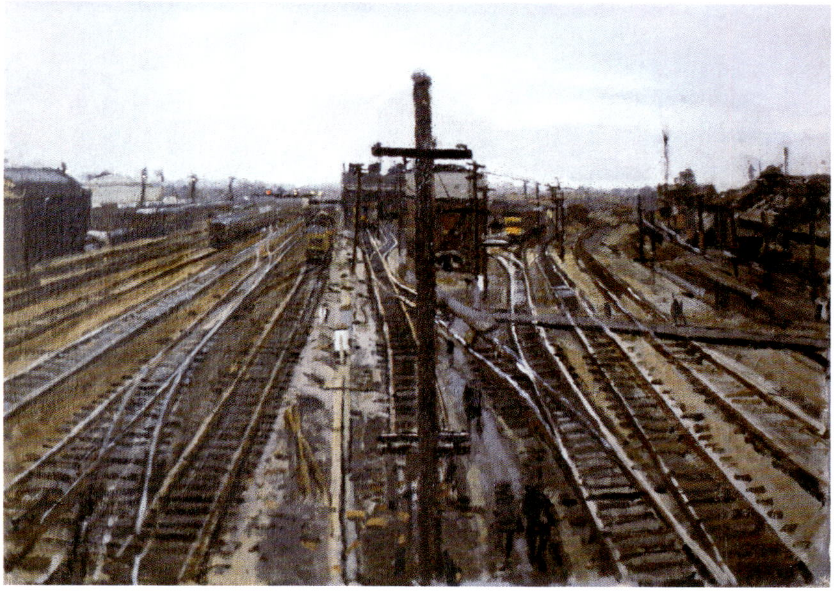

by and no letter came, I resolved to change my whole plans. I would give up all my teaching at the end of the academic year, except what was actually necessary for me to live on. I was still living at home, I didn't have any very expensive tastes, and if I just kept on a couple of days' teaching I would be all right.

No letter came, and at the end of the year I gave up my teaching at Berkhamsted and Ealing. I kept one day at Harrow and one day at Walthamstow, and I also kept the evenings at each school, feeling that as I had lost the day anyway, I might as well earn extra by teaching in the evenings. By this time, though, I realised that I liked teaching. I could recognise the dangers that were there – teachers for art schools were in demand and I wasn't bad at it, so I knew that in the end I would be offered a full-time position and that it would be tempting. But I had no responsibilities and I wanted to get right back into my work again. I had given up any hope of ever hearing from Chrissie, and I obviously never imagined that we would meet again after fourteen years.

During my fourteen years of teaching, my most interesting time was eventually at Walthamstow School of Art. I only taught part-time, about a day and an evening a week, but we had a most interesting group of students. They included Ian Dury (later of the Blockheads), Peter Greenaway, a future film-maker, Bill Jacklin, who went on to show with Marlborough in London and New York and now lives in New York, as well as other printmakers and painters. My experience at Walthamstow taught me that it is not the quality of the teaching that is most important, but the quality of the students. If you have got one really good student in the batch, such as Bill Jacklin, it spurs the others on, and they end up achieving their very best. The staff were all relatively young – I must have been about 31 or 32. Peter Blake also taught there, as did Fred Cuming, another Royal Academician, and Fred Dubery, who became Professor of Perspective before me at the Royal Academy. It was a good staff, but the quality of the students mattered most.

Ian Dury, for instance, went on to the Royal College of Art and became a very good Pop artist – very fashionable at the time – before he went into music. Peter Greenaway went into film, where his work was very influenced by his interest in painting. *The Cook, the Thief, His Wife and Her Lover* was almost like a Frans Hals painting and *The Draughtsman's Contract* was very definitely influenced by his knowledge of drawing (in which Walthamstow had a very good reputation). The quality of the students is confirmed by the fact that Walthamstow picked up around a third of the highly coveted 30 places to study fine art at the Royal College of Art – an incredible feat when you consider how many art schools there were in the country at the time. There weren't a lot of postgraduate schools in those days, so there was great competition for the 30 places at the Royal College in the Fine Art Department. The intense competition was reflected in the very high standard of the students who did get through.

The conditions at Walthamstow were also worthy of note. We hear so much about conditions at schools and are told that all schools must be new and modern, and yet those students at Walthamstow (basically a technical college with an art department) had very limited facilities. There were one or two art studios that were used by the painters. I remember that the life-drawing class was in a chemistry lab; the model used to be posed along one of the long desks in between Bunsen burners, while the students sat at the other long tables, laying their drawing boards against the table. So the conditions in which they worked were not very good. The students fought against that and achieved, despite the circumstances, not because of them. Later on, I remember, Walthamstow got a brand new art school. Maybe it's my fault, but I can't remember any students that have come out of Walthamstow since. There may well have been, but I don't remember any. Yet the quality of the students who emerged from Walthamstow when I was there was quite incredible. Of course, many of them were local boys and girls, some from what might now be termed deprived backgrounds. And they were probably working to get out of that – they wanted to achieve something, and many of them did.

Some quite funny stories came out of the art school because the local lads would look on art students as being rather 'namby pamby' or effeminate. The male students used to go down to a local pub and one night the local boys started taking the mickey out of them – at least this is the version I heard. One of the students, Bill West, who was a big lad himself, turned round and said, 'All right, I'll go outside with all of you, one at a time.' They did, and he fought and beat them all, one at a time, after which the local boys didn't take the mickey out of art students. It was very typical of the times, I suppose. Bill was certainly a very good draughtsman;

he went to the Royal College of Art and did some good paintings. I remember meeting him some years later in the Queen's Elm pub in the Fulham Road in London. We stood and talked and Bill asked, 'Do you remember when you gave me that criticism of my drawings on the third-floor corridor of Walthamstow School of Art?' I replied that I did, and he said, 'Do you remember you opened the window and threw the drawings out because you wanted to illustrate to me that they were so bad?' I remembered that too. Then he added, 'Do you realise you came close to following them out of the window?' We both laughed, but knowing Bill I could well imagine that I wasn't far from being thrown out of the window too.

There was a very rigorous discipline of teaching at Walthamstow. Later on a belief arose that you mustn't overteach because you would destroy the students' creativity, but in those days at Walthamstow we believed that you had to teach these youngsters drawing and the disciplines of painting. Before I got my day's teaching at Walthamstow the head came into my evening class. He quite liked the way I was teaching and told me, 'I would like you to do a criticism of the final-year students. If you come through that all right and I'm impressed with you, I will give you a day's full-time teaching.' You almost literally had an audition to see that you could teach. Schools were very different at that time because their heads were always the 'ideas men' of the school. They were always good painters in their own right and provided the inspiration to students there. Heads of schools would go around the studios and look at students' work and maybe even do a bit of teaching themselves. Meanwhile, the organisation and running of the schools was attended to by older women, maybe in their fifties, who got the institution to function effectively. I taught in about three different art schools which were always run on this model.

I remember the head at Walthamstow was a man called Stuart Ray. He was a bit of an eccentric as well as being a very good painter, and I remember that if he did take you on to his staff it was more or less understood that you would exhibit at the New English Art Club, in which he greatly believed. Also, he liked you to grow old roses – something else for which he had a passion. And although I wasn't a gardener I did start to grow old roses, as that teaching was very important to me.

It is worth at this stage saying something about the New English Art Club, of which eventually I became President. It was formed in 1886 by painters who thought the Royal Academy painters hadn't recognised what was going on in France. So the New English, or NEAC, was in fact an anti-Academy organisation. Many of its best members were eventually elected to the Academy, of course, because the Academy eventually caught up with what the New English had always been about. To some extent the New English lost its raison d'être – its members were now part of the Academy, which had caught up with Impressionism and Post-Impressionism, and certainly with Cubism. So the New English had many, many years in the wilderness, as it were. It was carried on by painters such as myself who very much believed in figurative painting and the importance of their own language, and who didn't believe that it was necessary to be particularly innovative or avant-garde. Then gradually it found its raison d'être again, because the Academy went on to embrace the avant-garde and was no longer about Impressionist and Post-Impressionist painting. The strength of the Royal Academy is that it could do this, and the strength of the New English is that it has kept to its vision. It became the bastion for good Impressionist and Post-Impressionist painting, and in the end gained enormously from the point of view of its members. In fact it began to replace the Royal Academy as the source of that traditional base. Today the New English has had a renaissance and is attracting new painters – not those at the cutting-edge who are into conceptual art, but young painters who believe in the basic value of drawing and figurative painting, as members of the New English have done for a very long time.

I have already touched on the staff at Walthamstow School of Art, a very diverse and interesting group of teachers. I taught an evening class and among the other teachers taking evening classes was a man called Clifford Hall, a well-known surrealist painter whose work comes up very often now at Sotheby's and Christie's. He was then in his late seventies, I suppose, and very bohemian in his way. He had been married three or four times, I think, and I remember walking home with him one night from Walthamstow to catch the bus back to town. I was complaining to him about the fact that my then wife, a dress designer, didn't seem to consider what I liked fashion-wise. She always wore very good, fashionable clothes that I didn't necessarily like. Clifford was amused. 'You're a bit of an innocent, aren't you, Ken?' he remarked. I asked what he meant. 'Surely,' he said, 'you realise that women dress for other women, but undress for men!'

On another occasion I was talking to Clifford about the fact that I couldn't manage to buy a *pochard*. I think the word actually means a box that would fit into a pocket; Impressionist and Post-Impressionist painters always seemed to use a *pochard*, in effect a little painting box. 'Oh!' said Clifford, 'I've got one that Sickert gave me.' Sickert, of course, was one of my great gods and I was a little dumbstruck. He said, 'I'll give it to you, provided you use it and don't stick it in a cupboard like a relic, as it were.' And I did use that box for years until it began to disintegrate. I've still got it in its very dilapidated state because I kept it as a Walter Sickert paintbox. I enjoy collecting the paraphernalia of painters.

I've got a Holman Hunt paintbox that I acquired from Christie's, as well as the paintbox of William Orpen and some of his brushes. I've also got Lucien Pissarro's paintbox, an easel that belonged to Robert Buhler and another that belonged to John Ward.

Eric Hebborn was another interesting member of staff at Walthamstow. He was a wonderful draughtsman, and we taught together at an evening class. I think he was a bit disillusioned that the art world had not recognised his skill as a draughtsman. Whether it was because of that I don't know, but he did become a very convincing faker of Old Master drawings. If you're going to become a faker, it's obviously much easier to concentrate on drawings, as modern technology can very quickly analyse a painting to discover whether the materials or the canvas is of the right age. All sorts of chemical analyses can be done with paint pigments, canvases etcetera, whereas with drawing it is easier to make a convincing fake. If you can get hold of an old book and use the endpapers, for example, then the paper would be of that period. It is also far more difficult to establish the exact age of charcoal, Conté crayon or chalk, whereas analysing the age of paint is now relatively easy.

Anyway, Eric became a very convincing faker of Old Master drawings. I don't think I'm speaking out of turn because in 1991 he published a very good book about his forgeries, entitled *Drawn to Trouble*. He eventually left England and went to live in Rome with his boyfriend, but was tragically murdered while he was there in the mid-1990s. The motive was unclear. No one ever discovered whether it was linked to his homosexuality, but it may have been. Or perhaps the dark side of the art market decided that it didn't want Eric, who was going to publish another book to say where the faked drawings actually were. We will probably never know. Eric's last book, *The Art Forger's Handbook*, was in fact published in 1997, after his murder.

Teaching in Walthamstow, and in other art schools, was very inspirational. I personally believe that one learns more from one's students than students do from their teachers. You are constantly confronted with ideas while you are teaching, and you see students do things that you have maybe, with some regret, allowed to slip away.

Teaching also had an impact on my private life. Before I met Chrissie, I had been totally against the idea of ever getting married, or even wanting to get married. Then my views had completely changed, leaving me, I imagine, in a slightly vulnerable state. In 1959 I was teaching at Harrow and I was keen – I liked the students very much and I organised some music for them at lunchtime. I didn't think they were sufficiently interested in music and there didn't seem to be the societies that had existed when I was at art school. My music group didn't get a massive turnout – probably around twenty students would come along, the same twenty, and I took them through the classics – I didn't play them very advanced music, even though some of the students used to ask me, 'Why can't you play us some Stockhausen?' or 'Why can't you play us some atonal music?' Nonetheless it became a fairly keen, close-knit group, and every Monday the same students would come along. I remember one Monday listening to the music when a new girl came in. She had only joined the school halfway through the term. She sat down and I remember seeing her ankles – I think I fell in love with them. By this time, of course, I had become quite eligible, although I had been totally ineligible as far as Chrissie's parents were concerned. In London I had sufficient teaching and I was still selling the odd painting. I was 27 or 28 years old, and, I suppose, reasonably attractive. Certainly I knew that the girls in the school were interested in the young tutors.

I started to talk to this girl, Annie, in the lunchtimes and discovered that her father was the Reader in Silversmithing and Jewellery at the Royal College of Art. He hadn't really wanted her to go to art school, however. Like most men of his age he had been through the war, and by the time it ended he had, I think, three children – eventually there were four. By the time he had finished studying after the war, he was offered a lectureship at the Royal College of Art because he was extremely good at what he did. I suppose he did a year of probationary teaching, then he was offered a lectureship which he had accepted. Eventually he was given a senior lectureship, and finally a readership. He never became a professor, which I think was a disappointment to him. Annie's mother was also a painter and she taught painting, in groups rather than in an art school, so to that family I was a very successful young man.

Her father, realising that the arts were very difficult to get into and conscious of his own experience, had advised Annie not to go to art school. In fact he had said she couldn't go to art school, but must do a teacher-training course instead. But after some weeks of this Annie made it clear to her father that the only thing she wanted to do was to go to art school. And once he realised that, being an artist himself, he agreed to it on one condition. Annie would have to study something at which he knew she would be capable of earning her living. So she came to Harrow to do dress design. In fact it was one of the best schools in England for the subject – one was Harrow, Walthamstow another, and I believe St Martin's at that time was also a good fashion school. As when I was at art school, everyone wanted to get to the fashion school at the Royal College and be one of the chosen few, as it were. So Annie arrived at Harrow, halfway through the first term. As well as seeing her at the music groups at lunchtime, the dress-design girls were some of my students in the life-drawing class, so I also taught her life drawing.

I realised fairly quickly that I was very attracted to her. She had a strange beauty about her, combined with a tenderness that was enormously appealing. Very soon I knew that I was in love with her. Of course I was 28 by this time, and Annie was 18. I was a teacher, and she was still a student. She had many young friends, while mine were older. At that age ten years makes an enormous difference so our relationship wasn't necessarily ideal or easy from the word go. But I admired her talent enormously and she seemed to like what I did, so we had mutual respect for each other's work. We shared our interests, although Annie's were more towards the popular side of music rather than the classical, and she naturally inclined towards the things that people a decade younger than me were interested in.

By the time Christmas arrived we thought it would be best to get engaged. We used to go out together, but of course the students didn't know this because we kept our relationship private. We knew that eventually it would leak out, however, and I decided, being rather proper, that it would be best to inform Mr Allison, the head of the school, about it first. In those days it wasn't really done for students and staff to have a relationship.

I remember that we went to the head's house at Christmas to tell him. When he opened the door he looked at me and said, 'This is holiday time, Mr Howard.' I asked if I could have a word and he enquired whether it could wait till next term. 'I'd rather tell you now,' I said, 'that I am going to marry one of your students, Mr Allison.' 'Oh, come in. What good news! Would you like some more teaching?' He had married one of his students himself and was therefore very sympathetic to our position. I didn't take any more teaching, in fact, and as we didn't have to hide our relationship any longer it went right round the school, of course. I suppose some of the girls were a bit jealous, but it became accepted that Mr Howard, a tutor, was going to marry Annie Popham. She, being so much younger, tended to be rather insecure in our relationship, and I noticed quite early on that she was a bit jealous. After several months, I realised that our relationship was very difficult and some tensions were starting to show.

That summer I decided to take Annie to Spain. We travelled down to the east coast, north of Valencia, and camped at Benicarló. In those days there didn't seem to be any great problem with camping: it was cheap, we were young and there were plenty of other young people on the campsite. I used to disappear early in the morning, at about six o'clock, and go up to a village called Santa Magdalena

Morning, Santa Magdalena de Pulpis, 1961
Oil on canvas, 70 x 90 cm

This small Spanish village, unspoilt in the '50s and early '60s, was a constant source of inspiration. The light and landscape sparked a language that I was to try and refine during the rest of my life.

de Pulpis, about four miles from Benicarló. It was a wonderful old Spanish village and in 1961 was still very unspoilt.

There was no tarmac road and there was a large well at the bottom of the village. Women used to come there in the morning, carrying their wonderful pottery water-holders on their heads in a very elegant manner. They dropped these into the well to draw water and then would stand there and do their washing. The houses in the village were fairly primitive. Early in the morning each day one would hear a Lambretta drive into the village with a sort of people-carrier on the back, from which one would hear a goat or a sheep or some animal. The animal and the owner would disappear into the butcher's shop and then, a little bit later, no more sound would come out of the butcher's shop.

It was an idyllic place and I was in love with it. I was still an extremely committed painter, even though I had a young fiancée, so I would disappear every morning at six, returning at about half-past ten. I would spend the main part of the day with Annie on the beach, and we would eat simply and relax. At about five in the evening I would go back up to the village and work until the sun went down.

When we got back from the holiday, Annie's father asked her if we had slept together. Annie said no and her father said to her. 'Is he queer?' I am not, but I certainly hadn't learnt anything from my first relationship, because again it would have been much better if we *had* slept together. Instead, I did my usual thing and put Annie on a pedestal. The following year we went to Spain again and this time we rented an apartment in Benicarló – it had a couple of rooms and was certainly more luxurious than camping. I followed my pattern of working very early in the morning at Santa Magdalena de Pulpis, a place to which I had become very attached. In the evening I went back again, and spent the long hours in between on the beach.

By this time the difference between our personalities was becoming very apparent. I realised when I got back from that holiday that probably my relationship with Annie wasn't going to work. Of course it was very public by this time – the whole school knew that Mr Howard was going to marry Annie Popham, and I knew that to break the relationship was going to be very hurtful and hard for her. Nevertheless, I thought it was better to do it now than go into a marriage that wasn't necessarily going to work. So I broke off our engagement, and Annie was devastated. I suppose you could say that she was broken-hearted. Her parents rang me up and said how upset she was and wouldn't I change my mind. To begin with I tried to be strong, but I was incredibly attracted to Annie physically and that was pulling me all the time towards her. This is why I said that if we had slept together and had a full relationship earlier I might possibly have stuck to my intention of

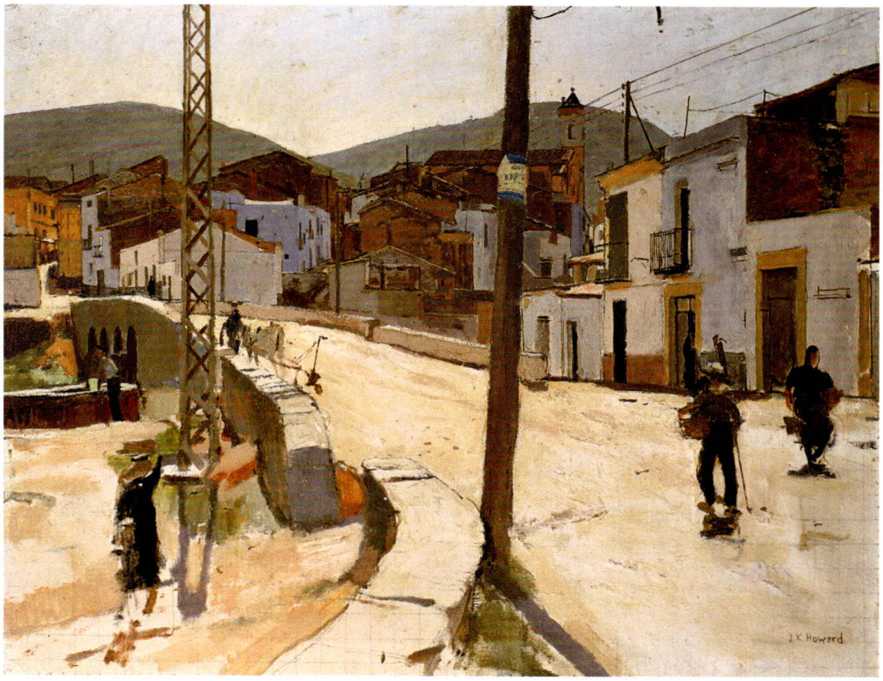

breaking the engagement. But we hadn't, and after a while I changed my mind. The family said that after we were married it would be different, and I wanted us to be different. So we put it together again and set a date for our marriage of 31 March 1962.

Once we got over this crisis things got much better and we approached the wedding with great confidence. I obviously thought that our relationship would become easier once we were married, and I was quite convinced that we would be married for life. Of course I should have known, even at that age, that it was ridiculous to believe that you could change each other in a marriage – and also wrong to hope that you could do so.

By this time Annie had nearly completed her course at Harrow. She had done her Intermediate and was studying for her NDD, and that year she was applying for the Royal College of Art. She was a brilliant dress designer who made clothes that people always wanted to wear, and only retired as a director of one of the largest fashion companies in the country in 2009. As I told her in the early days of our marriage, 'Annie, you are never going to design clothes that will change the face of European fashion and I'm never going to paint pictures that are going to change the world of European art. But you are always going to design clothes that people want to wear, and I'm always going to paint pictures that people will want to put on their walls and live with.' It was quite interesting how clearly I must have seen it. Who could really have known at that time how our two careers were going to develop?

Once we were married I found us a flat in the King's Road, right on the bend near the Man in the Moon pub. It was almost within walking distance of the Royal College of Art, where Annie was going to be studying for a couple of years. It sounds ridiculous now, but our flat in the King's Road cost £6.50 per week. In the early 1960s it was a very different King's Road. The Swinging Sixties were just about to

Below left
This photograph of Annie and I with friends was taken in Kent in about 1961. Second from the left is my old friend Maurice Cox. I taught him at the Working Men's College in Camden Town while still a student at the Royal College of Art in the '50s.

Below right
Fashion students at the Royal College of Art, 1964. My wife Annie is standing on the left, and seated in front of her is Ossie Clarke.

take off – and they did, with an explosive impact. I sometimes think that Annie and I were victims of the Sixties because everything changed so much. A huge thing, of course, was effective contraception; the Pill gave women the choice of when to start a family. As Annie was studying and then wanted to work at her profession when she finished, and as she was so much younger than I was, or seemed so at the time, we didn't start a family. I suppose in some ways we should have done, but by the time we were thinking about it our relationship was already creaking. We went through a time when she would stop the Pill for a month and we'd think that we'd have a child and that would sort things out. Then we'd get cold feet and Annie would go back on the Pill again for another month. Thus the relationship bounced back and forth.

It was an incredibly busy time, and from an outsider's point of view we must have seemed the ideal couple. Annie was doing well at the Royal College and I was beginning to establish myself as a painter. I'd begun to earn money and Annie had a grant, we were both young and we lived reasonably well in a very lively place. The flat that we had in the King's Road, spread over three floors, belonged to a man called Mallalieu. I'd taught with him at Harrow, and in fact he had taught me when I was a student at Hornsey. Mallalieu was a very good landlord; he was a bachelor who lived in his part and left us alone in ours. We lived there for two years while Annie studied at the college. She proved to be very bright and got

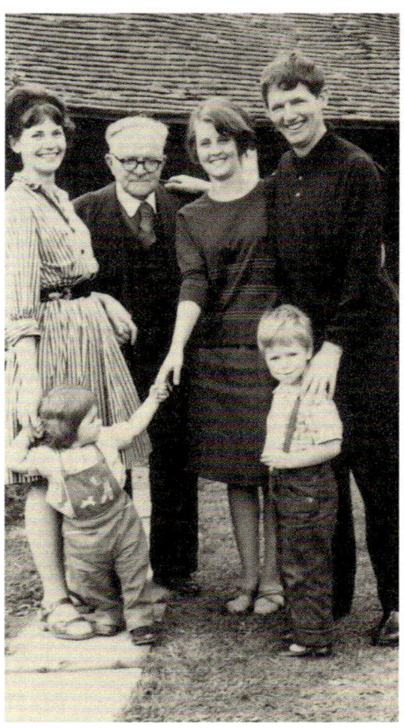

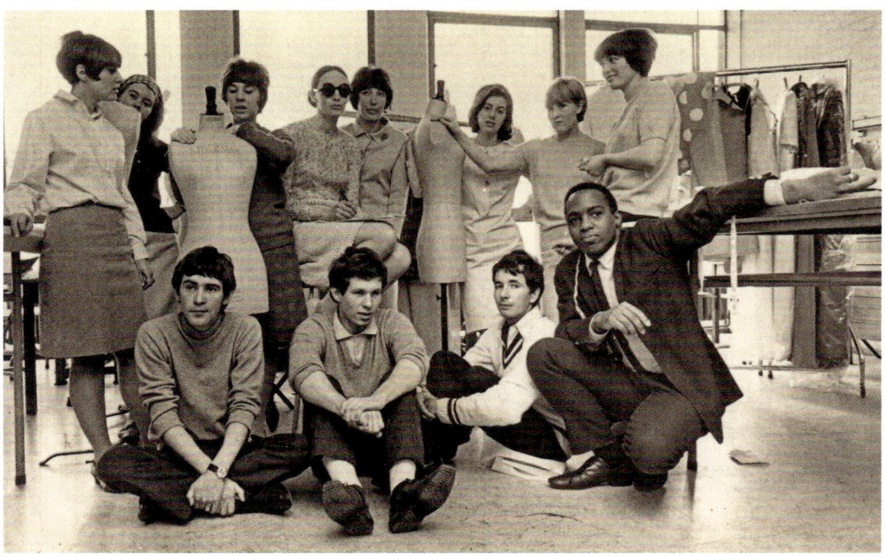

a good degree. She won a prize to go to America with Singer & Friedlander for a short period. When she returned, she was offered a post with Wallis Shops, a retailer she really wanted to work for.

At that time Wallis Shops was not so much a high-street shop as a company designing clothes for the wives of young executives who were able to afford good clothes. Annie designed the separates, including a marvellous range of suits based on Chanel for which Wallis was at that time renowned. She had one or two of those Chanel suits herself and looked absolutely superb in them, as she did in everything she wore. As I say, she had a strange beauty and a chemistry with which I was completely enamoured.

The physical side of our marriage seemed, from my point of view, to work well, but the emotional side was much more difficult. We used to go through difficult times, then end up in bed and make it all up, but then the next day we would be difficult with each other again. Of course that was no way to build up a relationship. When we had been married a while, after Annie left college, she was travelling a lot, visiting Modena for knitwear shows and going to Paris for the *prêt-à-porter*. I was also travelling a lot, doing commissions all over the country, so we were starting to spend more and more time apart. When we got together we still loved one another and it was good. It was like a honeymoon all over again, but after we'd lived together again for a while our temperamental differences would come between us. I couldn't analyse exactly what they were, but in retrospect the age difference was crucial. Marrying me at nineteen, Annie was still developing and forming her own unique personality, and this became curtailed. She suddenly had my older values, interests and friends to take on board, putting an inevitable brake on her own natural development.

Painters are by their very nature selfish – the inevitable consequence of a drive to fulfil something. Annie wanted more of me than I was willing or able to give. I saw my two loves as quite different, certainly not in competition, but Annie viewed my work as a rival, much more threatening than another woman. Deep down she wanted to be the centre of my life, as I suppose I was the centre of hers, for an emotional security that I was unable to give. There had also been a difference in upbringing, in family social status, in taste, but none of these factors were crucial in the breakdown of our relationship.

After Annie finished at college we bought our first house at Hampton Hill. It was called April Cottage, and it was beautiful. It had been done up very well and there was nothing that we particularly wanted to change, although Annie made it prettier still. It was extremely small – I suppose one would describe it as a 'railway cottage'. At the end of the garden lay a deep cutting, at the bottom of which was a railway line that ran into Waterloo. In many ways we were very happy there – the only problem was our two personalities. We bought the house for £2,650, which seems absurd now, and I wondered whether I could afford the £1,000 mortgage which I needed (I had already saved the rest). But we went for it, and two or three years later we bought a larger house round the corner. I remember we sold April Cottage for £3,650 and felt that we had made a fortune. When we bought our new house for £5,000 it seemed very expensive.

This was a large Victorian house. Annie brought her natural taste to bear on it and made it into a very beautiful home. We re-did the kitchen and made the two living rooms into one. There was a lovely garden, and Annie had as much feeling for gardening as fashion. Like many young dress designers she felt that fashion wasn't all that she should be about. She wrote a lot of poetry, she painted well and drew well, and she often toyed with the idea of going into the antiques business. But fashion was what she had been trained for, and fashion was what she was very good at. As the years went by she became more committed to it, and grew better and better as she began to understand it more. Couture was giving way to *prêt-à-porter*, teenagers stopped looking like their mothers, the perm gave way to the beautiful cuts of Vidal Sassoon. The world was truly changing in the Sixties and Annie was part of it.

Her time at the college had been a very good and extremely exciting one. She had been in the same year as Ossie Clark, Brian Walsh and Hylan Booker, all very talented students, and all the people from that year were destined to go into the fashion business. It was a good time for Annie to have trained and to have come out into that world as the Sixties defined and revitalised British fashion. It was the era of Mary Quant, Tuffin and Foale, and very soon, of course, Ossie Clark. Zandra Rhodes was in the year ahead of Annie and Celia Birtwell was coming on the scene. In the painting world, David Hockney was in the same year at the Royal College of Art.

And so our lifestyle became better and better in this exciting world. We had a large house, a good car and we travelled a lot. But there was a downside – something wasn't really working between us. Maybe it wasn't there, maybe it was the result of being young, when you can only see the parts of a relationship that aren't working. When you're older, of course, as I have learned, you concentrate on what is working in a relationship and you ignore the bits that aren't, because they aren't really important. When you're young, however, it's the other way round. You want to change the other person, which is a difficult thing to cope with in a relationship.

Looking back, one of the problems with our relationship was Annie's insecurity and that, of course, was my fault. Only I could make her feel secure, but I couldn't allay her fear – maybe it was because I had been a tutor and she had been one of my students. Whatever the reason, insecurity turned to jealousy, and Annie was constantly suspicious about whether I was having relationships with my students. Jealousy is a terribly destructive emotion, particularly when it is based on an imagined relationship or infidelity. I suppose if you've caused it you have to learn to live with a natural jealousy. When you haven't, it is very difficult to endure.

By this time we were spending quite a lot of time down in Cornwall during holiday times. Annie loved the sun; she loved to get brown and she always looked gorgeous with a tan. We did a few trips abroad to places such as Corfu and Spain, largely unspoilt in the early 1960s, but most of the time we went down to Cornwall, either with her family or to my family, who were by then living in Mousehole. I would carry on with my pattern of getting up early in the morning and going out painting, and then coming back and spending the day with Annie until about four o'clock, then going out painting again in the evening. This wasn't easy for a young wife to cope with. Eventually my logical mind decided that, as she loved the beach so much and I ought to spend more time with her, I should start painting the beach. Then I became obsessed with the beach and wanted to paint there all the time. I remember Annie storming off the beach one day and saying to me, 'I didn't know when I married you that I was marrying a paintbox.' It was quite a difficult thing for a painter to address.

As was almost inevitable, I suppose, I did eventually meet a student to whom I was very attracted. She was a part-time, evening student. Everybody in the school thought she was wonderful, and it turned out that she was in my class. She was attracted to me as much by my enthusiasm and my interest in her work as by physical presence. But my marriage was getting rockier, and I was getting accused more and more frequently of infidelity. In the end, on one occasion when Annie was in Paris at the *prêt-à-porter*, I went for a drink with the student after an evening class. We began a relationship which, strangely enough, I was quite good at managing. I found a flat in Harrow where we could meet and Annie wasn't at all conscious of what was happening. On the other hand, I was still incredibly attracted to my wife. Even when I made love to this girl, when I got home in the evening it was to Annie that I really felt drawn physically.

The affair went on for about six months, through 1972. That summer I said to Annie that I would go down to Spain alone and paint for six weeks so that we could have a really good holiday together. By the time she arrived I would be so 'worked out' that I would be able completely to relax and live on the beach: we would just eat and make love and have the perfect holiday. She seemed to like the idea so I went down alone to Santa Magdalelena de Pulpis. I got a room in the village and lived there for six weeks by myself. When Annie came down we moved into a flat in a village called Peníscola. It was right on the coast, and was in fact the village that was supposed to be Valencia in the film *El Cid*. As the name implied, it was a village high up on a very small peninsula – an idyllic setting.

At the beginning we went to the beach each day, where we swam and I read. We had a good lunch and then returned to our room and made love in the afternoon. In the evening we had good dinners, and it seemed to be a wonderful holiday. But on the third or fourth day Annie turned to me on the beach and accused me of being bored. I said that I wasn't in the least bit bored. 'The last thing I want to do at the moment is paint and I am enjoying this holiday no end.' 'No,' she said, 'you're bored. You don't like being here all day and you want to be painting.' I denied it again, but she just got up and went to our room. I lay on the beach feeling completely desolate. If a holiday like this couldn't help our relationship, I thought, what could?

I went up to the room. When I walked in Annie attacked me again, whereupon I turned round and said straight out to her, 'Annie, I've been unfaithful, I'm having a relationship.' She refused to believe me, but I told her it was true. 'I've been having a relationship for six months, and I think it's best if we now break up amicably and go our own ways.' Annie's reaction to that was that she didn't want our marriage to end – she wanted us to carry on, and that I shouldn't see this woman again. I said, 'I can't just finish things by letter. I have to meet her once more and have dinner and explain this to her.' But Annie insisted, so in the end I agreed and I wrote a letter to her. Of course Annie also wanted to know who she was, but I wouldn't tell her. She worked at it and she worked at it, guessing it was one of my students and eventually working out who. When she said that she wanted our relationship to go on, I said, 'How can it unless you can forgive me and not keep on about what has happened?' This, of course, she couldn't do, and our relationship continued to deteriorate.

The year 1972 was a really difficult one for me, although Annie and I seemed to be prospering in terms of our work. She had her very good job and I had a lot of commission work coming in – not always exactly what I would choose but still regular work, as well as my teaching. We had two homes, one in London and one an old school house on Dartmoor, a couple of cars and I suppose all the money we needed for a comfortable life. Both of us were in the arts and enjoying the same amount of success, so outsiders obviously couldn't or wouldn't have understood what was going wrong. From the outside it seemed as if we had a good life and were compatible with each other, and when we did separate only our close friends understood.

The following summer I told Annie that she should go off and have a holiday with her parents, who were going to Corfu. I told her it would be good for her to get some sun. I missed her terribly. When she came back we went to bed. She didn't seem to be particularly interested and when we did make love I knew very well that she had been with someone else. I sensed it and I knew it. About a week later we were driving to London Airport; Annie was on her way to Modena or Paris or somewhere for a dress show. We were having a row and I turned to her and said, 'Really, Annie, you are so suburban.' 'Yes,' she retorted, 'I'm so suburban that I've had an affair with a waiter from a restaurant while we were away on holiday.' My reaction was 'how much more suburban can you get'. In fact, I was deeply hurt and wanted to go on, provided that she never saw him again. She agreed to this and we staggered on.

A few weeks later we were going to a wedding in Richmond. We went into a pub to get a drink before the wedding and I told Annie I would get the drinks. She said she would, and as she opened her wallet I saw a postcard in it. She immediately pushed this further back into the wallet. I asked her who it was from and she had to admit it was from the waiter. He had followed her to London and they had in fact spent a night together. But away from Corfu she realised that he didn't fit into her fashion world, the fairly exotic art world in which we now lived, and that it was a mistake.

The damage was done, however. I said that she had broken her promise and I would get a flat in Hampstead. Then I very quickly discovered how hard it was to live in this impersonal place and leave all the comforts of our home behind. I missed Annie incredibly because all through this time, even when our relationship was so bad, there was still our physical bond. Of course my studio was also in the house at Hampton Hill; I was missing a place to work and a regular pattern of work. The various pressures brought me back home, but things were no better. A rather attractive art dealer who was trying to get my work set her cap at me and we had a very brief relationship. Annie again guessed, and that certainly didn't help our marriage. We were gradually slipping into very deep trouble.

I left home again and got another flat. Shortly after I had a surprise phone call – and can't now for the life of me remember how the caller got my number. It was Giordano of all people – the young doctor who I'd met in Italy along with Chrissie. I'd been his best man when he married an English girl a few years before. He told me that he built boats now and had a business in Australia. He had come to London for the boat show and wanted to meet for dinner, so we did. We had a good evening and I didn't say anything about my personal situation. At the end of the meal I asked him if he had heard anything of Chrissie. It seemed a logical question; I had heard nothing from her for about twelve years and I was curious. I certainly hadn't spent those years pining or wondering what she was doing. I'd been very, very involved with my marriage and my work, trying to reconcile the two in my life. Giordano replied that, strangely enough, they had kept in touch. She had married Hartmut and had two daughters. The following day he was going to a boat show in Cologne and he had arranged to have dinner with Chrissie that evening while he was there. I told Giordano to give Chrissie my regards and tell her that I hoped life had been good to her.

I'd given Giordano our home telephone number as I knew I would be returning home a few days later, as on the first occasion. Annie and I were trying yet again to make our relationship work. Then, right out of the blue, about three weeks later, I got a phone call from Chrissie. We talked and she told me that she had two daughters and was looking for a family to do an exchange with. Obviously Giordano had spoken to her about our meeting and, prompted perhaps partly by curiosity and also, as she explained later, by the fact that she had never actually forgotten me, she decided to ring and see if I could help with her two daughters. The timing wasn't good. My personal life was in a total mess, and I was certainly in no mood to become even more entangled.

So I did nothing about finding a family. Three months later Chrissie rang again to ask if I had managed to find anybody to take her daughters. So, literally for old times' sake, I thought I must make an effort. Through an old friend I found a family in the West Country who wanted to do an exchange with two young girls. I told Chrissie, and then she rang to say that she was coming to England to meet the family. She wondered if we could have dinner together while she was passing through London. I have to confess, strange as it seems, I didn't feel any excitement, but I agreed and asked where she was staying. She was going to be at the Kensington Court Hotel, just off Kensington High Street.

By the time Chrissie arrived in England, Annie and I had separated again. Our relationship had reached such a level that Annie had even attempted to commit suicide. This had scared me terribly, and I had decided that the only way was to move out, end the marriage and let her start all over again. After all she was still in her very early thirties and extremely attractive. She had a very good career and everything was going for her. The only thing that wasn't working was our marriage, which I felt was gradually destroying both of us. I let her know the telephone number and the address of where I was going to live in case there was any crisis and she needed to get hold of me. But I was determined that it would work this time.

When Chrissie was due to be in London I drove over to Kensington. I was in rather a sick state, trying to imagine what she would look like. I thought that as she had been married very young and had been a German wife for around twelve years, she would be fat. I then thought that she had money, so she would be wearing a fur coat. On top of that I thought she would probably be wearing pearls. I arrived at the Kensington Court Hotel and walked in through the swing door. And there stood a girl in jeans and a rather nice sweater, with loose brown hair. When I first knew Chrissie her hair had been permed, very much in the style of the times, but now she had a very modern, loose cut. But basically it was the girl who I had known in Italy fourteen years before, and I fell in love with her again immediately.

We went out to dinner together and she asked me how my life had gone since we had last been together. I told her all about my professional life and what I had been doing, and I definitely skirted around the personal side. I said nothing about my relationship with Annie, except that she was far too busy to come and have dinner with us. I asked Chrissie how life had been with her and she also skirted round her personal life with Hartmut. At the end of the evening I took her back to the hotel and returned to Hamilton Terrace, off Maida Vale, where I had a flat.

The following day I went painting in Hyde Park early in the morning, getting back to the little Mews flat at about half past nine. At ten o'clock a taxi drew up and Chrissie got out. I was astonished. She asked, 'Why didn't you tell me anything last night?' I asked what she meant and she said, 'I rang after we said goodnight, about half an hour later, and when Anna answered the phone she said you weren't living at home any more.' I invited her in and we sat down on the bare boards of the little Mews flat. It was strangely like the old days in Florence – we were back to a fairly primitive way of living. Chrissie had brought a lot of food with her as she said she had a plane to catch at three that afternoon. We sat down and we ate some breakfast together, and everything came out. I told her all about the previous thirteen years and how it had been. I explained that it hadn't worked, and that we were now living apart and were considering divorcing.

Chrissie then told me all about her marriage. After coming back from France she had decided to marry Hartmut, who in his patient, understanding way had then married her. Just as they had been friends before they were married, they had basically stayed friends for all their married life. In fact, they remained friends for the rest of their lives. However, the marriage had had no magic and its physical side had been almost non-existent. Chrissie told me how, after she had been married for six weeks or so, she had been walking along feeling deeply depressed and reflecting that life must be about more than this. She thought back to our relationship and realised that it had been more than that. Had our relationship been stronger, had it had longer to develop, she would have stuck to what we had agreed. She would have come to me in England and taken a chance on whatever there was to be. It was very sad really. She told me that over the next years, as the marriage went on and they brought up their family, whenever they were on the Autobahn and they saw an English car – a camper van, for example, packed with people and children and luggage – she would always look at it to see if I was in there. She had imagined that because of what we had said in Florence, my life would have developed in a certain way. In fact it had done nothing of the sort.

Chrissie and Hartmut had two daughters, Babs and Tina, with about two years, perhaps slightly less, between them. After that the marriage continued on a fairly even keel. Unlike with me and Annie, there had been no hurting. Chrissie was an extremely civilised person. As I learned later, she felt that it was demeaning to row. Hartmut had a very similar outlook, and Chrissie said that of course he should have been a doctor, or even a priest. Instead he had been drawn into the family business, much against his will, and therefore he was very unfulfilled as a man. Perhaps this did not help him to make a complete success of his marriage. But that's a very complex argument, and not one an outsider can judge.

So everything was out in the open. Once we had admitted to the lack of success of both our marriages and talked about our lives in general, we were very soon back to how we'd been in Florence, talking about all manner of subjects. Neither of us had enough time to talk as much as we wanted to, as the day went by and we had lunch sitting on the floor of the flat. At about half past one Chrissie went back to London Airport and flew back to Cologne. But somehow I think we both knew that a real bond had been forged, and that this time, ultimately, the story would be different.

Annie came and found me at the flat. She wanted me to go back home and after a while, of course, I did. The attraction was still there and I missed our physical relationship. I missed Annie and the home comforts and my studio – and I missed our life together. So I put everything into the car and moved back to Hampton Hill to try yet again to make our marriage work.

But by this time it had gone too far. A few weeks later, in the middle of an enormous row, Annie stormed out of the house and said, 'I'm going home. Sell the house. I'm definitely not coming back.' After she had gone I realised the only way to end this attrition was to do exactly what she said. Some friends of mine had asked me for first refusal if we ever sold Park House. I called them that evening and asked if they really meant it. They said they did, so I agreed to sell it for £22,000. That was it. The following day Annie came back. She said she was sorry about everything that had happened and could she come home. I just said to her, 'Annie, I've sold the house.' And it was as if, at that moment, her mind cleared and she realised what we were doing to each other. There was no enormous fighting – we just then wanted to talk logically about getting the divorce. We would have to live separately for two years, so it was going to take quite a time. We had to clear out the house, of course, involving the whole sad process of deciding who was going to have what. We made quite a simple agreement, totting up all that we had in the world (the houses in London and Devon, the cars, the money in the bank and so forth), and simply split the whole lot down the middle. Then, rather sadly, we just went our separate ways. Annie asked me to help her buy another house in Hampton Hill. She couldn't live in the main house where our marriage had been, but she didn't want to move away from all her friends in the area. So I helped her buy another house, not very far away, in School Road.

By now I had heard from a friend of mine, Michael Noakes, who was President of the Royal Institute of Oil Painters, where I was Secretary. He was giving up his studio in South Bolton Gardens because he had rented a house in London and he couldn't afford to keep both. He invited me to come and see his landlady, which I did, and she agreed that I could rent part of the studio in South Bolton Gardens. So it came about that, at the age of 42, I had my very own true studio in London. It was good to have, as I was about to start my life all over again. So much had come together in the last decade or so. Many things had happened, but suddenly everything was gone. I was at the beginning again, with, I felt, virtually nothing.

Life would be very simple if, when a relationship ends, you could just walk away from it and that would be that. But living with someone for twelve years creates a powerful bonding, both mental and physical. Even though I had met Chrissie again, she was still in Germany with her family; Annie was in London and I still loved her. As was inevitable, we eventually met up at a party and that proved too much – we went home together and started to see each other again. It only lasted for two weeks, as inevitably all the same problems were there. The physical aspect worked, but the emotional side was turmoil. It was as if I had been an alcoholic who had given up drinking, but had taken another drink when I thought I was cured. Now I can see that it was in a sense necessary; after those two weeks we did go our own ways and our marriage was finally over. Of course we had to start the two-year legal separation all over again. Annie eventually got married again, to another dress designer, and to this day we still occasionally communicate and are friends.

When I started to see Annie again, I wrote and told Chrissie. She immediately came to London and we talked at great length. Chrissie told me I was following the classic case of a breakdown in a relationship and asked did I really know what I was doing? I had to tell her I didn't know, but there was nothing I could do about it. She returned to Germany hurt and disappointed, but after Annie and I stopped seeing each other Chrissie and I started to write to one another again. Some months later, we met in Paris. Chrissie, typically, never mentioned what had happened and we re-started our relationship. She was a remarkable woman.

The next months were truly traumatic. I was living by myself, separated from Annie with Chrissie still with her family in Germany. I was working in Northern Ireland, continuously travelling, and I had been rejected by the Royal Academy Summer Exhibition for the third consecutive year. As was inevitable, I was drinking heavily at the Chelsea Arts Club, just down the road from my studio, and having a succession of casual relationships and one-night stands when I was in London. I was in my forties, and my life was in chaos. My real friends and Chrissie stood by me, thank goodness, as without them I think I would have gone under.

Despite my turbulent personal life during the '60s and '70s, of course, my professional life had continued to develop. Through all the ups and downs I remained determined to make my way as a painter and earn my living that way, not by teaching or the many other alternatives. When I left college in 1958, before I went to Italy, I had been noticed by a man called Colonel Jack Beddington. He used to go round the art schools and pick out those who he thought were up-and-coming painters. He saw my work and asked me to go and see him at Wildenstein – then a major force in New Bond Street, and one which, by a strange coincidence in my life, would come up very prominently many years later. When I returned to England after my scholarship I went to see Jack Beddington. I showed him the work that I had been doing in Florence and he reacted very positively to it. That December he included me in an exhibition called 'Some Contemporary British Painters', which featured six youngish, unknown artists. It did well, all my work was sold and they seemed keen to repeat the exercise the following December.

At the same time I was exhibiting as hard as I could at the societies. I had started to show again at the RA Summer Exhibition, and to get work accepted on a reasonably regular basis. I began to work regularly on the streets of the City of

London – as London was my base it seemed the logical place, and it was a subject I was still very excited by. I sometimes think of the City as it was, without all the developments that have happened since the '60s. I'm sure a lot of the new buildings are very significant, but they don't necessarily inspire me as an objective painter. (Sometimes I think the developers have done as much damage to the City of London as Hitler did, but that is purely a personal, painter's point of view.) Although I didn't realise that it would happen, people came out of their offices at lunchtime, liked what I was doing and asked if I would sell to them. Fairly quickly I saw that there seemed to be a market for my work in the City.

There was also a competition, I remember, called the Lord Mayor's Art Award. This started soon after I returned from Italy and it was always my ambition to win it. The first year I didn't – it was won by a friend of mine, but I persevered. The second year I won the first prize, and again the following year. So things were looking quite positive.

I also had a commission for illustration. A friend of mine, Olwyn Bowey, who had studied with me at the Royal College of Art and was teaching with me at Walthamstow, suggested to me one day in the mid-Sixties that I should go and see David Wolfers at Shell. He was the editor of the two Shell house magazines, one called *Catalyst* and the other *Land*, and he commissioned drawings for both. David used good painters who could draw, rather than professional illustrators, so I went along to see him at his office. I took my portfolio and David looked at my work, showing no enthusiasm for it at all, finally telling me that he would be in touch. That was all – no word that he liked it or that he thought that it had got something, just that he would be in touch. 'Well, there's no work there, for sure. He didn't even like what I did,' I told Annie later. Little did I know what a long association David and I were to have.

After a few weeks the phone rang and it was David Wolfers. He asked if I would go and do some drawings in Hertfordshire. I did, and worked very hard on them, although I remember they were very modestly paid. Then I took them to David who laid them out on his desk and looked at them. After a few minutes he looked up and said to me, 'Send me your invoice' – and that was it. Again, I thought that was my first and last piece of work for Shell, but a few weeks later he rang again, this time to request a series of drawings of Yorkshire. Fairly soon I got used to the fact that David obviously quite liked what I did, although he didn't show enthusiasm for it. By then I reckon I was paying my way. I was determined to earn money by painting because I already saw that, unless I could manage this, I would be drawn into teaching. And much as I enjoyed it, I didn't want to commit myself to teaching for the rest of my life.

Reims Cathedral, *c.* 1962
Oil on canvas, 122 x 91 cm

This was one of a series of paintings of cathedrals in England and France I made in the '60s. Untypically, I was very influenced by the early works of Maurice Utrillo. I often experimented with the texture of architecture at this time, mixing plaster with my paint and working with a palette knife as well as brushes.

At the weekends I used to go through the colour supplements to see who was using painting or drawings. On Monday morning I would ring the firm or the agents concerned and tell them, 'I saw your advert in the *Observer* at the weekend and I think I can do better.' After a pause they would usually ask me to bring in my portfolio. I would go and see them and they would be quite enthusiastic, although there was no immediate work. As soon as I got home I would write a letter thanking them for looking at my work, and of course that letter then went on file. Had I written to them first and not telephoned, the letter would probably have been binned along with all the other speculative letters they received. Anyway, it proved a rather successful approach and I eventually got quite a lot of work from Shell, BP, the Post Office and even, as I remember, the National Savings Bank.

So with the commissions and the illustrations and the tentative arrangement with Wildenstein, things were beginning to happen. In 1963 the Wildenstein work sold well again and they asked me to show again the following year. I managed to get work into the Academy, which was encouraging, and at the same time I was travelling around the galleries. I tried Roland Browse & Delbanco, one of the best galleries in Cork Street, but they weren't interested. I also remember going to the Beaux Arts Gallery in Bruton Place. It was owned by a Mrs Lessore, who was a very tough lady. She was very critical of my work when I showed it, but at the end, she offered to put something in her next summer exhibition. I was so demoralised by her comments, however, that I never went back. I had to get used to the fact that not everybody was enthusiastic about my work. When someone was, you took it as a compliment and as a great encouragement.

After the third show at Wildenstein they decided to do no more contemporary British painters. I believe that old Wildenstein had died and the son wasn't particularly interested in continuing. Fortunately, a graphic-design company north of Oxford Street had seen my work in Wildenstein. They asked me if I would like to show with them as they were using one of his floors as a gallery. It wasn't a very encouraging move, but it was something and I took the offer. That only lasted a year, however. When they closed, another small gallery along the road, the John Whibley Gallery, wrote to me asking if I would go to them. This was more encouraging – they were very professional and in my first show they sold more than half my work. By the last day they had sold about a third, and they rang me up and told me one of their main clients, Mr Barnet Shine, was coming in to have a look at the exhibition and would I come in to meet him. Barney proved to be a small man, Jewish and a multi-millionaire property developer. He went round the exhibition and had a good look. Afterwards, he

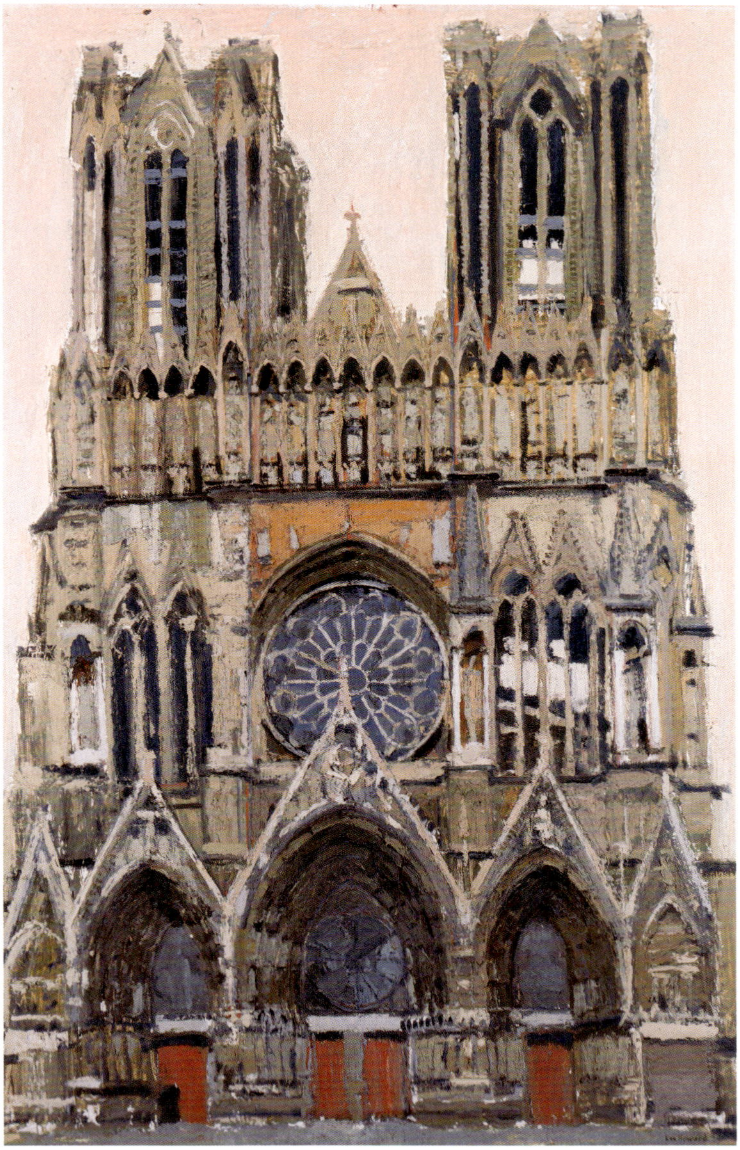

came up to me and said, 'I like your work, boy. I want twelve of them. It's an hour before the exhibition closes, but I'll make you an offer on those twelve now. Will you accept it? If I have to wait until one o'clock when the exhibition closes, there's no deal.' So naturally I told him, 'It's a deal, Mr Shine,' and that was that.

Barney Shine had built the tallest skyscraper in Boston, and he wanted me to paint it. I wasn't very pleased at the prospect. It was called the State Street Bank and wasn't the most interesting or innovative skyscraper in the world. So I quoted him a price of probably around £250, plus my flight and living expenses, while I was in Boston. Barney wrote back and said he would pay my £250 fee, but not my flight or my living costs. So I wrote back and said, 'We've got a good relationship, Mr Shine, but unfortunately I don't really want to paint the skyscraper anyway; can we forget it?' About two months went by and he tackled me again, 'I still want you to paint my skyscraper. I'll pay your flight and your £250, but I'm not paying your living costs.' Again I told him that I didn't particularly want to paint the skyscraper and that I hoped this wouldn't affect our relationship. After six months Barney wrote again and offered to pay all that I was asking. I wasn't able to go until the following Easter, but when I was flying in over Boston I looked down and realised that the State Street Bank was no longer the tallest skyscraper in Boston. One of the insurance companies had built one even higher.

Barney bought a lot of my work, I remember, and he came to my first show in the New Grafton Gallery in the early '70s. This was a small gallery just off Hay Hill – when Barney arrived in his Rolls Royce it was longer than the gallery itself. The private view was very full and Barney bustled in. 'Hello, boy,' he said, 'I'm in a bit of a hurry.' He looked round the gallery and asked which was the best painting of Richmond. I pointed it out to him, and the best Spanish painting, which he also asked for. Finally he said, 'It's my daughter's birthday tomorrow. What shall I give her as a birthday present?' 'That one, Barney,' I said, pointing to quite a small painting. 'Done, boy!' he said, got back into his Rolls Royce and drove away. I must admit that I hadn't picked out the most expensive Richmond painting or the most expensive Spanish one, which I could very easily have done.

Eventually Barney's directors decided that they wanted me to do a mural for the office – not an ordinary one, but an etched mural on big sheets of copper. They wanted it to be of London buildings and fairly two-dimensional like a mural. I should never have taken the job on and I can't remember why I did. It was a complicated business as the buildings had to be etched into these enormous sheets of copper. I had to get some very large tanks to put the acid in, which I did at our house in Hampton Hill as it had a fairly large garage. I got these large sheets of copper and drew the outline with a varnish. Then I put the sheets of copper into the large tanks. Of course, the smell was terrible. I wore a mask, but it didn't seem to have much effect.

I'd been suffering from ulcers for many years, since I was demobbed from the Royal Marines. They were getting worse and this particular job almost finished me off. The acid, or maybe the fumes, seemed to get into my stomach in some way and eat away at its lining. In the end I had to be rushed into the West Middlesex Hospital and have an operation to remove the ulcers. In the event they made a mistake, not uncommon in those days. They cut a main nerve in the stomach and it became paralysed. Although I went home after the operation, I couldn't get better. I ended up vomiting green bile and having to be re-admitted, at which point they discovered the reason and removed half my stomach. So from that day I have had half a stomach, but I have to say that it has only affected my life in minor ways. I don't particularly agree with the culture of suing doctors, although if it had been the culture then I could certainly have sued the surgeon who made the mistake in the first operation. The murals, of course, were never finished. They were never going to be very good so I don't think anybody lost from it, apart from me – the money, time, effort and pain that I'd put into the job.

My move to the New Grafton Gallery had come about unexpectedly. One day in the early '70s I was walking down Bond Street when I happened to run into David Wolfers. I hadn't seen him since I had worked for him at Shell in the late '60s and for some reason the work had dried up. I remembered that he had once told me, while I was working for him at Shell, that what he really wanted was his own gallery. I had turned round and said, rather pointedly, 'Oh, come on, David. If you really wanted your own gallery you would have it.' When I met him in Bond Street the first thing he said was that he now had his own gallery. 'Congratulations!' I said. 'Where is it?' He told me it was called the New Grafton Gallery, just round the corner in Grafton Street, near to Hay Hill, and asked me to come and see him there. A few days later I visited the gallery, whereupon David, in his usual understated sort of way, asked me whether I would be interested in joining it.

Although I was with Whibley I wasn't particularly satisfied there, even though they had moved to Cork Street. John and Lilly were a lovely couple, but I didn't feel completely at home with the gallery's other artists. I didn't necessarily feel that I fitted in, so when David offered me the move I took up the offer. He was a wonderful man, always very understated and never very overtly enthusiastic. I had about five shows with him, one every two years, and he never said anything positive about my paintings. At one point in the late '70s this got to me. I was due to go off and work in Hong Kong and before I went I sent him a letter. 'Dear David,' it ran, 'I've enjoyed my time with the gallery very much. Unfortunately I don't think you particularly respect my work and only show it because you can sell it, and therefore I think it is probably better that our ways part,' or words to that effect. A couple of weeks later I received a typically understated letter from David in Hong Kong. He had obviously been a little bit hurt and disturbed to get my letter. He wrote that he hoped I would have understood that he would never show work that he didn't respect, and that I should change my mind and go back and show with him. Of course I did, and I stayed with David for 30 years, until he died. I had fifteen one-man shows with him, more than any other artist. In the end we were selling out my exhibitions, much to his pleasure and, of course, mine.

So in 1973 I had settled into the Grafton. They were a really good gallery, and I much admired David Wolfers. I was exhibiting regularly in the RA Summer

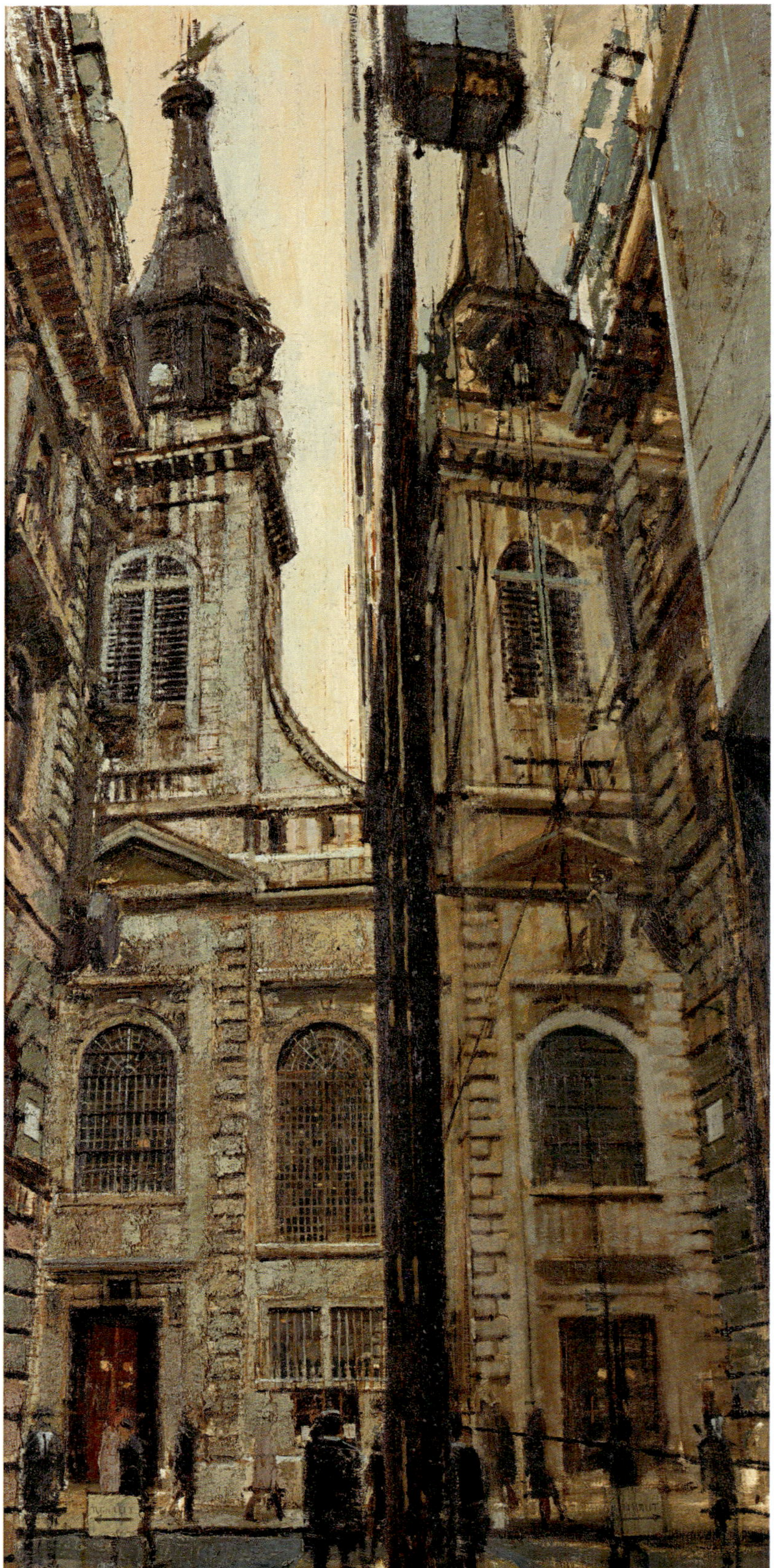

Exhibition and various other exhibitions, but I decided that I had to make a very positive move in my life. I took the decision to give up my teaching completely and earn my living entirely from my work. I suppose this partly came about because of the chaos in my private life. I wanted somehow to stabilise myself, although I can see that giving up the only proper job I had must have seemed a strange way to do so. I had also become dissatisfied with the teaching situation, however. When I started it seemed as though I could teach in the instinctive way in which I felt drawing should be taught, but by the beginning of the '70s, after the Coldstream Report and various other things that were happening in art schools, a form of teaching was emerging that I didn't feel completely happy with. I was quite pleased to think I was in a position where I could give it all up if I wanted to.

By this time I was in charge of intermediate drawing at Harrow School of Art, and one afternoon we had a meeting to decide on the terminology for this work. I always thought of it as drawing, I still do think of it as drawing and in my mind I know exactly what drawing is about. But the result of this long afternoon's deliberation was that drawing from now on must be called 'mark-making with intent'. This was typical of the direction in which the art schools were beginning to go. The focus was upon drawing up syllabuses, revising terminology and becoming increasingly removed from the nitty-gritty of teaching drawing and painting. I remember the head at the time asked me why I went into the rooms on the two days I was there to sit down with the students, to draw with them and for them. He told me that if I had delivered a lecture on Monday morning and got my terminology right, students would understand exactly what they had to be doing in the drawing studio. I wouldn't need to sit with them and show them how to do it. I realised then that art-school teaching was no longer for me. It was getting into the hands of people who were more interested in theory and organising, and it was time for me to resign.

First of all I had to work my notice, so having said at Christmas that I was going to pack up at the end of the academic year, I was told that if I taught up until Easter I could leave then. I wasn't entirely happy to be giving up teaching, as I had made some good friends among the staff and liked the students very much. I always remember that when I was in hospital with my ulcers the students would come to see me every evening. They brought me books and sat and talked to me, and that was very nice. I wondered why, really, because I was fairly severe with them. If I had a life class going and anybody arrived late, I would just say to them, 'Cheerio'. When they asked what I meant I would reply, 'Nobody comes in here once the model is posing. If you want to come to this class, make sure you are on time next week.' And they always were. It was an easy thing to do because the students really wanted

St Edmund King and Martyr, 1969
Oil on canvas, 180 x 90 cm

Part of a triptych which I showed in the Royal Academy Summer Exhibition in the late '60s. A large painting, I used to take it into the city on Sunday mornings on the roof of my car. Then I propped it against a wall and painted it on the spot. The main inspiration for the painting was the reflection in the wall on the right. Reflections have remained an inspiration all my life.

to be there. They weren't being forced to attend art school, and therefore you could command strong discipline.

As well as many good friends, I knew I would miss the whole atmosphere of the school. I would miss the contacts with both students and staff. The one thing I knew I wouldn't miss was the direction in which the art-school system seemed to be moving. I just did not feel it was sympathetic, although I appreciated that was just my point of view. In short, when I finally gave up teaching in 1973 it wasn't completely without regret. However, I never regretted leaving behind the politics that were starting to affect art schools at that time, making me choose to move on. Fortunately, during the 1960s and the early '70s my work began to be noticed.

One very good commission I received during those years was to illustrate the telephone directories for the Post Office, then Britain's national telephone company. The company was much more imaginative in those days, and it decided to have drawings in the telephone directories to make them more interesting. So the Post Office commissioned two or three different artists, draughtsmen or illustrators – whatever you want to call us – to visit the various parts of the country to do the work. This is a wonderful discipline and I really enjoyed it. We were only allowed to use a clear-cut line, no question of using brush or pencil, charcoal or any other medium because the telephone directories were printed on newsprint. It had to be done using a black pen line, which is quite a discipline. I drew all sorts of areas,

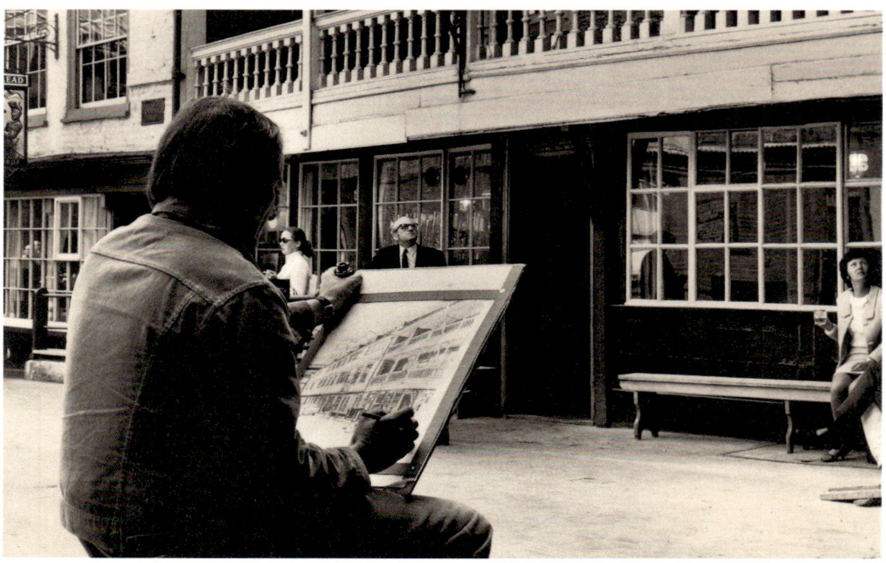

Hard at work on a drawing commissioned by the Post Office, *c.* 1965.

from Devon, Lincoln and Southampton, up to Scotland and the Lake District. Some of those drawings were taxing, believe me. If you want a difficult drawing to do, the Lake District in summer in pen line is very demanding. Usually I used to feature a cathedral in the area on the cover. I remember how much I enjoyed drawing Gloucester Cathedral. Lincoln Cathedral was another great job, as were Salisbury and Exeter. As well as being interesting and a challenge, the Post Office seemed in those days to be paying quite well.

It was hard work too. I was teaching on Mondays and Tuesdays, so I used to jump in the car first thing on Wednesday morning. I'd drive up to Cumberland or Scotland or wherever I was going, and draw for two or three days, returning on Sunday night ready to teach again on Monday morning. I had to be quite disciplined when I was on the road. I would get up early in the morning before breakfast and do one drawing, which I knew would be a write-off. Then I would go back to the hotel or guest house I was staying in, have breakfast and then go out again and do another drawing. By this time my hand and eye were in, and I knew the next drawing would work. Then I would drive to another town nearby where there would be another subject for me to draw. Each telephone directory had twelve drawings, one on the cover and several inside down the margins. I had held an ambition when I was young to have one thing in every house in the country. I nearly achieved this with my telephone-directory drawings.

As a result of my commissions, I was constantly travelling – another factor that damaged my marriage. Stowells of Chelsea decided to produce a calendar featuring twelve paintings of their various vineyards throughout Europe. They commissioned Norman Hepple and Christopher Sanders to do four paintings each, and me to do the other four. This was a flattering offer, as both Hepple and Sanders had quite high reputations at that time. But, of course, it involved a lot of travelling as I never took any shortcuts when I did commissions. I didn't go and take photographs, then try to do the work back in the studio. The Stowells calendar involved several weeks travelling in Europe at a time when my marriage to Annie was very shaky. We both had had affairs and it looked likely that we were going to separate. Yet absence, as they say, makes the heart grow fonder, and while I was in Europe I found myself, for the first time in my life, writing love poems to Annie in the evenings. I longed to get back to her, but, as always, it was fairly fraught when I did.

The first stop for the Stowells commission was Alsace-Lorraine, in the vineyards of a company called Gustav Lorentz. The wonderful thing was that they were so pleased to have me there that they gave me some of the best wine that I have ever drunk in my life to bring back to England. I then went on to Worms to do the Liebfrau Kirch in the Liebfraumilch vineyards. Then I travelled down to Lake Garda for the Bardolino, then from Bardolino up to Bernkastel to draw the white-wine vineyards there. It was an exciting trip lasting about three weeks. I remember that when I finished the last painting, at about 4 pm at Bernkastel, I decided I was going to get home as soon as I could, desperate to be with Annie again. I drove like crazy to the coast, got on the ferry (there was no tunnel at that time, of course) and finally arrived home in London at about 3 am. If only our relationship could have gone on as we imagined it would when we were apart, it would have been a wonderful marriage.

I was also exhibiting work, of course, not only with the galleries but also with many other groups. The first group to which I was elected was the ROI, the Royal Institute of Oil Painters. The President had seen my work for the Lord Mayor's Art Award and had decided that he'd like me to join; they asked me to apply, I did and they elected me. I was then elected to the New English Art Club, a group I had admired for a long time and whose members included Bernard Dunstan and Fred Cuming.

I remember that I had a one-man show up in Harrogate at the Harrogate Festival, where I was the featured artist. Before the Harrogate Festival opened the hotel rang to say that there was a black-tie dinner there to open the Festival, at which I, as the featured artist, was expected to speak. I wasn't too keen as that meant that I couldn't have a drink, but I agreed. About five days before the dinner I got a phone call from them asking how long my Saturday-night speech would be. I said I thought I'd speak for three or four minutes. The people at the hotel said that was not enough as Mr Bennett was planning to speak for three-quarters of an hour. 'That's a good idea,' I said. 'Let Mr Bennett speak for three-quarters of an hour…' and then it hit me. 'Which Mr Bennett?' 'Mr Alan Bennett.' When

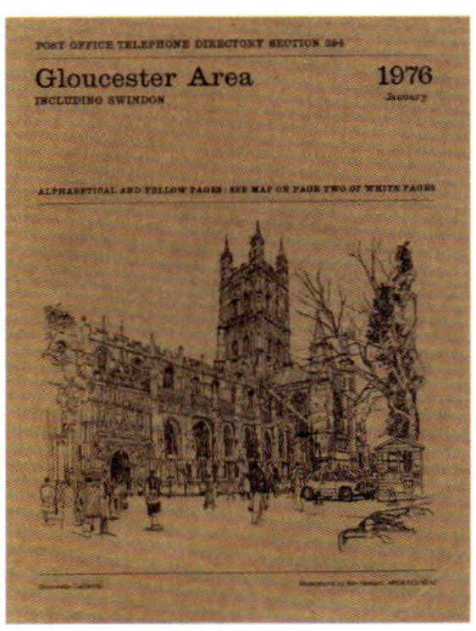

Gloucester Area Telephone Directory, 1976

A typical pen drawing of Gloucester Cathedral which I did for the cover of the Area Telephone Directory.

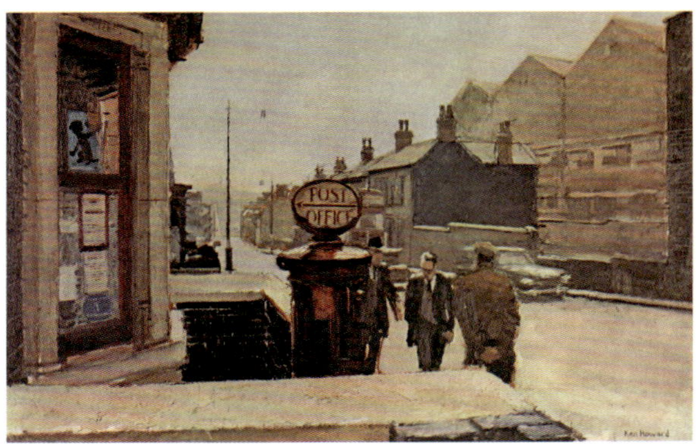

Poster: Street Scene in the Potteries, *c.* 1965

This poster was commissioned by the Post Office. In the background can be seen my small Triumph estate car. I had left London on Sunday morning at dawn, driven to Stoke, and returned to London in the evening with the finished painting.

they said this, I refused to speak second – no way was I going to follow Alan Bennett. In fact, the evening was a great success as we both spoke about similar subjects – he about his early life and me about mine. I got away with my speech because I went on first.

When I sat down at one of the two top tables, Alan was at the other one. My neighbour complimented me on my speech, and I explained that Alan Bennett was the real lead. I asked what he did and he said that he was the chairman of the Harrogate Festival. 'But that's not your proper job?' I queried. He admitted he was retired, and that he had been 'in retail menswear, on the management side'. Then, insisting I was the guest of honour that night, he began to talk to me about what I did. Suddenly someone on the other side of the table leaned over and said, 'Excuse me, Mr Burton…' 'You are not Montagu Burton, by any chance?' I asked. 'Oh no,' he said, 'he was my father. I took the business over from him.' I thought his career resumé was the most wonderful example of understatement I ever heard in my life: 'I was in retail menswear, on the management side.'

The Sixties had been a chaotic time. My personal life had been difficult: I had lost Chrissie and embarked on a difficult, complicated and totally absorbing marriage. I had struggled to establish myself as a working artist involved with several galleries, exhibiting at the Royal Academy and various societies and artists' groups. I had worked on diverse commissions and tried not to get too involved in teaching, which I enjoyed but knew was not the route that I wished to take.

The Sixties of course was an exciting time to live through, although it was only in retrospect that one realised it. This was despite the fact that Annie and I had a flat in the King's Road, the hub of the Swinging Sixties, when we first married. We were among the first generation on the Pill, we both had involving professional lives and we were becoming affluent in a changing society.

Although exciting, it was also painful. Annie and I were gradually finding ourselves and this didn't necessarily mean growing closer. It was not an easy process, often a painful one, and yet during that decade and the years of the '70s to come I produced some of the best work of my life. I realise now, looking back, that a period of chaos and the inevitable suffering is necessary to produce something special as an artist. The pain has to be deep and real, however; it cannot be manufactured.

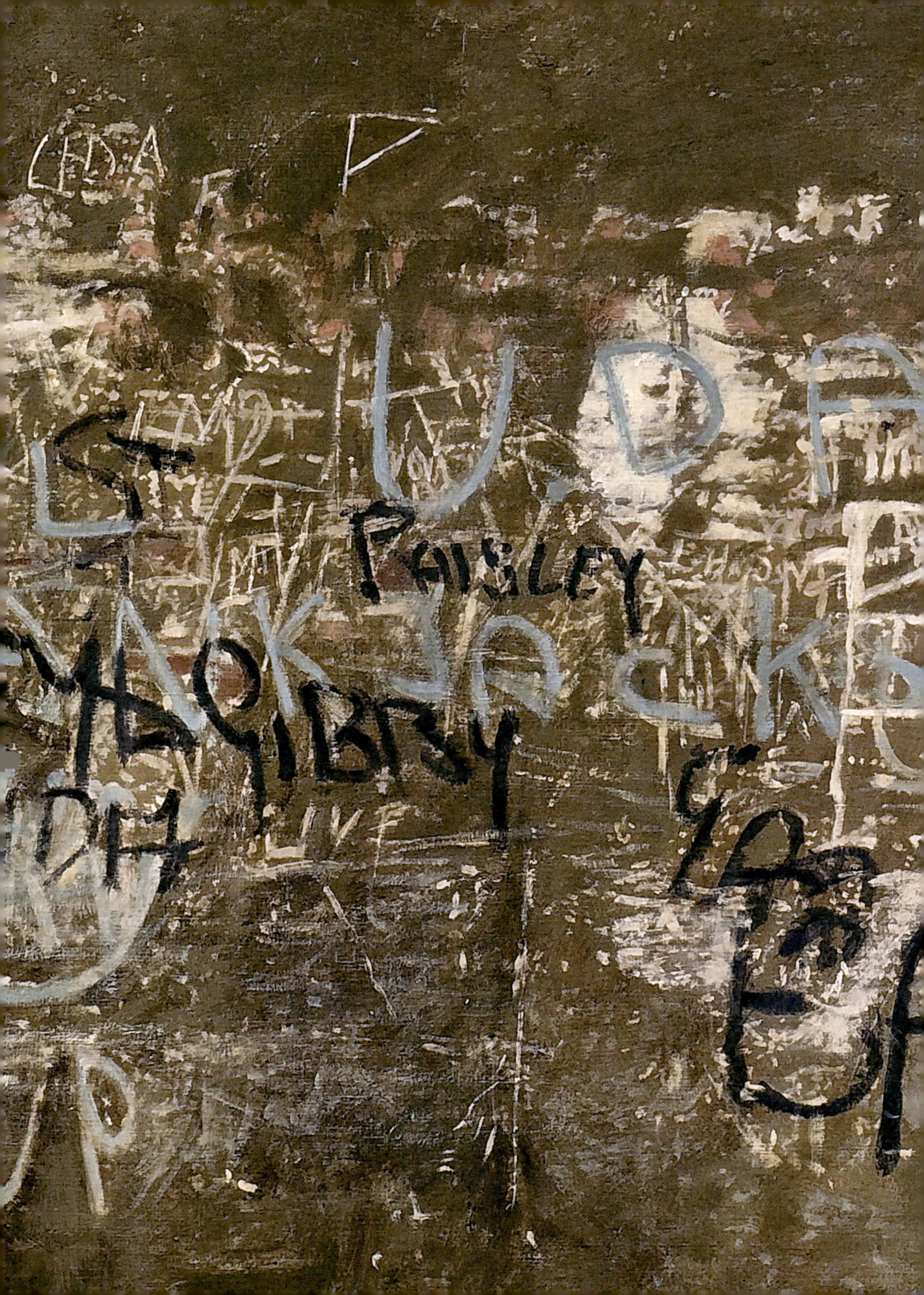
PAISLEY

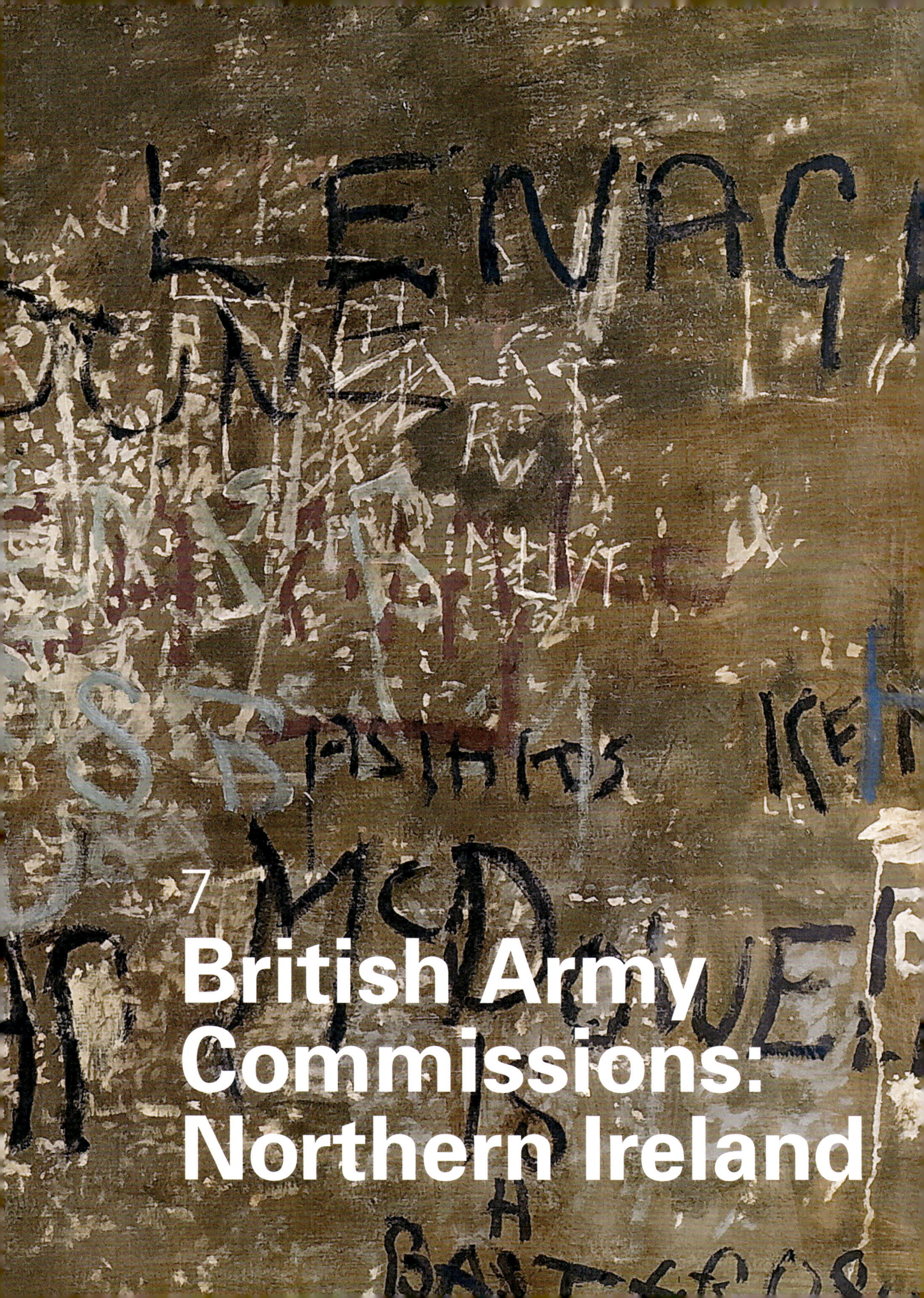

7 British Army Commissions: Northern Ireland

Early in 1973 I handed in my notice at the Harrow School of Art. I was set to leave at Easter and then, between Christmas and Easter as I remember, I received a commission to work for the Imperial War Museum in Northern Ireland. People very often ask me how this arose; it was very simple really. The Imperial War Museum had decided to commission an artist for the first time since the end of the Second World War. During that conflict official war artists were given a commission in a regiment – usually the rank of captain – and they worked for the Imperial War Museum all the time. Obviously my situation was very different. I wasn't in the Army and the commission was for a certain amount of money. It wasn't very much, only £500, but as I had just given up the only job I had, the prospect of earning £500 was very attractive. From the word go I found the idea of going to Northern Ireland very stimulating. War is a strange thing. I had lived through the Second World War as a child and absorbed the ugliness of war, the bombing and death, without being incredibly conscious of it.

But I knew that there was another side to war – a strange, terrible sort of beauty accompanies it. Certainly it speaks to artists. Some of the best artists are featured in the Imperial War Museum. Stanley Spencer, Graham Sutherland and Henry Moore were all official war artists, and naturally I felt very privileged to be asked to join that band. As I understand it, when the Imperial War Museum decided to appoint an official artist they wrote to the Royal College, the Royal Academy Schools and the Slade, asking each of them to nominate a possible candidate for the position. Although I had left the Royal College fourteen years before, Carel Weight, who had been my tutor, was still there. I suppose he thought, 'Ah well, Howard could do that job', and he sent my name off.

I think it was partly due to the fact that the year before, I had been commissioned by the doctors at Charing Cross Hospital to do a series of fourteen pen and wash drawings of the hospital. They covered the whole life of the hospital – the wards, the Accident and Emergency area, the operating theatre, the doctors' dining room, even the cook-house, and reflected all the aspects and architecture of the building. These drawings were made into lithographs, lithographic reproductions rather than lithographic prints, which were then sold to the Friends of Charing Cross Hospital to raise money for the hospital. I had done a set of around about fourteen drawings in pen and sepia ink which Carel had seen; I think that was partly the reason why he thought of me when asked to nominate someone to go to Northern Ireland. In addition to this, I had the sketchbooks that I had kept as a Royal Marine National Serviceman, and photographs of some of the paintings that I had done of life in the Marines. I also had the experience of being a National Serviceman, of course, and had reached a certain age – I was in my 41st year by then. Obviously the committee must have thought that I could cope with the difficult conditions out there. I don't think they really understood what conditions in Northern Ireland were like at that time, but they must have had some idea.

Anyway, I went along to the interview and got the job, which I must admit gave me quite a kick. Joe Darracott, Keeper of the Department of Art at the Imperial War Museum, told me they had £500 to spend and asked me what I would do for it. I told them that I thought the best plan would be to do pen and wash drawings, possibly the odd watercolour, rather than committing myself to any large-scale oils. Joe Darracott agreed to this. They then asked me how long I would go for, and I replied, 'Well, for as long as it takes.' I said that I would like to work there as much as I could, then when I returned the committee could take its pick from all the work done, up to the amount they had to spend on the commission. They agreed to this, obviously not wanting just to price it out time-wise. I could see already that Northern Ireland would excite me visually, and that I would like to be there for quite a long while.

I asked them to arrange for me to stay with the regiments in Northern Ireland while I was working, and this they did. It is worth remembering here how the regiments in Northern Ireland worked at that time. Basically they came to Northern Ireland from the British Army of the Rhine on four-month tours – something called a roulement – to fulfil what was quite a difficult role. They patrolled the streets and manned VCPs (Vehicle Check Points) in South Armagh and so forth. After four months they went back to Germany and another regiment would take their place. In 1973, of course, when I first went there, Belfast and Northern Ireland were full of soldiers. The Troubles had only been going for four years and things were very hectic, with army posts set up all along the Falls Road. I spent a lot of time in Hastings Street, which was a police station used as an army post. There were various mills and bus stations where the army was based throughout Belfast. Certain custom-built army posts, surrounded by corrugated iron (known to troops as wriggly tin) were in the very bad areas, such as Andersonstown and the Lower Falls Road.

By the summer of 1973 I was ready to go. I had given up my teaching, I didn't have a stable home life and I was looking forward to the experience. I asked the Imperial War Museum to arrange for the Army to look after me in whatever way they thought appropriate and I left for Northern Ireland in August. I really didn't know what I was going to find. From the papers you would have expected to be down on your stomach and crawling from the moment you got off the boat, as there seemed to be bombing and shooting in Belfast all the time.

In fact, it wasn't like that at all. When I arrived on the boat from Liverpool (I took my car with me) I was picked up by a young officer. He was a Major and had been given the job of looking after me and taking me around Northern Ireland so that I could see the various subjects that I might want to paint. Belfast wasn't completely a battleground. Some areas certainly were – down the Shankill Road, along the Falls Road and Sandy Row, for example, but in other areas you wouldn't really have known that there was anything going on. (The latter were inevitably Protestant areas rather than Catholic ones, but it still wasn't at all what I expected to find.) And when I got there the young officer assigned to look after me, who was typical of the Army, was meticulous and thorough in his preparation. He started to take me round the main areas – Belfast, Londonderry and what they called the country areas, including South Armagh, then generally known as bandit country. I always remember that one of the first areas we visited in Belfast was a newly constructed army post. It reminded me irresistibly of those Wild West wagon-train places. Instead of the wagons surrounding and making the loop there was corrugated iron, and inside there were Nissen huts and trenches. This was so that there was always some place to get down into when the IRA tried to bomb or mortar the Army post, and you pretty quickly learned the form.

So I arrived at this Army post and was met by the Colonel. He was quite thrilled to think that his regiment was going to be included in the Imperial War Museum's record of the conflict in Northern Ireland. He took me round this gathering of Nissen huts and I looked at everything. We went into one Nissen hut where we saw three men who had just returned from patrol. They had thrown themselves on their beds, their kit was all over the floor and their rifles were in the rack, while the walls were covered with rather lurid pin-up girls and nudes. I took one look and said, 'Wow, this is terrific. This will be my first subject. When I've been round Northern Ireland and seen all the possibilities, I will come back and make this my very first drawing.' The Colonel was absolutely delighted and off I went with the young officer who was looking after me. We went everywhere, but eventually I got back to this Army post. Again the Colonel met us, promising to give me anything I needed and inviting me to the Mess for lunch.

So off I went to the room that I thought I was going to draw, and it wasn't there. Instead I found a pristine clean room with three or four men and an officer who had been told what might happen, all looking very clean and well-groomed. I thought it was odd as it could not be the room where I was before. I tried the next room, but there was nothing there either. And after two or three rooms I went back to the Colonel and explained that I couldn't find the room I was supposed to draw.

He indicated the one I had looked over. 'No, I'm sorry,' I said, 'but it isn't that one. I've just been in and it's not the room I decided to draw.' 'Oh yes, it is,' he said, 'I'm certain it is. It's a very good example of an Army room in Northern Ireland and we've had it completely decorated and removed all the pin-ups.' I thanked him and went on my way, not very happy. On the whole, the regiments were very good with me, however, and very good to work for; they really did seem to enjoy the distraction of having an artist around the place.

I must have been something of a responsibility for them, but they didn't make me feel like that at all. It must have been difficult as I insisted on working in my usual way, sitting and drawing out on the streets. At first the soldiers said that if I was going to do that they would have to send some men to watch out for me while I was working. I told them I would prefer just to go by myself, to show myself to the locals and let them see what I was doing. I had a gut feeling that this would be the way to do it, and rather reluctantly they agreed to let me try. I must say that I never, ever felt threatened in Northern Ireland while working in that way. I was working on a drawing board and everyone could see exactly what I was doing; I clearly wasn't doing anything underhand or collecting information for Intelligence or anything like that.

As I say, most of the regiments and the Colonels in charge of me, despite the great pressure that they were under, were generally very accepting of me. One day I went up to the Creggan in Londonderry, a particularly tough area. The Army post was a kind of old garage on the edge of the Creggan Estate, and when I went in the Colonel didn't seem particularly keen to see me. He asked me where I wanted to work and I told him out in the parking area. I wanted to do a drawing showing the Army vehicles with the Creggan Estate in the background. 'Oh, you can't do that,' said the Colonel. 'It's far too dangerous.' I asked what he meant and he told me that the IRA, the Republicans, fired down onto this Army post from the council estate. He thought it would be far too dangerous for me to sit out there and do a drawing, and he wouldn't take the responsibility for me anyway. I was fairly obstinate, I suppose, and persisted. 'I've got to get this drawing done. Is there any time that I can work?' 'Well,' he said, 'they don't usually start shooting until about nine in the morning, so if you get up at dawn you can work out there until about half past eight. You should be all right provided you stay behind some of those screens' (indicating the big wriggly-tinned screens that the soldiers used when they wanted to move around the area without exposing themselves to gunfire). That was the best I could get.

The next morning it was pouring with rain. I'd got up at the crack of dawn, which was very early as it was summer, and I had to work from my car. I sat there

Patrol in Roden Street, Lower Falls, Belfast, *c.* 1975
Oil on canvas, 150 x 180 cm

This large oil painting was made from a watercolour and painted in a derelict part of the Lower Falls in Belfast. Eventually the houses were demolished and a new estate was built.

in the rain and did a pen and wash drawing of the troops on what I suppose you would call a parade ground, but it wasn't really. Beyond I could see these lines of houses on the Creggan Estate; to me it was very inspiring.

The rain made it even more visually exciting, creating wonderful reflections on the puddles and shine on the vehicles. There were some wonderful Army vehicles known as PIGs – they were armoured troop carriers, I suppose, and extremely ugly. I remember wondering if in 50 years' time people looking at my drawings would really believe that the British Army went to war in these old tin cans. They certainly weren't terribly pretty, they really did resemble armoured old tin cans, but that, of course, made them ideal subjects for drawing.

One of the wonderful things about Northern Ireland was the fact that it seemed to rain all the time. I remember sitting in my car drawing one day when an Irishman came up to me. He looked at what I was doing and commented, 'You're not looking very happy, mister.' 'No,' I said, 'it's your damned Irish weather, isn't it?' He asked what I meant and I pointed to the rain. 'Sure,' he said, 'it rains twice a week in Northern Ireland, you know – once for three days and once for four!' That about summed it up; an awful lot of the work I did in Northern Ireland was done sitting in a car. Obviously it could be restricting sometimes for the composition that I was making, but on this occasion up at Creggan it was quite all right. I sat there drawing until about half past eight, by which time I had finished what I thought was quite a good pen and wash drawing. I worked a lot in pen and wash at that time in Northern Ireland, usually in Half Imperial, which I think is about 15 by 18 inches. I would generally start by drawing with a brush and putting the main areas of tone in the composition of the drawing. I would then take a pen and draw it across the washes, then add more washes to coincide more with the drawing, and then define the drawing more and again with the pen. So I would be moving constantly from pen to brush and sometimes a bit of pencil or whatever was needed, until the drawing finally came together.

I went in for breakfast and when I entered the rather grumpy Colonel came towards me and asked how I had got on. So I showed him my work on the drawing board and his eyes lit up. 'Oh, oh,' he said, 'I like that!' I thanked him and he asked if he could buy it as he was leaving the regiment at the end of that tour and wanted to give them a farewell present. He thought the drawing would be ideal as a memory of the Creggan. 'I'm terribly sorry,' I replied, 'but I can't sell you this one as I am on commission to the Imperial War Museum and I must show them everything that I do.' He tried to persuade me to make an exception, but I was firm. 'Well,' he said, 'I know what we can do. You can go out again tomorrow morning at six and do

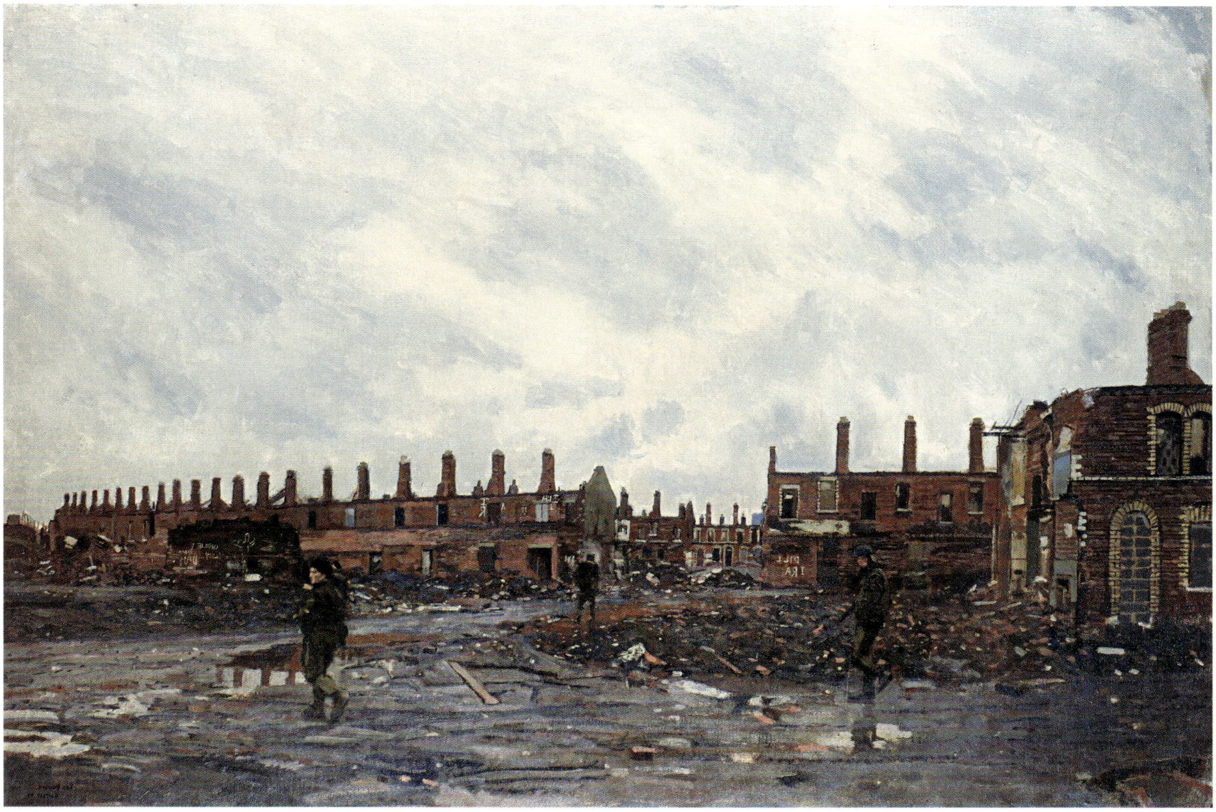

another one.' 'What if there are Irishmen shooting at me all the time?' I asked. 'Oh, no, no,' he assured me, 'you'll be all right. You go out and do me a drawing tomorrow morning.' Suddenly his whole attitude to my being there had changed because he liked my work. He did in fact buy the second drawing I did for him, so it must be hanging in a Mess somewhere in the world.

Northern Ireland proved to be quite a happy hunting ground for me and it suited me wonderfully. It was extremely dramatic visually – in 1973 there were still quite a lot of very run-down, near-derelict houses. There were bad areas as you went into different parts of the Creggan, but I couldn't have asked for a better commission because it harked back to my origins. The place reminded me very much of the working-class areas of Neasden and Cricklewood, with the factories and the terraced houses, although those in Cricklewood were a bit nicer than the ones in Northern Ireland. These were very 'drawable' subjects. The fact that it rained so much was also ideal for me, strangely enough. Although later in life I inclined more and more towards strong sunlight, at the beginning I mainly worked when it was overcast. The reason is quite simple really – if the light is strong the image changes very quickly and you have to work very fast. As I got older I could work faster and capture effects more instantly, but when I was younger the image stayed longer if it was overcast, giving me more time to work on whatever I was doing. Also I found that when it was overcast and grey the colour became more intense and richer. Very often in sunlight the sun bleaches the colour out and the shadows become

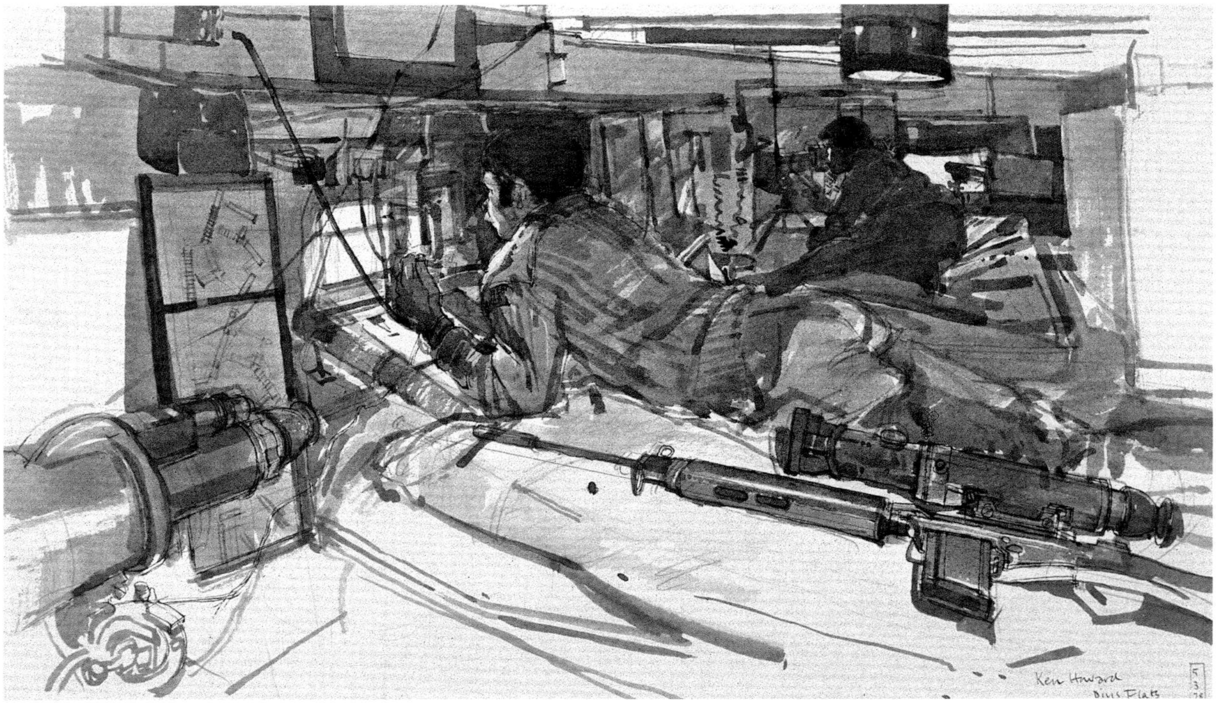

OP in the Divis Flats, 1978
Pen and ink and wash,
37.5 x 55 cm

This drawing was made in an OP (observation post) on the top of the Divis Flats. I had to crawl in and make the drawing in a restricted space, lying on my stomach. To get to the OP we had to go up by lift, which was sometimes sprayed with bullets by the IRA. I was lucky!

dark. I know that we were always taught at art school to find colour in the shadows, after the Impressionists, but when it is sunny there is a much stronger sense of dark and light, which of course is gradually what I became much more about. But Northern Ireland's grey, or rather silver light suited me very well.

I worked in the Creggan quite often. One day when I went up there it was pouring with rain and I hadn't brought my car. I went into an Army post and there was an OP, an observation post, on the edge of the estate. These were usually structures resembling concrete bunkers with a slit on each wall; the soldier would sit inside and observe the area where he was. It was up to him to make notes about who was around – usually a line of photographs was fitted above the window in the OP, presumably of the most active IRA members in the area. The soldier would report on whether he had seen so-and-so in the area, or whether he was reported to be around. One knew, despite IRA propaganda, that soldiers didn't shoot people from those observation posts.

On this occasion I was in the Creggan and it was raining. Three or four soldiers were each taking a turn in the OP, one of them with a particularly striking head. I asked him to sit for me and I did a small oil portrait of him (I did have some oils with me as well as watercolours). When I had been commissioned by the Imperial War Museum initially they had said that I could do whatever I liked when I was out there, but that they didn't want portraits. So I did this one thinking, 'Ah well, this is one for me.' and just carried on with the tour.

When I got back after my first tour in 1973 and went to take the work in to the Imperial War Museum, I decided to take the portrait anyway. It was like an exam at school – I took all the work in and sat outside while the Imperial War Museum

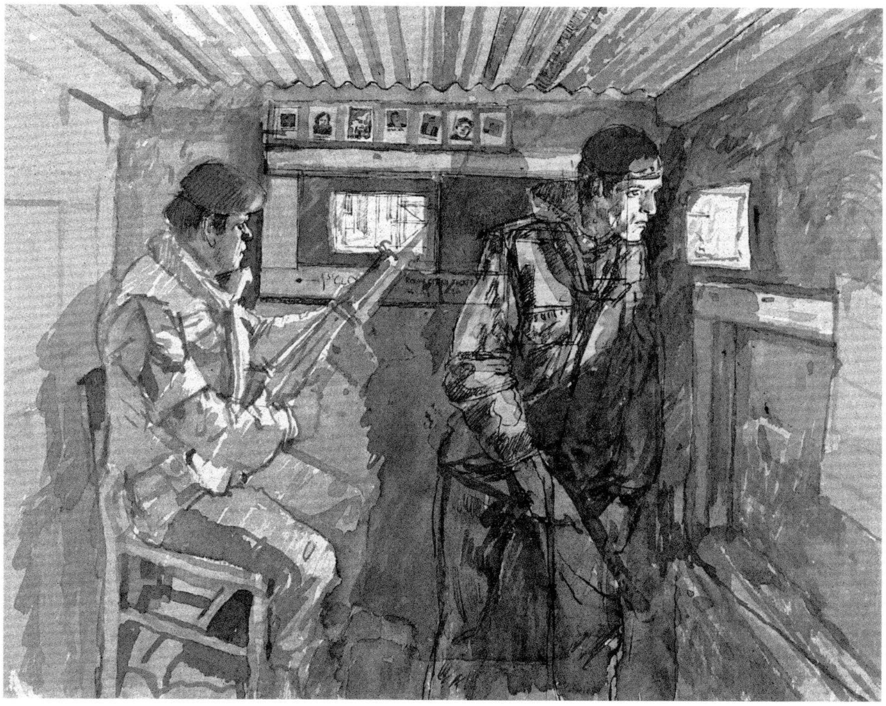

The Sanger, 1973
Pen, ink and wash,
37.5 x 55 cm

This drawing clearly shows my approach to drawing at the time. The figure on the left, who was there for only ten minutes, was drawn with a brush to establish the main tones. Then the figure on the right appeared. He was there for two hours, so after the initial tonal statement I developed the drawing with pen.

committee looked through it. In those days the committee naturally consisted mainly of people from the museum, along with a General in the British Army and a Royal Academician, or an independent painter. On this occasion the Army General had been a General in the Royal Engineers, and he was later in charge of the Royal Hospital, Chelsea. He was known as 'Splosh' Jones, by the way, because as a Royal Engineer he had apparently been very adept at dropping Bailey bridges into rivers.

After the committee had looked at my work General Jones came out. He told me that he liked my work, particularly the portrait of the soldier, which he'd like to buy. And I thought that as the Imperial War Museum wouldn't want it anyway, which they didn't, then I could certainly sell it to Splosh. 'Yes, sir, certainly,' I replied, although I can't now remember what price I asked for it, probably about £100. The General was delighted and the following week I got a letter from him which said, 'I love my painting, but from the badge it looks like he is a Royal Engineer and that's why I bought it. I wondered if you could do a little bit of research when you are next over in Northern Ireland and find out what regiment he was in and what his name was.' So when I went over to Northern Ireland a few weeks later I began to enquire what regiment had been at the Creggan on that particular day and which unit had been up in the OP. Unfortunately it emerged that the cap badge was that of the Royal Artillery, not the Royal Engineers. Obviously, working the way I do, the cap badge was just an impression so it could have read as one or the other.

A little bit embarrassed, I wrote to Splosh and explained the position, offering to take back the painting if he wished. I received a very nice reply saying, 'Of course not, it's the painting I like, and even if it's not an engineer it doesn't matter. But would you mind finding out the name of the soldier for me?' By this time I was travelling back and forth to Northern Ireland quite a lot, so the next time I went I checked again. I found out which exact regiment would have been up there and in the OP at the time, and I discovered that the soldier's nickname was 'Regiment', funnily enough. Unfortunately 'Regiment' had deserted and no one knew where he was. I was now even more embarrassed, but I wrote to Splosh to tell him that the boy I had painted had since deserted. Again I offered to refund his money and take back the painting. But Splosh, to his credit, refused to do so. He wrote a very amusing letter back to me saying, 'Of course none of this matters because I love the painting.'

One further twist in the tale of this painting took place some months later. The *Observer* colour supplement decided to do an article about the official war artist in Northern Ireland and they chose 'Regiment' for the front cover. I have to confess that it wasn't a very good article – in fact the journalist who wrote it had no sympathy at all with my attitude to working there and I had finally to complain. She eventually had to apologise to me – something that doesn't happen very often. But the cover stayed with me. I remember I was driving into London that weekend, speeding past some billboards on the Cromwell Road, and there was 'Regiment' in all his glory, smiling down on me. 'Well, it wasn't all negative,' I thought, and wondered where the young soldier I painted could be.

My day at the Imperial War Museum, when I took in the work for selection, had another nice outcome. Joe Darracott, who commissioned me to do the paintings, told me how much he liked the work and that the committee had selected the ones they wanted. Originally the commission had been for £500, but he said that they had managed to afford a little bit more, so they bought work worth £1,000 in total. He pointed out what they were buying and said that he would very much like one of the other ones for himself. Although he hadn't got a lot of money, he had a small work by Whistler, which he said he would be very willing to swap for one of my small drawings. Of course, I immediately agreed. The Whistler lithograph still hangs above my stairs on the way up to my studio, and it gives me great delight.

Things were still very hairy during my first tour in Northern Ireland. In fact I was to keep visiting the province for the next ten years, although I didn't know it at the time. The Imperial War Museum commission was just for one trip, to do work up to the cost of £500. But things developed from there, as the regiments liked what I did very much. My traditional approach to the job, in which I saw myself as a visual journalist, has been unusual really. Since I went out the painters sent by the Imperial War Museum have often been more controversial, as you might say. I certainly didn't want to make a political statement in my drawings: to me that wasn't what

I was there for. Political statements can be so subjective. I wanted to make drawings from which people could take some propagandist or political statement if they wanted to, but certainly not to impose it on them. I like to think, however, that when people look at my drawings in the Imperial War Museum in 50 years' time they will really get a feel for what life was like for the British soldier serving in Northern Ireland.

If this is your aim people will always say, 'You were very sympathetic to the British Army.' My answer is that this isn't necessarily so. I just happened to get a boat to Belfast and then lived with the British Army. If I had got off the boat and stayed with a Catholic family I would certainly have had some sympathy with their point of view. If I had got off the boat and gone and stayed with a Protestant family in Sandy Row, I'm sure I would have had some sympathy with their point of view. Such feelings are inevitable. I saw the incredibly difficult position the British Army were in, set between these two warring factions and experiencing hostility from both sides, and certainly it is true that I was sympathetic to the position that soldiers on the ground were in. But I didn't make my drawings overtly speak of that sympathy or reflect any broader political views.

I must confess that as time went on I became more and more concerned with the plight of Northern Ireland's children. I thought that the attitude of the Catholic and Protestant adults was their own affair, but a generation of children were losing their whole youth, something that could never be replaced. When I went back some twenty years later and revisited my old haunts, I saw youngsters standing on corners. These young men and women must have initially been small children at the time of the Troubles. Even then, although things had changed vastly, they were still living in a very disruptive and unnatural environment. And this sympathy for the children began to find expression in the work that I did for myself while I was in Northern Ireland.

I suppose the major work that resulted from all the time I was there was a piece called *Ulster Crucifixion*. The work now hangs in the Ulster Museum in Belfast, I'm pleased to say, because of all the places in the world that is the museum and the city where it truly belongs.

It came about one day while I was working in the Lower Falls. It was a near-derelict landscape in 1973, very dramatic with the sort of terrible beauty that often occurs in war zones. (When I returned later the area had been redeveloped with new houses and all the original atmosphere had gone.) One day I was drawing in the Falls, down at Roden Street, and I saw a boy playing. He climbed up a lamppost and hung from the crossbar that is usually on lampposts – there is no lamp on the top, just the post and the crossbar. It struck me that it was just as if he was being

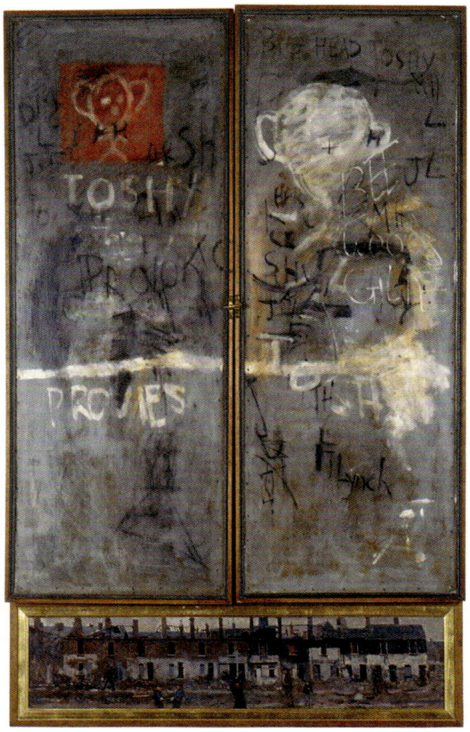

Ulster Crucifixion, 1978
Oil on canvas, 120 x 180 cm

This is an unusual painting for me as it was both challenging and political. Normally my paintings are inspired by a purely visual stimulus, much of the time by light. Of course the original stimulus for this work was also visual, the strange beauty of graffiti walls.

crucified. And when he came down I offered him 50 pence to climb up again and hang there for long enough for me to draw him – it wouldn't take too long. He agreed, shinned up the lamppost and hung there. I made the drawing of him with his striped shirt and his baggy trousers, and that was that. The drawing remained in my sketchbook.

About a year later I was down in the Protestant Shankill Road area. In a funny way this was appropriate as I never wanted the work I did in Ireland to be about one side or the other. I didn't want it to be 'for' one and 'against' the other

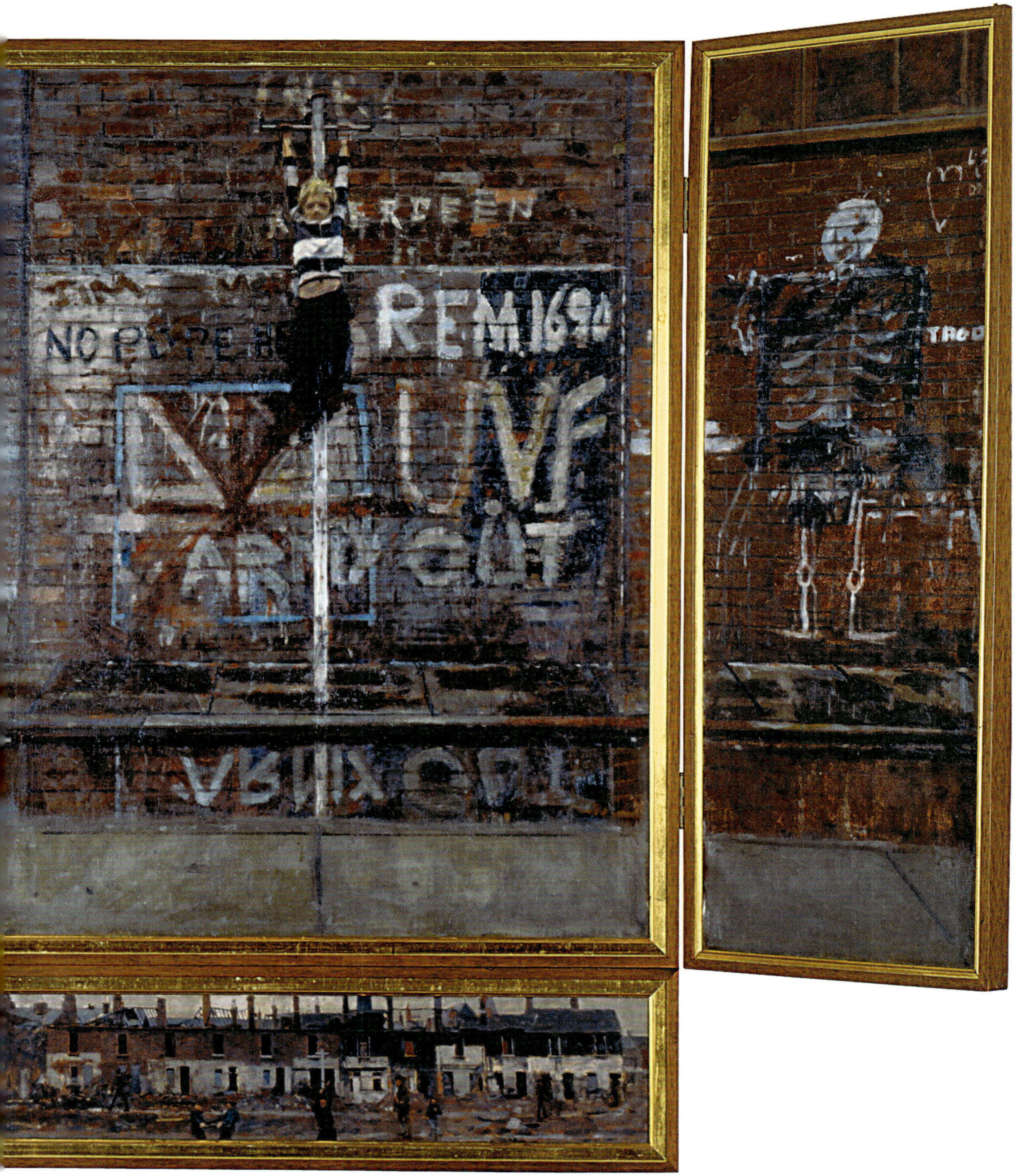

NO POPE H
REM169
UVF

because I didn't feel that that was what my painting was about. Anyway, I was in the Shankill Road and I had become incredibly interested in graffiti in Northern Ireland. I have a studio in Venice now, and I find that one of the awful things in the city is how the graffiti hooligans have covered all the walls. They don't create the sort of graffiti that I saw in Belfast – which was fantastic – but terribly repetitive stuff, like a sort of bad signature. It is just like a little dog peeing against a wall to leave its mark. In Northern Ireland the graffiti in the early '70s was quite incredible; I took masses of slides of it and I've still got the collection. One day I will have to get that into the Imperial War Museum too.

Anyway, I saw this wall in the Shankill Road which, if you had put it into the Tate, would be a work of art in itself. What very often happened with Northern Ireland's graffiti was that the locals would produce some graffiti with a strong political message and then somebody else would come and paint it out. Then the original people would come and paint it back again. And then it would get painted out again – perhaps by the Army or maybe by those from the other side of the street, who were likely to be of the other persuasion. Belfast was incredible. It wasn't a case of half the city being Catholic and the other half Protestant. In Belfast a few streets were Protestant and a few streets were Catholic, an inevitable source of tension as one side would rampage in the streets of the other. This, of course, was the original reason why the British Army went to Northern Ireland. The B Specials (a Protestant paramilitary organisation) were attacking the Catholic community and the British Army was sent to keep them apart, essentially to keep the B Specials away from Catholics. A few weeks later, of course, both Protestants and Catholics had been shot, and both sides were against the British Army. But that's another story.

There was an intriguing mix of graffiti on this wall in the Protestant area. One said '1690 – remember 1690', this being the year of the Battle of the Boyne, a crucial date for the Protestant community. Alongside it was printed, 'No Pope here', and underneath that was painted 'UVF' – the Ulster Volunteer Force, a Protestant paramilitary group. At the bottom it read 'Army Out'. I am not a particularly religious person, but it struck me that these were all the reasons why Jesus Christ was crucified. 'No Pope here': religion. 'UVF': politics. 'Remember 1690': the force of history. 'Army Out': it could have referred to the Roman Army. Unlike a lot of the Protestant walls which are painted very carefully, this one had weathered; it had been painted over and the result was a very dramatic graffiti wall. I remembered the boy who I had seen hanging from the lamppost and suddenly I saw these two images come together.

When I went back to London I began to paint a big sketch of the boy against the graffiti wall. Then the idea began to grow on me, and I decided to make it like a triptych as it was a religious conflict as well as a political one. I painted two side panels that could close like two doors to cover the centre panel of the Crucifixion. I also remembered that there are often saints on the two side panels of triptychs in churches. I had seen some graffiti walls in the Catholic areas, again very dramatic in their colour and texture because they were even more painted, painted out and repainted. They featured skeletal figures and the names of those who must have been local heroes. I remember one said 'Tago', which I suppose could have been the nickname of an IRA member in that area, and another said 'Big Ears, Toshy'. There was also almost a caricature of a figure with big ears and that too had been painted out and then repainted. I thought that those two figures could act as the saints in a way. The boy hanging from the lamppost would be in the middle, and the graffiti on each side would be the equivalent of saints, heroes or whatever. On the backs of the doors I decided to paint mug shots, inspired by the lines of photographs in the OP. By now it was beginning to develop as an idea for a religious painting, I suppose. I wanted to have a predella at the bottom, and I decided that this should feature a long line of derelict houses with an Army patrol walking across it. So finally in the triptych of the *Crucifixion* I had all the elements involved in the Northern Ireland Troubles: Protestant, Catholic and Army.

I worked on the painting for a long time, I remember. At that time I wasn't a member of the Academy, but I nevertheless decided to send it to the Summer Exhibition. It was hung and got on quite well, but it was a time when I didn't necessarily sell paintings at the Academy and I didn't sell the *Crucifixion* that year. When I got it back I had it in my studio; I quite liked it and it was my second wife's favourite picture. Next door at the time lived Jania O'Hana, the widow of a Bond Street dealer, Jacques O'Hana, who had died some years before. Jania pushed a competition form for the John Moores exhibition in Liverpool through the door. 'Why don't you send your *Crucifixion* to the John Moores?' she asked me. 'No,' I replied, 'John Moores would think I am much too traditional – John Moores is more innovative and new.' But the painting was hanging on the wall, so in the end I decided I might as well send it there. It would be out of the way for a while, and you never know – I just might get it hung at the Moores, although it was about something that wasn't really me. I sent it off and a few weeks later received a letter to say that I had been awarded one of the prizes in the John Moores. Not only had the painting been hung, but I had actually been awarded one of the prizes! It wasn't one of the first prizes, of course, as these went more to the avant-garde works, but

Shankill Wall, 1978
Oil on canvas, 150 x 180 cm

Ruskin said 'beauty is in the eye of the beholder', and this graffiti wall in Ulster was sublimely beautiful to me.

it was very gratifying to think that I was probably one of the first really figurative painters to win a prize at the John Moores.

When the *Ulster Crucifixion* came back I hung it in the studio again. Eventually, one night in the early '80s, I met a fellow painter in the Chelsea Arts Club. He sadly is no longer with us, but he painted portraits of oil men in America a lot and obviously he had someone out there who was a dealer. He used to buy pictures and take them to America, so when he asked me if I had anything he could buy I invited him back to my studio. I was thinking of one of my church paintings or something like that; I did a lot of paintings of city churches and cathedrals, and I thought one of these might be right. He came back with me and bought a city church painting. Then, as he was going out of the door, he said, 'Oh I like that'; it was my *Ulster Crucifixion*. He asked how much I would charge for it, I told him the price and he agreed. Then he called a taxi and left with the paintings. The next day my wife returned and as soon as she walked into the studio she asked where the *Ulster Crucifixion* was. I told her that I had sold it the day before and suggested we had dinner that night. But when she said it was one of her favourite pictures, I knew I would have to try and recover it.

A few nights later I met the painter again at the Chelsea Arts Club. I explained what had happened and that I'd be happy to give him his money back. He told me that if I gave him five times the amount he'd paid me, he'd get it back for me. Obviously it had already been sold to the American dealer. So the picture disappeared for many years, and then I got a phone call out of the blue from a dealer in Gloucestershire. 'You won't know me,' he said, 'but I know you. I've got your *Ulster Crucifixion*.' I said I thought it was in America and he replied that he had brought it back and had just sold it to the Ulster Museum. He wondered if I would like to see it before it went. That picture had a long history. I have to confess that if I had to stand by one picture, if I was to be remembered by one picture when I drop off the perch, then I think that the *Ulster Crucifixion* is the one that I would point to and say, 'That's the one I'm going to stand by.'

I did several large pictures for myself when I was in Northern Ireland. Several of them were based on graffiti because it was incredibly evocative, particularly at that time – beautiful in the terrible way that characterises images of war. I remember seeing a wall in the Shankill Road that had become just a mass of words written across it. More words had been written over those, some of them had been scratched off and then others had been painted over again. The whole wall had gradually accrued an extremely beautiful texture of black and white and grey. It was as if the people who had done it had deliberately thought about the colour, but what

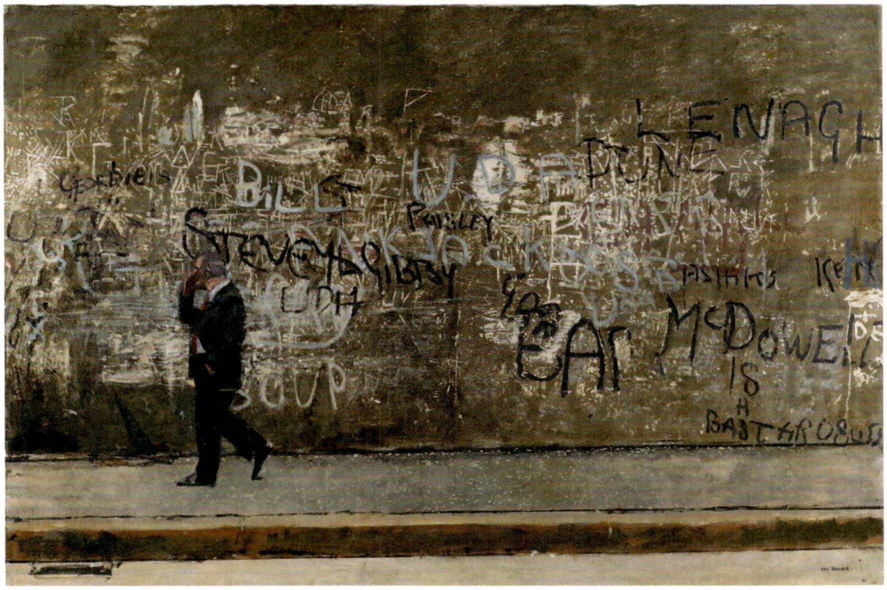

had happened, of course, was that the colour had been weathered. It was a beautiful wall – most people would have looked at it and thought it was just graffiti, but to me that wall was as inspiring as any landscape or any other image. Everyone knows the saying 'Beauty is in the eye of the beholder'. To me, looking as an artist does, even a graffiti wall in the Shankill Road can be beautiful.

The painting I did of this wall also had an interesting history. I sold it to Lord Belmore who lived in Castle Coole in Northern Ireland. After a couple of years he wrote to me and said that unfortunately the painting was, as it were, so loaded with a sense of the Troubles that he couldn't hang it in his collection; could I advise him on where he should sell it? I wrote back and said that I would buy it back from him, and that I would pay him exactly what he had given me a couple of years ago. When I got the work back I gave it to my stepdaughter. It hangs in my studio today – the only painting that I wouldn't sell and I suppose that it is the only painting, in a way, that I haven't sold.

So Northern Ireland produced a good body of work for me off my own bat, as it were, as well as the commission work. I have a feeling that this was the work – quite powerful, quite edgy in a way – that I have exhibited the most at the Royal Academy at different times, and I think it was possibly this work that finally got me elected. I remember that in 1983, the year before I became an Associate Member, I had sent a particular work to the Academy as my prime work. I was driving back through France and we had just got to the point where you can pick up the English radio; as we had been away for some weeks, I wanted to catch up on the news. Then they started to talk on the radio about the Summer Exhibition at the Academy, at which my former teacher Ruskin Spear had been the senior hanger. (Of course, once you have submitted works to the Summer Exhibition you are always on tenterhooks as to whether they would hang them or not. Even though I had got my pictures in regularly for years by that time, I still never took it for granted.) Ruskin

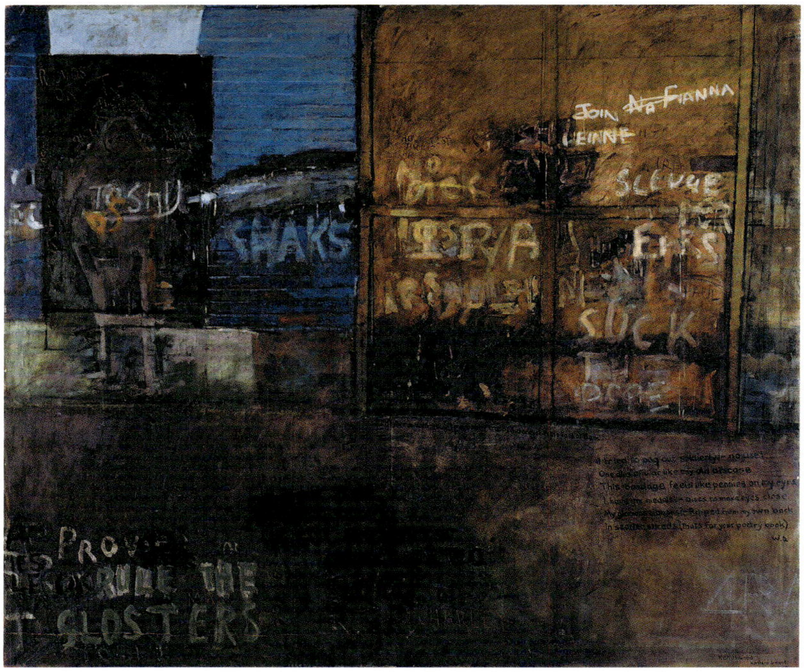

Spear was talking and his interviewer was being rather critical of the show, saying that the Summer Exhibition was not really about life as it is. It was too concerned with nice pictures and so forth. Ruskin turned round in his usual gruff way and said, 'Oh, come on now. What you are talking about? There's that big painting by Ken Howard of the graffiti wall in Belfast' – and that was how I learned that I was in the Academy that year. I must say that the rest of the drive home was very pleasant.

To return to Northern Ireland, when I worked there I would draw in the street most of the time. People would often suggest that I should bring a camera and take some photographs for safety's sake, but that wasn't my way of doing things. I think drawing is about revealing things to yourself and copying photographs isn't.

In any case, the locals got to know me quite well as I worked on the streets. This happened fairly quickly, in fact, because of the television programmes over there. I particularly remember an evening news programme called 'Scene Around Six', which I was on a few times. I think if they were a little short of news they used to wonder if that crazy English painter was still sitting around in the Falls Road and I'd be invited on the programme. 'Nationwide', a popular current affairs programme, also came over; they were doing a programme on Belfast and thought it would be original to have a war artist on the programme, so I was brought on. Through a little television exposure the Belfast citizens became more familiar with that English painter who was working on their streets.

One day I remember being in the Falls Road when a taxi drew up beside me. Not many buses ran down the Falls Road in the early 1970s. Most of them had been burned or blown up or taken out of commission and the taxis had taken over their role. In those days they would come down the Falls Road loaded with people going into the shopping area – prams were stacked on the top and people were hanging out of the windows. Such a taxi stopped by the side of me as I sat drawing away on my stool. A large Irishman stuck his head out of the window and said, 'See you're back again, mister.' 'Yes,' I said, 'that's so.' To which he responded, 'See you're back again, doing more f—in' propaganda for the Brits.' I looked up at him, smiled and said, 'Well, it's a job, isn't it?' He scratched his head and said, 'Yes, I suppose it is, mister.' Up went the window and off they went. It was this sort of regular banter that I believe kept me safe on the streets of Northern Ireland.

In fact I never, or very seldom, felt threatened on the streets there. I remember working in an area called the Markets – not a wholesome spot to sit around and paint at the beginning of the 1970s, when I think some sort of feud was underway between the Provisional IRA and the Real IRA. Certainly the citizens of the Markets weren't very keen on the British Army. Anyway, I was sitting in the street one day doing a drawing for one of the regiments stationed in the Markets at the time. The locals would come out, take a look at what I was doing and say, 'That's very good, mister.' It didn't seem to matter what the subject was – the fact that I was drawing aroused interest rather than animosity. If you were sitting in the streets drawing, people knew what you were doing – there was nothing suspicious or concealed, they could all see it quite clearly. But you never considered using a camera in Northern Ireland as that was dangerous. If you went along the street surreptitiously taking photographs you could have been doing anything. You could be a member of the SAS or just a civilian collecting information. So as well as artistic preference, security was a very good reason for not using a camera.

Anyway, I was sitting in the street doing my watercolour drawing or my wash drawing, whichever it was, and the locals were very pleasant. They brought me out tea and sandwiches and beer, and then we talked a lot and it was an enjoyable experience. Then I went back and stayed at the Army post in a church on the edge of the Markets, but I still had to finish the drawing. The next day I went back to the street where I was working. I sat down and began to draw, then suddenly became conscious of a different atmosphere. People who had been talking to me the day before seemed to scurry past. They didn't want to recognise me sitting there. Nobody came up and spoke; instead people went inside and closed their doors. Whether they were trying or not, I eventually got the message, packed up and went back up to the Army post with my stool. As I walked back into the Army post I heard reports coming in on the radio from various places. Then this report came in to say that there had just been a shooting in the street I had been drawing in.

I then realised the simple truth. I was sitting in the very position where they had made plans to ambush the next patrol that was coming down. This had been

Wall in the Lower Falls, *c.* 1980
Oil on canvas, 150 x 180 cm

When you are elected to the Royal Academy you have to give a Diploma Work, an example of your work. As I had only just given up working in Northern Ireland in 1984, the year I was elected, I gave this Ulster wall. It was first exhibited in 1984 under the title *Ulster*.

Soldiers preparing for an anticipated riot in Belfast, 1973. I am standing on the left, drawing the group of soldiers as they wait under the motorway.

decided in advance and then of course this mad Englishman had come and sat in the middle of it all, just at the wrong moment. They couldn't have told me to go away – that would have been too obvious. By the vibes they set, however, they knew that someone who had been around as much as I had would sense something was wrong and would pack up. That's what I did, and I suppose that's why I survived all the time I was in Northern Ireland without really feeling a sense of danger. My instincts were in tune with the atmosphere around me, and that was so important.

On the theme of not using a camera, I did use one once. I had been in the Province working for myself (that is, not on commission) and in those days there was nowhere you could stay in Belfast in that capacity. There was one international hotel called the Europa, but it was blown up every week so one never thought of going to stay there. So whenever I went to Belfast in those days I would ring up a regiment that I had known or worked for and ask if I could stay with them. They were always very good; I was quite well-known in the British Army by this time, so they would say yes and give me a bed in some suitable place. It was never very comfortable, of course. I remember sleeping in the bicycle shed at the back of the police station in Hastings Street for about three weeks when I first went to Belfast. At other times I slept in buses or in old ruins, but I always found somewhere to put my head down. It was very helpful to be able to say to the Army, 'can I come and live with you?' I suppose things were a bit easier in those days. Anyway, I stayed with various regiments when I wanted to do some studies for my future paintings, or whatever I was working on at the time.

On a Saturday morning, when I was catching a plane in the afternoon, the Colonel asked me if I would do a painting for them to commemorate their tour. I explained that unfortunately I hadn't got the time to do it as I had to catch a plane that afternoon to return to London. He suggested I could take some photographs and paint it for them in London. I suppose I felt a bit guilty: the regiment had put up with me all week with no charge for board and lodgings. I just ate with the fellows and then stuck my head down on a bed wherever I could find it. Nevertheless, they had entertained me for the week and I felt an obligation. I agreed to do something and asked if there were any patrols in the area that morning. They said there was one in the Clonard – a fairly difficult area in those days, I must admit. So I went down and stood on a corner where I knew the patrol would come round eventually, with a camera around my neck. Along came the patrol and I stopped and they went off down the road. Obviously British Army patrols wouldn't normally let people photograph them, so it was somewhat unusual for someone to be clearly snapping them as they went past and getting no reaction from the troops.

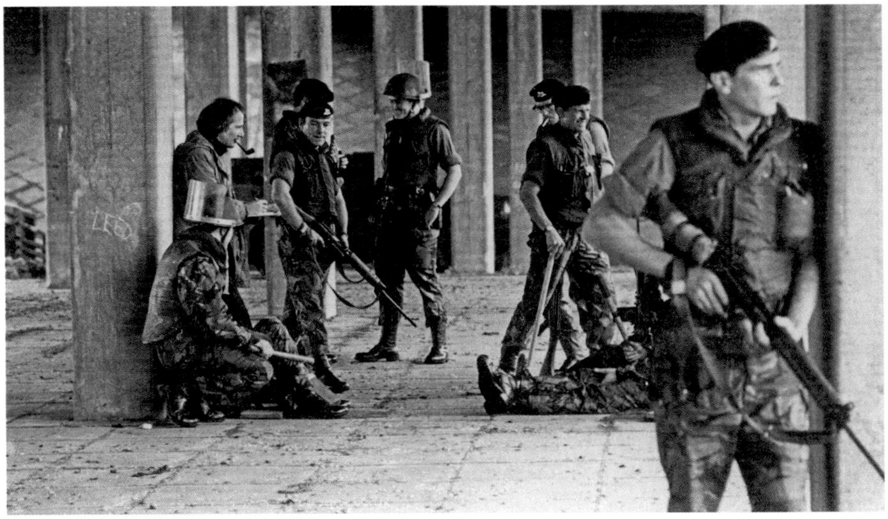

Suddenly an old lady appeared out of a door on the other side of the road. 'Why don't you f— off?' she shouted across the road. I looked over and replied, 'I'm sorry, madam, but I'm only doing a drawing.' 'No, you're not,' she said, 'You're with the British Army.' I showed her my passport, which said I was an artist, but she wasn't impressed. 'That means nothing, mister,' she said. 'You're with the British Army. They would never let someone stand on the corner photographing them without knowing him.'

I realised I was in trouble here, and she was very aggressive. Suddenly I saw that there were telephone lines going into her house. A few trips before I had done drawings for the Belfast Telephone Directory and my drawings were all over it. There was a drawing of the City Hall on the cover, with my signature on it. 'I'll tell you what,' I said. 'You go and look on the front of your telephone directory and that will prove what I say.' At first she refused, but I persuaded her to go and have a look; I had to get out of the situation somehow. She disappeared into her house rather reluctantly. A few minutes later she appeared at the door with a big grin on her face. 'You're f—ing right, mister,' she said, 'you're on the front of the telephone directory and your name's underneath it. You are an artist – come in and have a cup of tea.' I didn't go in for a cup of tea, however. I left, but I thought then that never again would I use a camera on the streets of Belfast.

Generally the locals did take to me. I think that in a funny sort of way everyone loves an artist. I remember once working up in Derry, doing some drawings of the Creggan Estate. All of a sudden an old man came up and started to talk to me. He said that he was an artist so we exchanged stories a bit and he asked me to come and have tea with him. I thought for the sake of public relations I should go and have a cup of tea with him, so we set off. Eventually we got to some flats – the ones that had been at the centre of Bloody Sunday. Of course I had realised by this time that I was in the middle of the Bogside – not the best area to be in, especially if you were English and connected to the British Army. And you could be absolutely sure that the people in the area knew about these connections. The IRA system of intelligence was incredibly sophisticated and well-developed, and I never kidded myself that the people there didn't know exactly what I was doing.

This old man took me in and gave me a cup of tea. He showed me the drawings and the watercolours that he did and we talked about them. Then we got to discussing the Troubles, and we had a completely normal conversation. He was obviously a devout Catholic and a Republican, but there was no sense of aggression from him and I didn't in any way feel threatened or in danger. I must admit that when we walked into the Bogside past the Derry Wall I began to feel a little bit nervous. It was about 1974 and Bloody Sunday was still an extremely emotive subject. The wound was still very raw with the local people.

I had so many experiences out there that they would fill a book on their own. In Butler Street, one of the hardest streets near to Flax Street Mill in the Protestant part of Belfast, I was drawing one day. Some rather heavy boys came up with the opening gambit, 'Why don't you f— off, you're with the British Army?' 'I'm only drawing,' I said. 'I'm drawing for a museum in England.' 'Oh, that's for a museum is it?' they asked, and I explained that their street would be famous in the Imperial War Museum. That was the end of the aggression and the boys even asked me to come into one of the Republican clubs in Butler Street for a drink. I have to confess I didn't go.

On another occasion I was sitting in the middle of Divis Flats. At that time this was the real Republican centre of the Falls Road area of Belfast. Some lads approached me and said, 'You're with the SAS, aren't you?' I denied it, but they said I was. 'We've seen you coming out of the Army base over the road at the back of the police station.' So they knew exactly what and who I was. But because I was sitting there drawing they began to look at my work and got interested in it. Then they said, 'Oh, come into the flats and have a cup of tea. You must be cold.' So often I encountered this rapport, no matter whether I was working in a Protestant area, a Catholic area or just sitting in the barrack room with the fellows. That is one of the best things about the arts: somehow it breaks down barriers between people.

Northern Ireland wasn't all doom and gloom, I must say. There was also a great sense of humour. One of my favourite stories was when the regiment asked me to do a painting that commemorated one of their incidents. I didn't normally do that sort of thing, but then they wrote to me and asked me again. I said I couldn't do anything unless I could actually see it. But they persisted and it was the Colonel of a regiment that I had done quite a lot of work for, so, eventually, I decided to do a watercolour and asked them to send me whatever reference they had. I received a very bad photograph from the front cover of the *Belfast Telegraph* showing smoke and a derelict car and people running around. The sergeant had cleared the street of civilians because of the burning car and the great danger before it blew up. The photograph wasn't going to be much use to me, but I had now got the bit between my teeth. The next time I went over I visited the police station where the regiment was based. 'Can you let me have some soldiers for a few hours?' I asked. They lent me some soldiers and we went out the back of the police station, where the soldiers posed for me in various positions. They did whatever I asked them to do, so I soon had the figures I needed.

Then I went down to the main street where the incident had happened. I did a watercolour of the street, with its old back-to-back houses, and all I needed was the blown-up car. So I went to the Ops room and asked if any cars had been dumped and blown up recently. They told me there was one near the Divis Flats down in Roden Street. So I went off and found this burnt-out car. I sat a little way away from the derelict car on a grey and miserable afternoon and began to draw it into the watercolour. I was surrounded by rubble and derelict back-to-backs; that whole area of Belfast was gradually disintegrating. So I sat there on this gloomy afternoon. I had a bottle of ink beside me too, as I usually worked with pen and ink and wash and watercolour.

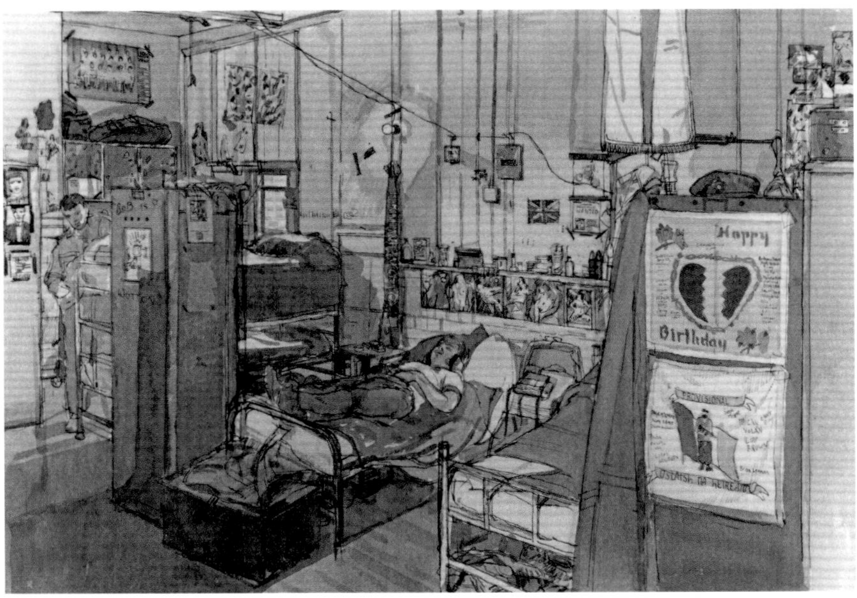

Barrack Room, Belfast, 1973
Pen and sepia wash, 37.5 x 55 cm

This pen and wash drawing was made in a barrack room near the prison at Long Kesh. On the right are two handkerchiefs, adapted into birthday cards and signed by the prisoners.

Suddenly a very large boot landed on the top of my bottle of ink. It had been a miserable afternoon with the drizzle and I was not amused. I was about to say, 'Why don't you look where you are treading?' when I noticed that the boot was a Doc Marten type of boot, which in Northern Ireland at that time were called Stampers. They were part of the gear that the young boys and Republicans at the Divis Flats wore, and this one was rather large. And I then saw the sawn-off wide jeans to just below the knee (they were called 'parallels'). I looked further up the parallels to a jeans jacket and there was a rather large youth looking down at what I was doing. As it was a drawing of an Army event I was naturally very slightly nervous, but all he said was, 'I feel bad about treading on your bottle of ink, mister.' 'It doesn't matter at all,' I replied. 'I've got another bottle in my bag.'

Then he looked more closely at the picture and remarked, 'That's dead on, mister' – a typical expression of the boys of the area. I thanked him and he said, 'That was done in Dun Louis Street, wasn't it?' 'Good Lord,' I thought, 'he recognised that a bit quickly!' I said it was. 'Round about April last year or some such date.' 'Yes, that's right,' I said, feeling again a bit nervous. 'Sorry about treading on your bottle of ink, mister.' 'No, no, really, it doesn't matter at all. It's quite all right.' So he carried on looking at my drawing. 'That's dead on,' he said again. 'That was the day the Brit won the Military Cross, wasn't it?' He does know what I'm doing, I thought, but I just said, 'Yes, that's right.' He went on looking at the drawing for a while, and he repeated, 'I feel bad about treading on your bottle of ink, mister.' Once again I said that it was all right. 'Tell me, mister,' the boy said, 'you're sitting there drawing that derelict old car in front of you, and in your painting it's burning and there's smoke and everything. How did you manage to do that?' I explained that sometimes, if it was necessary, I had to make things up, even though I wasn't very good at it. 'I see what you mean, mister,' he said. 'I do feel bad about your ink.' I told him again not to worry, but that I had to concentrate and I couldn't do that and talk at the same time. 'I'm putting you off, mister, aren't I?' 'Well, yes, a little bit,' I conceded, so he said he would push off, but that he still felt bad about that bottle of ink. 'No, no,' I said, 'it doesn't matter at all.'

So, anyway, he disappeared and I went on with my drawing. I can never to this day quite realise how it happened, but all I can say is that car was among all these derelict buildings, so it was possible to approach it without being seen. All of a sudden I saw smoke coming out of the car, so immediately I thought, 'That's handy, just what I needed.' The smoke increased and then the engine of the car sort of blew up, I suppose because of the petrol remaining in it. The whole car was enveloped in black smoke going up into the heavens. I couldn't believe my luck and I worked away on the watercolour. Then all of a sudden, the boy came back through the smoke. He stood in front of me and with great pride pointed back to the car. 'Does that make up for the bottle of ink, mister?' He'd set the car alight for me.

I worked in Northern Ireland, on and off, over a period of ten years. Most of the time I was working on commissions for the regiments or the Imperial War Museum. There was an incident at the Imperial War Museum when some of my drawings got damaged in a fire in the basement. I always thought it was a bit strange that the fire had started in the corner where my drawings were. I asked the museum whether there was anything suspicious about it, but they denied it completely. In fact my drawings were never shown because I suppose that, even up to recently, the Irish situation was still volatile and maybe they felt that it would be inappropriate to display them. Anyway, they commissioned me to go again after the fire and I did some new drawings all over Northern Ireland. I don't believe they were as interesting as the first ones, however. The derelict areas were being redeveloped by 1979; the old graffiti was disappearing and Belfast, and Northern Ireland in general, felt more sanitised. This was a great improvement for the local inhabitants, but for an artist like me it was less inspiring. Northern Ireland wasn't as visually interesting as it had been in 1973, nor was it so overtly dramatic.

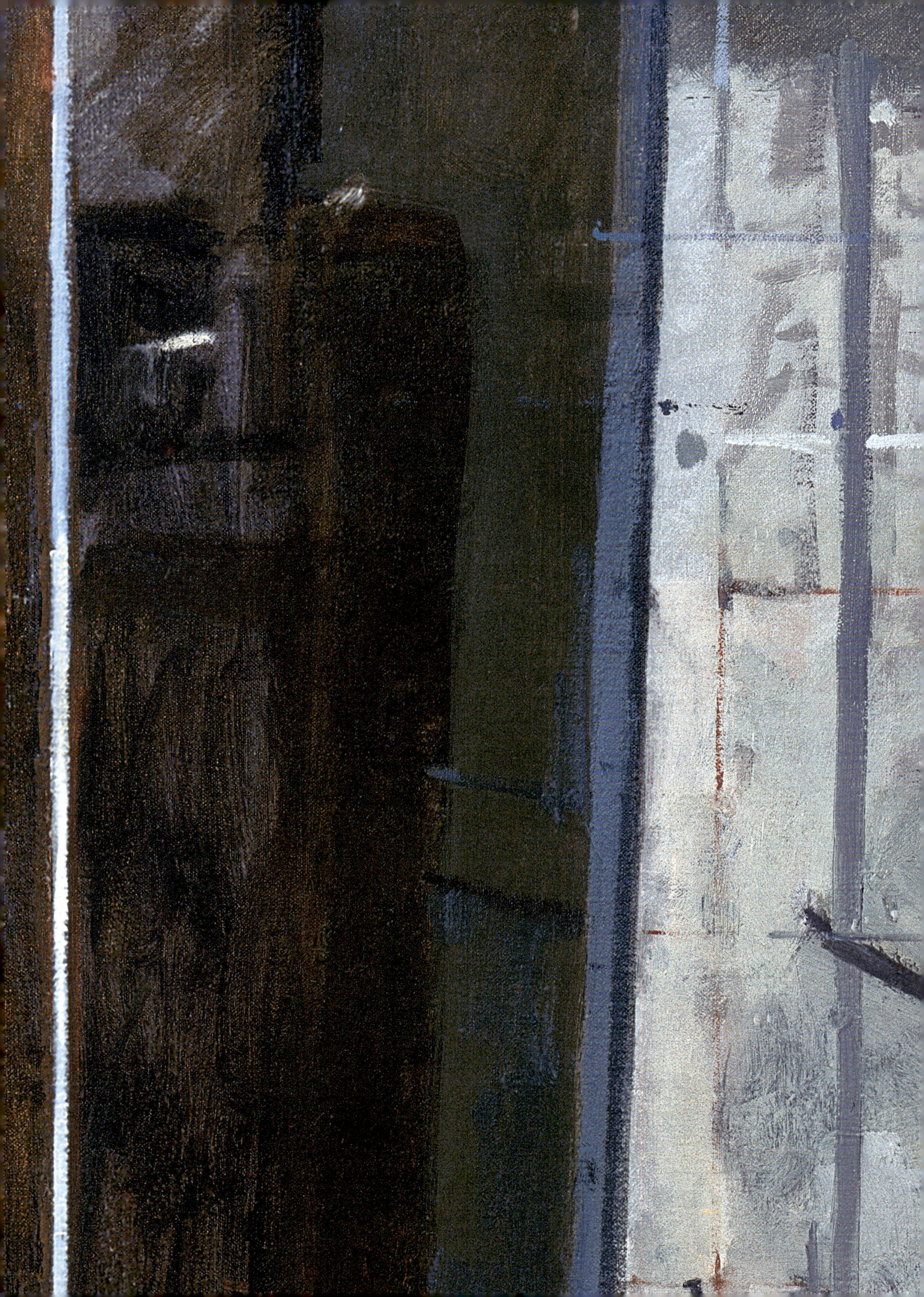

8

Portraits

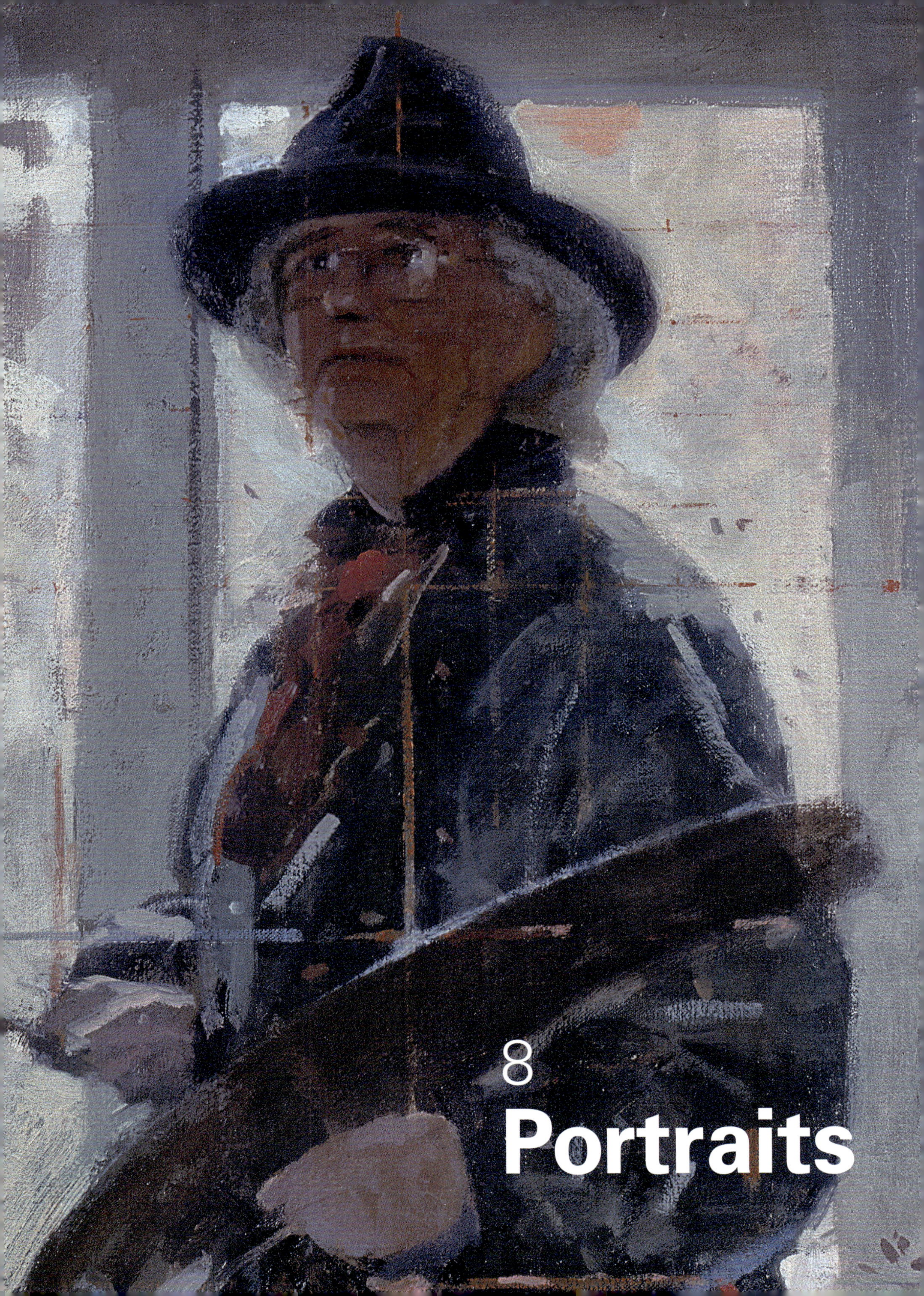

By the mid-'70s, as well as doing commissions and my own work, I had become very practised as a draughtsman. I could do a portrait drawing very quickly and convincingly – if someone sat for me for five or ten minutes I could get a drawing just right. It all started in Northern Ireland when I was living in a barrack room. In the evening the boys would ask if I could do a drawing to send back to their wives, girlfriends or parents, and I would do these at a fiver a time. The soldiers were very happy to have a drawing, and as I could do, say, ten in an evening it could make quite a considerable difference to my earnings. Hundreds of these drawings from Northern Ireland are still around, and I still get letters from people along the lines of, 'We've got a drawing of my father from when he was in Northern Ireland signed "Ken Howard" and we saw your work at the Academy', or 'Are you the same Ken Howard who drew my father in Northern Ireland?' This gives me great satisfaction, as I believe art should be for everybody and the more people who have my work the happier I am.

As I worked more closely with the regiments, I travelled to other locations with them to draw and paint. On one occasion I was coming back from Cyprus – I had been working with the Sherwood Foresters – and we flew back from Cyprus to Lyneham in a propellered aeroplane. I can't remember the name now, but they were big, troop-carrying aircraft with propellers, not jets, so the flight took a long time. There were about 60 fellows on this plane when we were flying back. When they saw me they asked if I would do some portraits and I agreed as it would fill the time between Cyprus and Lyneham. I ended up drawing all the men on that plane; there were about five I hadn't completed as we drew near to Lyneham and they urged me on: 'Come on, Mr Howard. Get on with it; we want our portraits drawn as well.' So I drew an entire planeload of soldiers on one six-hour flight. Later on I remember doing some watercolours as some of the officers asked for them, so I also got to be quite a dab hand at doing watercolour portraits.

I never went in for portrait-painting in a big way, however, as it wasn't something I wanted to do. I have always believed that portraiture is a rather impossible task, as everybody sees their loved ones or people they're close to in their own terms. If you live with someone for a long time, you stop seeing them objectively any more. Instead you see them, at least in part, as they have always looked. I remember when I lived at home as a boy, my mother never seemed to age from the day I first remember her, even though I was a very visual person from early childhood. I was conscious of how things looked around me, but nonetheless, from the very beginning until I left home aged about 27, it didn't seem as though my mother had aged. Then I didn't see her for several months after my first marriage –

and when I saw her again I realised she was an old woman. Of course, she had been growing older all those years, but I hadn't noticed it. In the same way you don't really see what you look like when you shave in the morning: you see what you think you look like. So I always thought that portraiture was a fairly impossible thing to do.

I've done a few, of course, mostly men. I painted Gerald Durrell for the zoo in Jersey, when he had his zoo for endangered species. He would go off and bring these endangered species back to the zoo and breed from them, and then take them back to their natural habitat and get them to breed there, thus saving the animals from becoming extinct. I painted Gerry and I learned a lesson then about portraiture. If you do a portrait and someone makes minor criticisms – 'that's like so-and-so, but don't you think you've got the left ear a bit big?' or 'don't you think the eye is staring?' or something like that – you know you might as well start all over again because you just haven't convinced him or her. He or she has looked at the portrait and not really recognised the person. There may be a likeness, but it isn't convincing. I remember when I painted Gerry, however, his second wife, Lee, an American zoologist and a lovely woman, came in to the room when the portrait was finished. She looked at it and her first words were, 'Gee, Ken, that's Gerry,' and I knew that I'd won, I'd captured him. There was no worry about his eye, his nose being a bit big, him looking a bit serious, or anything like that. That was the portrait that I still believe wasn't bad. Usually I like painting men with beards, because I always say that if you can get the eyes right, everything else looks after itself. Gerry did, in fact, have a very full beard and the painting was quite convincing.

I also painted the Queen on one occasion. In 1974 I was commissioned by the Parachute Regiment to paint a picture of the four battalions receiving new colours. This was at the Rushmoor Arena in Aldershot, and it was the first time that I had ever done a ceremonial picture. I finished up doing quite a lot of them, regrettably – like everything in life, if you do something and it works you get asked to do more and more. That's why I don't exhibit portraits; I know that if I did I would get requests to do more of them.

When I painted the Queen, I had a sitting at Buckingham Palace. This happened because she presented the colours at Rushmoor Arena. I went down there as it was my first ceremonial commission and I wanted to get everything right, and went to rehearsals for a week before the event. The four battalions had to be drilled and everything had to be absolutely correct. As I watched I realised that there were particular aspects of the ceremony that I wanted to paint and for which I needed studies and people to pose for me.

Gerrald Durrell, 1979
Watercolour, 30 x 22.5 cm

This was the original watercolour study I did for the Durrell portrait and in many ways I prefer it to the finished oil. Watercolour is about finding an equivalent for the subject in paint. It leaves so much to the imagination that it allows viewers to see what he or she wants to see. This I believe is the secret of good portrait painting.

Unfortunately it rained each day. Every time we got to the point where the Queen was going to do her part, the General at the time, a man called Roly Gibbs, had to call off the rehearsal because he didn't want the men to get their dress uniforms too wet, as they had to be in good condition for the following Saturday's event. By the end of the week I still hadn't really seen the exact moment that I was supposed to show – the Queen giving a colour to one of the Colonels, while the other three Colonels, having received theirs, were kneeling down.

When it came to the Saturday morning, realising I hadn't got this study, I had to go out with the press when they went to cover the event. Strangely enough, that morning was fine – I always said that the Queen commanded it not to rain that day, but I didn't know what I was going to do without that key study. So I took a camera with me, but of course the press knew the ropes and so I got squeezed out. After the event I still hadn't got what I needed and I told Roly that I couldn't complete the commission. He said he would get me a sitting at Buckingham Palace, but I didn't believe him. Lo and behold, I got a letter from the palace the following week saying that they had been asked to arrange a sitting with the Queen so that I could do a study for the painting.

I must admit that this was probably the only time in my life when I've been really nervous. I was shown into the Yellow Drawing Room on the first floor where the Queen always sits – if you're looking at Buckingham Palace from the front, it's on the first floor at the left end. I went in about an hour before the sitting was due and drew from the window before the Queen arrived. I wanted to get my eye in and feel in practice, if you like, so that later I wouldn't be fumbling around.

Eventually she arrived and stood for me by the window in the pose that she took in the final painting. I did two small studies, which unfortunately I haven't got any more, and it wasn't as terrifying as I thought. She made general conversation while she was posing, asking me about where I lived, my general experiences with the Army and so forth. She was extremely nice and not at all terrifying. At the end she looked at my studies and approved of them. 'I've enjoyed meeting you, Mr Howard,' she said, and then she left. It's something I'll always remember.

I remember a story about Peter Greenham when he went to paint the Queen at the palace. He was very much more bohemian than I am, much more what one thinks of as being an artist, and he wasn't necessarily the best-dressed man in the world. He also smoked very heavily, so there was usually cigarette ash on the front of his suit. When I went to the palace I took an easel box along, but Peter had a paintbox with him as he was doing a large portrait and an easel was already set up for him. So he arrived at the gate with just his paints in a modest paintbox in his

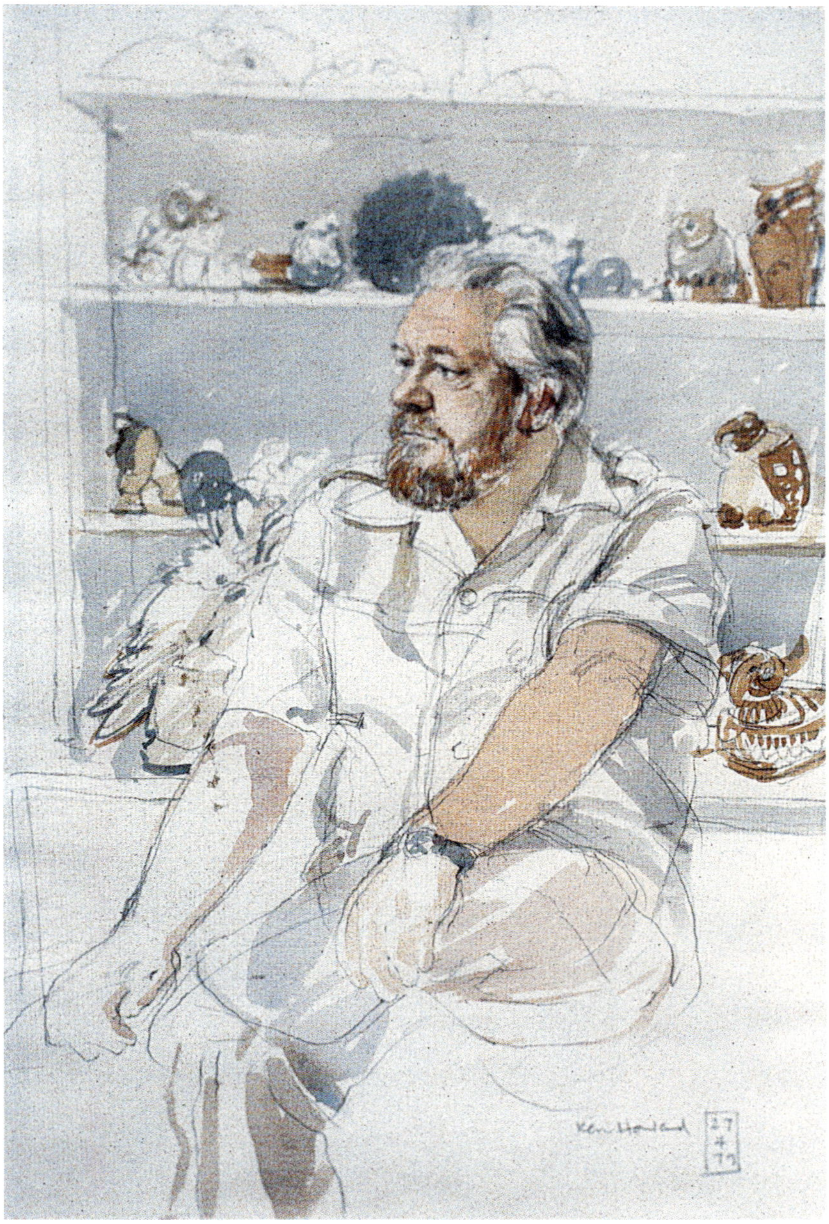

hand. The policeman on duty asked where he was going as Peter went through and Peter explained that he had come to paint the Queen. 'Oh, have you, sir? That's very nice,' said the policeman, rather sarcastically. 'And does Her Majesty know, by any chance, that you've come to paint her?' 'Of course she knows,' Peter said. 'I've got a sitting today.' The policeman advised him to go over into St James's Park and do a little landscape instead.

And Peter, being such a nice man, didn't argue. He went over to St James's Park and started to paint, but after about ten minutes the Queen's equerry rushed up to him in the park. Apparently he had gone to the gate and asked if anyone had seen a painter, to be told by the highly embarrassed policeman that he'd sent one over to

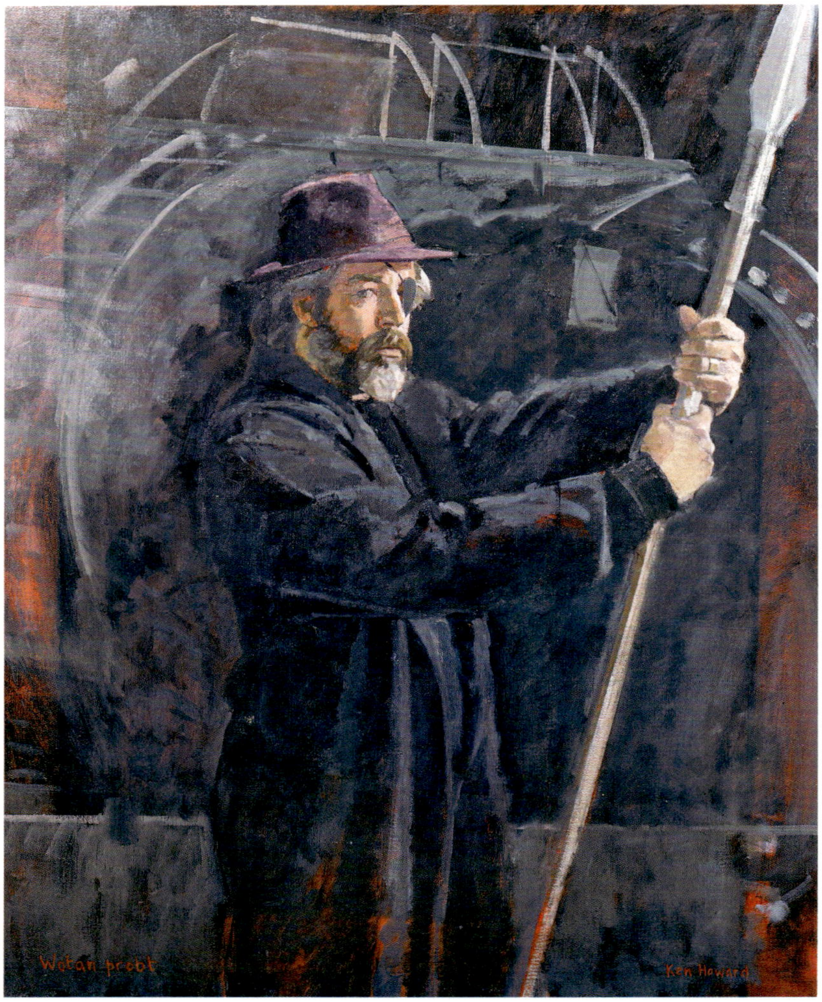

John Tomlinson, *c.* 1995
Oil on canvas, 120 x 100 cm

I made this painting of my friend Sir John Tomlinson in my London studio after hearing John as Wotan in Harry Kupfer's production of Wagner's *Ring*. I couldn't get the exact costume from Germany, but created something similar. John now has the portrait.

St James's Park. 'The Queen has been waiting for a while to sit for you, and she was wondering why you were late,' explained the flustered equerry, but it was just because Peter had done what he had been told.

I remember some time later one of the Sunday colour supplements had an article on what the Queen spoke about when she was sitting for a painting. They must have asked the Palace for four names of four painters to interview and I was one of them, although I had not done a major painting of the Queen, just the studies I mentioned. We four painters got together and discussed this. We guessed that the press were going to try to get us to say something amusing that would embarrass the Queen, and we decided we would plan in advance so that there was no way that would happen. The journalists took us out individually. I remember going to lunch and having a glass or two of wine; they presumably hoped that this would increase my storytelling abilities. In the end it was a bit embarrassing as I had decided to tell a story about the Queen's answer to my question as to whether she was being painted by anybody else at the time. She had replied that she was being painted for a picture for the Canine Club. The Queen smiled at me and said, 'He's very good at dogs, but

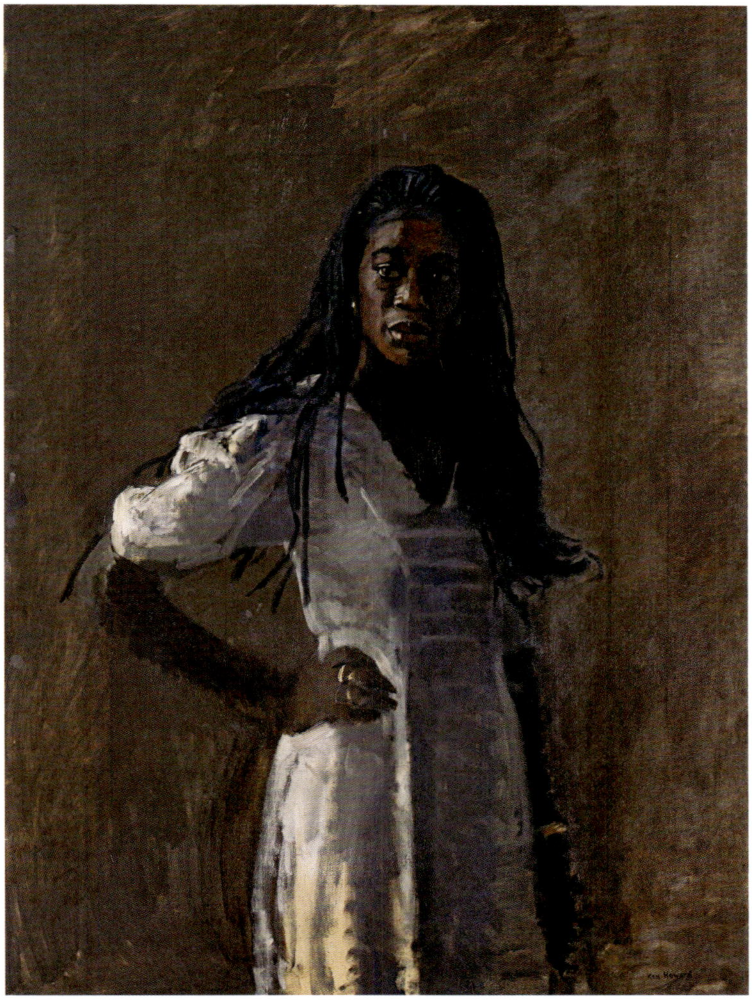

Malreth, 1986
Oil on canvas, 120 x 100 cm

After I had made a painting of a cook (overleaf), I wanted to paint a Caribbean woman. I was introduced to Malreth by her brother, to whom I gave a lift from Bristol to London when he was hitchhiking. She was a remarkable girl, a jazz singer, a social worker, a wonderful model and many other things. I painted this large portrait in one 'wet' (one sitting).

not very good at me.' I thought that this was a story with a bit of humour that would keep them satisfied, but I was careful not to give the painter's name as that would be embarrassing for him. Being the press, of course, they went and found this painting and discovered who the painter was. In the final article they quoted his name and showed a reproduction of the picture. I had been fairly friendly with this painter, though I didn't know him very well, but I don't think he ever forgave me for that story. I was really quite angry about what had happened.

In 1986, soon after I was first elected as an Associate of the Royal Academy, I was invited to the National Portrait Gallery for an exhibition of paintings of the Queen. I presumed I was being invited because I was an RA, and expected to see all the RAs there. When I arrived at the National Portrait Gallery, however, where Princess Margaret was due to accompany us into the exhibition, there were only two other RAs there: Peter Greenham and Norman Hepple, who were both portrait painters and had paintings in this exhibition. I didn't associate myself with having a painting in at all, but suddenly David Poole, then President of the Royal Society of Portrait Painters, came over to me. He said he liked my painting, and I was baffled. 'I'm sorry,

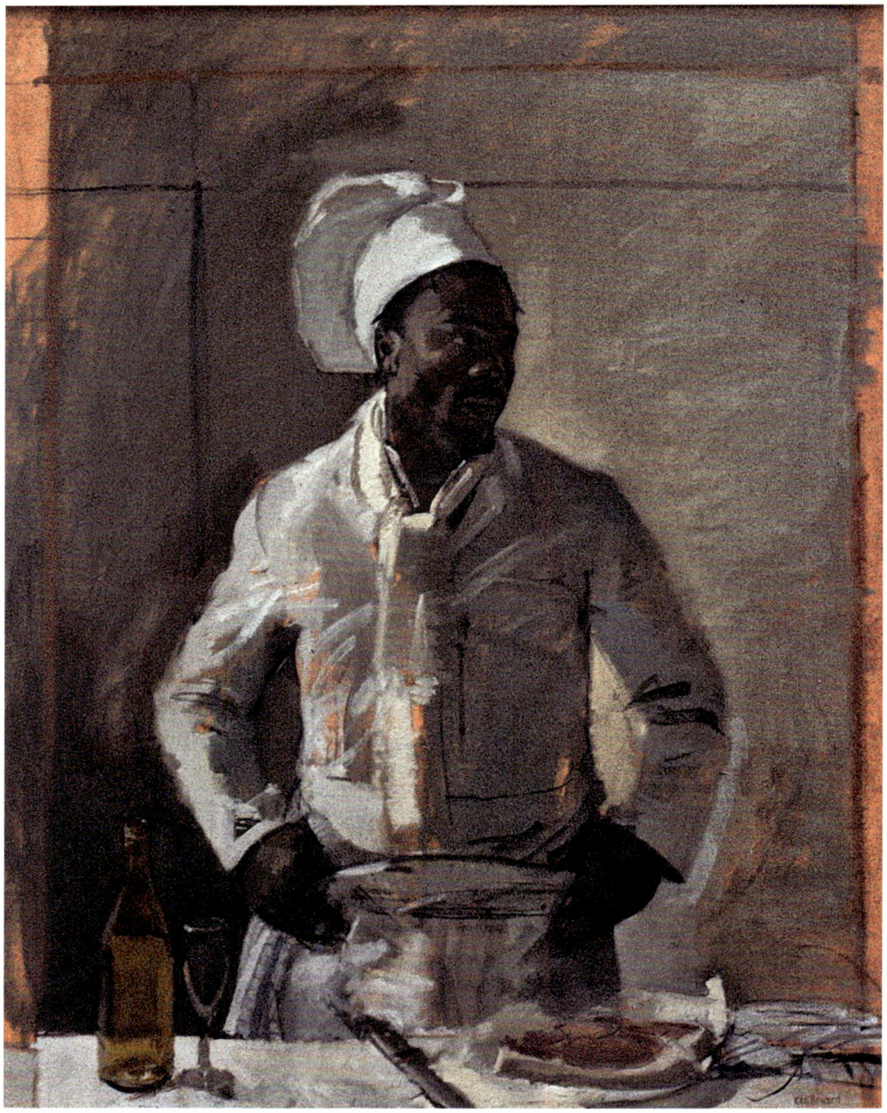

David, you've got it wrong. I haven't got a painting in this exhibition.' He assured me I had, but I said I had never painted the Queen. I hadn't painted a big formal portrait with many sittings, and I didn't think that my smaller studies for the painting to hang in the Parachute Regiment's Mess counted as having 'painted the Queen'. Anyway, David opened the catalogue and there, over a double-page spread, was this little study that I'd done in 1974 of the Queen with the Colonels kneeling with their colours. I'd sold it to the dealer John Brandler for £200.

I remembered how this had happened. In the early 1980s I often had requests for work from dealers and galleries, as I have always been relatively saleable. John Brandler had visited my studio, but I said that I didn't have anything on this occasion. He asked if there was anything behind the curtain (where I kept my studies) and I said that he could have a look if he wanted. John went behind the curtain and dug out one of the two studies I'd made of the Queen at Buckingham

Palace. It was quite a small panel that I had painted of the Queen while I was at the palace, and afterwards I'd fitted in the Colonels who were receiving their colours. So in a way it was a sketch of the middle of the big painting. John asked if he could buy this, but I hesitated, pointing out that it was just a study I had done for a commission. 'Well, I'd like to buy it,' he said. 'How much do you want for it?' I told him that he could take it for a couple of hundred pounds. He agreed and we did the deal. The next week he rang me up. 'I thought I'd let you know, boy,' he said, 'that I did well with your sketch. I sold it for £600 a few days later.' 'Congratulations, John,' I replied, thinking he'd come and buy some more work anyway, so it would benefit me in the long term.

A few weeks later he rang me up and told me he was furious. He'd just seen the sketch in a dealer's in St James's – it was in their window priced at £1,800. 'What are you worrying about?' I asked him. 'You bought it off me and sold it for three times that, now they've bought it off you and they're going to make three times as much – surely that's fair enough.' He still grumbled, but I just said, 'Oh, come on, John!'

So when Princess Margaret took us all in to the event at the National Portrait Gallery, there was my little study. It was beautifully framed and hung between two rather boring full-length portraits of the Queen. I must admit that it looked a million dollars – far more alive and vital than practically anything else in the exhibition.

If I paint portraits, which I do now and again, it is always because I have chosen the sitter. Rather as one views a landscape or a cityscape, I have seen them and thought, 'Ah, I can see a painting in you.' One of my best portraits is of a cook. When William Orpen was elected as an Associate of the Royal Academy, the work he presented to the Academy as his Diploma Work was called *The Chef at the Hotel Chatham, Paris*. It features a cook in a big chef's hat standing by a table with a bottle of wine and some meat, and I have always admired it. One day in the Royal Academy restaurant I saw an Afro-Caribbean guy coming out of the kitchens in his whites and I thought, 'Wow, that's terrific. I wonder if he would sit for me.' I decided to do a 'Homage to Orpen', repeating the composition with this black chef replacing the figure in the Orpen picture. I asked the chef if he would sit for me; he was flattered and agreed.

He came to the studio with his whites and I set up the scene, placing a bottle of wine on the table, as in the Orpen picture, along with a pork chop. He stood there and I began to paint, then suddenly he began to sweat profusely. I asked if he was all right and he said no, he wasn't feeling very well. I told him to sit down away from the table, and after a few minutes he seemed to have recovered fully. I asked him if we could carry on and he said he was all right now. He returned to the table, but

Homage to Sir William Orpen, 1985
Oil on canvas,
137.5 x 110 cm

I painted this portrait on a burnt-sienna ground, which is unusual for me. However, it gave a real lift to the predominantly grey colours of the painting.

Self-portrait with Borsalino, *c.* 2000
Oil on canvas, 120 x 100 cm

This large self-portrait was inspired by a self-portrait by Goya, although his work was on a smaller scale. Goya was my first influence as a painter and his work has continued to inspire me all my life. This is the first self-portrait I did wearing a hat, partly because in my later years I feel almost undressed without one, and partly because Goya wears one in his portrait.

after a while he began to sweat profusely again – I thought he was going to fall over. So I told him to sit down again, as there seemed to be a real problem. 'Well, Mr Howard,' he explained, 'unfortunately I'm a vegetarian. Unless you take that pork chop away, I think I'm going to pass out.' I took it away immediately and from then on everything was fine. I went on to do one of the best portraits that I've ever done. It was bought in the Academy, funnily enough, by Nicholas Goodison, at that time Chairman of the Stock Exchange. I had recently been doing a commission of the floor of the Stock Exchange, which he bought.

Nowadays I have to admit that almost the only portraits I do are self-portraits. I think all artists are intrigued by self-portraiture, and there are many advantages in it. The model is always there when wanted and does not move because you are looking in the mirror at your own image. When you look away as you are painting, you are not looking at the image anyway, but when you return to the image, it's as it was before. Certainly you get to know your own head very well, its proportions and facial expressions, and I have done a few self-portraits over the years. One of the first I painted, when I was sixteen, is now in the Royal Academy collection after hanging in my studio for many years. I still have another that I painted aged 72 – and I must admit that I have changed a bit across the years.

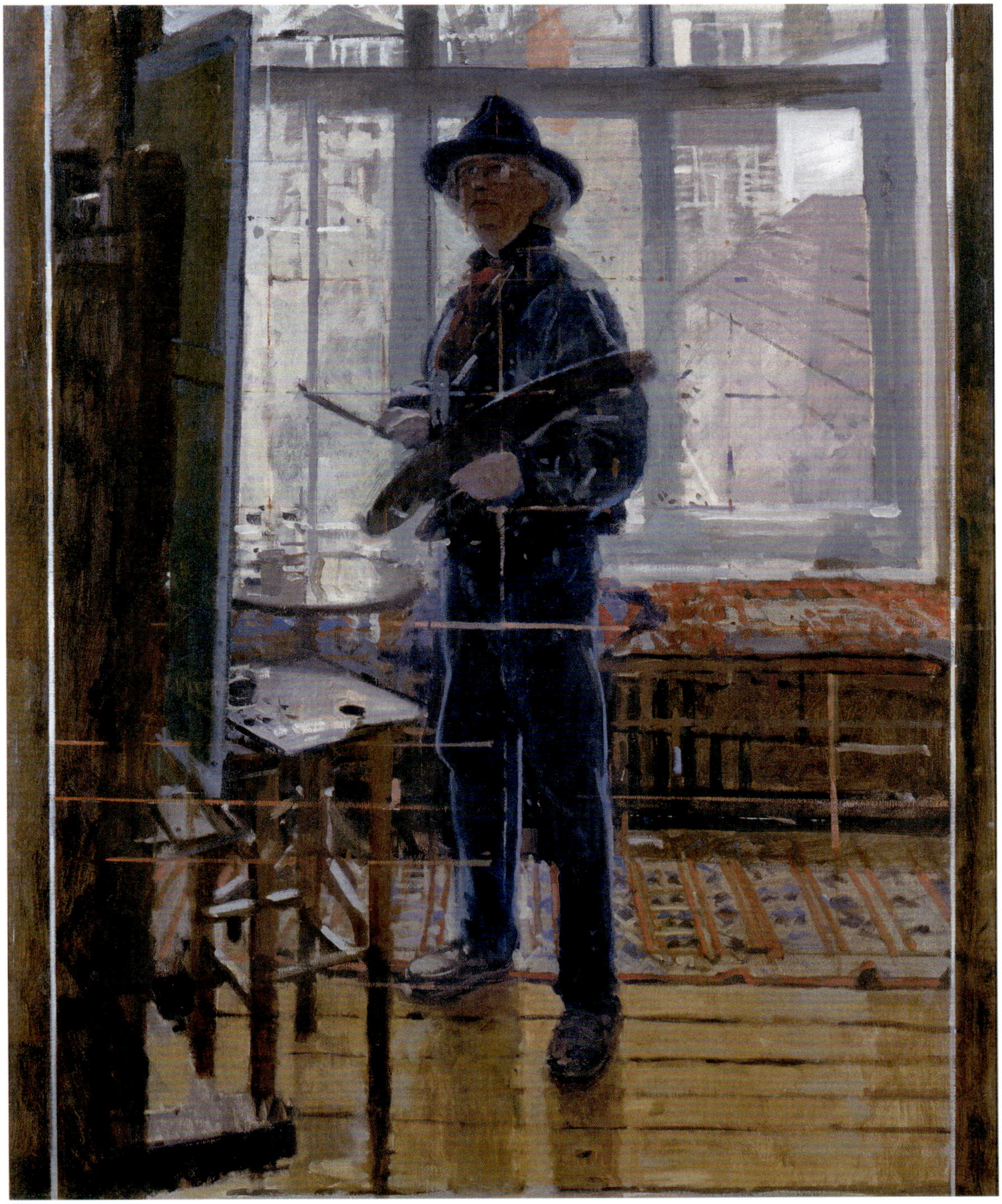

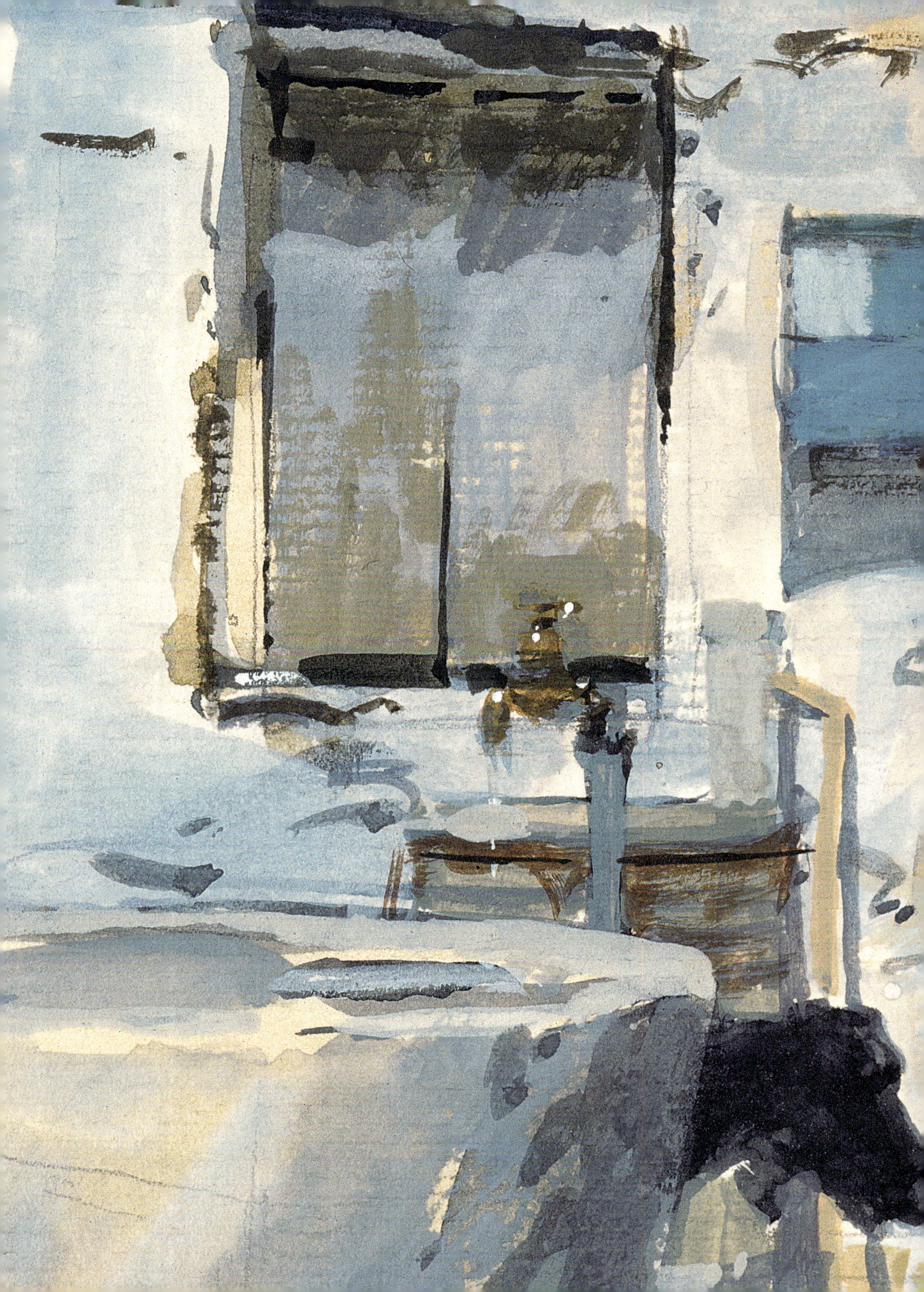

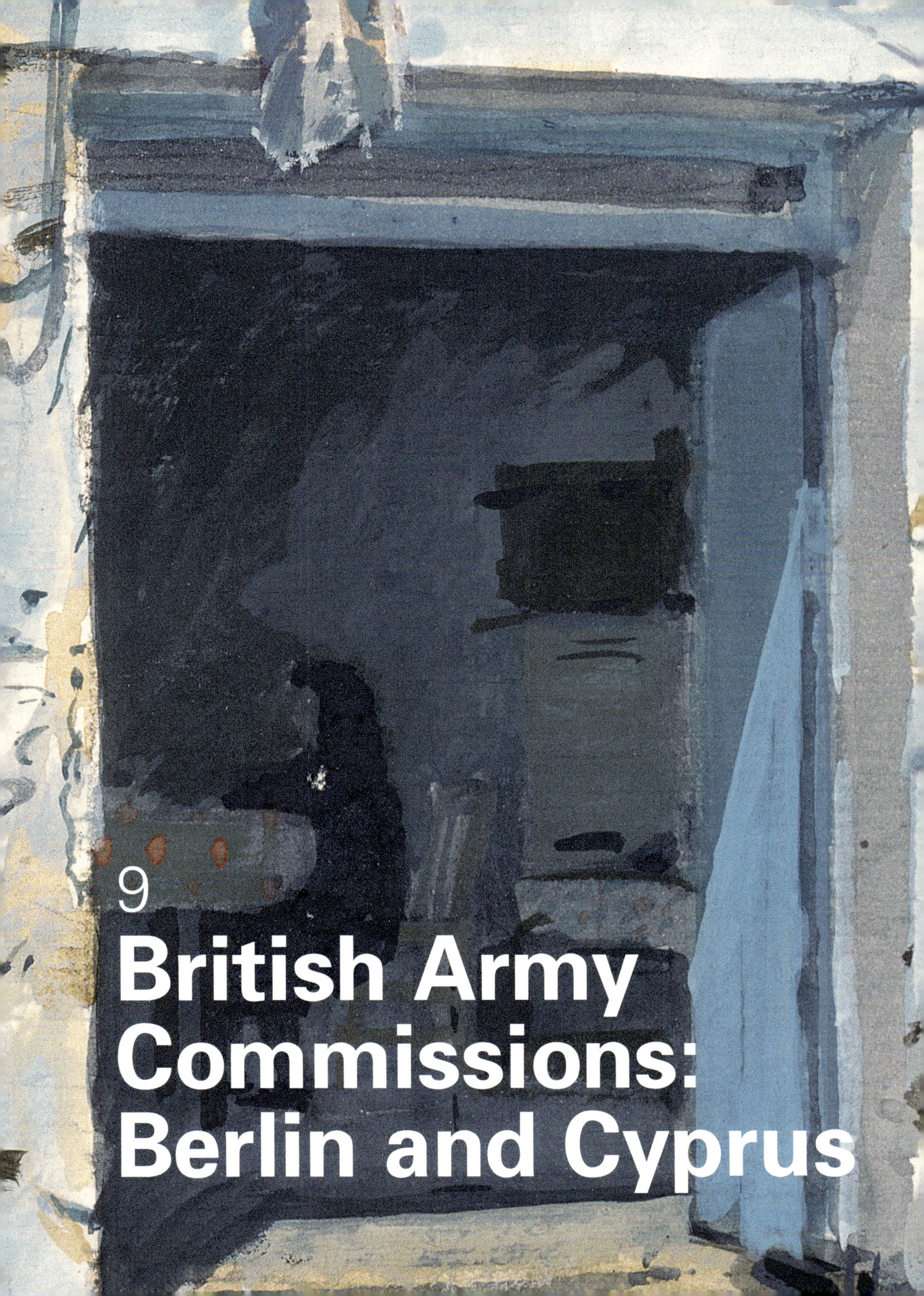

9

British Army Commissions: Berlin and Cyprus

Snow at Sampford Spiney, 1978
Oil on panel, 30 x 40 cm

This study was made near my Devon studio in 1978 on a freezing cold day and completed in front of the subject. Snow makes everything beautiful as its whiteness intensifies the richness of the landscape's dark, neutral colours.

Working in Northern Ireland opened up many other doors of course during those ten years. Although it was very important to my work at that time, I only actually spent two years on the streets of Northern Ireland; the rest of the time was spent partly doing my own work back in England. I was working a lot on Dartmoor, where I still owned the old school house that Annie and I had bought, and in Cornwall, where I had bought my parents' cottage in the village of Mousehole. I had given up painting London by that time because the redevelopment didn't stimulate me, but I was working a lot in England on landscapes and cityscapes. I had also started working in Venice – nothing like the amount that I do now, but I did work in Venice from time to time.

In addition to the Northern Irish work, however, I started to receive commissions to travel with regiments to other countries. Under the four-month roulement, or change-over system, in Northern Ireland, the regiments regularly returned to the British Army of the Rhine (the units in Ireland all came from Germany rather than the British mainland). I suppose they liked the work that I had been doing in Northern Ireland and their Colonels would ask if I could do some work for them in Germany. So I began to do two trips to Germany each year to fulfil commissions. I was reasonably organised about this and I didn't go until I had enough work to last me for at least two or three weeks.

At this time these commissions formed my basic living; I wasn't teaching any more and I had given up any form of illustration work. I started working for the regiments in Germany and then, as they were also serving in such places as Cyprus, I started to travel there as well. I went all over Europe, including Berlin, where I worked a lot, and then the Far East. There I worked with the Gurkhas in Hong Kong, India, Nepal and even down in Brunei. It was a great life which also included commissions in Canada and America, and at one point down in Belize. I was never still and I relished keeping on the move – quite good therapy, having been through a divorce. I was so busy that I never had a chance to get depressed.

Over time I worked out a sort of circuit. I would do a tour of the British sector in Germany, covering the area around Osnabrück and Münster, along to Hanover and Bielefeld, and then up to Hamburg, Kiel and the Lüneburger Heide. The regiments would then be deployed somewhere else in the world, at which point they often asked me to go and work for them from there. In this way, my Army commission work really built up through the mid-'70s.

Although I took the opportunity to visit Chrissie in Cologne when I was over, my main reason for going to Germany was to fulfil commission work. Münster had

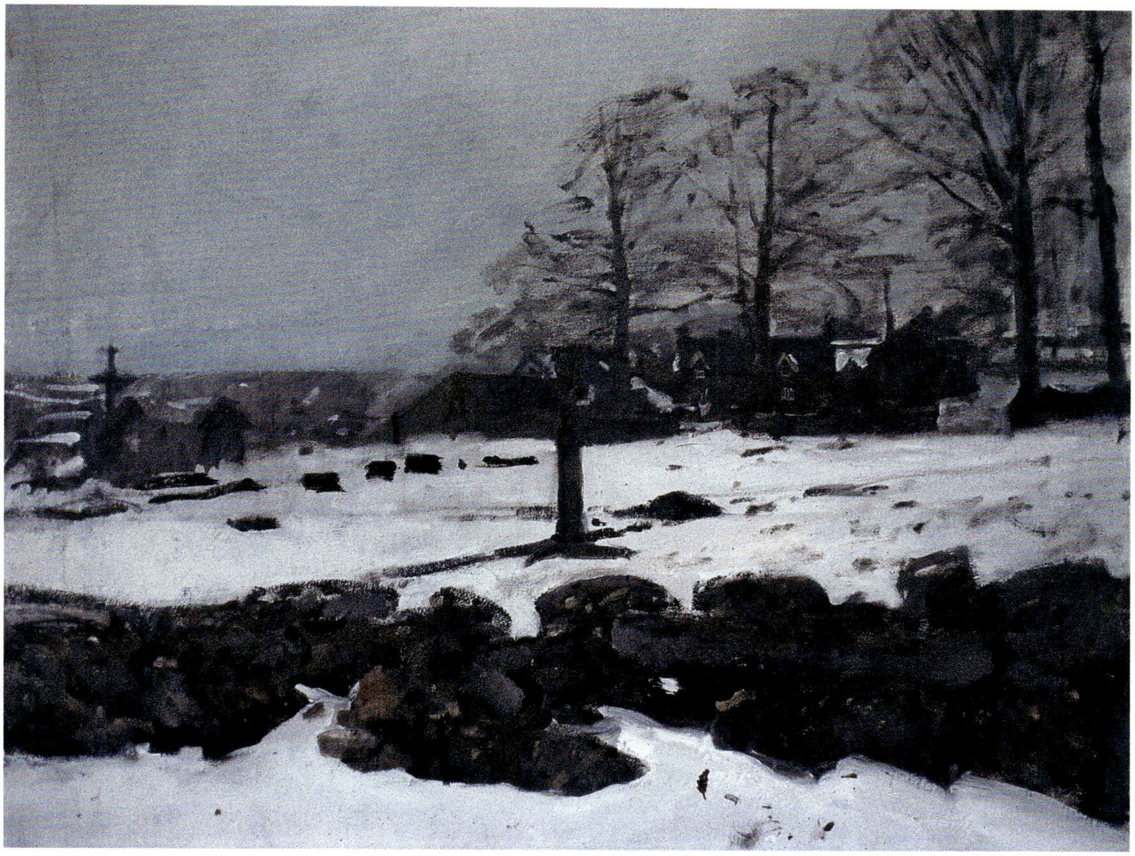

a lot of tank regiments when I was there, I remember, along with a large training area. I was commissioned to do a painting that featured the Challenger tank, a very large machine, and I went up onto the training area to watch tanks on manoeuvres. I remember that I damaged my hearing doing that; I didn't take the soldiers' advice to wear ear defenders and ended up too near the tanks when they were firing. My back also suffered a bit from sitting so much in cramped conditions, working in the back of lorries or under canopies.

Anyway, I went up onto the training area near Münster to do a painting of a Challenger tank with a regiment that recruited mainly in Scotland. After the day's work the soldier in charge of the tanks asked if I would like to drive a tank back to the main road. I told him that I had never driven a tank in my life. 'Well, it's not very difficult, Mr Howard,' he assured me. 'You get into the driving seat and I'll show you the brake and the accelerator. Then you pull this if you want it to go right and you pull that if you want to make it go left; it's really very easy, Mr Howard.' In for a penny, in for a pound, I decided, and let him put me into this sort of cockpit – at the front of the tank, as far as I remember. The others all piled on top of the gun turret for me to drive them back to the main road, probably just a couple of miles away.

I started driving rather gingerly, then began to get more confident. I put my foot down on the accelerator and felt it start to gather speed; I thought it was

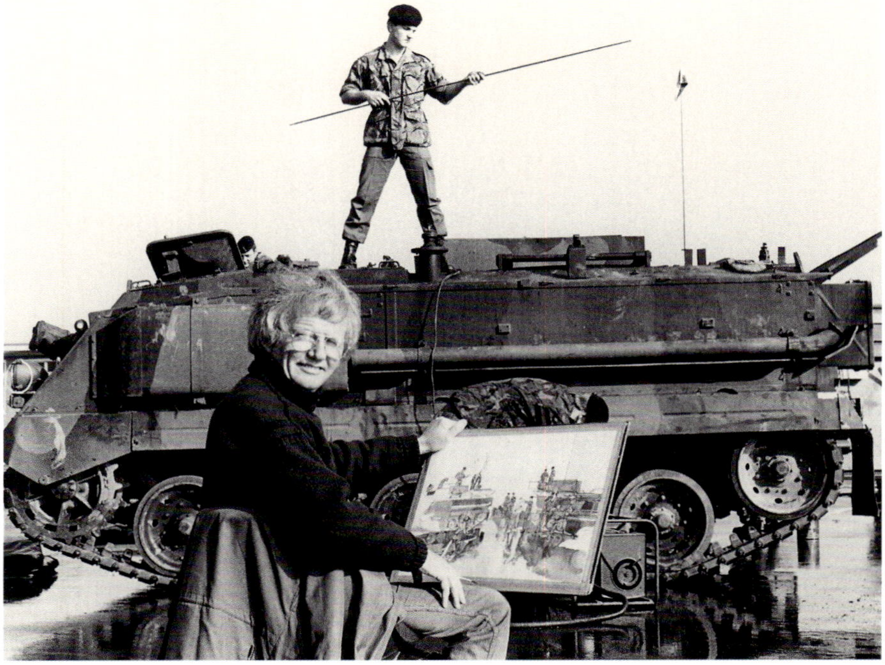

wonderful. By this time I had forgotten about the troops hanging on to the gun turret on top of the tank; I began to motor and the tank took off at some speed. Up on the training area there were dips and lumps and bumps, and eventually I saw a very large crater appearing in front of me. I had to decide very quickly whether to brake or just go on and hit the crater. It seemed best to carry on motoring, so I went down into the crater and up the other side. It wasn't that deep, but the tank took off and then landed in the mud and dirt. I drove on, finally getting close to the road. I felt that I had now done my bit and pulled the tank over to hand it back to the proper guys to drive me back to the barracks. There was a pregnant silence. I sat there waiting and then, all of a sudden, a red-faced Scotsman appeared above me. He was upside down because he was leaning forward from the top of the tank to look at me. In a very strong Glaswegian accent he enquired, 'Tell me, Mr Howard, have you ever had any f—ing trouble getting a driving licence?' That was all he said, while I realised that all the time I was motoring along, enjoying myself, those poor fellows were hanging on top of the tank for dear life!

The great thing about working for the Army was that they were incredibly efficient. I knew that when I was going to be doing a trip to, say, Osnabrück, the regiment would tell me well in advance what they wanted me to do there. If they were a tank regiment, for example, they might want to show a group of tanks drawn up in the forest, so the watercolour would need to feature the tank, the men and what they did. But there would be no time wasted in arranging things. Everything would be organised ready and that was an incredible help. If I were to write to the regiment and say I was arriving on Monday 5 July and would be working with them all day, starting at 6 am, and that I would need to have three tanks in a wood nearby, and ten men available for the day to pose for studies, you knew very well that it would all be in place when you arrived. That was really important to me. It is a little bit the same with models really – you get all keyed up for the painting you are going to make and if the model doesn't turn up it is incredibly frustrating. I can't work with models that aren't reliable as they distract and annoy me too much.

At work after rain in Herford, Germany, *c.* 1975. I posed this soldier of the Royal Signals to fit into a complex composition I was working on for the Corps.

The figures in my Army commissions were always recognisable because I am a good draughtsman. They might be very small, but they were undoubtedly Sergeant Smith or Corporal James or whoever it might be. I suppose such things are part of the paintings' appeal, though there was a slight drawback in being specific because these watercolours were really to represent the whole regiment. However, this never seemed to be a problem. I remember doing a watercolour in a forest near Münster very early one morning. The sun was coming up and one of the sergeants went to the edge of the wood to have a pee. I saw him standing there with the sunlight coming through this stream of pee. By this time I was working very fast, you had to if you wanted to get things down straightaway. 'That's a wonderful effect of light,' I thought, and I painted this sergeant into the picture with the light coming through his pee. It caused a lot of hilarity, and to this day that watercolour is showing sergeant whatever-his-name-is peeing on the edge of the wood, with the tanks and all the other paraphernalia around him.

By the late '70s I was working all over Europe. I went up to the Arctic Circle with the Marines who were training there – very difficult painting conditions because the days were so short. As far as I remember it didn't get light until about 11 o'clock and it was dark again by 2, so you had a working day of about three hours. It was also bitterly cold, of course. The Marines had what they called snow cats – little tanks pulling behind them a small, troop-carrying vehicle that could hold about six men. They let me use one of them to do a particular painting showing a patrol of men in a snow-covered forest in the Arctic Circle. The towed vehicle, where I would sit and work, took heat from the vehicle that pulled it, enabling me at least to keep warm enough to work, and this was the only way that I could do the job. And, as always on these trips, I did a lot of work for myself, including watercolours of Norwegian landscapes.

I also worked in Belgium for SHAPE (Supreme Headquarters Allied Powers Europe), as well as in Lahr in southern Germany, where the Canadian regiments were. Berlin was another important place of work. Germany was still divided in the late '70s and the Russians still controlled part of the city. I can still remember the ritual I had to go through when I drove to Berlin for work. First I went to a place called Helmstedt, at the beginning of the Russian zone, where you had to book in with your car. They noted the mileage and checked that you had enough petrol to get to Berlin without stopping: it was a real performance because the Russians did not want you to leave the road for any reason whatsoever. You could have been spying or anything, so they timed you to ensure that you hadn't left the road. It was all carefully calculated. The Russians knew the approximate time it took to drive from Helmstedt to the checkpoint on the edge of Berlin; you were timed out when you left and the Russian checkpoint checked you in when you arrived. They confirmed your time, petrol and mileage to make absolutely sure.

It was quite an eerie feeling, like going out into a sort of no man's land, and when you were in Berlin it was incredibly claustrophobic. I wouldn't have wanted to live there – the city was still completely divided. The Russian sector with Checkpoint Charlie was there, and the atmosphere was very redolent of the early John Le Carré books, such as *The Spy Who Came in from the Cold*. I was commissioned on two or three occasions to paint the Berlin Wall, I remember, as well as the area dividing the two parts of the city. There were towers all along this no man's land. Every bit of the ground could be seen so that if anyone tried to get across, they could be shot by a marksman in one of the towers. Many people were killed. I remember how creepy it was because there were wires between the towers, to which dogs were fastened. They had a sort of chain that ran along the wire, so that the animals could run between one tower and the next. Even if you escaped being shot as you tried to get across, you might well be attacked by one of these ferocious patrolling hounds.

I often wondered what the Russians really made of me. They must have reported back that a strange Englishman was sitting on the edge of no man's land again, doing a drawing and looking over into their side. Whether they claimed that I was a sort of spy I don't know, but I never had any serious problem. The only 'local difficulty' I ever ran into occurred when I had been working in Berlin for two or three days and had to get to Hanover the following day, to work with a regiment there.

There were some sad and sordid sides to the city. I found it depressing that when you stopped at the Russian checkpoints the young Russian soldiers always wanted Western cigarettes. You took care to have some spare cigarettes with you, and the boys would surreptitiously offer you a belt buckle or a badge in exchange. 'Oh Lord,' I thought, 'this wonderful state that they believe in so much, and yet they will swap their insignias for some cigarettes.' One night the young officers took me over to eat in East Berlin as they were able to go there. Just before Checkpoint Charlie I remember a park area filled with prostitutes in fur coats; they would suddenly open their coats as you were driving along, to reveal they were naked beneath. I don't know where you were supposed to have sex with them – behind a tree, I suppose – but it was all a bit sordid and East Berlin was very depressing. The centre was incredible – the authorities had restored all the old buildings, such as the Opera, so that it resembled old Berlin. Then, very quickly, you came upon lines of the most boring high-rise flats that you had ever seen – far more boring than anything being built in London at the time. There were some nice sights too, of course. There were still steam railways, which was great. I hadn't seen steam trains in use for years, but the Russians were still running them in 1970s East Berlin.

West Berlin was also fairly seedy in the '70s, perhaps not surprising in a city full of troops. Whenever I worked with the regiments in the city the young officers would want me to go on the town with them; I usually declined because I had a heavy workload, but one evening, when I had only to drive to Hanover the next day, I agreed. They took me down the Kurfürstendamm, which in those days was a red-light district; I was in my forties then and thought I had seen life, but I was actually fairly inexperienced in some matters. We went to a live show where a couple had sex on stage – not the least bit erotic and frankly rather boring – and then progressed through several bars. At about two in the morning we arrived at a bar where I was propositioned by a beautiful blonde girl. After buying her champagne she invited me to 'go around the back' with her, but fortunately at that moment I touched her hair – and, although very drunk, I realised with a shock that it wasn't real. I then noticed that she had an adam's apple and that her fishnet stockings covered some very masculine muscles. She was a fellow! I have never got out of a bar so quickly in my life.

The following morning a very hungover painter turned up at the Berlin checkpoint, ready to drive to Hanover. I left very early in the morning and was extremely tired, plus by this time I had become so used to all the procedures that I got a bit lax. Stupidly, I didn't check my petrol, and the Russians didn't bother to check either. I started to drive out along the Autobahn to Helmstedt, and after about two miles I suddenly looked at my petrol indicator. To my horror I realised that I had no petrol – I had forgotten to fill up. 'What do I do?' I thought, trying not to panic. 'If I run out of petrol I am stuck in the middle of the Russian zone, and if I try to go back by crossing the hard shoulder in the middle of the road I may get shot at.' I was still near enough to Berlin to be visible from the observation towers along that bit of the road. In the end the only thing I could do was to bounce over the top and drive back to the Russian checkpoint. All hell let loose, I remember, and there were reports going back to the British sector about this Englishman in a car who had come back without adequate papers. It wasn't pleasant, but that was the nearest I came to getting into trouble in Berlin.

I also remember one funny story from this time. I had just bought a new car, a Volvo 940 estate. On these trips I took everything with me – paper, paints, drawing boards. I had a sort of mobile studio in the back, so an estate car was essential. I bought this one new before I left London, then drove it all the way to Berlin. I'm not the most mechanical person in the world, but I noticed that the gear lever showed five gears – something I'd never had before. I believed I had only four gears, and drove right through Germany using just the four. As I was driving in from the checkpoint to Berlin, I suddenly realised that I had gone into fifth gear and thought I must have done untold damage to the car. When I got to Berlin I contacted a Volvo agent and rather shamefacedly admitted what I had done. He was unperturbed and didn't think I would have done any damage to the car.

On another occasion when I was in Germany, I remember going to stay with the Scots Dragoon Guards – one of the wealthiest regiments in the British Army at that time, formed out of the Scots Greys and the Carabiniers. I had met them in Northern Ireland, but I later went to work with them in Germany. When I got to the Mess there was a wonderful car outside called a Scimitar, which you'd describe as a sort of sports estate car. I wanted a Scimitar as soon as I saw it. It was a fantastic car, and the only car in my life that I have enjoyed driving. It was like being in an aeroplane somehow, and incredibly responsive. Once when I was going through Germany I was driving really fast – there wasn't a speed restriction on the Autobahns in Germany at the time. I must have been doing about 100 miles per hour, when all of a sudden my seat gave way and I was lying almost horizontal – it gave me quite a fright. Another of my nine lives gone, I suppose.

During the 1970s, when I was travelling the world and still working in Northern Ireland, Chrissie and I continued to see each other. This wasn't on a very regular basis, but we did meet in Germany, Holland or Italy. In the summer, if I was in England, Chrissie would come over for five or six weeks; we would drive down to Dartmoor and go walking and paint together. She absolutely loved the old school on Dartmoor, especially its privacy. A church stood behind the building and a farm was across the way; otherwise the nearest town was Tavistock, some four or five miles away.

Chrissie was a natural landscape painter and she loved the flow and rhythm of landscape. I remember when we first met again we went to the Black Forest and she eulogised about the mountains there. I myself had very little feeling for them. I have always been a vertical and horizontal man, more interested in cityscape than landscape, and preferring interiors to still-life – something with which Chrissie was rather obsessed. Her favourite painters were those such as Giorgio Morandi and Jean-Baptiste-Siméon Chardin. One day we were talking about my visit to Morandi in Bologna some 30 years before, and I told her that the artist had offered me one of his paintings for £50 and I hadn't had the money to buy it. Chrissie laughed and said, 'Oh, Ken, if only you'd bought that Morandi for £50, I think I would have had the strength to stand up to my parents, and the whole world, and come to live with you in England!' She was joking, of course, but she did have an obsession with Morandi's work that definitely influenced her own paintings.

I remember a conversation that summed up the really great qualities in her work, and in a way the weaknesses in mine. We were walking on Dartmoor and it was a wonderful day. We used to walk up to a pub in the middle of the moor; it was about four or five miles, but Chrissie, like many Germans, was very keen on walking. As we walked I suddenly saw a landscape that I thought was wonderful. I threw up my hands to make a rectangle of my fingers through which I could look at the scene. Chrissie teased me that I saw the whole world through a rectangle. 'Yes, of course I do,' I said, 'because I am a painter and that is how I see it.' But Chrissie didn't agree. 'When a landscape strikes you, first of all you should hear it, smell it, sense it and then see it – and then decide what you want to do with it.' She was undoubtedly, I think, a great painter.

I was very much about the excitement of looking at the scene. Seeing was in fact everything for me, and I suppose in that sense I am still very close to Impressionism and Monet's theory about standing in front of nature. But Chrissie wasn't like that at all. One day when we were in Cornwall she was working on a still-life, and she worked on it from ten in the morning until the light went at the end of the day – it was summer, so the light must have gone at about 10 o'clock. When the light failed and she stopped, I looked at this picture. 'Chrissie, that is quite miraculous,' I said. 'There is only thing that worries me, and that is it hasn't got much to do with what you're looking at.' She turned to me in astonishment and said, 'It's got everything to do with what I'm looking at.' She sensed it, smelled it, heard it and finally she looked at it – and the painting was a summation of all these things.

Such an intense pattern of working was very typical of Chrissie. I would start in the studio with a model who came at about 7 am. Chrissie would get up at about 8 am, look into the studio to say good morning and then go off to do whatever shopping needed to be done and put the washing in the washing machine. She would then start to work at about 10 o'clock, from which point nothing else interested her. At lunchtime I would sometimes offer to make her a sandwich,

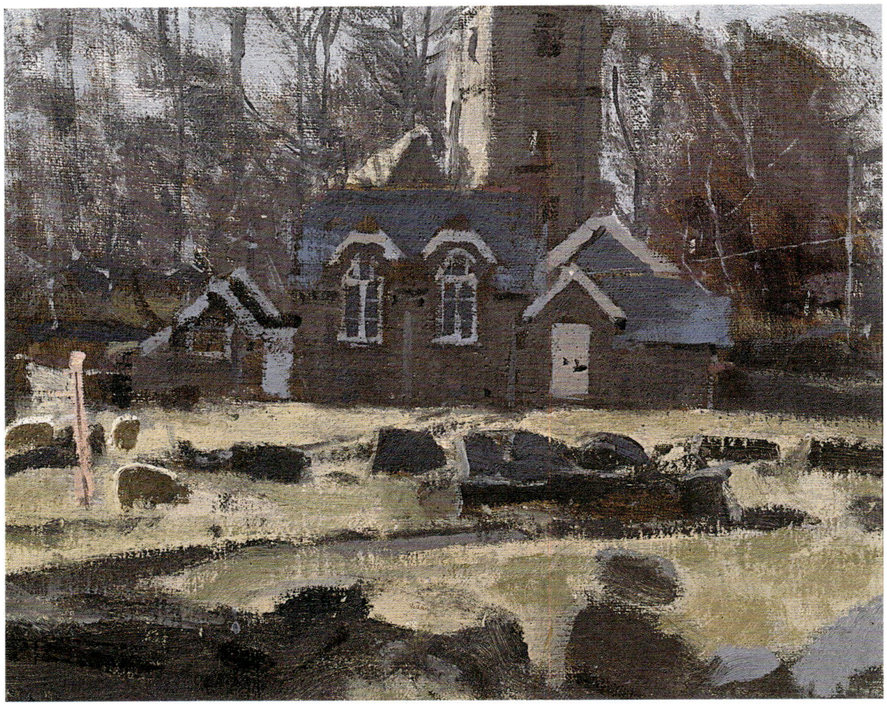

Sampford Spiney Studio, *c.* 1975
Oil on board, 30 x 25 cm

This small panel shows my studio at Sampford Spiney. I bought the Victorian schoolhouse, situated on Dartmoor in front of a church, to have a base from where I could paint snow.

but she never wanted anything. At teatime I would suggest a cup of tea, but again she would say no. She would just work obsessively on this still-life all day.

Of course, to my way of thinking this wasn't the way to work. Chrissie could sit in front of a still-life all day, working while the light and everything changed around her, but she still carried on with her painting. By contrast, I worked in short bursts while the light was doing something, and when the light changed, I did. But the way that I worked was draining too. I used to work for maybe two or three weeks without a break, after which I would be exhausted and excessively depressed. This was the case with everything that I was doing until I felt that I couldn't paint any more. Chrissie, with her typical insight, suggested that I should paint for six days a week and rest completely on the seventh, not even thinking about painting or anything to do with my living as a painter, such as business letters or anything like that. Instead, on that one day off we should talk, go for a walk, perhaps see a film, maybe go out, but get completely away from work.

As an artist, Chrissie understood the demands that painting imposes, and I welcomed her suggestions. In fact it was only during the '70s that she had started to study again, being accepted as a mature student at the Cologne School of Art in her mid-thirties. It was a bold decision on her part: ever since she was a young girl and her father had made his thoughtless remark that there wasn't any talent for art in the family, Chrissie hadn't really painted. When I met her she was studying art history in Florence, but soon after the break-up of our relationship she had married Hartmut, and had two children. She had been a very attentive mother to her daughters, even coming home at lunchtime to give them a meal and make sure they were set up for the afternoon before she returned to class.

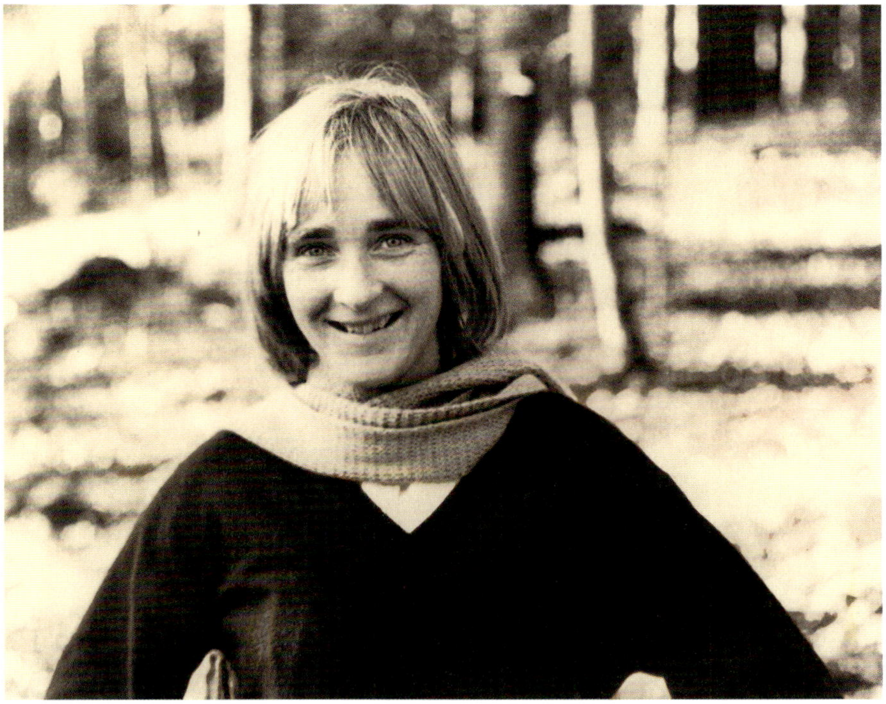

This photograph of Chrissie in the Black Forest in southern Germany was taken soon after we met up again, in around 1975. At the time I was working for a Canadian Regiment at Lahr.

Typical of Chrissie, however, she threw herself one hundred per cent into her painting. She became one of the school's top students and was eventually awarded one of the best degrees in her year. A lot of the students were much younger and didn't have the same work ethic as her, but they looked upon Chrissie as a mature person, even a sort of mother figure. She became a great favourite in the school as she was so wise, with such a good attitude to work. One of the boys in her year, aged only seventeen or eighteen, actually fell in love with her. He was quite talented, but he became obsessed with Chrissie, doing paintings of her and her house. He became quite a problem and Chrissie was such a giving, open sort of person that she didn't recognise what was happening until it was too late. She was very disturbed by the whole situation, and in the end the boy had to be transferred to another school. A teacher at the Cologne School of Art was also very close to her. He recognised a good student who was closer to his age than the younger pupils, and was very attentive, helpful and encouraging. He died some years later, but I still have one of his works in my studio in London.

I remember that towards the end of my commission work, in the early '80s, it was becoming more difficult for the regiments to find a seat for me on a plane. In the beginning, if a regiment was travelling to a place they could always find a spare seat on the plane where I could get tucked in. It wasn't always very comfortable – I remember one flight in a Hercules where I was right on the side with all these Scimitar tanks down the middle, I think it was up in Norway. But it was always an interesting, if not a very comfortable way to travel.

I remember working in Cyprus quite a lot, just after the Turkish invasion of Northern Cyprus in 1974. This was one of my first foreign commissions, to what

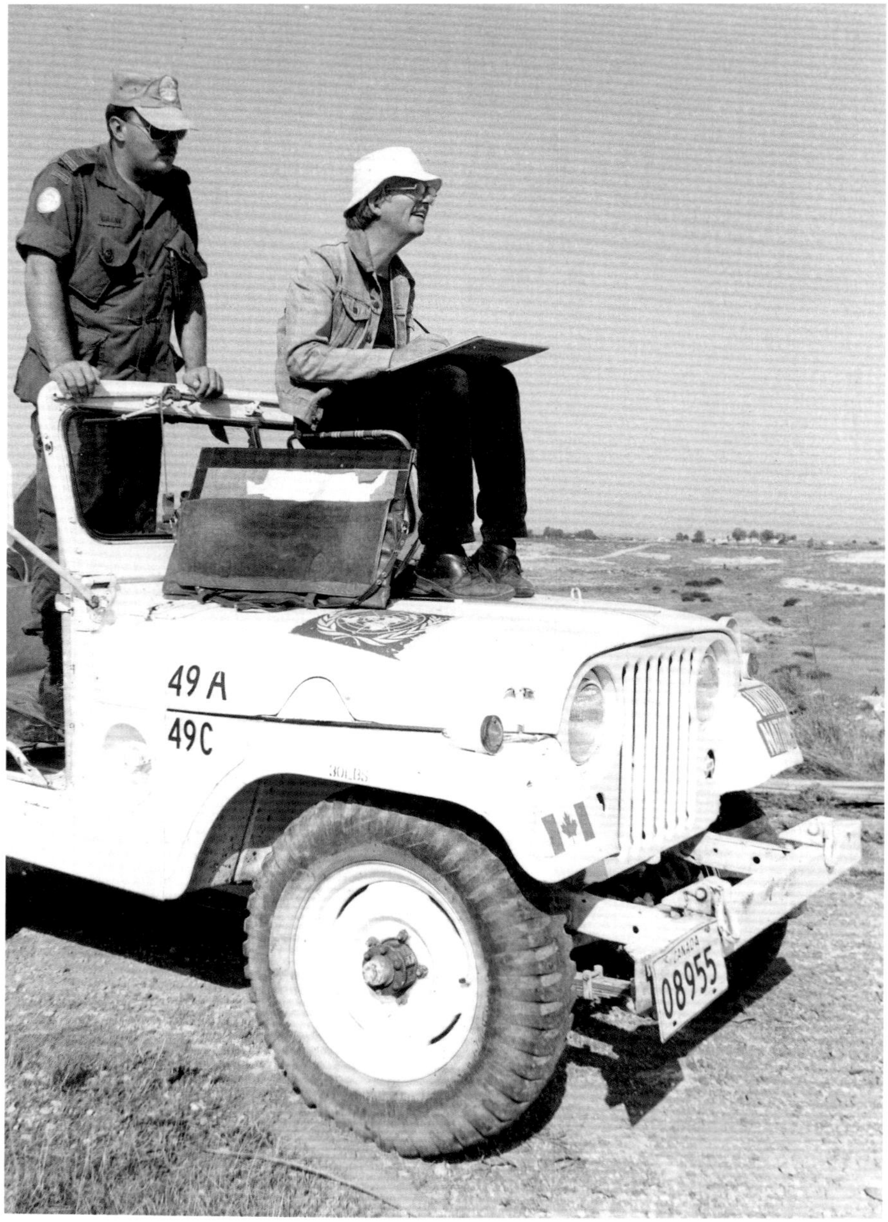

was a sad island in those days, with everything in turmoil. I saw Turks being taken in buses from the south to the north, and Greeks from the north to the southern area. There was a sort of ethnic cleansing going on. Whole villages were suddenly uprooted and you came across eerily deserted ones where no one at all remained. There was something incredibly surreal about these places. I found it quite fascinating. Even in the middle of the capital, Nicosia, things were in a strange stasis. I remember seeing a car dealership with four brand new Toyotas in the sale room. They were seven years old, but had never been moved, let alone driven. They were probably the oldest completely unused Toyota cars – real collectors' pieces I suppose.

I loved Cyprus, and if anything would ever get me to go back and do a commission it would involve a return to Cyprus. In those days, the mid-'70s, the island was still relatively unspoilt; there were holiday towns, but nothing like I understand it is now. There were still lovely little villages, such as Pissouri near to Akrotiri, where I spent quite a lot of time. Donkeys were still ridden in the streets and there were no cars. As well as working on commissions, I took the chance to do my own work, either in the early morning before I went to work on my commission, or in the evening. In the end I started to have exhibitions in some of the places I visited. I remember having one exhibition in Nicosia, featuring work that I'd done all over Cyprus.

This is typical of the way I had to work when I was with the army. To get the particular perspective I wanted, I perched myself on the bonnet of this United Nations jeep in Cyprus.

The commission work was quite interesting, not least because there was still technically a state of war. A 'Green Line' ran between the Turkish north and the Greek south, into which no one was allowed to go. The line actually ran through Nicosia, and there was one street into which neither Greeks nor Turks were allowed. I was one of the few people able to go to these places with the United Nations patrols, gathering reference material for the work I was doing. There was a restaurant in that street and I remember being told that when the Turkish invasion happened, the people who had been in the restaurants had all fled into their respective Greek or Turkish areas. This restaurant had literally not been touched since that day; it was quite spooky. There were still tables with food on them, long since gone mouldy, of course. You could almost think the restaurant was still functioning; only the cooks, waiters and diners were missing, and would never return.

The Green Line went out into the country. It ran the full length of the island and was about a mile wide in country areas, as far as I remember, but only a couple of streets wide in Nicosia. At this time I had a commission to do a sketchbook of watercolours for the United Nations, which they were then going to print. I think they were looking at printing around 500 copies, to be sold to the various nations keeping the peace in Cyprus.

There certainly was a range of nations involved in this. There were about five at any one time; Canadian troops were there, I remember, as well as British and Swedes, and the General in charge was a German; I did a portrait of him. When I arrived on the island the troops said they would show me the whole of the United Nations area. They flew me in a helicopter from the east end of the island to the west. It was an amazing flight; we went more or less along the Green Line because the United Nations were posted on the edge of it. The pilot pointed out the various posts and we would go down and land so that I could look around. I noted the ones

Midday Light, Cyprus, 1982
Watercolour, 17.5 x 22.5 cm

I made this watercolour, for myself when I was working with the United Nations. I saw an old woman in a village sitting in a darkened room and wanted to capture the effect. I tried again and again, but couldn't get what I wanted. Eventually I gave up, almost weeping with frustration, and accidentally poured a glass of water over it. Miraculously, as it dried the effect I wanted was there. I realised at that moment that some of the best results come about by accident.

that were most stimulating and to which I wanted to return to do a drawing or watercolour. In the end I was there for six weeks. It only rained once, on that first day. An enormous storm came in and caught us in the helicopter, so we had to land on top of a mountain while it passed.

To digress a moment, one of my favourite colours has always been raw umber. Ruskin Spear, who taught me at the Royal College, had suggested that I got a tube because I wasn't very good at colour. He said raw umber would help me out. This raw umber was a wonderful green-brown really – brown with a cool touch to it – and I used it a lot. It was more green than red, in fact, although you normally think of green as being a warmish colour. Some years later, this wonderful colour that I depended upon changed. It was no longer this beautiful green-brown, instead it was a rather boring brown-brown. I wrote to the artists' suppliers Winsor & Newton to ask what had happened to the raw umber. The company's chemist wrote back to explain that unfortunately they had lost their supply. I thought this was most likely an excuse; they were probably cost-cutting and trying to produce a synthetic raw umber.

However, my trip to Cyprus had an unexpected result. After the storm had gone, the helicopter took off again and we continued to fly along the Green Line. Then the pilot suddenly said to me on the intercom, 'Look down there. There's that marvellous copper mine, and doesn't it look incredible after the rain?' I looked down and saw this lovely green colour of the copper mine – no longer worked, of course, as no one was allowed into the Green Line. Everything – fields, mine, buildings – was deserted. Then the pilot told me that next to it was an umber mine. I couldn't believe it, but he said that it had been an umber mine before the war. I realised that it wasn't just any umber mine – it must have been *the* umber mine. I saw straight away that the wonderful green colour in the old raw umber had come about because of the proximity of the copper mine. The green of the copper had gone down into the earth. Winsor & Newton had been telling the truth all along – they had indeed lost their source of raw umber.

Two days later, when I had returned to Nicosia, I told this story to the German general. 'Oh, there's no problem, Ken,' he assured me. 'We'll fly you in and you can get a couple of demijohns of your raw umber.' A couple of days later both sides agreed that I could be dropped into the umber mine by helicopter and allowed to dig up some raw umber with a bucket and spade. In due course I brought this back to England. I flew back from Cyprus in a British Army plane, and went through customs at RAF Lyneham – even the Army have to go through customs when they come back from service overseas. I had two demijohns with

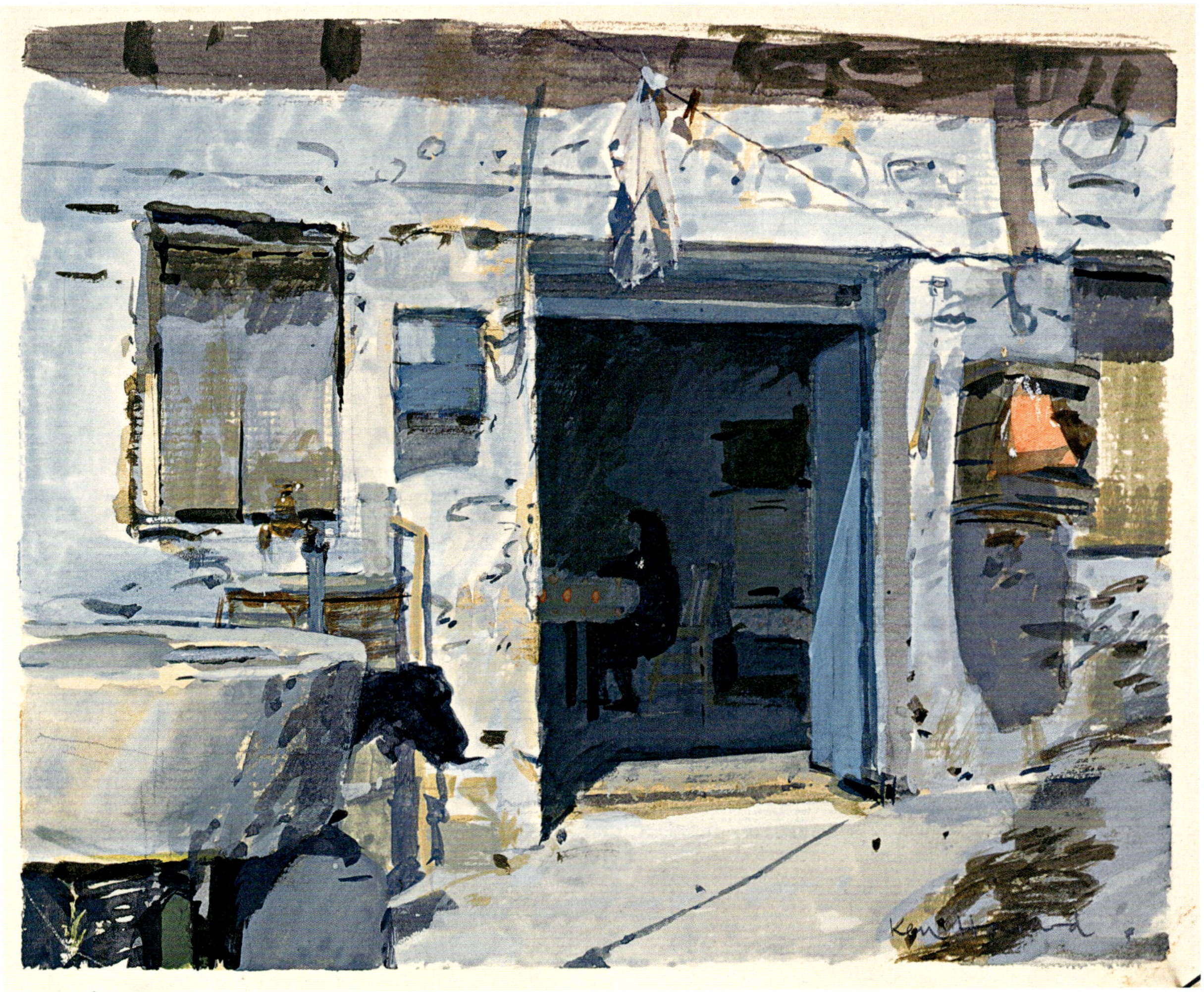

earth in them and the raw umber had started to go a bit solid. When I presented them to the customs officer he was baffled. I explained that it was raw umber and he asked what I meant. I told him it was an earth colour, but he demanded to know what was hidden beneath. Then they turned the demijohn upside down, convinced that I was trying to smuggle something into England and had covered it with mud. Of course, they didn't have a clue what raw umber was.

On another occasion in Cyprus I was asked to do a watercolour of an old school. It was a very famous place that had been attacked by the Turks. A band of Greek soldiers had defended it with incredible heroism and all died – a modern version of Thermopylae. I was asked to do a watercolour of the school because it stood on the Green Line near to Nicosia. I sat on the edge of a dirt track that marked the delineation point between the Greek and Turkish sides. The Green Line was quite narrow as it was near to Nicosia and there were still some Turkish trenches in the area. I was busy drawing the school and these trenches, when all of a sudden a Turkish patrol approached. They couldn't actually come on to my piece of ground, but they were not welcoming. 'What are you doing drawing our positions?' demanded the Turkish officer. I explained that I was drawing the school, not their positions, and he ordered me to give him my drawing. I refused; I had been working on it for a long time and it wasn't a bad watercolour. He gave the order again, so I held up the drawing board to show him. 'I don't care. You're drawing our positions,' he repeated, and he went on and on. In the end it looked as though things were going to get ugly, so I took the drawing off the board as if I was about to give it to him, then tore it up; he was furious. I ripped it up into little pieces and gave him a handful of these bits of paper. At this stage he sort of reached for his pistol and I thought, 'Oh, my God.' For a minute I was a bit worried in case they just grabbed me and pulled me over to the Turkish side. Dreadful visions of *Midnight Express* began to rise in my imagination and I wondered what on earth I had got into. Fortunately by this time the United Nations had seen what was happening from an Army post nearby. One of the little armoured cars came along the dirt track and they sorted out this potentially difficult situation.

Being with the United Nations, I had access to places that civilians hadn't been allowed to visit for years. I remember that they took me to the end of Famagusta, deserted since the day of the invasion and the Greeks fled to the nearby British Army base at Larnaca. They believed that this would be all over in a couple of days and that they would return to their shops and houses and lives in Famagusta. But of course it didn't end and Cyprus is still divided. The United

Nations took me into this deserted part of Famagusta which they ran and it was really eerie. I remember the film of Nevil Shute's novel *On the Beach*, in which a submarine comes up and lands in a deserted city. They must have got permission from the UN to shoot the film in that completely abandoned part of Famagusta.

The only time I got really scared during this time was when I went to Beirut to do a commission for a cavalry reconnaissance squadron based there. I had been working in Lebanon for this reconnaissance unit and was asked if I would go and do a watercolour of the Place des Martyrs in Beirut. As usual, I managed to get a lift on a military plane – a bit like hitchhiking round the world. Beirut in the late '70s was experiencing huge problems, including numerous kidnappings, which worried me somewhat. I always refused to have anybody with me when I was working in Northern Ireland because I thought that protection from soldiers was asking for trouble, but Beirut was different. It was the first time I agreed to a job on the condition of having a cover round me, to prevent kidnapping or anything else. So I drew and painted in the streets while the soldiers covered me – rather a stressful experience and not one I was keen to repeat. The city's American base was blown up while I was there, too, which was a bit traumatic. Yet it was certainly a compelling place at that time; the imagery in Beirut was quite surreal. I remember going into the town and passing the camps where all the fighting had been going on, and noticing how the trees had all been stripped completely bare like those in the battlefields of the First World War. I remember there was a helicopter stuck on a low block of flats just where it had come down; it looked like a strange piece of sculpture, poised on the top of the flats. The whole place was very creepy and disturbing – tense and ready for violence, like a coiled spring. I was very pleased to get back to Cyprus without having been kidnapped.

This period of working with the Army had come at an appropriate time in my life. Financially it was very helpful as I had given up my only regular income. I was also going through a difficult time in my personal life and the travel was a welcome distraction. I was rootless, as with divorce I had lost my home comforts; it was not difficult to travel at the drop of a hat. I had constant companionship in what would have been a lonely existence, had it not been for the time I spent with Chrissie.

During those years I realised the children, the graffiti and the suffering all became part of my life, and this was expressed in my work. However, I gradually came to find the commissions repetitive and I knew that for the sake of my painting I should only do them for a limited period.

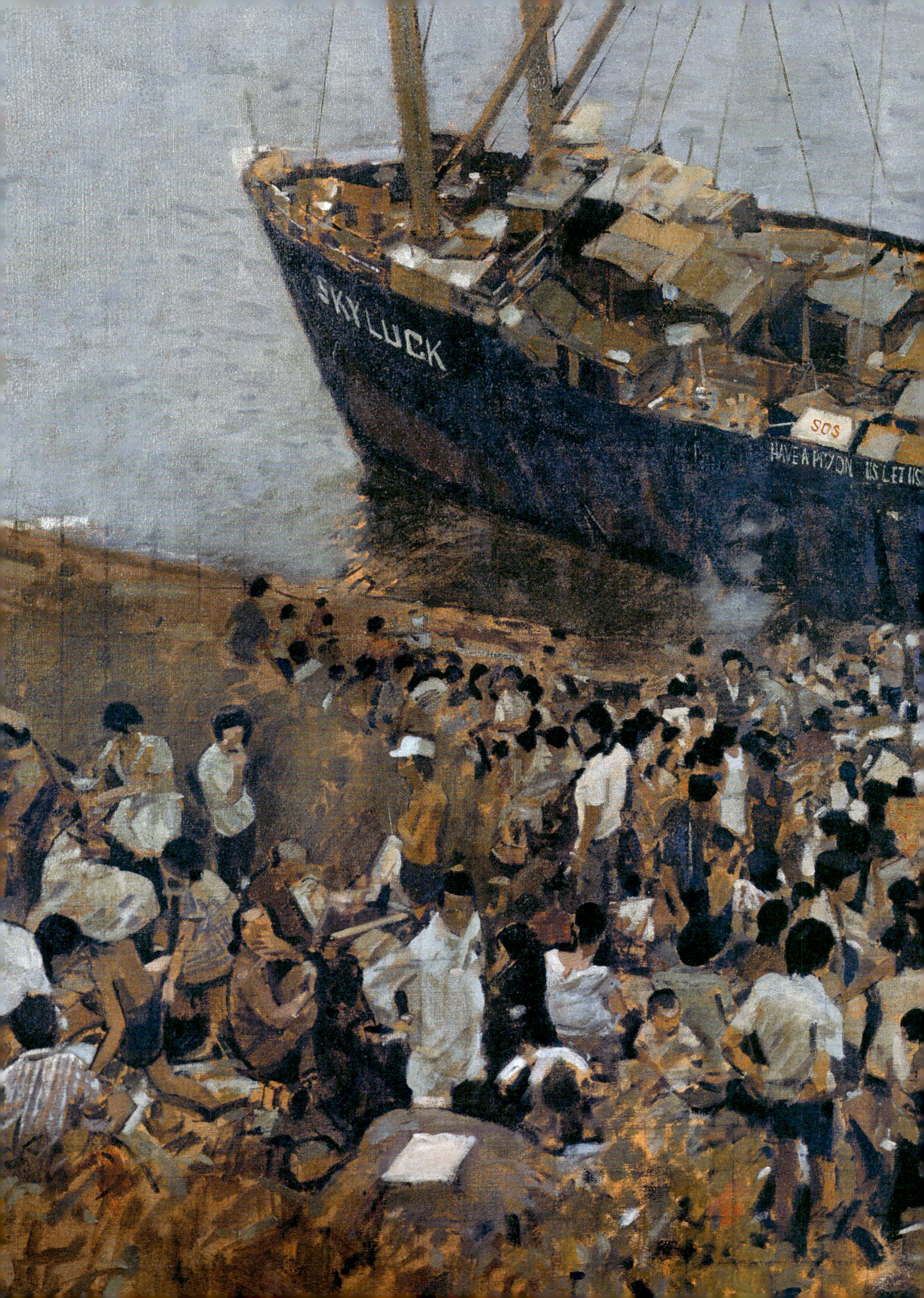
SKY LUCK
SOS

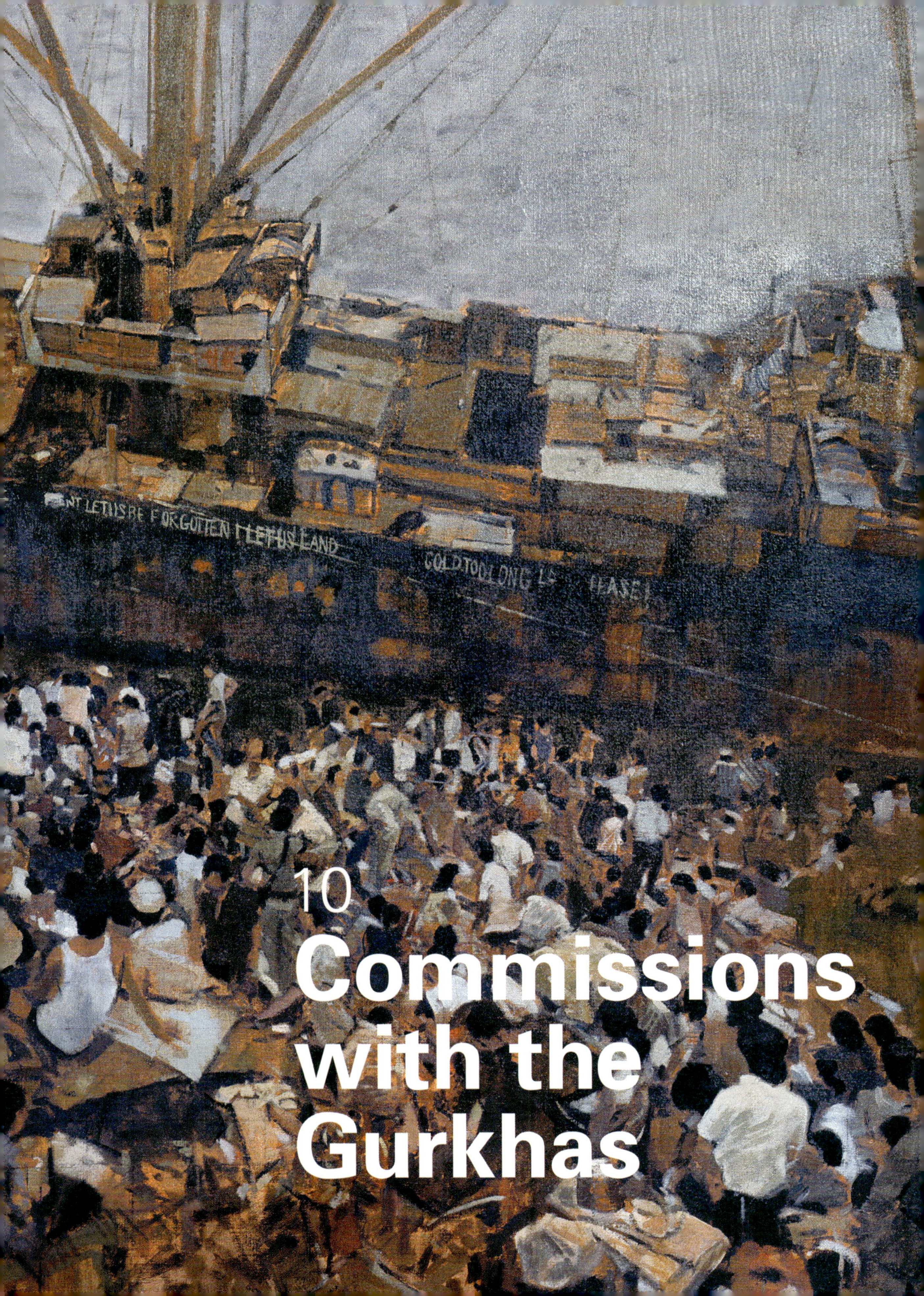

10

Commissions with the Gurkhas

Street Scene, Pokhara, Nepal, *c.* 1972
Pen and sepia, 38 x 56 cm

While I made this drawing the children gathered around and I tried quickly to capture their ethnic characteristics. The child on the far right was from near Tibet, the boy in front from China and those to the left from near to India and China. Drawing must always be about the particular.

After Cyprus my foreign commissions gradually built up. A particularly interesting one occurred in 1979, when I was asked by Peter Duffell, a Colonel in the Gurkhas, to do a series of drawings. He was writing a book on the life of a Gurkha in Nepal, focusing on his life in the village rather than time in the services. He wanted to explore where the boys came from and what they returned to afterwards, and how their lives developed after their time in the army; it sounded very interesting. However, when Peter asked me to do a set of 30 drawings on a Gurkha's life in Nepal I had to tell him, rather bluntly perhaps, that I didn't think he could afford to commission so many. Instead I suggested that if he would take me to Nepal for no charge, I would do the 30 drawings and give him reproduction rights to them all. In other words, I would make transparencies of them all and provide all the drawings he wanted for his book for free. In return I would keep the drawings as my income from the trip. Peter agreed immediately. All he really wanted were the drawings for the book, so he was happy to accept.

As Colonel of the First Battalion 2nd Ghurkha Rifles, Peter Duffell had to go on what was called a 'pension trek'. I don't know whether they still do, but at that time a senior Gurkha would go on trek through the villages and pay the veteran Gurkhas their annual pensions. It was the perfect opportunity for our trip. Peter paid for me to fly to Hong Kong with him and then travel to Kathmandu, from where we set out on this trek towards Annapurna. We visited several different villages, I remember, and I did a whole series of drawings.

It was a wonderful trip – and an unforgettable experience. When we arrived at our hotel in Kathmandu, I took the chance to walk round the city before it got dark. It was a rather basic hotel in the centre, but Kathmandu was still fairly unspoilt. When I walked through the city that evening Kathmandu seemed absolutely magical, with all its temples and people in their traditional dress. 'What an incredible place it is!' I said to Peter when I got back.

I was too excited to sleep that night – for the first time in my life. I just lay awake all night waiting for the dawn. Next morning I went out into the streets at first light, something I will remember until my dying day. There was a sort of low mist rising among these old temples and an elephant went past with someone sitting on top. I felt that I had never seen anything like it in my life before. The people had become attuned to tourists, though. I remember Peter had told me not to buy anything on my first evening as I would be charged far more than it was worth. And of course while I was walking around someone did come up and ask me if I wanted to buy a woman's bangle. They were rather lovely and I thought Chrissie would like one for her wrist. The man asked for about £20 but, mindful of Peter's advice, I said

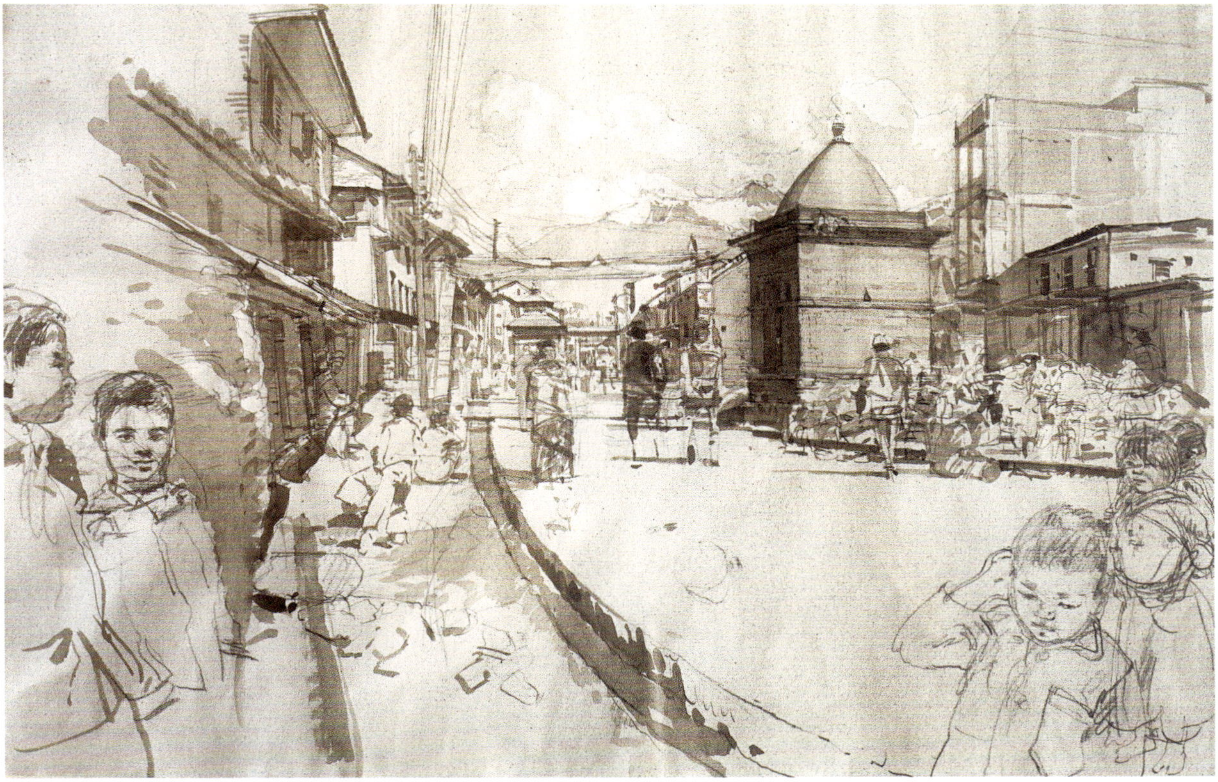

I couldn't afford that. The price gradually came down and down and I eventually paid him around £5, which I thought was a good deal.

When I returned to the hotel Peter asked me if I had bought anything and I told him about the bangle for £5 – he was too much of a gentleman to tell me at that point that I had been done, but of course I had. At the end of the trip I went out again to draw in the city. As I was leaving the temple where I had been working, at the end of the day, another vendor showed me some things left on his tray. I told him that I didn't have any money, which was not far from the truth as it was the end of my stay. When I looked at the tray, there was the very same bangle that I had bought on my first night in Kathmandu. 'Oh, come on,' he said, 'I will let you have this very cheaply.' I asked the vendor his price and he offered it to me for five shillings. I knew immediately what Peter had meant when he warned me about paying too much for the first thing I bought.

A few days later we went to a place called Pokhara, down the road from Kathmandu, by jeep. It seemed quite a long way and we saw lots of little roadside teahouses that were incredibly busy. We had to recruit some boys at Pokhara to carry our stuff, as we were going to be trekking and living in tents for several days. Peter recruited four porters, one of whom was a boy who wanted to become a British Gurkha – the usual ambition of all boys in Nepal at that time. There were Indian Gurkhas and British Gurkhas, but British Gurkhas were preferred as they paid more. Boys who got into the British Gurkhas also had the chance to travel: they would serve in Hong Kong and they would even go to Church Crookham in England

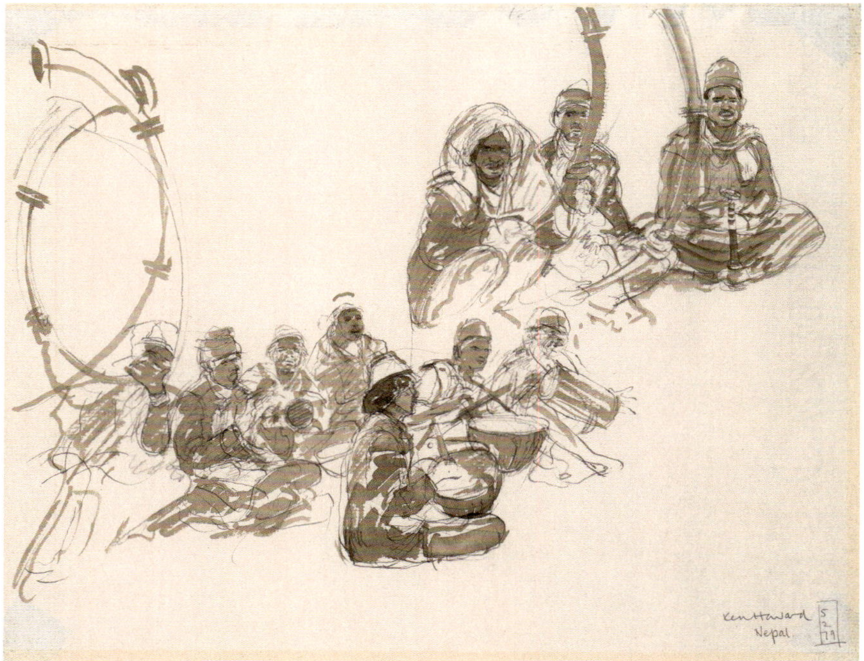

for a period of time. The Gurkhas were also regulars at any place of conflict; in 1982 they went to the Falkland Islands, I think.

So Peter had little difficulty in finding four porters. He came back and said that he had got four, but one was a town boy and he wasn't really sure that he wanted him. Anyway, the next morning this boy came to Peter and begged to be taken, so Peter agreed to give him a chance. 'He just won't be up to it,' he said to me, 'not with all the walking and climbing.' But obviously this boy wanted to get into the British Gurkhas and had decided the best way was to impress the Colonel on the trek. He came with us and proved to be incredible, out-walking the other three experienced porters and going up hills like a deer.

After we had been out for about four days we got to the top of a mountain. Peter looked across the valley to another peak and told me, 'On the other side of that mountain is the village we are going to.' 'I'm sorry,' I said. 'You're going to go to the village on the other side of the mountain, Peter, but not me – I just can't go on with this sort of pressure.' 'Oh don't be such a wimp, Ken.' he replied. 'Of course you will come with me.' But I was determined, so he agreed that I could stay in the valley until he returned.

The next day Peter left me there with the other porters. He took just his bag (with the pension he was going to pay out) and the boy, who was to carry the overnight things for their stay in the village. They went off up the mountain – probably a hill in their eyes, but it certainly looked like a mountain to me. When Peter returned the next day he told me that I had been right. 'You would never have climbed that mountain,' he admitted. 'It almost broke me and I am pretty fit, but the boy was incredible and went up it with no difficulty whatsoever. I completely take back all I ever said about him being a soft, towny boy who wouldn't be up to this sort of thing. If I can recommend him to get into the Gurkhas, I will certainly do so.'

The trek was physically hard and demanding. When Peter left me in the valley we were camped by a river and I went off to one of the villages to draw. On my return I was crossing the river on the stones with my portfolio under my arm when I slipped. I thrust my hand out with the portfolio to save that from falling into this very shallow river, managing to thrust it onto a rock. The portfolio stayed above the water, but I split the nail on one of my fingers and badly bruised and cut the finger itself. By the time Peter came back I was in great pain and the finger was throbbing. We were very remote and he said that there was nowhere we could get treatment for about two days – I was going to have to walk with that finger. Peter bandaged it and told me to keep it up to my chest; this would stop the blood running down into it, so it wouldn't be quite so painful. When we finally arrived in the small town, the doctor's surgery was pretty primitive. It was very dirty, and I thought that if anything was going to kill me it would be having treatment in this surgery. In the end it all worked out, however. I got it anaesthetised and was able to carry on.

In those days I had quite long hair. I didn't have a ponytail, but it was quite long and loose. This caused a funny incident when we arrived at one village. We had been walking for several days and were approaching this village through the hills. They had obviously sent out a runner to look out for us; he spotted us and ran back to report we were coming. We were met on the outskirts by the headman and the Damai band, the village band. They welcomed us and escorted us through the village to the local school, where children danced for us. It was incredible – the villagers garlanded us with flowers and treated us like royalty. Peter was walking with the headman as we entered the school and he suddenly burst out laughing. 'Can I come in on the joke?' I asked. It turned out I was the cause. 'They sent out a runner,' Peter explained, 'and he came back into the village saying "The Sahib is coming, the Sahib is coming – and he's got his Memsahib with him".' They imagined I was a woman because of my long hair, which Peter thought was hilarious.

All the villagers turned out to greet us because Peter was a sort of god in a way – the Colonel of a British Ghurkha regiment who everyone wanted to impress because they wanted their sons to get into the British Gurkhas. As I say, the headman and the Damai band met us on the edge of the village and marched us through, and there was a great fiesta held for our arrival. At that time dancing was mainly performed by men and boys, and it was considered a great honour for girls to dance, which they did for us. I remember that night we drank a bit too much

Damai Band, Nepal, 1979
Pencil and wash,
25 x 32.5 cm

This was one of the drawings I made for Colonel Peter Duffell. At the time I felt it was an impossible subject, but from this drawing I learned it was better to attempt something big and miss it than to achieve something small. The musicians playing have far more intensity than the resting figures, which were relatively easy to do.

of the local whisky, which I think they called *rashti*, and I didn't get to bed until about 2 am. The party was still going on and the drums were beating when I crawled into my tent, but I managed to get some sleep. I got up at about 6 am when everything was quiet; it seemed a good moment to go and work. I crept out of the tent, under-slept and over-drunk, and started to draw. Immediately the villagers appeared with breakfast for me – boiled eggs and goodness knows what. It was a great experience.

There is a caste system in Nepal, the musicians and tailors of the Damai being a fairly low caste, but the Damai band was quite wonderful. I remember Peter asked me to do a drawing of them in the field, beating their drums and blowing on these enormous horns that resembled elephant tusks. For once in my life I felt that I was beaten by this request – I was feeling hassled because of the walk and everything, and in the end I told Peter he wanted the impossible. I went out across the fields and he came after me saying, 'Oh, come on. Do me a drawing.' I gave in and went back. The Damai band stopped playing for a while and I drew them seated with their instruments. I also did a drawing of them playing their instruments and moving and beating their drums, which, in fact, turned out to be one of my best drawings of the whole trip. It captured the feel of the music and the movement, whereas the drawing I did when they were seated with their instruments was just another drawing of Nepalese people.

One of the things that drawing in Nepal reinforced for me was this business of the particular in drawing. When I first got to Nepal, all Gurkhas, even all Nepalese, looked the same to me. It's as if you have two black cats – the first time you look at them they appear to be the same black cat, but when you live with them you can soon tell then apart. The more I drew the Gurkhas, the more I appreciated the differences between Gurungs, Limbus and Rais, for example, who all came from different parts of Nepal. The Gurungs were mountain people used to hard living, and there were many of them in the Gurkha regiments. A Gurung looked very different from a Limbu, who in turn looked different from a Rai, while a Rai looked different again from a Damai. Eventually I could distinguish the different types. I remember the first time that somebody looked at a sheet of drawings of various Gurkhas and said, 'Good Lord! He's a Gurung, he's a Limbu, he's a Rai.' I realised that I had captured a very particular thing in these drawings. They were not highly detailed, they were quickly done – in portrait drawing the person usually hasn't got time to sit for you for very long. Yet I'd managed to grasp the particular character of that person, and it did really teach me something about drawing.

We didn't stay in a house in any village, as Nepalese houses were fairly primitive. Their owners cooked in them and a simple chimney in the roof meant they were quite smokey. Instead the porters always set up our camp on the edge of a village, which gave us both space and privacy.

Nepal had a great romance about it. The clothes that the people wore, especially up in the hills, were very distinctive, as were the buildings, and the simple architecture of the villages. There were no roads up into the villages, so everything that was used for building had to be carried across country. The Nepalese could carry sheets of corrugated iron that they would use for roofs on their backs, but there was no glass in their windows or anything like that – they simply couldn't bring it across the hills.

It was all quite primitive but extremely beautiful. Some years later I went back again, in a private capacity, with Chrissie and her half-sister and husband from Norway. We employed our own porters and trekked up from the main road to the ancient city of Gorkha, once the capital of Nepal.

My history isn't very good, but I believe that the soldiers originally came from Gorkha to fight the East India Company. They were such good soldiers that they forced the East India Company out of Nepal and back to the Indian border. When a truce was arranged, part of the agreement was that the British could employ the Gurkhas, who they had realised were extremely good soldiers. So the Gurkha regiments were established, to become an important and honoured part of the British Army.

I've worked with Gurkha regiments all over the world, from Borneo and Hong Kong to the Guatemalan border in Belize. I remember making a terrible faux pas one night in Belize, just after we'd returned to base camp, following two or three days in the jungle. I stripped off and went into the base shower, to find all the Gurkhas in there were wearing swimming costumes. When I got back to the Mess I asked Peter Duffell, the Commanding Officer, 'Why do all the Gurkhas wear swimming trunks in the shower?' 'Oh my God,' said Peter, 'you didn't go into the shower with the Gurkhas in the nude, did you Ken?' I said I had, and he told me that exposing yourself to a Gurkha is the greatest insult you can give them. 'It's lucky they didn't have their *kukris* [a cross between a sword and a dagger] with them,' he added. Of course, I didn't have a clue. I always went into the shower in the nude and that was that.

On another occasion I remember having dinner with the Gurkhas at Church Crookham in Hampshire. The Gurkha Major had invited me into the Gurkhas' Mess, not the British Officers' Mess, for lunch. It was a chance to enjoy their particular

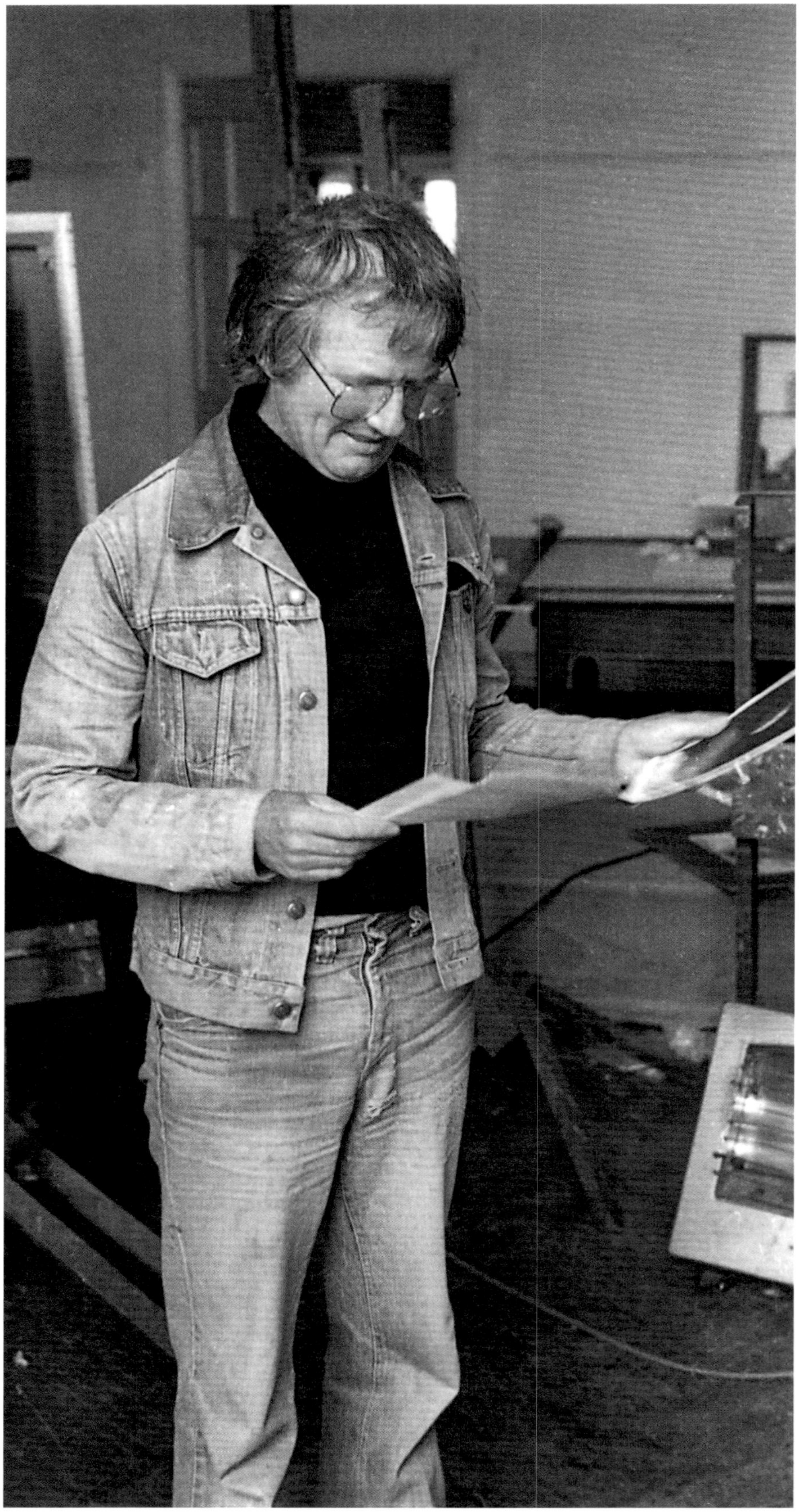

food, especially the distinctive curries that the Gurkhas made wherever they went. I was seated on the top table with the Gurkha Major, and I thought I'd watch whatever he did. I saw him take a chilli from his curry and, as I thought, put it in his mouth. In fact, I took my eyes off him for a moment and didn't realise that he just nicked the chilli with his teeth – just to release the flavour, I suppose. Anyway, I put the chilli right into my mouth. The flavour was incredibly strong – I think my hair stood on end, I was sweating and must have gone bright red. But the Gurkhas, being so courteous, didn't show any sort of amusement or let me feel embarrassed. They were complete gentlemen and behaved wonderfully.

Checking the mail in my London studio between foreign work trips, *c.* 1980. Jeans were almost a uniform for me in those days.

As I say, I've worked on commissions for the Gurkhas across the world, and I have an enormous admiration for them. They were incredibly smart men, always impeccably dressed when they were out and about, and they had equally impeccable manners. In Hong Kong I stayed in a place called Gun Club Hill, which was a Gurkha base. Whenever I visited the guard on the gate gave me a very strict salute. I was embarrassed by this and told him there was no need to salute me, I wasn't an officer. But he continued to do it.

Misunderstandings could occur, but their courtesy was unruffled. Once in Hong Kong I remember looking for a loo, in the days when my hair was quite long. I was up on a veranda in a very typical Gurkha base when a Gurkha major came along. He didn't know me and I asked him if he could direct me to a toilet. 'Oh yes, Ma'am', he replied, 'it's along there', and he pointed me to the ladies'. Of course Gurkha soldiers never, ever had long hair – it was always well-groomed and short.

I worked with the Gurkhas in Hong Kong in the late '70s and early '80s, a time when many Chinese were still trying to get over to Hong Kong. They could see the bright lights of Hong Kong from the Chinese mainland and heard about what life was like there. Some of them would do anything to get across. They either swam to the island or tried to get there in boats. The rules at that time were rather odd: Chinese who managed to get across to the mainland and reached Hong Kong proper could record their arrival and register, in which case they were allowed to stay. If they were caught on the way to the centre of Hong Kong, however, they were taken to an interrogation centre and then sent back to mainland China. As the authorities didn't really want to have floods of Chinese coming into Hong Kong, the island was patrolled by army, police and other guards, including the Gurkhas, so being caught was highly likely. I actually went to one of these interrogations to do some drawings. I remember they asked a young man how many attempts he had made and he said five. 'Well, you're going back again,' they said. 'Yes, and I'll try again,' he replied.

Boat People, Hong Kong, 1979–80
Oil on canvas, 150 x 180 cm

This large oil painting was made after a trip to Hong Kong in 1979. I was criticised because I didn't show the people as unkempt and dirty after their long ordeal on the *Sky Luck*. However, I painted what I saw, as despite the conditions on the ship they came off clean and well kept. People should not have preconceptions about subjects – it is the truth that matters.

The Chinese who were sent back were, so to speak, re-educated in how good the Chinese state was. Some were incredibly determined, however, trying again and again and again until they finally got out. I was never absolutely convinced that the Chinese authorities were that worried about such attempts – there were probably then too many people in the villages and towns, and if a few of them went over to Hong Kong, so be it. Very high barbed-wire fences were in place all along the border, which was constantly being patrolled by Gurkhas. One of my commissions was to show the different things the Gurkhas had to do to prevent the illegal immigrants entering Hong Kong.

Eventually I even held an exhibition in Hong Kong. I was going out there to do some commissions for different regiments and I was asked to do an exhibition by Caroline Cornell – her husband, Johnny Cornell, was then the Colonel AQ at Fort Stanley. I said it was too far away from England and I wouldn't be able to organise it, but Caroline said if I did the work she would arrange it all. And she went on to organise a show that did very well.

When I went out to do the commissions and have the exhibition I stayed with Johnny and Caroline. They picked me up at the airport and took me to the arts centre where my exhibition was to be, and of course I had nothing at all ready for the exhibition. Well, I did have one, a watercolour that I had done of Hong Kong on a previous visit. I took that with me so that they could get a card printed, as I knew that the publicity would have to be put in place before the exhibition opened. I also knew that I had to make up the exhibition from the six weeks' work that I was embarking on, so when Caroline and Johnny took me along to the arts centre for the first time I really panicked. It was a big space and I thought I would never produce enough work in six weeks to fill it.

The day I arrived we had some drama at dinner. As we were sitting at the table Johnny and Caroline's *amah*, or servant, suddenly backed into the room from the kitchen. Her eyes were wide and we wondered what the matter was. She was followed by two drenched Chinese boys who had swum over from the mainland. They had arrived at the bottom of the Cornells' garden and come up the hill to the house. Caroline immediately offered to put them in the boot of the car and take them to where they could register so that they would be able to stay. But Johnny said no, as this would have severely compromised his position in the Army. So I'm afraid they had to be handed over to the powers that be. No doubt they swam over again some weeks later, and maybe that time they succeeded; I don't know.

Meanwhile I had to get on with the painting. Caroline dealt with all the framing and cataloguing, so all I had to do was go out and paint. I worked solidly for

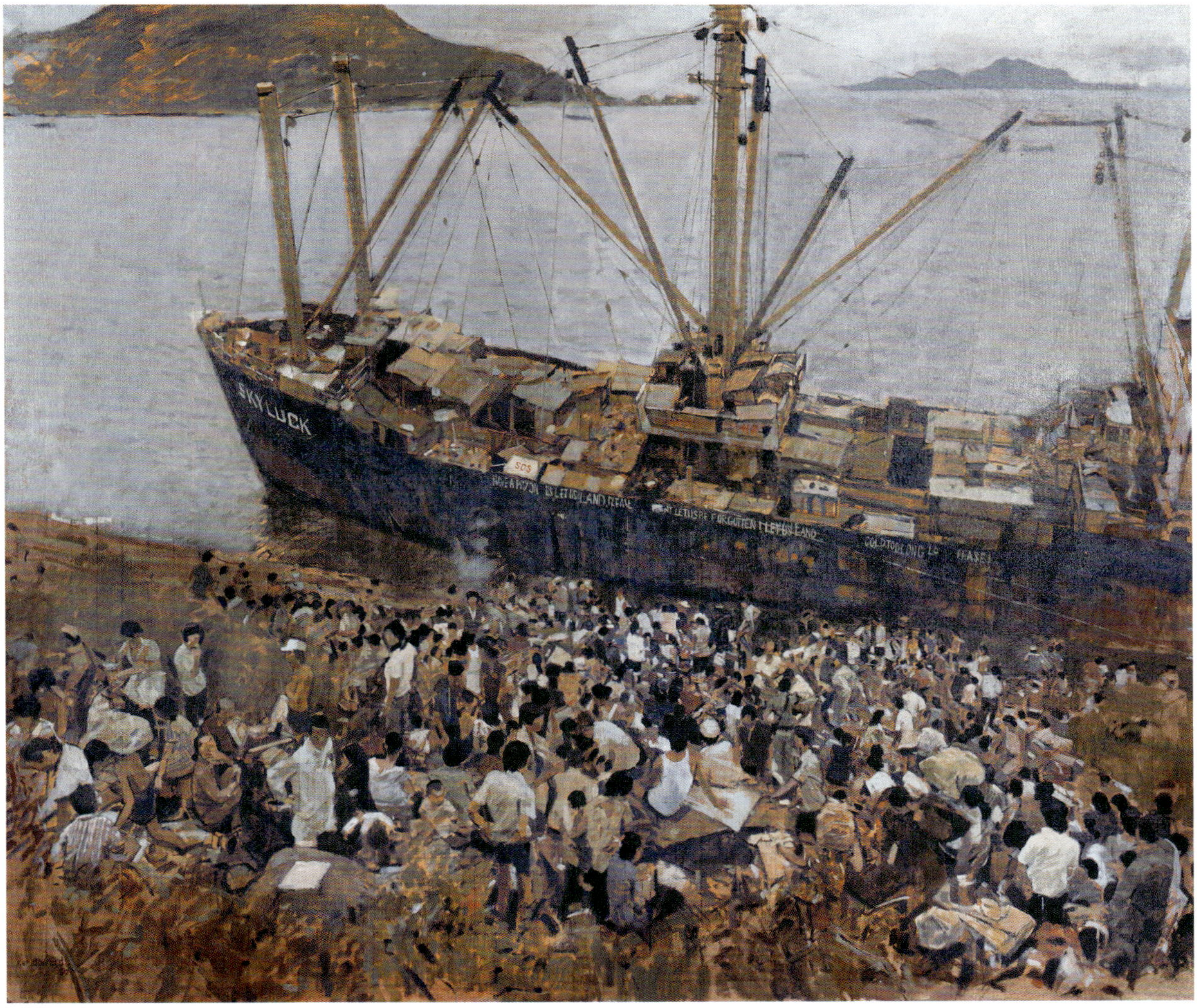
SKY LUCK

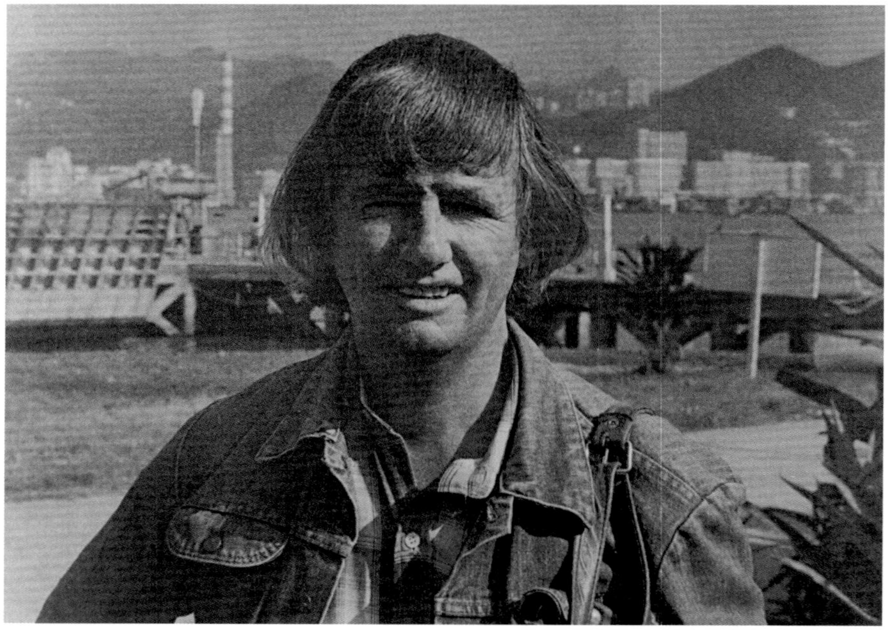

A moment of relaxation on a trip to Hong Kong, where I worked for the Gurkhas, *c.* 1980

six weeks, during which time the sun never went in once. I would go out early in the morning and paint right through the day, and I really got in tune with this particular Hong Kong light. I painted 80 small watercolours and the exhibition material really came together. I had a bit of luck, too, with the light.

A couple of nights before my exhibition opened I met an American at a dinner party. She asked if she could attend the exhibition and I arranged for Caroline to send her an invitation. The American lady duly came to the exhibition's private view. When she arrived she saw six red spots (indicating sale) on the watercolours near the door. She immediately turned to her husband and said, in a very loud voice, 'Gee, Wilbur, they're nearly all sold!' The Army people were there, of course, and obviously quite a lot of diplomats. There were also rich Chinese who quite liked the idea of owning a small painting of Hong Kong by a Western artist. Everybody heard this very loud voice saying that nearly everything was sold and things really took off. People who had been trying to make up their minds whether to buy or not, and which one to buy, suddenly panicked. All 80 watercolours disappeared on the opening night. At the desk they took down the names of people who hadn't managed to buy a painting and had asked if the next time I had a show in Hong Kong they could be invited and have first choice. Unfortunately this was the only exhibition I have ever had in Hong Kong.

I remember one day near to Christmas when I was drawing in the streets of Hong Kong. The place was crowded and the buildings were particularly beautifully decorated, with all those wonderful banners hanging down covered in Chinese calligraphy. Suddenly a Chinese man came up to me and looked at my drawing. He was obviously an educated man and he said in English, 'Oh, so you speak Chinese!' I said no, I didn't speak Chinese at all. 'But,' he said, indicating to the drawing, 'you write it perfectly.' And I realised that I was copying the scene in

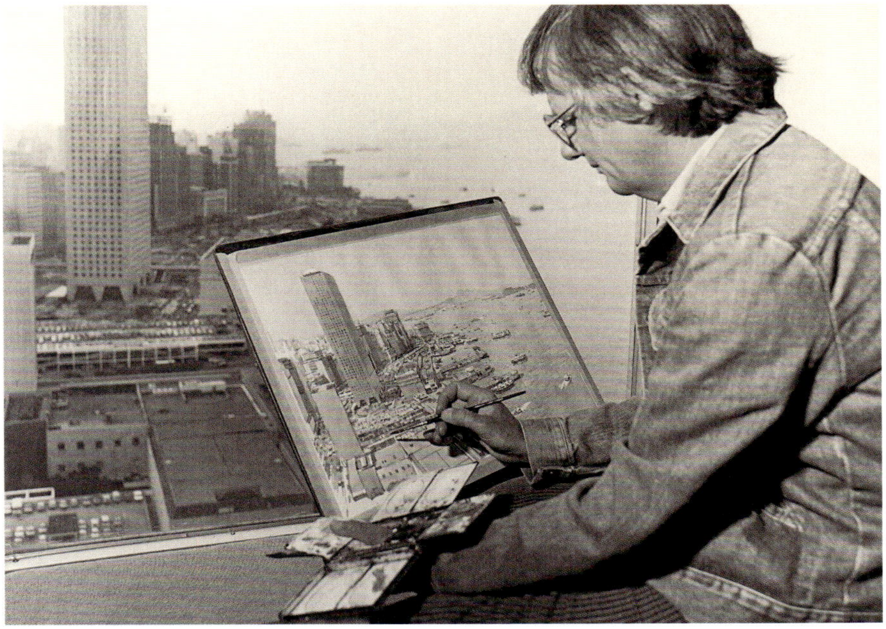

Painting outdoors in Hong Kong, *c.* 1980.

front of me, and my drawings were always very accurate if they weren't very detailed. By this time I suppose my style was getting freer in a way, but any marks I made were extremely accurate. The marks that I put down for this Chinese calligraphy obviously spelled the words that they were supposed to spell, even though the language was unknown to me. Once again, it taught me about the importance of the particular in drawing.

This reminded me of an outdoor drawing lesson that I had taken years ago when I was teaching at Walthamstow School of Art. The students were drawing a shop front, but when I looked at their drawings I noticed that between them they had spelled the name of the shop in three different ways. They were just generalising, not really looking at what they were drawing – and drawing for me is about the particular, not about the general. It may be about an overall breadth, the whole, but it is about the *particular* whole.

While in Hong Kong I worked a lot up in the New Territories outside the main city. They contained villages and wonderful fish farms, with lakes that reflected the mountains behind. The views were almost like scenes from Japanese prints, if you like. I worked in a little village called Sha Tau Kok, which I think must have been on the border with China. It may even have extended into China, because there were Chinese guards across from where I was with the Gurkhas. It was a point of confrontation and the Gurkhas were there to stop people coming across.

While I was in Hong Kong I received a message that the Sultan of Brunei wanted me to do some drawings of the landscape. He was going to build a polo club and he wanted a couple of watercolours painted to show the landscape before the club was built. I thought that this would be interesting – it was a time in my life when I was keen to see anywhere new. And when I arrived I discovered that there were regiments there, including the Brunei Malay Regiment. I then got commissioned, as normally happened, so I was able to do more than just the two watercolours.

The Gurkhas were there, too, because there was a lot of oil in Brunei, which was part of Borneo. All the oil was in Brunei itself and therefore not in the other two countries which made up the island. Insurgents were coming over from Sarawak to try and undermine the Brunei government in order to get control or obtain some of the oil revenue. So the Gurkhas were there to guard the oil fields and this gave me another opportunity for work.

A plane was sent up from Borneo specifically for me – that was the way they did things. I sat in with the pilot and when we landed and I descended from the plane I saw a Mercedes at the bottom of the steps. The aide-de-camp to the Sultan, who was there to meet me, told me it was for my use while I was in Brunei. In the corner of the field there was a helicopter: that was my transport if I wanted to go out and see the longhouses and go into the jungle. I could call on the helicopter whenever I wanted. It was incredible really – here was I, a slightly unkempt painter in an old pair of jeans, with rather long hair and a drawing bag over his shoulder, and yet I was being treated like royalty.

While I was in Borneo, I did a commission for the Brunei Malay Regiment. Whenever I went on these trips I was initially going to do one job and then it always developed into several and I ended up staying for several weeks. I painted in the jungle and worked with the Gurkhas in the oilfields. It was interesting, but not a completely happy experience. I remember that when I was doing the watercolours for the polo club, for example, I was near the sea. There I encountered these little flies that bit you all the time; I called them 'teeth with wings', and there was no way you could keep them off. The climate was also a problem – it was so hot and humid in Brunei that it was almost impossible to do watercolours as they would never dry. When I stayed with the Gurkhas in their camp I had an air-conditioned room, and when I emerged it was just like stepping into a hot, wet oven. So the working conditions weren't very easy, but it was still a great experience. I went up into the longhouses and was entertained by the locals. I was wined and dined, and even encouraged at one stage to be attracted by the headman's daughter. I don't know whether he thought it was a good way to get her back to England or what, but I didn't find her a particularly attractive girl. I must admit that I was quite pleased to get on the helicopter and get back to the city.

The jungle was especially difficult to work in because it was so tropical. I had to get the soldiers to rig up a couple of car tyres on planks of wood, and then I could get my stool onto these. In that way I could sit in the jungle and do my watercolours on the spot. I got thoroughly bitten for my pains, but, as always, that was the way I wanted to work.

Another jungle I experienced was in Belize, a British protectorate to which I was taken by the Sherwood Foresters. They asked me whether I would go over and do some watercolours and, as always when I got to these places, the commission expanded. I went to work for the Jebel Regiment in Oman and I finished up working for the Oman Gendarmerie, the Oman Artillery and pretty much every regiment in the Oman Army. When I went to Belize I also worked with the Air Force, who had Harriers out there, the Royal Navy, the British regiment stationed there and the Gurkhas – whoever was there.

It was particularly difficult in Belize. In most places, such as when I worked in Norway or went to Hong Kong, I could reckon on finding materials if I ran out of anything. When I went to Belize, however, I was told to take every single thing I needed because there was no way you could get any art materials unless you went to America. So I took all my materials and a stock of paper, because I knew I would get other commissions while I was out there. When we landed at Belize and got off the plane, it was sunny. The sergeant told me to leave my stuff on the tarmac and come and have a drink. Mindful of my materials, I suggested I should first take my kit into wherever I was staying. 'Oh no,' he said, 'don't worry about that.' We went over to the Mess and while we were having lunch there was a storm. The rain just bucketed out of the sky, and halfway through I realised that my kit was still out on the tarmac. I went to get it when the storm was over; everything was sodden. My portfolio, full of paper, was absolutely wet through. I had to spend the first couple of days drying the paper out, stretching it with gum strip and then drying it out flat. I vowed then that never again would I leave my kit unattended.

There were some wonderful things in Belize, however. I remember at weekends we used to go out to the cayes – long thin strips of sand, just off the coast. The officers would get a boat on a Sunday, take a picnic and do a bit of snorkelling. I'm not really much of a swimmer or a snorkeller, but even I couldn't resist it. I was snorkelling off one of these cayes and looking down at the completely clear seabed. Suddenly I saw this shark and thought, 'Oh, Lord! What do I do now?' I gradually flipped my flippers, trying not to make any excessive movement, and nervously swam my way back to the caye. As I got out I said to the officer, 'Oh God. I've just had a real fright. There was a big shark underneath me in the sea.' 'Oh, don't worry about that,' he said. 'It wouldn't have attacked you.' But I wasn't going to wait to find out. Yet even that day ended in magic. I remember the sun was setting as we travelled back to Belize in a motorboat.

Dolphins came and swam alongside the boat and bounced on the hull; it was glorious. That evening I thought how people would pay a fortune for that sort of thing, whereas I was actually getting paid to be there.

Not all experiences in Belize were so elevating. I remember being in a shower when we had come back from the jungle – not with Gurkhas this time. We were all in little shower cubicles, in the nude, when suddenly one of the officers entered with a jam jar. Inside was a tarantula. The officer held up this jar with its big hairy spider and asked, 'What will you all do now if I put this on the floor?' He gave me the fright of my life – you feel especially vulnerable naked in a shower, and if someone brings a tarantula in you nearly die of fright.

I travelled on commissions for the British Army for about ten years, between 1973 and 1983. Towards the end of my time I was asked to go to Canada, and this was one of the few times in my life that I missed a flight. I had been travelling somewhere else in the Far East and when I got back to London I only had a very short time before I turned around and hit the road again. The letter had said that my flight was at 09.00 hours on Friday, and because I was looking for time I willed myself into thinking that it was nine in the evening (21.00 hours), when I should have known full well that it was nine o'clock in the morning. When it came to about six in the evening I went to find the car to drive up to Brize Norton. Suddenly it dawned on me that I should have been getting the flight at 09.00 hours. I rushed back into the studio and rang Brize Norton. The person who answered the phone immediately said, 'Is that Mr Howard?' I said it was and he told me I had missed my flight that morning. I asked what I should do and he told me to come up to Brize Norton, sleep there overnight and go on the flight in the morning. I remember stopping at Greenland on the flight out. I have never been to such a desolate place in my life – arid, empty, cold and icy. It was absolutely terrible and I never wanted to go there again.

When we arrived in Canada we had to get to a place called Medicine Hat, about a hundred miles from where we had landed. In between there was nothing, just a straight road going on and on into infinity. The landscape itself was flat and barren, with about one tree, but the skies were absolutely incredible – the landscape was all in the sky.

When I got to Suffield, a British Army Training Unit, it proved to be a vast range where tanks and guns could be fired. I got to know the Canadian Brigadier who looked after the training area, and he was mad keen on wildlife. So when we weren't working he used to get me into his four-wheel drive and we would go out on the prairie, towards the Saskatchewan River. We stood and just watched the wildlife there – quite undisturbed, strangely enough, by all the noise and goings-on at the training area.

The trip to Canada was near the end of my travels with the British Army. I suppose I had been doing it for nearly ten years by then, and I was beginning to find it, in an odd sort of way, rather restricting. It had been a very good living and very exciting in terms of travelling experience. I could have written an entire book about things that had happened to me all over the world – India particularly, but also working with the Gurkhas and down in Brunei. Yet I was starting to feel the commissions were taking over my life. I was quite popular with the regiments, I suppose, and by about 1982 or 1983 I must have had work from practically every Mess in the British Army. But in the end I decided to give up all my commission work and depend solely on my gallery (I was still with the New Grafton Gallery), exhibiting at the Royal Academy and anything else to which I still belonged, such as the New English Art Club and the Royal Society of British Artists. I never do things by halves: when I gave up teaching, I gave it up completely, and when I gave up commission work for the Army, I cut this out completely too.

This was not a whim, though; I had good reasons for doing it. In 1983 Chrissie had at last come to live with me in England, so obviously I no longer wanted to be travelling all the time. I had also realised, of course, that she worried whenever I was in Northern Ireland, even though I tried to convince her that I was in no danger. Furthermore, while painting and drawing all over the world had been exciting and stimulating, working to sometimes repetitive commissions was, I felt, limiting my development as an artist. After ten years I knew it was time for a change.

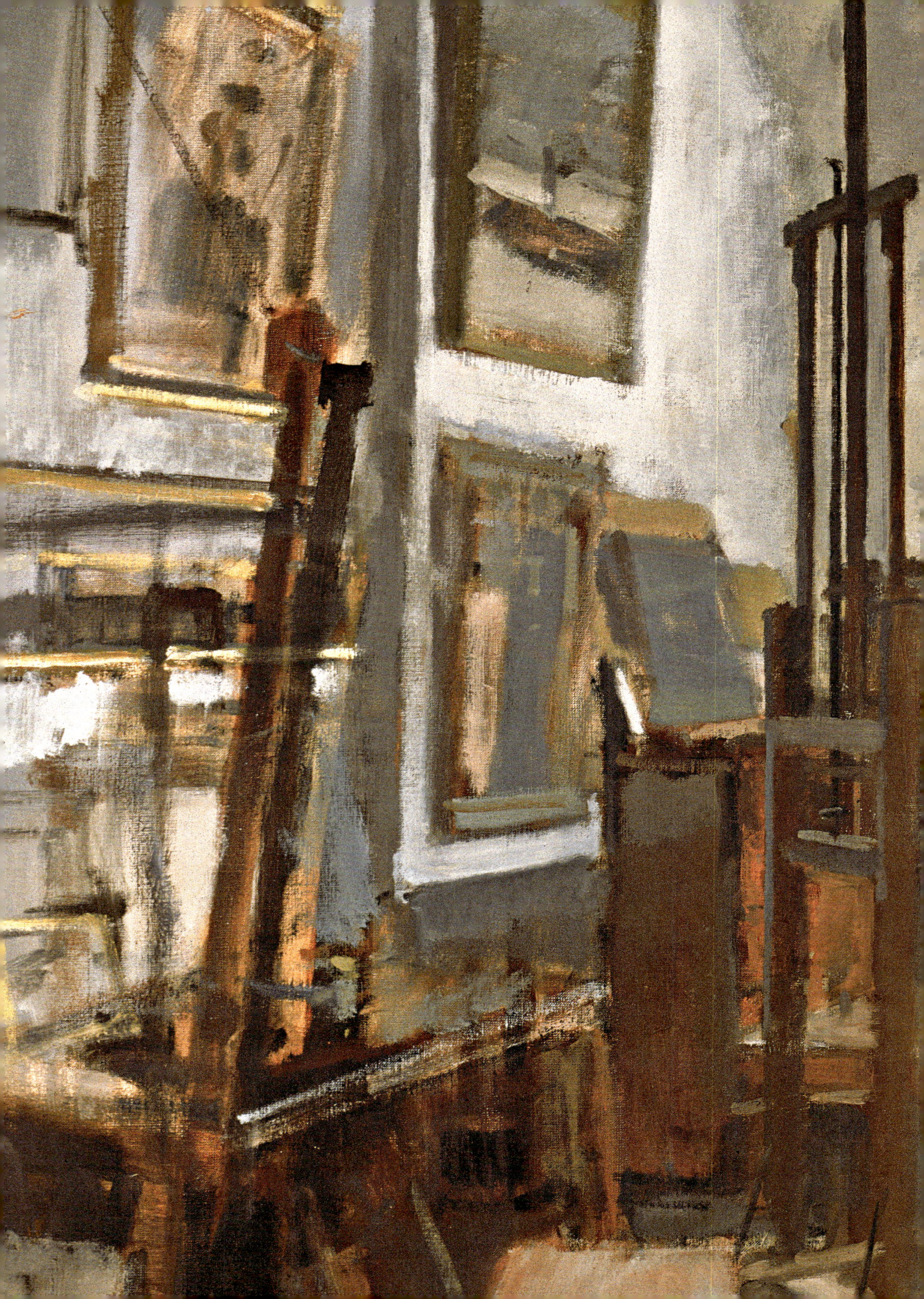

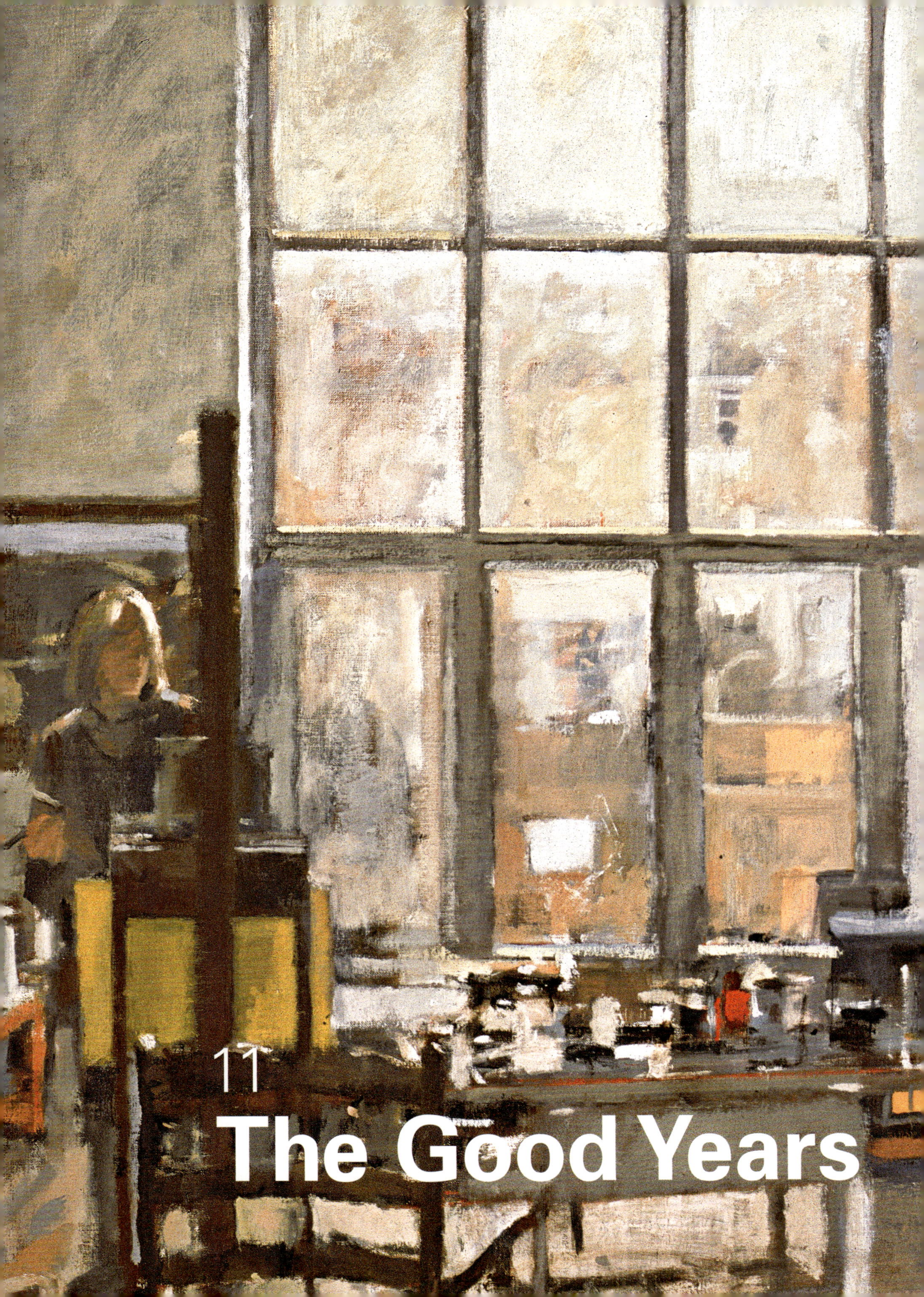

11

The Good Years

Saskia at St Clement's Studio, *c.* 1982
Oil on canvas,
122 × 102 cm

This is one of the first interiors I painted after buying St Clement's Hall and Studio.

Early in the 1980s, 22 years after we had first met in Florence, Chrissie finally came to live with me in London. It was a defining moment for me. I had stopped going to Northern Ireland, I was hardly doing commissions and my work reflected what I wanted to do. Above all, I was living with a woman who I had loved and wanted to be with, and our life was shaping up just as I had imagined it. I remember the long letter I had written to Chrissie after we met for the first time in Cologne. On my return to Florence I described to her how our future life would be. Of course it was all imagination, but in the end it had all worked out pretty much as I had described. By the time that Chrissie came to live with me we had our studio in London and a place in the country. I was earning enough from my paintings to give us a lifestyle where we could travel and do the things that we wanted to do. Life was good.

When Chrissie came to live with me I immediately wanted to marry her, but she preferred to wait. She explained that she had hurt Hartmut enough by leaving him and Germany, and that she would only marry me when – or if – he wanted a divorce in order to re-marry. We felt as married as two people could be, and as Chrissie didn't want another child the formalities didn't seem necessary. We were together, and at the beginning of the 1980s life seemed about as good as it could be.

There were some difficult aspects to surmount, of course. Chrissie's daughters, Babs and Tina, took their mother's decision to leave Germany in completely different ways. Babs, who was always very direct, simply said when Chrissie told her, 'Why didn't you do it years ago?' Tina, on the other hand, was very upset and cried a lot. I was working in Jersey that summer and Chrissie came to be with me there when she left Germany. Tina joined us from Sardinia, where she had been on a holiday, whereupon Chrissie took her for a walk and told her everything that had happened.

The strange thing is that the girls had no idea that there was anything wrong between their parents. Chrissie and Hartmut were both extremely civilised people and Chrissie couldn't stand any sort of tension or arguments. That was typical of the way Chrissie went on in life. She tended to be very direct, with no beating about the bush, but she didn't lose her temper or foster states of tension, such as I had experienced so often in my life. Chrissie was extremely sensitive in that way. Even if she was in a room with two other people who weren't relating very well to each other, she would have to leave the room.

We lived together for eleven years without having a row. When I say that 'we' never had a row, I did attack Chrissie on one occasion – verbally, I must add. I had been working in the studio that morning and had got into a terrible mess with the painting that I was doing. When Chrissie came in I must have said something aggressive to her and she didn't respond, but two evenings later she said to me,

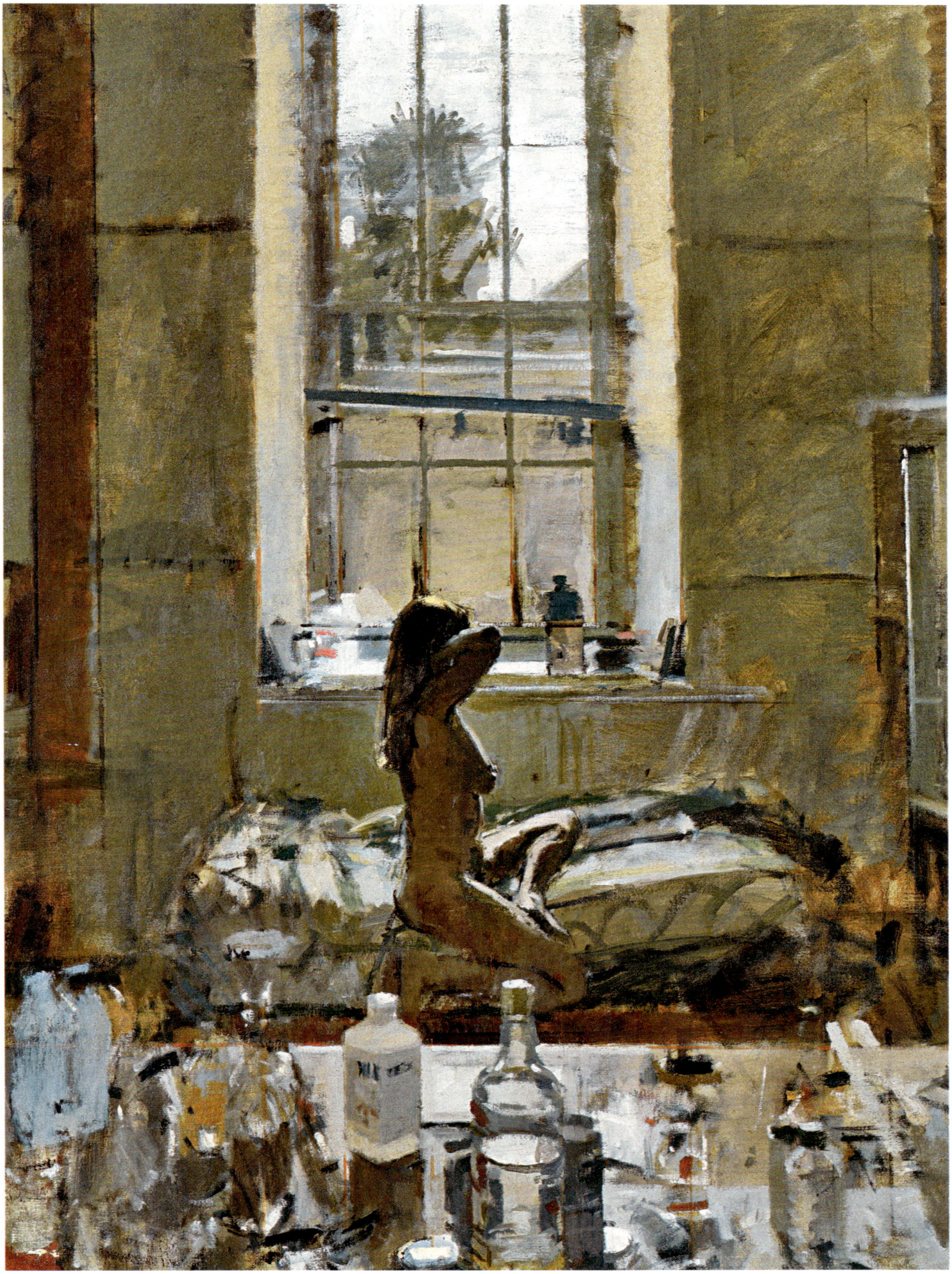

'Oh Ken, you shouldn't lose your temper with me like you did the other day in the studio; it doesn't belittle me, but it belittles you.' And she said it with such feeling, not wanting to see this man, who for some reason she loved, bringing himself down or belittling himself. I realised then that when we respond to somebody's belligerence, it does no one any good, and that it's much better if you treat it in a sort of Gandhi-esque way. Chrissie's words taught me a lesson that I never forgot, and I never lost my temper with her again.

It may seem strange that the girls had no concept of what was happening in the family. They saw me arriving and sometimes staying when I was in Cologne, and they knew well that in the summers Chrissie would sometimes go away working in Italy with Ken. Yet they didn't imagine for a minute that Chrissie and I were lovers, or that their parents' marriage had any problems. I thought that was rather wonderful. When Chrissie came to live with me they didn't hold it against me, and the girls and I have been firm friends ever since. I suppose it's easier being a kind of stepfather, because the girls could speak to me about their problems in a way that they probably wouldn't have to their father. Soon after Chrissie came to England, Tina was studying dress design in Paris and Babs had gone to a Rudolf Steiner school, where she was doing a course in eurythmics, a form of dance. They used to visit us in England and of course Chrissie could easily fly back to Germany if there was any sort of problem.

In 1982, the year after I gave up commissions, I won the Hunting Art Prize. It wasn't a vast amount of money in those days, but £5,000 was still a reasonable amount. I asked Chrissie what we should do with it and her reply was heartfelt. 'Let's do something special. Don't let's spend it on petrol and materials and things like that, let's do something special.' And so she suggested that we should go to India and have two or three months just painting. This did have a certain attraction for me because in those years India still had a vast and wonderful steam-railway network. I'd never really got my love of railways out of my system and the Indian Railways had real appeal. After Neasden and Cricklewood I'd worked a lot at Southall in west London, but by that time it was diesel, which wasn't as visually exciting as steam. Ever since I was a young man I'd dreamed of experiencing steam railways once again, in countries like South Africa or India, which still had such networks. So to me this was a great idea – and we could plan it for the right time of year, which for India means December, January and February.

Before I left England my decision to paint the Indian Railways received a couple of mentions in the *Daily Telegraph*'s Peterborough column, as well as in one or two other papers. Another fellow with a great interest in the subject read about me in the paper and invited me down to Brighton to see his collection of photographs of the Indian Railways. He showed me all his slides of these pristine railway trains. They were very beautiful, but not very visually stimulating in terms of a painting. I also found out before leaving England who the head of the Indian Railway was and got a letter of introduction. He turned out to be a charming man who gave me all the papers I needed to work. There was a lot of concern about security as it was a time of heightened tension between India and Pakistan, so I knew I would need permission to work at places like Jhansi and various other railway sidings. Armed with his papers, I thought that it would be all right to work wherever I wanted to.

By this time Johnny Cornell, my friend from Hong Kong, had become the Military Attaché in Delhi. Neither Chrissie or I knew very much about India and we realised that it was quite a complicated place to visit if you were completely green about the conditions, where to stay, what food to eat and so on. I got in touch with the Cornells, who had always said, 'Come to India and stay with us.' I asked if the offer was still open and they said yes. It was getting near to Christmas and Chrissie, as always, wanted to spend the holiday with Hartmut and the girls in Germany. Because Christmas was so special to her, she suggested that I should go ahead to India and she would join me there, flying directly from Germany after Christmas. So I flew out initially by myself and she came out to join me in January. I spent virtually three months in India and she spent six weeks. We had an absolutely wonderful time together.

It was getting close to Christmas when I finally got there. As soon as I arrived in India I found myself inundated with commissions again – maybe Johnny had told people I was coming, or my reputation as a military artist had gone before me. As Johnny was the Military Attaché I undertook commissions for certain regiments and for people who might help to give him an 'in' with the powers that be – those, in effect, that I felt that I should do. I remember one colonel who commanded a tank regiment down near Jhansi, in roughly the centre of India. It was a big railway town where they made the film *Bhowani Junction*. When I met this colonel he said to me, 'While you are in Jhansi, will you come and do a commission and paint my tanks?' I didn't particularly want to, but I thought that this would give me somewhere to stay while I was down there. He assured me that if I came I could be his guest in the Mess; everything would be supplied and arranged for me. As it was just before Christmas, Johnny and Caroline were going to a resort further south for a short holiday, so they offered to drop me off in Jhansi at this regiment's base. I went into the Mess and walked up to the bar. Indian Messes were still extremely English in those days – very proper and somehow more English than English ones, with paintings round the wall and beautiful furniture and officers in their finery. But

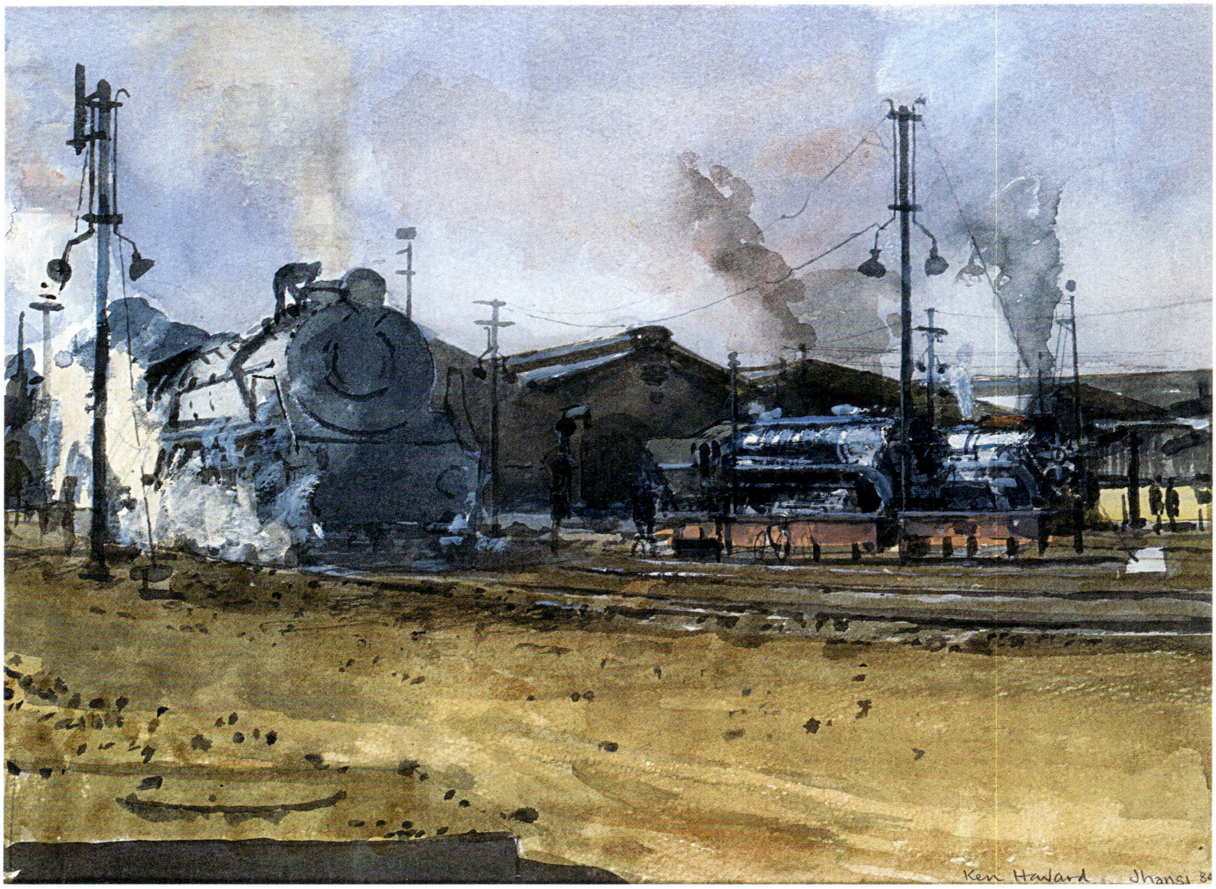

although this was certainly a rather splendid Mess, I suddenly registered that no one was expecting me. When I told the adjutant that the colonel was expecting me, he said that he knew nothing about me. I repeated that the colonel was expecting me, so the adjutant took me to this man who had asked me to come and paint this picture. It was as if he had never seen me in his life before.

The Indian Army was incredible at that time. When I got back to Delhi I learned that the tanks that this man had asked me to paint were in fact Russian. When the Ministry of Defence heard about this they were furious: no way was an English artist going to paint top-secret tanks. So the colonel decided simply to forget about it. He didn't tell me not to come because in his own mind he would forget that he had ever even invited me. So it was obvious that I wasn't going to be able to stay in the Mess. I was left on my own, extremely embarrassed, so I went to find a hotel to stay in and ended up in a rather grotty one near Jhansi.

The next day I went to the railway yard at Jhansi, which was amazing. Things seemed to be looking up and I started to draw the steam trains. They were slightly dirty – well, not dirty exactly, because the Indians kept their trains very well turned out, but there was smoke and steam and ash, and all the paraphernalia that you get round railway yards. I had been there about an hour when an officious little man came up and asked me what I was doing. I explained that I was drawing the trains

Jhansi Loco, 1984
Watercolour, 37.5 x 55 cm

When I originally worked in watercolour I kept to transparent thin colour. By the time I made this study I mixed Chinese white, gouache and pastel with the watercolour, my main influences being Turner and Hercules Brabazon Brabazon. Chrissie was completely uninhibited in her watercolour technique, and in that way she influenced me.

and that I had all this paperwork. 'Where's your passport?' he demanded, and because I had expected to stay with the regiment and be looked after, I hadn't brought it with me. As soon as I couldn't produce a passport he declared, 'I am arresting you as a spy.' I told him that it was ridiculous, but he marched me off the railway sidings and told me that he was taking me to the police station on the other side of town. By this time I was getting pretty furious and I refused. 'I am not walking to the other side of town,' I said. 'You'll have to get a taxi.' He insisted that I was going to walk, so I just sat down and said, 'I am not moving from here. If you want me to go to the police station, you will jolly well find me a car and get me there.' Eventually he did, then he duly marched me into the police station, where they started interrogating me. It went on and on, and in the end I got really angry. I started to pretend I was falling asleep so they nudged and poked me so that I would 'wake up' and they could ask me more questions. Of course, I was no more a spy than a fly. At the end of the day I said I wanted to know if there were any English officers in the town and they told me there weren't. I told them about people I knew at the Mess, but that didn't do any good either. In the evening they released me and said I had to be back at the police station in the morning to carry on with the interrogation. The following morning I got up, feeling pretty miserable, and lo and behold Johnny and Caroline appeared. They were going back to Delhi and had stopped by to see how I was. When they found I wasn't at the Mess they came to find me. I told them the whole sorry tale and of course Johnny immediately started to pull strings. He got hold of the Provost Marshall and eventually I was released with an apology. Thankfully I returned to Delhi. Incidents such as these really got me down to begin with, until I learned how to cope with them better.

I have to confess that India was probably the most disturbing place I've ever been to. After I had been there for two weeks by myself I was ready to pack up and jump on a plane back to England. If it hadn't been for the fact that Chrissie was looking forward to it so much, I would certainly have left India behind. I remember one day I was painting in Delhi, working on a watercolour of the Ministry of Defence, which was in a building designed by Edwin Lutyens in the middle of the city. It was an incredible morning – very hot and very humid, with quite amazing light. It was actually like looking at a Monet painting. Anyway, I was halfway through this watercolour when a policeman came up and said he was going to arrest me. I asked why and he replied, 'You're painting the Ministry of Defence, therefore you are a spy.' I did have my passport that time and in the end I convinced him that I really wasn't a foreign agent. But when I asked if I could finish my watercolour he said simply, 'No,' and that was that.

India was difficult for me technically as it was nearly impossible to work in the streets. A million people would gather round if I set up to work; crowds formed quickly as there were always lots of people with nothing better to do than stand around and watch. It's as if the people there don't really understand what you're doing, whereas in England, if you're working on the spot, people will come up and admire what you're doing, and maybe say a couple of words about it. People in India didn't seem to grasp the concept of outdoor painting – crowds just swarmed round you and blocked off whatever you were looking at. I normally tried to work up on roofs or on balconies or temple steps – anywhere where you could get above the crowd and enjoy a clear view.

On one occasion in the town I got so fed up with being crowded and unable to find any balcony or roof to work from that I went to the local police station. I said to the officer there, 'Look, I'm trying to draw out on the street. If you will give me a policeman to keep the crowds back, I will do your portrait.' He was delighted, of course, and I sat down and did him one of my line-drawing portraits. It was a dead likeness and he was thrilled. He gave me a policeman and we went out on the street together, but in the end it made no difference. The poor policeman was left fighting with the crowds as they were all insisting that they should see what I was doing – it was very edgy and almost became a riot.

I remember once getting onto a roof at Lucknow. I found a man who had control over this particular roof and gave him a small amount of money to access it – in India you can do anything if you give a tip. After I'd been up there a few minutes he told me that I had to leave – obviously he wanted some more money. But I was firm. 'No, I'm not leaving this roof until I've finished what I'm doing.' He started to get really annoyed but I wouldn't budge. I just said, 'If you want me off this roof, you will have to throw me off, I'm afraid.' And I stayed up there and carried on painting.

Everything about working in India seemed to me to be difficult – there were stomach bugs to contend with, the whole bureaucratic system was complicated in the extreme, and when you went out of Delhi and into the villages it was very primitive. I remember once going to a village to do some drawings. Caroline ran me out in her car and left me there, telling me that I could come back whenever I liked (there was a bus that went through that village that would bring me back into Delhi). It sounded fine.

When I got there I went to the edge of the village to draw a fantastic mosque that I could see. Of course the youths of the village came out and found me completely unique and amusing. Maybe they had never seen anyone actually painting on the spot before. I imagine that what I was doing seemed completely foreign to them, and the language I was using in the painting may have appeared very rough and unfinished in comparison to the style of art that they were used to. The children obviously didn't have very much to do in the village, so they decided to amuse themselves by annoying me – including grabbing my brushes and generally disturbing me.

I finally packed up, deciding that I should go across the fields and work in the landscape for a while, then come back to the village later on. The children followed me and after getting bored with trying to snatch things they decided to start throwing stones. Some of them hit me and I began to feel alarmed. I remembered the film *Suddenly Last Summer*, when a man gets waylaid on a Mediterranean island by a group of youngsters who eventually kill him. It was time to get out of there, so I ran into the village with these children following me, shouting and throwing stones. I saw the bus coming and when it stopped I tried to get on, but they caught hold of my drawing bag and tried to pull me back. It was a pretty frightening experience.

However, the Indian Railways were wonderfully exciting. This was around about the middle of the 1980s, when the railways still ran on steam. I always remember the first day I was there and I asked Caroline to take me down to Delhi Junction. She dropped me there and I went to a gate at the side of the big marshalling yard – I didn't bother to ask whether I could go in. For the first time since I was young I caught that particular smell – a mixture of steam and smoke and all the things associated with steam railways – and my whole youth flooded back to me. The engines themselves were magnificent, of course – they were like great animals, powerful and almost alive. They were far more exciting than the ones I had experienced in England as a boy on the Great Western or the London, Midland and Scottish Railway.

The series of watercolours I did of the Indian Railways at Jhansi, Delhi and elsewhere were a very exciting group of paintings. I also did a number of paintings in Lucknow and went and worked in Kashmir. At the end of the trip Caroline put on an exhibition of my work at the Military Attaché's house in Delhi. It was a large residence and the exhibition was very successful. We sold everything, except for the railway paintings that I refused to show. I wanted to take them back with me.

As well as the railway paintings there is one commission that stays vividly in my mind. There was a regiment called the Deccan Horse and they asked me to paint their former Lieutenant Colonel, who had become the Chief of Army Staff in India. His name was General Vaidya. When I first went to see him I explained that I would need about three or four sittings; it wasn't going to be a very big painting, I was

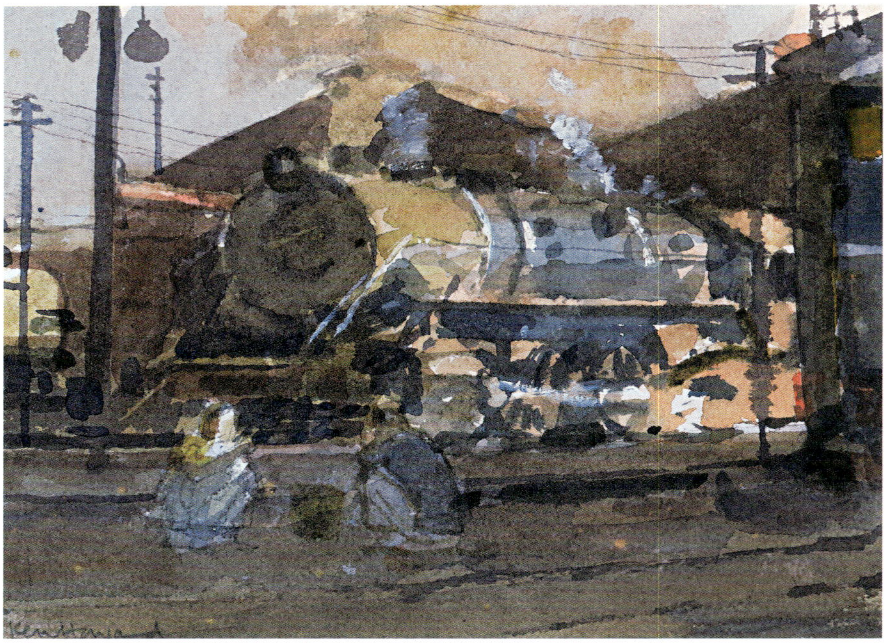

Jhansi Loco, 1984
Watercolour, 12.5 x 17.5 cm

This small watercolour was made in approximately fifteen minutes. I love to paint subjects that may disappear at any moment. It concentrates the mind, forces one to be selective and keeps a sense of excitement.

thinking 60 x 50 cm, but it had to show all his medals and decorations. We arranged a time for the first sitting, in his house, and I was driven over there. There was a guard on the gate because of Vaidya's position as Chief of Army Staff and he asked what we wanted. 'It's Mr Howard,' the driver explained. 'He has come to see General Vaidya.' The guard informed us that Vaidya was at the Ministry of Defence building. I said that he couldn't possibly be as I'd arranged a sitting for ten o'clock that morning. But the guard insisted he was at the Ministry of Defence. By this time I was getting really edgy in India and I didn't care that he was the Chief of Army Staff – Vaidya had let me down and made me waste the day. I was furious and I told the driver to take me to the Ministry of Defence.

When we got there I went straight in. I knew from Johnny how difficult it was to get into the inner sanctum; as Britain's Military Attaché, Johnny was always trying to see the General or somebody in the Ministry. But I was too angry to think about that and I just marched in, headed for the desk and said, 'I've come to see General Vaidya.' They directed me into a lift and we went up to the second floor. I found a door that led directly from the lift into his office and there, sitting behind his desk, was Vaidya. He looked up and said, 'Oh good lord, Mr Howard!' 'Yes, that's right, General Vaidya,' I replied. 'I've been so busy,' he explained, 'and I am so busy now that I just can't sit for you today. I am so sorry. Could you possibly do this commission from photographs?' 'No, General Vaidya, I couldn't,' I told him. 'Quite honestly, if your regiment wants this portrait you will have to give me these four sittings.' 'I always have Sundays off. Could you fit these sittings in on the next four Sundays?' Vaidya suggested. I assured him that I didn't mind when it was as long as I could have the sitting when I came.

So that was our arrangement, and I think he was rather amazed that I didn't just salute and agree to work from photographs. Anyway, I started going to his house every Sunday and having lunch there. Vaidya was charming and a wonderful man to paint: very good looking – dark, with silver beginning to show in his hair and a fine moustache. I got to know him and his family over the Sunday sessions, and the painting was successful and well received.

Some months after I returned to England I turned the radio on to hear the news headlines. The lead item that morning was the report that General Vaidya, Chief of Army Staff in India, had been assassinated by his Sikh guards. He was in charge of the Army and although I can't remember the exact details, his death was linked to Sikh anger over an attack on the Golden Temple at Amritsar, a major Sikh holy place. Vaidya had been assassinated as he was in charge of the Army; such events were later to claim Indira Ghandi's life as well and spark terrible violence across India. For me, his death was a personal grief. I had got to know this man and found him delightful, as was his charming wife and family.

Chrissie and I always travelled together very easily and the later stages of the trip were wonderful. In the day we were both happy to do our own thing and in the evening we ate together and enjoyed company. Kashmir, where we went some weeks after Chrissie arrived, was quite incredible. We stayed on a houseboat and because it was after Christmas it was bitterly cold. Snow lay by the big lake near the capital city, but visually it was quite wonderful. Like India, however, Kashmir proved

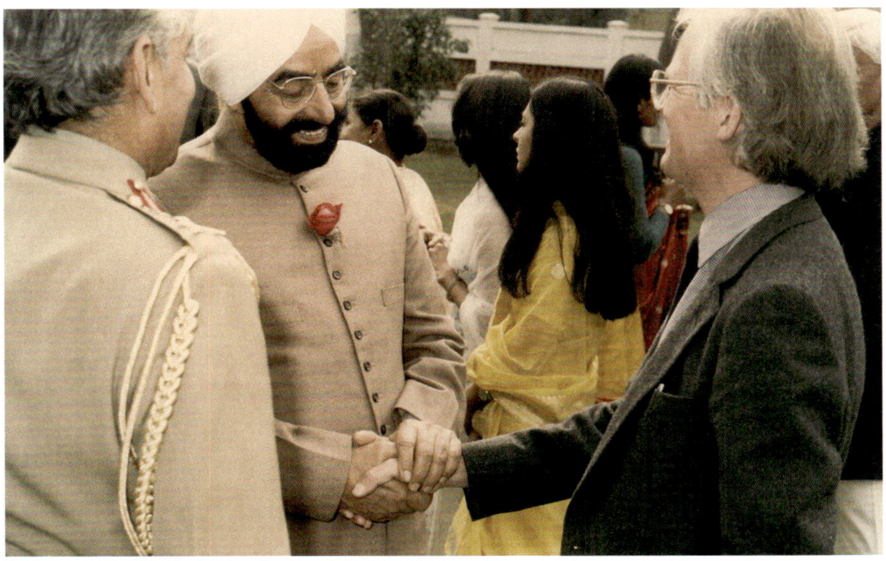

Meeting the President of India in 1984. General Vaidya, whose portrait I painted, is on the left.

a very frustrating place to work. There didn't seem to be many roofs or temples that I could work from, so we used to take a boat and go out into the middle of the lake to work from there. But as soon as the locals saw that we were out on a boat they piled into their own boats and came alongside us, trying to sell us cigarettes or whisky, so we still couldn't get any peace.

When we arrived in Kashmir and got off the plane we set off into town. Glancing out of the car window I thought it was very strange that all the women looked pregnant. They wore a heavy sort of kaftan that bulged at the front. It was only after a couple of days that I realised the bulge was due to the small container of charcoal they carried under their kaftans to keep themselves warm. Years later I had a similarly strange experience when I got off a plane in Yemen. Everyone seemed to have a swollen cheek and I thought, 'Good Lord, all these Yemenis' teeth must be in a dreadful state!' I only discovered a few days later that they used to chew a sort of vegetable to give themselves a high. This drug wasn't sold until midday, but by the afternoon everyone was chewing it.

Towards the end of our India trip we arranged for Chrissie's half-sister, Bibi, to fly down from Oslo with her husband, Haakon. The four of us had a few days together in Delhi, then went on to Nepal. Ever since I had trekked there with Colonel Duffell some years earlier I had promised Chrissie that I would take her on a trek. We hired some porters from a trekking company set up by a Gurkha Major in Kathmandu when he retired. He arranged everything for us, including hiring our porters and a Sherpa who spoke English to lead the party, and we literally had nothing to carry. This was a bonus as by this time I needed a stick. I wasn't as agile as Chrissie. Transport was provided to take us to Pokhara, which along with Kathmandu was one of the main cities in Nepal. We were dropped off near Pokhara and began to trek into the hills towards Gorkha, the old capital of Nepal. It was a very memorable experience.

The porters would walk ahead and set up a camp at lunchtime. In the afternoon we would walk on and again they would be ahead of us; by late afternoon they would have set up a camp for the evening. Chrissie and I would then go off and do some watercolours in the last couple of hours of light. Haakon and Bibi would read and generally relax round the camp, and in the evening when we got back Haakon and I would drink from large bottles of Scotch and brandy which we had brought with us – I have to admit that neither lasted very long and after about four days we had run out of both. The girls didn't drink, in fact, so it was only Haakon and me, but he was a very big man. He was the epitome of a Viking – around 6'3 in height, with a large frame. While not in any way fat, Haakon was very well built; he could absorb more alcohol than me, too, though I did soak up a fair amount!

Anyway, on about the fourth evening we got hold of a porter and asked if he could go to the local town and get us some of the local brew. I think it was called *rashti*, a form of Nepalese whisky. He returned with a bottle. He had obviously just taken the money, however, as when we came to have a drink after dinner we realised there was no alcohol in it at all. It was full of rather unpleasant-tasting water, probably from a local river, and we realised he must have pocketed the money, thinking we wouldn't know the difference. This was fairly unusual because the Nepalese were generally wonderful, very honest people.

At the end of the trip, on the very last night, I remember we all sat round the fire talking. By this time we had got to know our porters very well and we asked what they were going to do next. They said that after this trip they were going back to their village to go on building a school. They explained they were building it themselves as they didn't have the money for professional builders; I can't remember what they got paid per day by the trekking company, but it was a very small amount, perhaps around £4 a day, and all the money they earned went back to the village to help complete their school. All they needed to finish it was £25 to buy corrugated iron for the roof, which to us wasn't a huge sum. We promised to give them £12.50 each at the end of the trip so that they could finish the school's roof. Naturally they were delighted.

Around the same time I won a prize in an international art competition in Germany, organised by Sparkasse Bank. There was always a given subject, which that year was a 'figure in an interior'. A friend who ran a gallery in Basel sent me the form and suggested that I enter. I wrote back to him saying that I wasn't that sort of painter; I was sure that they would be looking for more innovative work than mine. I mentioned the competition to Chrissie and she reminded me that a very good friend of hers, Klaus Schwantes, lived in Karlsruhe. 'Why don't you send a painting down?' she asked. 'Klaus can give it in for you and there won't be any problem.' I said I thought that it would be a bit of a waste of time, but why not? I sorted out a 120 x 100 cm canvas. It was a big preparatory oil sketch – rather like Constable did before he painted a big canvas. I had done a large sketch for one of my studio interiors and although it was a very lively bit of painting, it was still figurative.

I packed the picture and put it on a train, contacted the organisers and let them know it was coming. Klaus picked it up and when it came to sending-in day he delivered it to Sparkasse Bank. I had forgotten about it completely when, a couple of months later, I received a phone call. A voice spoke in German, so I said,

'I suppose you want to speak to my wife.' 'Nein,' he said, 'I want to speak to Herr Howard.' His English was quite poor, so I called to Chrissie as I was sure it was her they really wanted to speak to. I wandered off and when she put the phone down she said, 'You have won the critics' prize in Karlsruhe and they want to fly you out next week for the prize-giving.' I was astonished. I went the following week for the prize-giving and I saw this quite selective exhibition of pictures from all over Europe and Russia. The strange thing was that mine was the most figurative painting in the exhibition. Many of the others were abstract or Tachist; they referred to a figure, but were not representational. As mine was the only truly representational painting in the exhibition, it looked incredibly original and strikingly different from everything else; that must have been why the critics gave me the prize. I'm sure it wouldn't have happened in England, but in Germany my picture did look quite original.

After three months in India I returned to London with Chrissie early in 1984. I had spent all the money I had won in the Hunting Prize and a tense time was approaching. Every year in the spring I would have a crisis – it had gone on for years. It was all to do with sending work in to the Royal Academy Summer Exhibition, something hugely important to me. I was obsessed with the idea of trying to get elected to the Academy for a few reasons. Several of my good friends were in the Royal Academy and I wanted to join them. I also realised that the title RA would give people who liked my pictures the confidence to buy them. People often admire pictures, but aren't sure that they are worth the prices or doubt whether their opinion is right. I felt that the stamp of being an RA would help to get over these sorts of problems.

Every spring I would prepare my three best pictures to send to the Royal Academy. I would work on them between Christmas and spring, during which time they would totally obsess me – I even dreamt about them. Often I would be dissatisfied with them and Chrissie would find this quite funny because she did not care about belonging to the Royal Academy or similar places. 'Oh, Ken,' she would sigh, 'I wish the RA would elect you and then you wouldn't go through this pain every springtime.' (When I was elected to the RA I still went on worrying about the pictures I sent in. I realised that I would be hung alongside my fellow painters, to be judged against their work, so I always wanted my work to stand up to that quality.)

By 1984 I had been exhibiting there for 32 years, between the ages of 18 and 50. Election was something that I wanted all my life, ever since Bob Whitmore, my art master, had told me that if I wanted to earn my living painting, I needed to become a Royal Academician. I suppose it was always niggling at the back of my mind, and as the years passed I got to know friends who were in the Academy, such as Bernard Dunstan and John Ward, people that I really loved dearly. I very much wanted to join the same club, but it had always eluded me. Every year when the elections came up I naturally wondered whether I might be elected this year, but never was. I stayed on the candidate list, however; every five years you come off, but if enough Academicians want you to stay on the list, you get put straight back on. I had been put back on it three times.

I will always remember the day in 1984 when I was finally elected a Royal Academician. The phone rang and it was Bernard Dunstan, who'd just been to the General Assembly. New members are elected to the Academy when an existing member dies; in those days you were first elected as an Associate. Gradually you went up the list. As roughly two or three people tended to die each year, or became Senior Academicians, you could expect to become a Royal Academician after about ten years. Originally, when the Academy started, some people stayed as Associates for ever, never being voted up to full members, but by the time I became a member it had become a natural progression – the artist who had been an Associate longest took the next vacant place.

Bernard rang me and told me that I had been elected. It was a fantastic feeling after all those years of exhibiting – sixteen of which I had been a candidate. It certainly shaped my future. Bob had been right: being an RA was to make all the difference to the possibility of earning a living without teaching or commissions. My time at the Academy has been great – I'm a natural 'belonger' to such things.

I remember a very funny story surrounding my election. For years I had been painting for the City companies – commissions that had come through the RA, funnily enough. By that time the RA was beginning to move away from painters who did typical traditional commission work, but I was happy to work for the Drapers' Company and the Haberdashers' Company, along with various financial houses. Anyway, a lot of this work had come through Sir Hugh Casson, who was President of the RA at the time and had been for a number of years. When I saw him at exhibitions he would always nod and say, 'Hello, how are you?' 'Very well,' I'd reply, and doff my hat with respect as he was President of the Royal Academy and I wanted to become a member. When I was elected I got a letter from Sir Hugh. Typical of him, it just read, 'Dear Ken, Hip hip ARA! Good to have you aboard!' I remember thinking, 'How very nice!' and the next evening I had to go to my first banquet as a member. When you arrive your name is called out as you go forward, but Hugh was busy talking to the previous guests. When I got up to him I said,

'Thank you very much for your letter, Sir Hugh.' 'Oh, oh,' he said, 'Yes, yes. You read it all right?' I said that I had and thanked him again. 'Oh, good,' he said, and we went on in to dinner. During the drinks before, whenever I caught his eye or he caught mine, he had a sort of quizzical expression on his face.

Anyway, I went off to India the following day for about six weeks to work. When I was in Delhi, where I was going to have an exhibition, Sir Hugh came to give a lecture and I thought I would go along and listen to him. When I walked into the building he said, 'Good Lord, what are you doing here?' I explained that I was working in India and was going to have a show. 'Well, it's nice of you to come to my lecture,' said Sir Hugh. I told him the pleasure was all mine, and when the lecture was over he came up and asked me how I thought it had gone. 'Brilliant as always,' I said, quite truthfully as he was a remarkable speaker. 'What are you doing now?' he asked, so I said that I was preparing for my show, due to open in a fortnight. Sir Hugh then said that he had a couple of other lectures to do in India, and we went our separate ways.

There was a big opening at the Royal Academy when I got back to London. Academicians were expected to attend such things and, being a new boy, I thought I'd better. Along I went and there, when I walked in, was Sir Hugh. 'Good Lord,' he exclaimed. 'Back from India then?' 'Yes,' I said, and he asked me how I'd got on. I told him that the show had gone very well and asked after his lectures. 'Oh, they went very well,' he said, and we sat and talked for a few minutes. Then I said, 'Well, I suppose we should go and do our duty,' by which I meant mixing with everybody and talking. 'Yes, good idea,' he said, then, as we turned to separate, he suddenly turned to me. 'By the way, when you were in India, you didn't meet a fellow called Ken Howard by any chance?' I just didn't know what to say – all those years we had met and chatted to one another and he'd never had the nerve to ask who I was. I understand that completely. When I go to exhibitions, I find there are people I've been seeing for years. At the beginning I never made a note of their names, and then you just become too embarrassed to ask who they are after about ten years of passing the time and chatting.

I always encouraged Chrissie to send work to the RA and I well remember the first year when she sent in one of her rather dark oil-painting still-lifes. It was hung in Gallery I, which in those days was *the* gallery to be hung in. There were always several RAs in that gallery, as well as the pick of the non-members' work. And the first year Chrissie sent in, her painting was hung in that room. I had been sending in for nearly 30 years and in all that time I had only once had a picture in Gallery I.

There was never any jealousy or rivalry between Chrissie and me. She was happy for everything that happened to me and I was happy for everything that happened to her. Deep down inside I knew that she was a much finer artist than I could ever be. Maybe that seems a silly thing to say – how can you judge painting? It's not a simple formula: two and two don't make four. Yet if you live with somebody and see the way they feel and think, and everything about them, you can come to an objective view of the quality of the person and his or her work. I always knew this and I told friends that Chrissie was a much finer painter – I sometimes used the word 'better', which is silly because one painter is not 'better' than another. You can't judge art in that way, to calculate that Piero della Francesca was a better painter than Picasso, or that Velázquez was a better painter than Monet, for example. It's a completely impossible thing to do, but I had an enormous admiration for the work Chrissie did. As with Annie and her dress design, I was convinced that one day Chrissie would fulfil her enormous potential – it was only a question of time before she would come fully into her own. As I said, life in the 1980s was as good as it could get. I was really happy. I was content with life – despite the struggles with work and the occasional dissatisfaction with what I was doing.

When you are young you imagine that you could be the next Goya or Velázquez or the next Rembrandt – these are the things that keep you going, ridiculous as they are. This is what gives you the energy to work when nobody is interested in what you are doing, maybe when you are not doing particularly well at art school. You still have to believe in yourself. And Chrissie said, 'but eventually you have to see where you stand in the total picture'. She said it quite simply and directly, not even very critically, but very, very truthfully. She never praised pictures unless she really liked them. There was no easy, 'I like that' or 'that's good' unless she really believed it. She would very often rather say nothing than be critical, but every now and again she would say, 'You know, Ken, that's a really good picture,' and you then knew that it was.

I remember once I was painting in the studio and was in a terrible mess. I was painting a girl called Lorraine and I thought the picture was the absolute end. When Lorraine had left Chrissie asked how the morning had gone. 'Absolutely dreadful,' I told her, and she came into the studio. When she saw what I was doing she said, 'That's one of the best paintings you've ever done!' Rather ungraciously I retorted, 'Oh, you're just trying to cheer me up,' even though I knew Chrissie never, ever did such a thing. 'Turn it around to the wall and don't look at it for two or three days,' she suggested. 'Then turn it back and if you want to go on with it, do so. But it's done and in three days' time you will see that it's done.' And she was right. I turned it round to the wall and then, three days later, I turned it back again. Sure enough, it was one of my better pictures.

Funnily enough, I frequently stay with some very close friends who live on Dartmoor, and they still have that picture . Whenever I see it I remember Chrissie's words, and realise how right she was. I really think that she was an exceptional painter.

Chrissie and I were privileged to have a wonderful circle of friends. Many of them were painters; some of them, such as Bernard Dunstan, Diana Armfield and Fred Cuming, were fellow Academicians. Others came from elsewhere in the arts: the opera singer John Tomlinson was a very close friend. One day I got a letter from another friend in Switzerland who was a great admirer of John's and also liked my work very much. He wrote and said he wanted to give John one of my paintings as a very special present. Could John come to the studio and choose one and then he, Werner, would pay for it? John eventually arrived at the studio, but during the course of the evening we both decided that Werner couldn't really afford to give John one of my pictures, so we made out that he wasn't attracted to any of them. John and I became good friends, and he and Chrissie had a particular empathy. I think in a sense he and Chrissie were closer, possibly because their characters were more alike.

I think the first time that we heard John perform was at the Coliseum in London, where he was singing Mephistopheles in *Faust*. He gave a wonderful performance and at the end the audience were shouting their 'bravos'. We had agreed to have dinner afterwards, and ten minutes later we met this man at the stage door who wasn't that different from Chrissie and me. John had a wonderful wife, Moya, and three children. His daughter wasn't very well at the time and he and Chrissie discussed children and families for the whole of dinner, while I sat there feeling a little left out.

The 1980s were not just a happy decade for me and Chrissie; they were a boom time in the art market. Margaret Thatcher and Nigel Lawson had put money into the pockets of the wealthy and the art market flourished as a result. It was a very good time because, no matter in what style you painted, the fact that the market wasn't controlled by any government body or the Arts Council meant that it was up to the individual to decide what sort of paintings he or she wanted to buy or support. If people loved abstract painting, they bought it. If they loved figurative painting, they chose that instead. Fortunately I never had any particular problem selling my paintings, maybe because people react to my work immediately; it seems to communicate with them as it isn't excessively complicated or ambiguous.

When the art market took off in the mid-'80s, I was poised to enjoy one of the most prosperous times in my life. It was quite strange really, because for the first time I realised that I was earning as much as a captain of industry – which is no longer the case, I hasten to add. Today, captains of industry in the City obviously earn vastly more than any artist, even the most successful. But in the 1980s, if you were doing reasonably well, you could earn an income equal to the top incomes in the country.

I was still with David Wolfers at the New Grafton Gallery. I had been there since 1971, had many shows and was becoming his longest-standing artist. When David left Hay Hill he went into Bond Street, in a gallery above Agnew's, then he decided to set up a smaller gallery in Barnes, where he lived. He was getting older and didn't want to come into town every day, preferring to work nearer to home.

When David went out to Barnes he asked me to go with him. I said I would – I felt I owed it to David as he had started me off. He had taken me on when he was earning very little from what I painted, but he had some good artists, such as Carel Weight and people like that. What he earned from them sustained him, so that he was able to support young artists who weren't necessarily earning him any money. I think this pattern is the ideal way for galleries to function, although unfortunately I don't think all galleries do. Another unfortunate thing is that artists often get picked off by more senior galleries when they become successful. David would often build people up, only to have Agnew's or one of those galleries in town come along and encourage the artist to join them instead. I had one or two such approaches myself, but I was very happy being with David, particularly when he was in town. When he moved to Barnes I told him that I would go with him, but if I was offered a show in central London I would do that as well. David agreed that was fair enough, as long as I kept doing my bi-annual show with him.

David didn't do a lot of business between shows, and the bi-annual show was the only money I made from the gallery. By this time he was selling me quite well, however, and my show gave me a substantial income, along with what I sold at the Academy or the New English. Dealers were beginning to come to the studio and they didn't take work on sale or return – they actually bought it. As I didn't have a contract with David, I could do this. My only obligation to David was to have a good show for him every two years. At Christmas he had a mixed show and I would let him have a couple of things, then in the summer he had another mixed show and I would do the same. But I was free to function with other people, and this I did.

The most important dealer at this time was Manya Igel. She originally wrote to me and asked if she could buy some work and I replied that unfortunately I was over-committed. During the following year I kept getting sales slips from open

Oriel Autumn, *c.* 1985
Oil on canvas, 120 x 100 cm

If I had to paint one subject all my life it would be my studio at Oriel. Every year each season is different. So is every week, day, hour, even each minute. It never repeats itself or bores me – it is continually fascinating.

exhibitions with Manya's name on them. After that, of course, I invited her to the studio and the outcome was that every year for the next ten years Manya bought enough work between exhibitions to give me a steady income. At that time the form was for dealers to take work on sale or return, but Manya was the first dealer to pay a cheque upfront. We became good friends, but when I went to Richard Green it was an exclusive arrangement, so I couldn't let Manya have any more work. For some time our relationship was strained, but time has healed it, thank goodness.

About the time that David moved to Barnes, I was asked to do a commission for a man called Lord White. I was beginning to get a bit of a reputation on the strength of my studio paintings and I suppose he knew me for these. Gordon White – I don't think he was Lord White at that stage – was part of a business called the Hanson Trust. He and his business partner, James Hanson, made a lot of money buying up companies, then selling off the bits that weren't profitable and keeping those that were. They were a real power in the business world in the 1980s.

Gordon White had just moved into a house in Tite Street; it had originally belonged to Sargent and was next door to the studio that Sargent had used. Being Gordon White, he went to the National Gallery and asked their advice on who might do him a painting of his house as it had been in Sargent's time. The National Gallery informed me of this and I was approached. 'Gordon White is quite a collector of pictures,' I thought, 'and it isn't too onerous a task to do another studio interior – even one that is, in effect, a historical reconstruction.' So I agreed, but only as long as it was a small-scale work. White wanted a large canvas, but I told him I would do one at 60 x 50 cm.

When the painting was complete White sent his dealer, Peter Johnson, to see me. He had a gallery opposite the Carlton Tower called Oscar and Peter Johnson. His father had been Oscar Johnson and after he died Peter had continued to run the gallery. He used to sell a lot of work to Hanson and White. Peter rang me up and explained that Gordon White had asked him to come along and see the commission and confirm that it was all right. I admit I felt slightly miffed because I felt it was a commission – whether it was all right or not, you've got it.

Anyway, Peter came to the studio in South Bolton Gardens as he only lived round the corner in The Little Boltons at that time. He walked into the studio where I had been doing a painting of Marika, a standing nude, earlier that day. The painting was still on the easel and he saw it as he entered. 'Oh, I like that,' he said. 'Can I buy it?' I said, 'Sure', and he looked on the wall where there was a beach piece. 'And I like that. Can I buy that as well?' I agreed, thinking that this was going all right. Then he

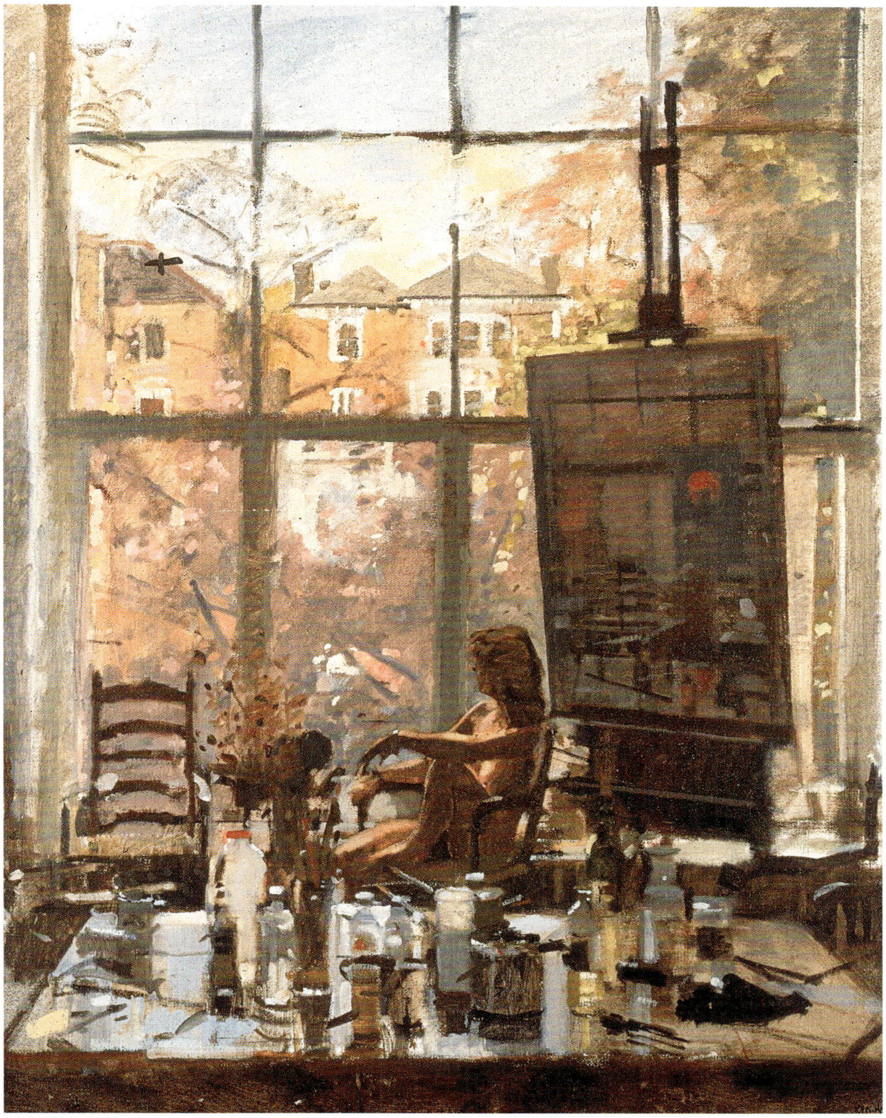

said, 'I'd better look at the commission,' so I showed it to him and he said it was fine. He looked at some more work and then he went. The following week he rang to say that Gordon White had liked the commission as well and he had suggested that Peter should give me a one-man exhibition. As I had agreed with David Wolfers that I would show in town if I was approached (I wasn't particularly looking for another gallery to put on a show as I had enough on my plate with David, the Academy and the dealers), I said that I would do it. I told David, who immediately said that he would give me a show every year if I would just show with him. Peter responded to this by saying that he would also give me a show every year if I left David Wolfers. But I said no to both of them and stayed with David. I did a show with him every two years and I did a show with Peter Johnson in the intervening years. This worked well in the '80s; it was the first time that I had ever had a show that sold out completely at the private view.

It was a crazy time. Galleries were springing up outside London as well, and they were also asking for shows – it seemed as if once again I had fallen on my feet at the right time. Just as I decided finally that I would live by painting, along came this period when the art market really took off. In addition to the shows I did every other year with Peter and David, Peter put on a show of my watercolours every Christmas, which also sold very well. A gallery in Burford called the Sinfield Gallery also started giving me shows outside London. All of a sudden, the fact that I had given up my regular income when I had stopped doing the commission work for the Army had been taken care of through this big demand in the art market.

Inevitably the market turned downwards in the late '80s and early '90s. It turned right down, in fact, and there were terrible stories in the papers about art dealers committing suicide and everyone going broke. Just as the press had built the market up, they knocked it right down when it turned. Funnily enough, I've always managed to survive these things somehow. I think it is partly because I've never charged excessively for my work, even when the market went silly in the middle of the 1980s, when people said the work of anyone selling out exhibitions must be too cheap and I should put my prices up. But I resisted.

Racing Dinghies, Marazion, 1986
Oil on board, 15 x 22.5 cm

I was on my way home at the end of a long day's painting when I saw dinghies coming across Mounts Bay near Penzance. I immediately realised how exciting it would be when they hit the beach and set up my paints. I made this, one of my favourite studies of light, in approximately ten minutes.

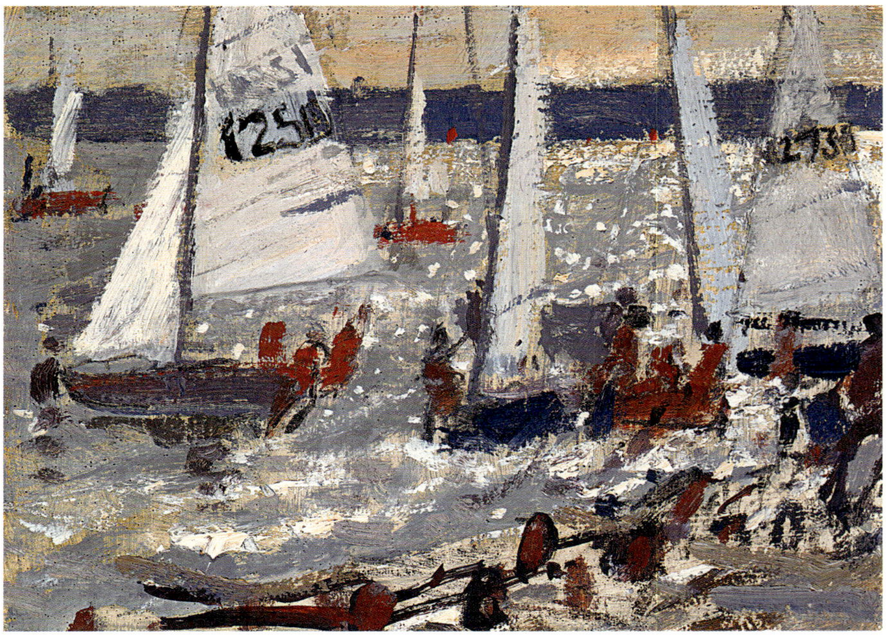

They were my prices. I put them up a little bit each year and in that way I kept my market together. In contrast, a lot of artists put their prices up dramatically in that period, and when the bottom dropped out of the market they couldn't reduce them again. If people had bought at one figure and then seen prices on new work go down, the bottom would obviously fall out of the market. Even when the market turned down my prices still seemed to be quite reasonable, and so I managed to keep on selling work.

At this time I was getting four figures for some of the larger canvases. Even the small ones were going for several hundred pounds, which was quite good, and because I was very productive, working six days a week, my output was quite considerable. A lot of people have told me that I should reduce my output because then my prices could go up and people would value the work more. But I always cite artists such as Turner and Monet – not that I am comparing myself with them! However, both of those men had enormous outputs and it certainly did not affect their markets. I think it is wrong to try and manipulate anything. You can only do what you do, in the way that you do it; if you do produce a lot of work, fair enough. There was no way I was going to stop painting because I was producing too much work. I wouldn't hoard work under the bed and save it for my old age, because for me part of the process ends with exhibiting the work and hanging it on somebody's wall.

Anyway, in the mid-1980s my work in the Academy was beginning to sell very well. When I started exhibiting at the Academy I didn't expect to sell, but my sales took off at this time and they became a regular part of my income.

Strangely enough, I have now had something like 30 exhibitions in London and many more outside the capital, as well as in places like South Africa and America. Yet I have never, ever had a proper review in a national paper. I've had reviews on some things, for example my work at the Academy or for the New English, but I have never received an actual review of a one-man exhibition – and it seems to have made no difference whatsoever. I began to get to the stage when I thought it was better that I didn't have reviews because a bad one might frighten away my patrons, the people who did want my pictures.

In fact, that isn't likely to happen, as whenever I do get reviews for work in the Academy they are invariably bad. Certain critics, such as Richard Dorment in the *Daily Telegraph* and William Feaver in the *Observer*, really did dislike my work and gave me terrible reviews. I remember Feaver once wrote a piece in the *Observer* in which he said that I was more or less the epitome of everything that was wrong with the Royal Academy (he wasn't particularly an admirer of the Academy in any case).

San Marco Morning, 1986
Watercolour, 27.5 x 22.5 cm

The limpid light in Venice is ideal for watercolour, as Turner proved to us so often in his wonderful evocations of the city. This transparent sketch, made early one summer morning in San Marco, was the first of hundreds of watercolours that I made from this one spot. When critics say that Venice has been overdone it shows their lack of understanding of the subject. It is like saying the human figure or a tree has been overdone. Venice is organic and has a life which constantly renews itself.

He picked my six pictures in the Summer Exhibition that year and rubbished them, to the extent that letters of protest appeared in the paper the following week, saying that what Feaver had said was quite wrong. Yet the year that he completely rubbished me I trebled my income, again showing that critics make very little difference. I find that if I get an editorial piece, which happens to me quite often – either an article about the studio or travel or a piece in the *Daily Telegraph*'s Peterborough column, or something along those lines – then that is quite valuable because it makes people conscious of me and my work. There is a saying that no publicity is bad publicity, and I think that is probably true.

Having said that, bad criticism does get to you, and it does hurt. It's as if someone says that your children are ugly, and it's no good responding that you don't care what people say because you do care – you want people to say good things. With a painter it is less crucial than with a performer, I think. I once asked John Tomlinson about his attitude to reviews and he told me that he never read them until the end of the production. I can understand that completely; your task is to interpret a part in a particular way and if a critic were to comment that you were doing this or that wrongly I suppose you could be affected by that the next time you went on stage. As a painter you have completed the work by then and it is on the wall. Possibly it may affect your next batch of work, although I personally don't think it does. I just carry on painting the way I want to paint, regardless of whether the critics like it or not. I have had one or two good reviews from critics of the exhibitions in the Academy – fortunately at one stage Brian Sewell, a fairly tough critic, did seem to approve of what I did when he first did crits of the Academy, and he has continued to do so in more recent years. At other times I confess that he has gone for the jugular and it is no good denying it, it does hurt. Bad reviews do affect you, so in many ways it's probably better not to read them.

I remember one day I was travelling by Underground to the Academy for the private view which started at ten o'clock. I opened the *Daily Telegraph* and Richard Dorment had reviewed the show; he had hit me quite hard, with throwaway remarks and so forth. 'Oh Lord, that's done for me this year!' I thought. 'Nobody who reads that paper is going to consider buying any of my pictures.' I arrived at the Academy at about quarter past ten and looked on the board which indicates what has sold and what has not. To my amazement I observed that all my six pictures had gone in the first fifteen minutes. Somebody rushed up to me and said, 'I've been wanting one of your pictures for years and finally today I have managed to get one.' I couldn't help but ask if he had by any chance read the *Telegraph* that morning. He said, 'Oh yes, yes, I have read that. What a lot of rubbish that man writes. I shall write

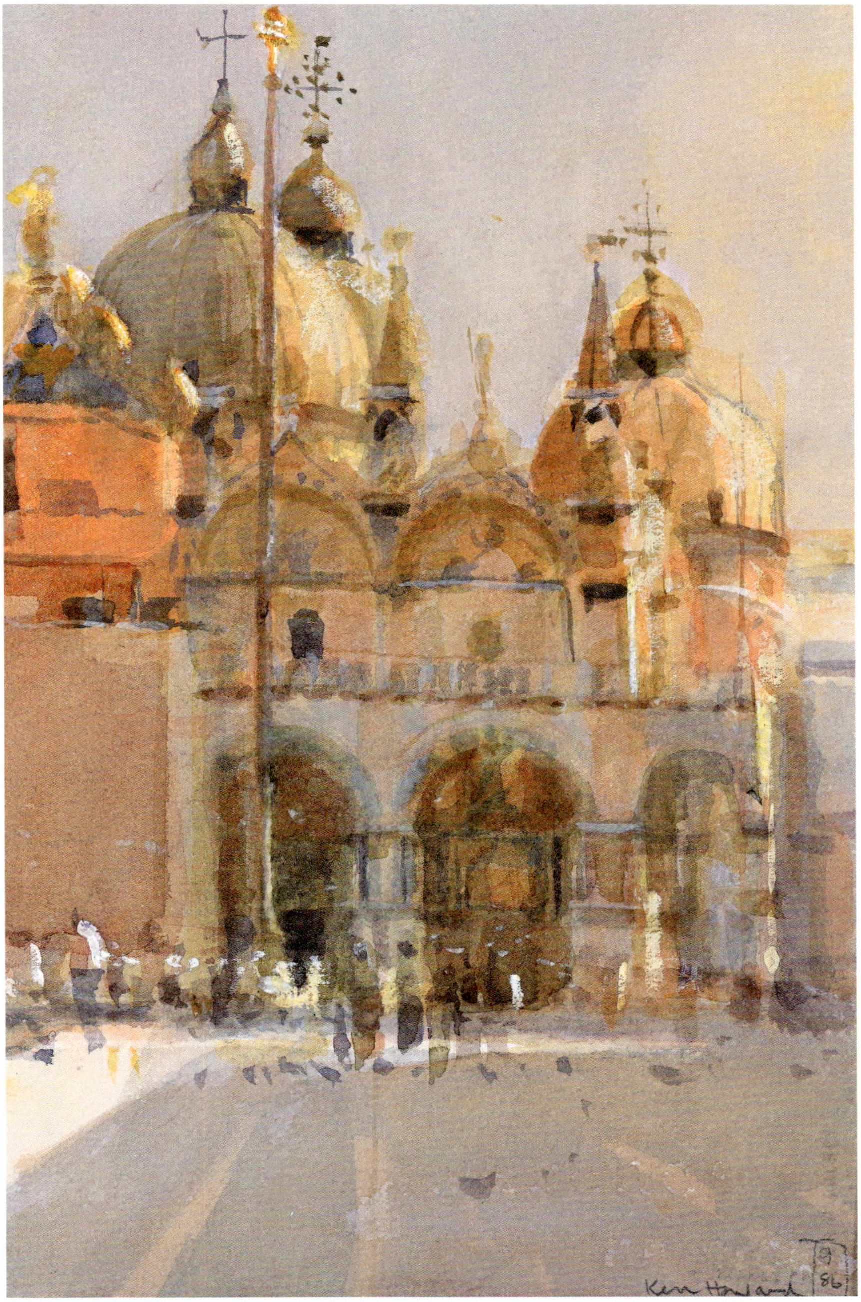

a letter and object to what he said.' So in the end people do not buy pictures because a critic says they're great (unless they're buying them for investment, I suppose, which I don't approve of anyway); they're buying them really because they love them and want to live with them, and they're not influenced by what the critics say.

I remember once there was an exhibition at David Wolfers's gallery by an artist called Dick Lee. He's sadly no longer alive, but I've probably now got half a dozen of his paintings which I have bought over the years. He had a show at the New Grafton and got a wonderful rave review from the critic of the *Daily Telegraph*. This journalist used to write very considered reviews of figurative painting and he ended the piece by saying that anyone with some spare money should go along and buy one of Lee's pictures. In fact I think I'm right in saying that after that review no more of Lee's pictures sold – the exact opposite of what you'd expect.

I stayed with Peter Johnson for about six years, I suppose. I had three one-man shows with him and then the shows at Christmas, but in the end I felt it was all getting too much. I decided just to stay with David and give up showing with Peter. I didn't feel that I needed to be in town because David had built a good business in Barnes; he had taken a lot of his clientele with him and it was in many ways a good spot. Barnes is, of course, on the west side of London, and a lot of the art-buying public come from places like Richmond, Twickenham, Sheen and Wimbledon. They were quite happy not to have to go into London for private views. In fact, in the last show that I did with David Wolfers, in 2000, just a little time before he died, we had our first sell-out at a private view in Barnes. David told me that it was the first time that he had ever sold out an exhibition, and particularly at the private view. It was in a way the perfect finale to my 30 years with David.

After that show people had again been saying that I should be back in Bond Street – it wasn't enough just to be out in Barnes. So when Richard Green offered me a show I decided to do one; he had not requested exclusivity, of course, as this was the first show. So although David had said that he would prefer me to show only with him, he didn't object to my show with Richard Green. After the first show Richard Green said that he wanted me to go exclusively with him; and by that time, unfortunately, David had died. So I was saved having to make the choice between them. Had I had to do so I would have told Richard, 'Well, David Wolfers is now well into his eighties. As long as he keeps the gallery, I must still be able to do one show with him every two years, and it will probably be only one more show.' In the event, however, I didn't have to do that. For the first time in my life I chose to go exclusively with one gallery, and in a way it was right. By now I was in my late sixties, approaching my seventies, and I wanted a simpler life really.

During the 1980s Chrissie and I were both working very hard. We both loved our work, our life and each other, and it really was a golden time. Not that this was necessarily the thing to bring out the best work. Sometimes one needs the dark underside: a bit of pain or some difficulty. Chrissie had been very good for my work, however. I remember on one occasion, when I had been working on a canvas for about two months, she challenged me, 'But Ken, why do you keep on re-drawing it? You draw well, and when you start a picture it has always got some life and vitality about it, but sometimes you go on for far too long.'

Chrissie really taught me something: that a painting is done when it gives you back the sensation you had when you first got the idea or the subject. Once you have captured that sensation in the painting, as it were, then it's finished, and completion has nothing to do with putting fingernails on or dotting the 'i's or crossing the 't's.

By this time Chrissie was being noticed by the galleries and getting attention in exhibitions; she had her first show in London in 1984. David Wolfers had come to the studio to see my work. He saw some of Chrissie's and said, 'Oh I like that' and 'When did you do that?' I explained that it wasn't mine, I wished it was, but it was Chrissie's. He began to get interested in it and eventually asked Chrissie if she would do a show at the gallery. Peter Kuhfeld, another good friend of ours, was a very good painter who showed with the New Grafton at that time, and David suggested that Kuhfeld and Chrissie did a show together. They showed about twenty paintings each. Then she started to show in the Academy and in various other exhibitions and was gradually becoming more confident in what she was doing. It had taken time, but she had got over her father's unfortunate remark that 'there was never any talent in our family'.

Also I think she had got over any sort of self-consciousness about working in the same studio as me. We both had an effect on each other. I think any good

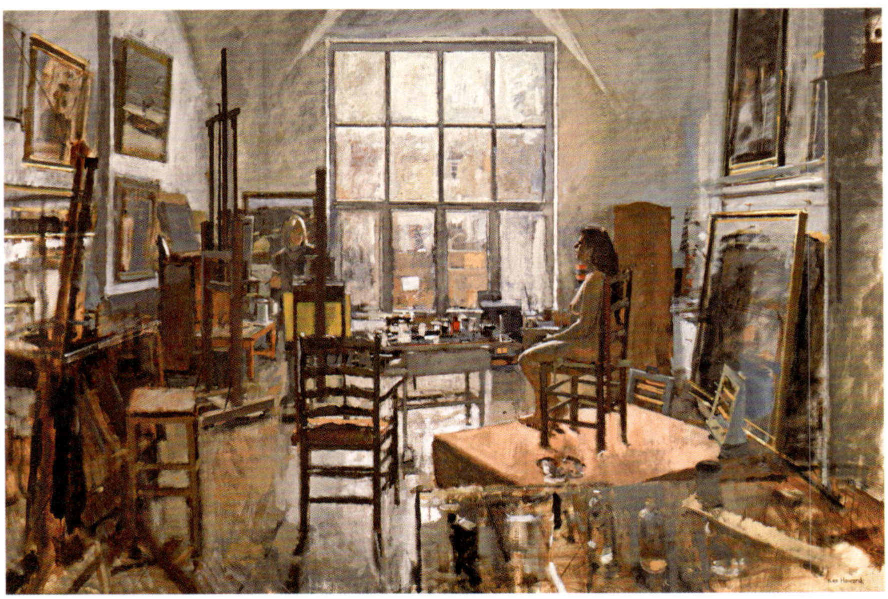

The Studio, 1980–81
Oil on canvas, 150 x 180 cm

This was the first painting I made of my studio interior at South Bolton Gardens. It was a revelation to me. After painting all over the world for eight years, I realised that all I wanted from a subject was literally on my own doorstep.

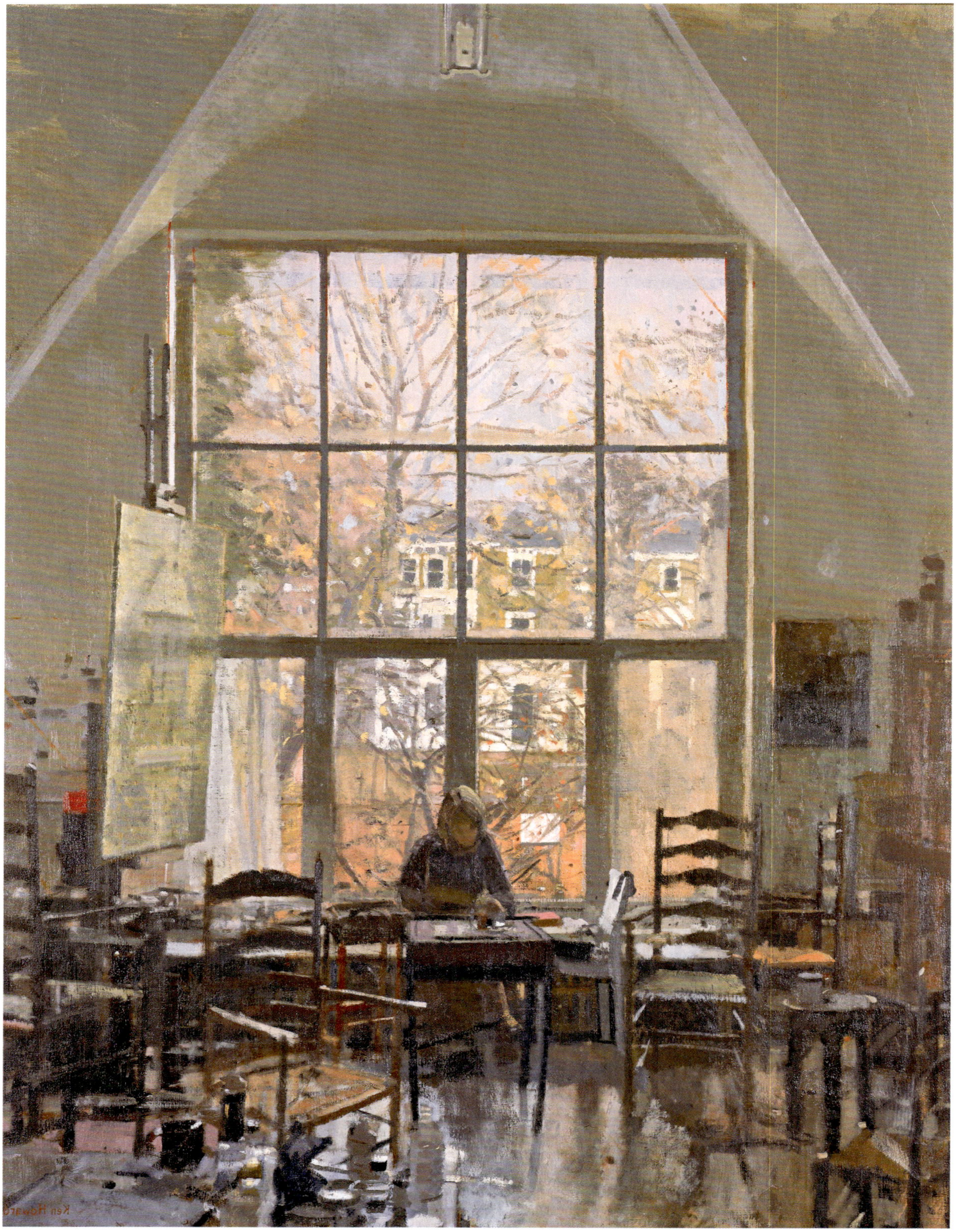

things that came out of my work in those years arose really because of Chrissie's influence, and I think she was influenced by me as well. We were two completely different painters, but Chrissie had become, as it were, more figurative and representational than if she had stayed in Germany. Had she remained in Germany I think she would have gone further down an abstract route. Living in England, however, she mixed with my friends who were also basically figurative painters. She got to know my friends from the New English and from the Academy, as well as the various societies that I belonged to. Chrissie had naturally absorbed some of their preferences, but interpreted them completely in her own language. There was no question of her paintings being, so to speak, mock-Ken Howards. Her work was completely Christa Gaa's – she exhibited under her maiden name as a lot of painters do. Even after we were married she still used her maiden name and never exhibited as Christa Howard.

The '80s were the good years for me from so many points of view, both personal and professional. Most importantly, of course, was that Chrissie came to live with me, so many years after we had decided we wanted to marry, and it was just as I had imagined it would be – harmonious and full of love.

From a professional point of view, the high point of the decade had been my election to the Academy, again after waiting many years (I was in my fifties and had first exhibited in the Academy when I was eighteen). I also won the Hunting Art Prize and the Sparkasse Bank Prize. This was also the time I stopped doing commissioned work and managed to support Chrissie and myself purely on my own work. The art market was buoyant, we were travelling and living in London and Cornwall. Chrissie's work was winning recognition and she was beginning to exhibit widely.

I have to admit that sometimes I thought that life was almost too good, and that there must be a price to pay. Yet little did I realise in those halcyon years just how heavy that price would be.

Interior at Oriel, 1982–84
Oil on canvas, 120 x 100 cm

This interior with Chrissie developed over a period of two years of continually questioning the composition. Originally the figure was quite different and I could not make it work. Then one day, in a moment of revelation, I saw Chrissie painting by the window and it all came together in a couple of hours.

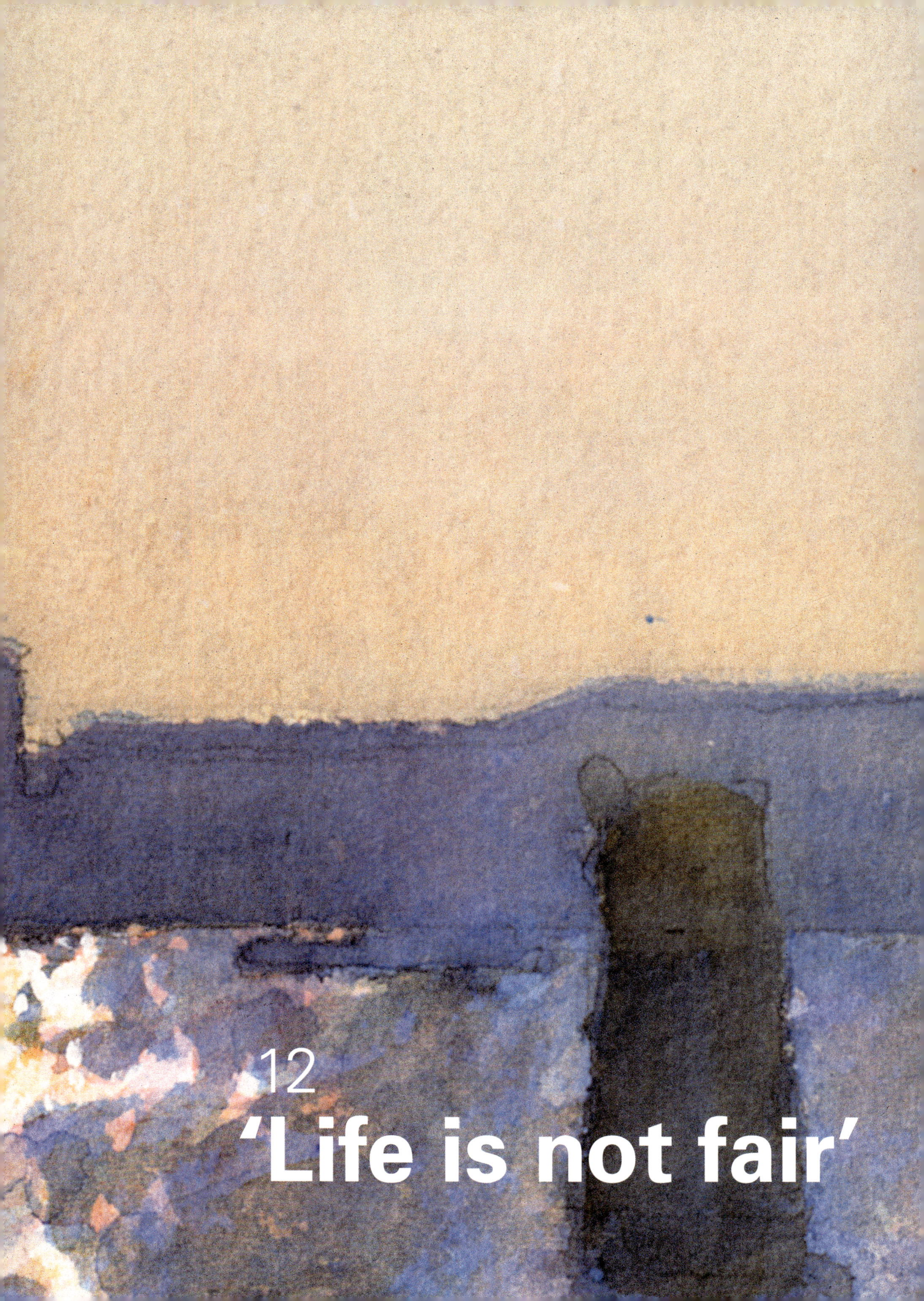

12 ‘Life is not fair’

Sennen High Summer, 1988
Oil on canvas, 140 x 280 cm

This large painting was made over a period of one year in the studio from many small studies done on the spot. Unusually for me I was facing north and thus the tonal contrast is less important; instead, the orchestration of the colour dominated the process.

I still remember clearly how one morning in the mid-'80s Chrissie and I were lying in bed talking and Chrissie touched her breast and said, 'Ken, I've got a little lump here,' to which I jokingly replied, 'Chrissie, you've got two little lumps there.' We had a little laugh, and then she said, 'No, I really have got a little lump here and I must go and see a specialist to make sure it's all right.' That again was typical of Chrissie; she wasn't someone who would just do nothing about it. She was very practical – very German, I suppose, in that way. Chrissie wanted to go and see a particular gynaecologist in Kingston who she used to visit for a check-up every six months, but he was away on holiday. His stand-in saw Chrissie and told her, 'Oh no, that's quite all right. There's nothing to worry about. If you are still bothered, by all means come and see Dr Digory when he gets back, but I don't believe there is any problem there.'

Chrissie didn't talk a lot about things and it was as if she had forgotten about this. The first I knew was about three weeks later she said to me, 'I am going to Kingston to see Dr Digory,' and off she went. She returned home in a sort of panic because Dr Digory had said there was in fact a problem and it had to be dealt with straightaway. The following day Chrissie flew to Germany. She went to see an eminent doctor in Cologne, a very good friend of hers. In fact he had brought her daughters into the world. She was immediately admitted to hospital for another check-up. They confirmed that the lump was cancerous and decided that Chrissie had to have a mastectomy.

This was incredibly traumatic both for Chrissie and myself. Partly it was the speed of events – she had jumped on a plane the next day and gone to Germany, when we didn't really know for sure whether there was anything to panic about. Immediately after the diagnosis Chrissie was on the phone, asking me what she should do. I said there was no question at all: 'You must have the mastectomy as soon as possible.' It was the only thing to do, but it was very hard for her. Chrissie was extremely sensitive about her body and after the operation she seemed to withdraw into herself. It took me quite a while to convince her that I didn't love her because she had two breasts; I loved her because she was Chrissie, a total being, and the fact that she had had a mastectomy made no difference. But it did affect her extremely. She became much more sensitive about going on the beach in a swimming costume, and also about revealing herself to me when we made love. Gradually she began to accept it, however, and as time passed we began to think that everything was going to be all right.

We obviously knew about the history of breast cancer. The following year, just after we seemed to have got over that first trauma, Chrissie realised she had a lump

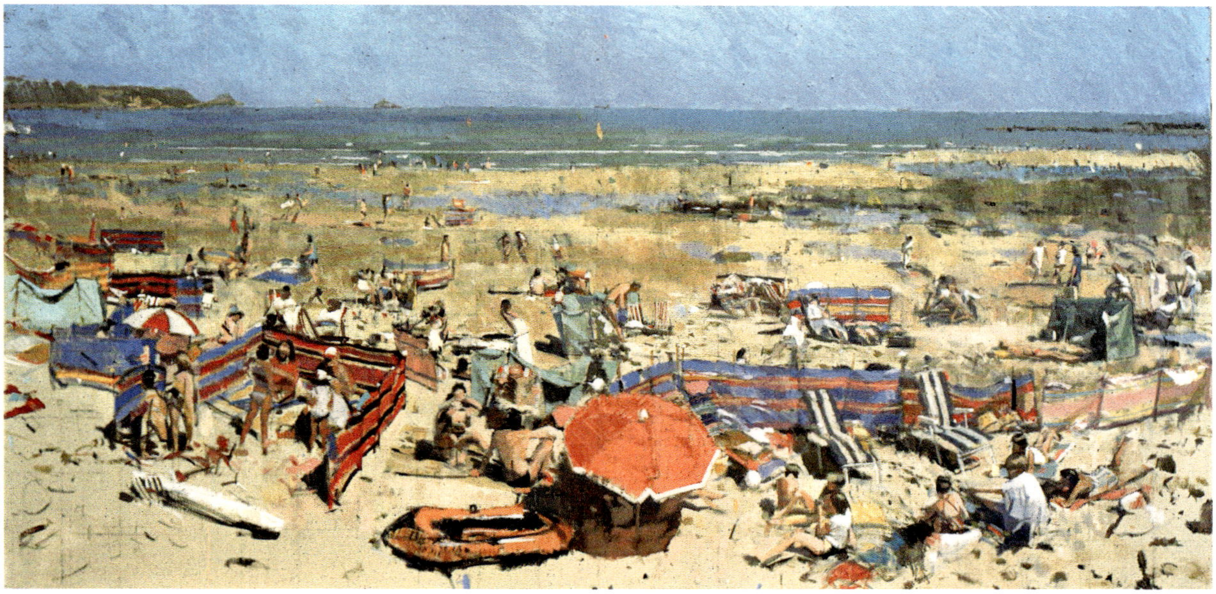

in the other breast and she immediately went to Germany again. Once again they did a biopsy and reported that they didn't think that this latest growth was malignant, but that they couldn't be absolutely sure. Chrissie asked me what I felt and, again, I told her, 'The decision is completely up to you, but my opinion is that you should have another mastectomy because that is the safest way. If there is any malignancy there, at least it will be removed and we won't have to keep on worrying about it. It will in a sense have been dealt with.' I think that was what she wanted to hear. I remember at that time I jokingly said to her, 'Chrissie, I always wanted to live with a boy anyway, and the fact that you have lost your two breasts makes no difference to me whatsoever.' I was speaking the truth: it honestly didn't make any difference to me. Anyway, she went off to Germany and had the second mastectomy.

At that time I was working in Jersey. I had become quite involved in Jersey in one way and another, including painting Gerald Durrell for his zoo on the island. I also had a one-man exhibition in St Helier and had been commissioned to paint a big composition of the Queen opening the Jersey Parliament. I was still earning my living purely from my work. I wasn't teaching any more, I had given up all my Army commitments, and David Wolfers and other galleries and dealers, such as Manya Igel, were taking my work and giving me an income. The various societies to which I belonged also took my paintings, of course, as did the Royal Academy Summer Exhibition, where by that time I was beginning to sell regularly.

So in that summer when Chrissie went back to Germany to have the second mastectomy, she insisted I went off to Jersey and carried on with the work that I had already taken on. It was a pretty busy trip and we were constantly on the phone to one another. It may sound rather strange that I didn't immediately drop everything and go to be in Germany while she was having these operations, but although Chrissie was living with me in England, many of her friends were still in Cologne.

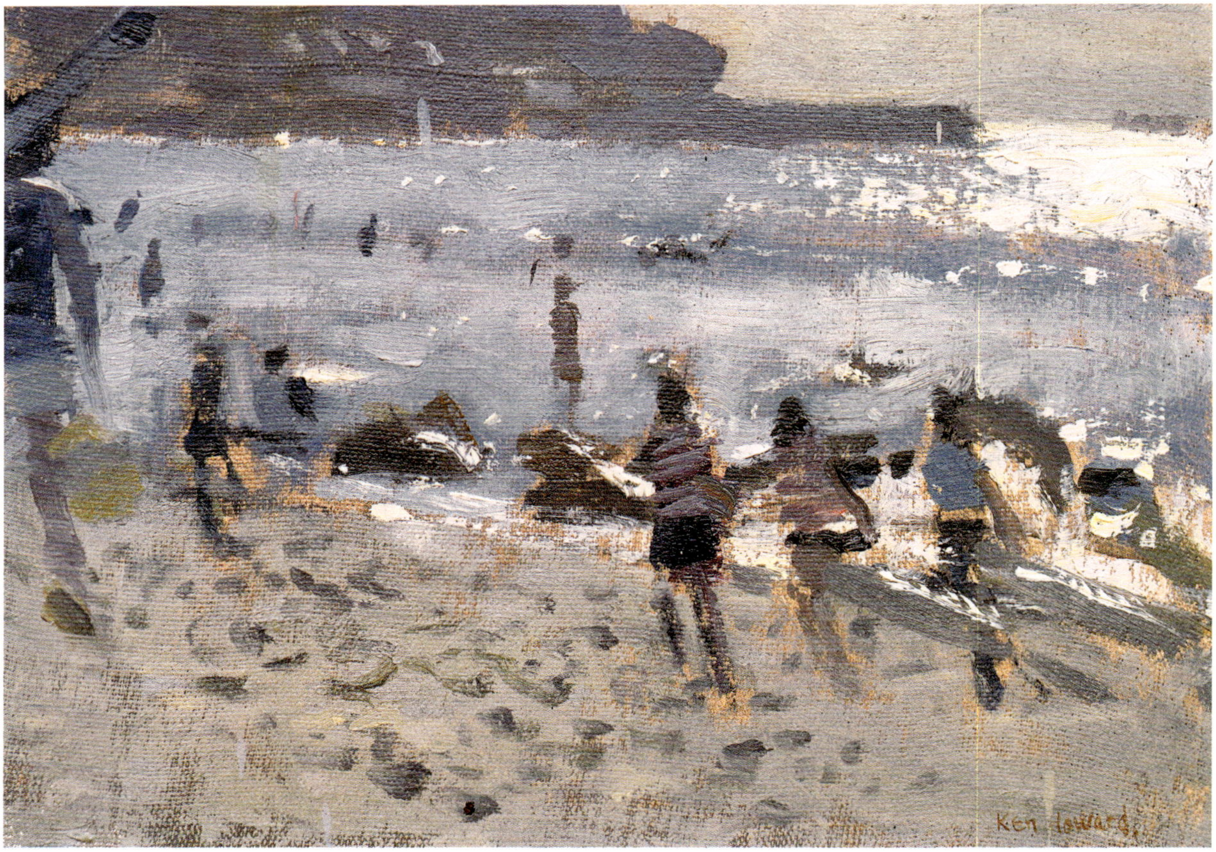

So were her daughters and her husband Hartmut, with whom she was still very good friends, so Chrissie had a lot of support. People were visiting her and helping her through this time, and she made it clear to me that she just wanted me to get on with my work and not be completely disrupted by this situation. That was very like Chrissie. I suppose many other men would have just dropped everything and gone to Germany, but I have always said that artists are strangely selfish people who have this sort of obsession with their work. It is often called an illness – the only way they feel they are living, in a way, is through their work. Chrissie recognised this completely and I appreciated it when I saw it in her.

When Chrissie had finally had the second operation and was ready to leave Germany again she came directly to Jersey. By that time I had become very friendly with Sir Peter Whiteley, the Governor of Jersey at that time. We had known each other for some years; he had been Commandant General Royal Marines and eventually became Commander-in-Chief Northern Europe. When Peter retired he was appointed the Governor of Jersey, which often happens with very senior officers in the armed forces. We had known each other for some time because, years before, without really knowing me, he had bought a couple of my paintings of Mousehole, where my studio was. It was a special place for them as Peter had actually proposed to his wife, Nancy, in Mousehole, so he bought these two paintings. We got to know each other and he liked my work, so he bought some more. In fact, I think Peter and Nancy have the largest collection of my work, probably 40, maybe even 50 paintings.

While I was working in Jersey for the painting of the Queen opening Parliament, as well as Gerry Durrell's portrait, Nancy and Peter very kindly invited me to stay with them at Government House. When Chrissie had finally finished in hospital she came to join me there. Peter and Nancy insisted that she should come to recuperate at Government House when the operation was over; they had a large staff who could look after her and help her to get strong again. There was no point in going back to England, with all the normal pressures of living that would entail, but it made perfect sense for her to come to Government House and live there with me.

There was an amusing story that as Chrissie flew into the airport in Jersey she saw a Rolls-Royce come onto the tarmac and pull up at the bottom of the steps of the plane. Chrissie, watching from the window, wondered who the famous person was who would be collected in it. Then the stewardess asked if there was a Christa Gaa on board. The stewardess explained that the car had arrived at the bottom of the steps for her. Chrissie was incredibly embarrassed about it – she had no feeling for things like that and she was travelling with plastic bags that she had brought over from Germany. Everybody in the plane watched as this woman – not smartly dressed and loaded with carrier bags – went off down the stairs. The Rolls-Royce had been sent by Government House, of course, to pick her up.

When she had the second operation Chrissie immediately decided to have a breast implant. At the same time she asked whether they could put an implant into where the original operation had been done. And although it was much more difficult in the earlier case than with the recent mastectomy they did it, and they did it extremely well. She was able to wear a bikini again and had much more confidence; the change was incredibly important to her as a woman. Naturally I was delighted for her that this had happened. Anyway, we lived in Jersey for a few weeks with Peter and Nancy, and I finished the commission work that I had undertaken. It was summer and Chrissie relaxed completely at Government House. She got on extremely well with the staff, who enjoyed her open and lovable personality, and they all looked after her. There was a bit of social life, which, after all the trauma, I suppose she was ready for, and then we returned to England and resumed our normal lives, if you can put it that way.

The year 1990 proved to be a very busy one. I had my usual show at the New Grafton Gallery in the spring, we travelled a lot that year and I was the featured artist at the Harrogate Festival. Later on in the year we heard that Hartmut wanted to re-marry, so he and Chrissie needed to arrange their divorce. Chrissie and I realised that we would at last be able to marry. On 13 October 1990 (13 seems to have been a lucky

Sennen Evening, *c.* 1990
Oil on board, 20 x 25 cm

This small study was painted in the late afternoon, my favourite time for working. Made quickly on the spot, with very little detail, I tried to capture a sense of that time of day.

Chrissie and me at the Arts Club in Dover Street on the day of our wedding. It was 31 years after I had proposed to her in Florence.

number for me – many things in my life that have been good happened on the 13th), 31 years after we had first met, Chrissie and I were finally married. When we had our wedding breakfast at the Arts Club in Dover Street I had to make a little speech. I said that I had always known that Chrissie was very cautious when she made decisions, that she never made a decision quickly without due consideration, but that I thought 31 years to decide was a little over-cautious! It was a joke that went down well, thank goodness, and Chrissie found it very amusing. We had a wonderful wedding celebration and then came back to the studio. It was one of the most wonderful days of my life.

Before our wedding in early September we had been to Venice and then down to Tuscany, because Chrissie particularly liked painting there. We had found a flat in an old converted *castello* just south of Florence. It was called Montegufoni and had been the summer home of the Sitwell family. When the last Sitwell had died it had been bought and converted into holiday flats. That sounds dreadful, but in fact the castle itself, when you entered, looked no different from how it had always appeared. Only when you got into your apartment did you become conscious of the modernisation.

We went with a couple of very good friends – my oldest friend, in fact, Brian Harper, whom I had known since we were at grammar school when we were eleven years old. Brian has remained my closest friend. He wasn't in the arts, but it was to him that I would turn if I wanted advice, a man who always gave me an honest appraisal of anything I was doing. (He didn't always tell me what I wanted to hear, I must admit!) He and his wife Mavis came down to Venice with us for the start of our stay. I remember that Chrissie and I went shopping for our wedding and it was generally a very happy time. John Bratby – the well-known painter of the Kitchen Sink school of the '50s – and his wife also happened to be in Venice, and we spent an evening with him having a drink on the Piazza San Marco. Venice was a great meeting-place for people in the arts. I always said, and it was true, that I never went to Venice without unexpectedly bumping into someone I knew well. It's a little bit different now, as after having made all the films about working in Venice, people do tend to come up and talk to me because they have seen them. In the early years there was nothing like that, however, and I just ran into people I knew.

After Venice we went down to Montegufoni and Tina joined us, I remember, along with her little daughter, my step-granddaughter. Chrissie absolutely adored children and she doted on little Alexandra; the three of them used to sit round the pool. Chrissie painted a certain amount, but not with the energy that she normally put into work because once her daughter was there, with her grandchild, they became

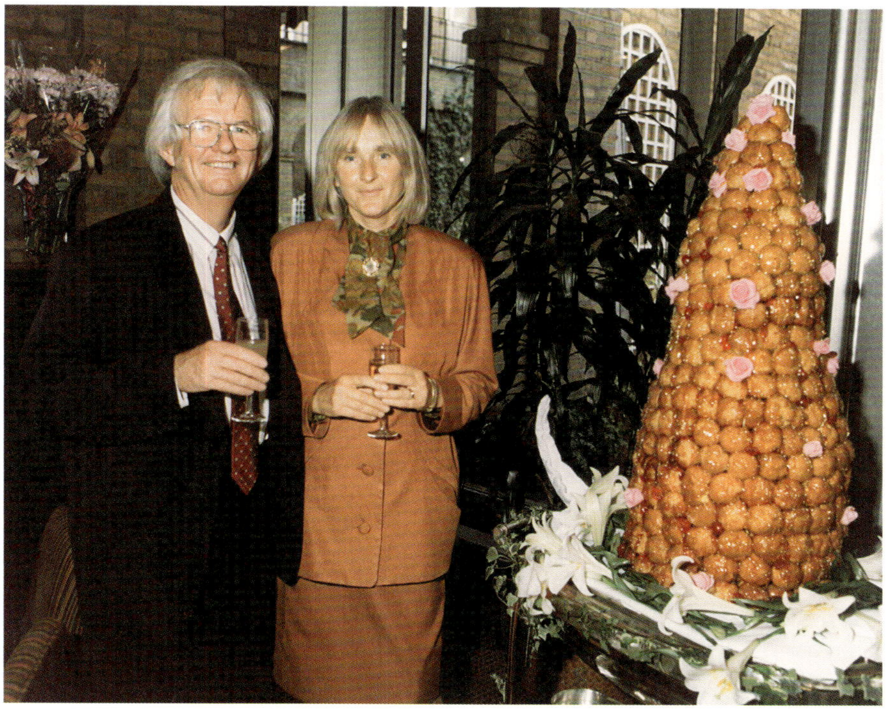

the prime focus; painting in a way took a back seat. In that sense she was extremely feminine. Women, I think, have a much stronger bond with their children than most men do, and their children very definitely come first. I used to joke with Chrissie that in her life her children came first, then her work and then me. I didn't say it with any resentment. I recognised completely that her children were her greatest love, her work was an obsession and then I came along. But Chrissie had so much love to give that she had enough for all of us and I never felt in any way deprived.

A couple of years earlier we had taken a converted farmhouse near Arezzo, on another trip with Brian and Mavis. They were very good companions because they never resented the fact that Chrissie and I disappeared off with our paintboxes for the whole day, so the four of us would spend just the evenings together. I remember when we arrived at this house it was incredibly damp and Mavis decided to put the electric blankets on to dry the beds out because they were impossible to sleep in. She turned the electric blankets on and then went to prepare a meal. All of a sudden smoke began billowing up the stairs from where the bedrooms were – a bed with an electric blanket had caught alight. I remember it was quite a panic and I had to take photographs of all the damage for the insurance.

At the end of that trip Chrissie and I were supposed to be going to Cyprus, where I was to paint a portrait of Lee Durrell, Gerald's wife. Because Gerald had been so pleased with his own portrait he wanted a watercolour of Lee to go with the one he had bought from me, which was a study for the big painting for the zoo. At the last minute we got a phone call to say that Gerry and Lee had been caught up in Russia, where they were making a film. They couldn't get back to Cyprus, where they had a house near Kyrenia, so I couldn't do the portrait. Chrissie and I decided that we didn't want to go back to England early (Brian and Mavis had already returned home); we decided to stay on, but we couldn't rent the house we were in.

Chrissie had made friends with some farmers when she was painting in the landscape and one of them offered us a room close by in his big medieval farmhouse. It was a memorable week – the Italians can really entertain people well. Why they took such a shine to Chrissie and myself I don't know, but they treated us like royalty. I remember on the last night what seemed like the whole village came in to a big room in the middle of this medieval farmhouse. We all sat there eating our meal at a big table in the middle and the villagers sat round the edge on long benches and watched us eat.

We had had some warning of what was to come earlier in the morning, when Chrissie first got up. She looked out of the window and said, 'Oh, Ken, the farmer is murdering all his animals' – a funny way of putting it, but he was killing chickens and rabbits and generally getting ready for this great feast that night. Being in Italy, of course, as well as being in Chianti country, there was a great deal of wine. When we were at table, every time my glass was a quarter full, the farmer would immediately top it up again. After a while I was absolutely intoxicated and realised that if I didn't leave the room now I'd risk falling off my seat. So I made the lame excuse that I was going to the bathroom, struggled to my feet and staggered out. By this time I was so drunk that I just settled down on the bathroom floor and fell asleep.

After about half an hour Chrissie was beginning to get a bit worried because I hadn't come back. 'I wonder what's the matter with Ken,' she said, 'we ought to go and find out because some other people will want to use the bathroom.' The farmer told her not to worry; it was a very modern bathroom which they had only had for about five or six years and nobody ever used it – they just went out into the country to pass water or whatever was required. So they let me sleep and I don't remember another thing until I awoke the following morning. They had carried me to bed and undressed me, but the following morning, amazingly, I had a completely clear head. I said to the farmer, when we were thanking them for their hospitality during the week, 'Your wine must be wonderful; I was completely drunk last night, but I have got no sign of a headache or a hangover this morning!' He looked almost offended that I should even have considered having a hangover after drinking his wine.

It had certainly been an eventful few days. A couple of nights before, Chrissie had got up in the night to go to the toilet; being one of these old medieval farmhouses, our bedroom was off a sort of central hall, with other rooms off it. As Chrissie walked across the central hall, a door opened to the side and there stood one of the farmer's sons, a lad of about eighteen or nineteen. We had gathered during the week that he was the buck of the village. There he stood, completely naked, with an enormous erection, exposing himself to Chrissie. With great presence of mind she just looked sideways, glanced at his penis, said simply 'Olé' and walked on into the bathroom. The poor boy was so embarrassed he just shut the door. Chrissie told me this story with great hilarity when she came back to bed.

One of the wonderful things about painting is that you do meet so many people and people feel they can relate to you. They can talk to you about what you're doing, and this was perhaps why the farmer offered us the room in his house. Obviously it was a room that had been used by the family's unmarried daughter; she was kept by the family and seemed to be a general dogsbody around the house. So when the farmer decided that he was going to offer us a room, of course he offered us hers. I don't know where she had to go and sleep, but I always felt a little bit guilty about that.

After Chrissie and I married our life went on in much the same way. We were very close and spent a great deal of time together; we were both of us working hard and travelling, and all in all it was a very happy period. Chrissie seemed to be working even harder than before. I knew that she had an exhibition coming up at the New Grafton Gallery, so I just accepted the fact that she was working so hard towards it, although that was actually very unlike Chrissie. She resisted working to order, as it were, preferring to work extremely hard and put in long hours in a purely instinctive way. She had not worked for exhibitions before.

In that same year – we were now into 1991 – she mentioned to me that she had a great desire to play tennis again. She had been an extremely good tennis player in Germany and she wanted to take up the game again. Typically, she didn't just want to take a racket and go out and do it like a hobby. She had been quite a serious player, so she decided to get some lessons with the professional at the tennis courts in Penzance. Chrissie used to go off for her tennis lesson early in the morning when I was working with a model, then she would come back and paint for the rest of the day. Her ability was clear and within a few weeks of starting lessons the professional at the club asked her to partner him in the mixed doubles of an approaching tournament. He had recognised what a good player she was and Chrissie was obviously very flattered by this. When she came home I would ask her how the lesson had gone and how she was finding playing again. Chrissie replied that she was beginning to get a feel for the ball again, but that she hadn't got the energy that she had had before. 'That's not really surprising, Chrissie,' I said. 'You are now in your early fifties and you were a girl in your teens when you played tennis before.'

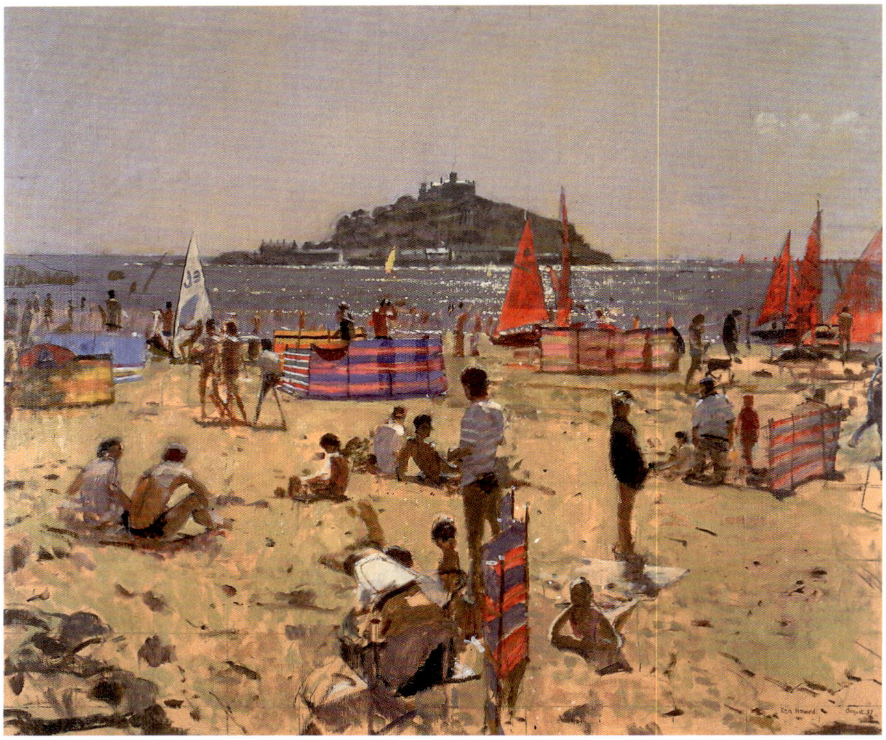

But something obviously still worried her. She used to come home and say, 'I was really striking the ball and playing for about fifteen minutes and then I just had to sit. I really needed to sit down and take a rest before continuing playing.' I didn't read anything particular into this. I thought that tennis was a newfound exercise, and it was demanding, so it was natural that she became tired and breathless and needed rest.

At the end of the summer we prepared to go to Venice for our usual September trip; we were also planning to go down to Montegufoni and take Tina with us. Suddenly, as we packed up in Cornwall, Chrissie said, 'When we get back to London I am going to take my exhibition to the framer.' I was surprised at this as the exhibition wasn't due until the following spring or early summer, so much so that I commented, 'Good Lord, Chrissie. That's most unlike you to be ready so far in advance.' 'I know,' she replied, 'but I am. I have got the work ready and I'm going to get it to the framers while we are in Italy.' I thought no more about it and we came back to London and did what we needed to do after a summer away. We then set off for our September in Italy, and Tina and Alexandra came and joined us.

When in Venice we worked quite hard in the day, going in the evenings to eat in the Campo Santa Margherita or somewhere like that. Chrissie would sit there watching her granddaughter, this miracle of a child as she saw her, running around. Alexandra could just about walk by then and she staggered around the Campo in front of the restaurant where we were sitting outside eating. After about a week I was in our room and Chrissie came in, breathing very heavily. I said in concern, 'Chrissie, you shouldn't be breathing like that after coming up a flight of stairs.'

St Michael's Mount from Marazion, 1987
Oil on canvas, 100 x 120 cm

This morning subject is all about tonal contrast and scale: the scale of the figures against the smaller St Michael's Mount, and the contrast of the figures against the light warmth of the beach. Painted on a large scale in the studio, it was based on many oil sketches. It has always been my ambition to take a canvas of this size to the beach and paint on the spot, but I have never had the courage.

'I realise that,' she replied. 'I am going to see a doctor because I have no energy and feel tired and breathless.' So the next day she went off to see a doctor and he did some tests. Immediately he told her she had to come into hospital straightaway. The last thing Chrissie wanted was to go into hospital in Italy, so we realised we'd have to cancel Montegufoni and drive back to Cologne.

The last evening we were in Venice together I remember very clearly. A very good friend and fellow painter, Peter Greenham, and his wife Jane, also a very good painter, had come to Venice. They had suggested we should have dinner together and we ate in a lovely restaurant in Dorsoduro. We explained that the following day we were going to head back to Germany because Chrissie wasn't particularly well, but that evening she seemed so full of life. The Greenhams' son, David, was with them, and Chrissie had always been close to David and liked him very much. We hadn't met him that often, but the two of them were very friendly; Chrissie had a fantastic ability to relate to younger people. Anyway, we all enjoyed dinner and said we would meet up again in London. In fact, we were never to meet up again.

We left early in the morning. Tina made her plans to go back to Cologne with Alexandra, while Chrissie and I drove through Switzerland to Cologne so that she could see a doctor there and have some more tests. On the way, Chrissie told me that she thought it was her old trouble again, referring to her cancer. I resisted the idea. 'No, it can't be, Chrissie – you have been so active, working so well and playing tennis and living so fully this year.' I suppose deep inside I just couldn't face accepting that it might be the cancer. Chrissie had thought further, however. She said, 'If it is my old trouble, I don't want to have chemotherapy or radiotherapy. If I've only got a few months left, I want to live them as fully as possible. I don't want to be under that sort of debilitating treatment all the time.'

I began to think back to that summer before. I have always believed, in a strange way, that if you listen to your body it tells you when there is something wrong with it. I think Chrissie had subconsciously been aware that her body wasn't right, which had prompted her to finish her exhibition and get it off to the framers early. She had felt the need to play tennis because she wanted to prove to her body that she was still strong and active – that there wasn't anything really wrong with it. But I think something deep inside her was telling her that things were going radically wrong.

Chrissie was always a 'liver' who never wasted life, but that last year before our final trip to Venice she seemed to live doubly actively. Her perspective had changed a little, too. I remember one day we were having a discussion which must have touched upon one of my weaknesses. I'd said, rather lazily, 'Well Chrissie, I suppose that's just me.' Her response was passionate. 'Oh, you can't say "that's

San Giorgio Maggiore, Venice. Brilliant Light, 1990
Watercolour, 17.5 x 27.5 cm

Painting Venice is a constant revelation. The city reveals herself to you, and you reveal her to the viewer. She is like a beautiful woman: continually exciting, surprising and always evoking love.

just me". If we don't try and improve ourselves during the years that we are on this earth, what is the point of being here? If we just accept our weaknesses and say "that's just me!"'

When we arrived in Cologne it was late September and Chrissie's birthday. We had been going to spend it in Tuscany with Tina and Alexandra, and when we arrived in Cologne she was determined not to see any doctors or have any tests until the day after her birthday. 'I want to enjoy my birthday.' And we did all enjoy it tremendously. Both her daughters came and we were all together. Chrissie was really sublimely happy and seemed for that evening to have put the thought of anything being wrong out of her mind.

The next day she went off to the hospital close to the house she owned in Cologne. She returned saying that she had had some tests done; the results would be through in two days. We went to the hospital two days later and saw her friend, the doctor who had done the two mastectomies. 'I'm afraid it's your old trouble back again,' he told her. She immediately said to him, 'I don't want chemotherapy or radiotherapy,' to which he replied, in that direct, very German way, 'You will live for two weeks.' Chrissie looked at him and said, 'I don't have a choice then, do I?' 'No,' he answered, 'you must start chemotherapy immediately.' We were both in a complete state of shock. I had been trying to put the possibility out of my mind, and I suppose Chrissie hadn't really wanted to accept it, although her body was telling her that there was something radically wrong. I remember that we just cried together. We couldn't understand how this had happened after all those years of separation, when we had finally got together and been able to marry. We were just completely shell-shocked.

The following day Chrissie started chemotherapy – it was obviously that urgent. Her lungs were filling up with liquid and, although they had drained them, the chemotherapy had to stop the process. Very typically of Chrissie, one of her main fears was losing her hair. She was very conscious of her physical being and asked to have ice packs put on her head when she was having the chemotherapy in the hope that they would prevent her hair from falling out, which they did. The ice obviously froze the roots and thus stopped the chemo reaching them, which apparently is why people lose their hair. She kept the ice packs on the top of her head all the time she was having chemotherapy. Afterwards, even Chrissie was very sick and depressed, due, I suppose, to its physically debilitating nature. Eventually they told her that they couldn't do any more; she could leave hospital for a period and then come back again to continue with the treatment. So Chrissie left the hospital in Cologne and we returned to England.

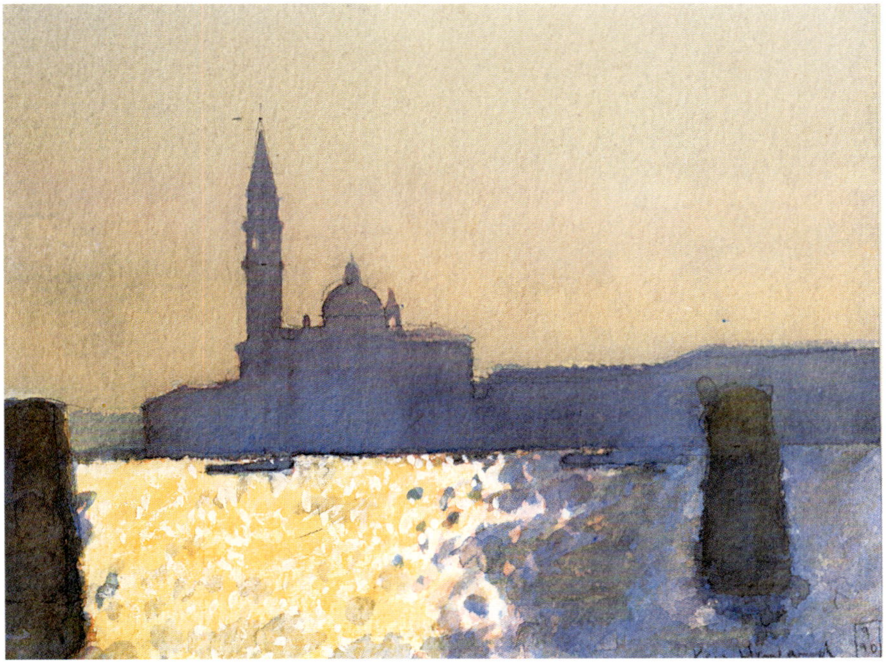

She immediately threw herself into things that were happening here. We had started to restore the studio and put in a new kitchen and bathroom, and she wanted to be involved in this and in buying new furniture. We also drove down to Cornwall and spent time in Mousehole as she wanted to go to Cornwall and see friends there. But it was a very fraught time, a very sad time. Although we were glad to be together, the reality of what was happening began to hang very heavily upon us. Eventually we went back to Germany again to continue the chemotherapy.

I had, of course, dropped everything, although I had some shows in England at that time. All my work just got forgotten, everything was put to one side. I could only think about Chrissie's condition and so we went back to Germany together. I vividly remember the first day she went back to continue chemotherapy. I was sitting in the corridor outside the room where they were administering it when suddenly I felt a pain in my eye. I didn't think much about it until I went into the room after they had finished. Chrissie was lying down on the bed and she looked up at me and said, 'Ken, you look like Dracula!' When I asked her what she meant she told me that my eye was full of blood and immediately sent me several floors up to the hospital's specialist eye department. When I went in the doctor asked me if I was under any particular strain at the moment. I didn't see the funny side of it; I just said to him, 'You could say that.' He explained that the tension and strain I was under had caused a blood vessel to burst. He was not surprised and he told me not to worry about it. 'Within two or three days it will just subside and your eye will be completely normal again.'

By this time Chrissie was obviously getting weaker. She was losing weight as she went through the chemotherapy and she was beginning to lose some of her

Sennen Evening II, *c.* 1988
Oil on canvas, 150 x 180 cm

I made this large painting in the studio during the evenings, after working on small studies on the beach during the day.

hair. I was still staying in the house that Chrissie owned in Cologne, along with her brother, who was also living there. I used to go back there alone if Chrissie was in hospital, otherwise she would come back and stay there with me. After a time, however, Chrissie said she thought that I should return to England. She had finished another course of chemotherapy and had decided to go down to southern Germany to spend some days with Franz and Constanza Buhler. They were, I suppose, two of her oldest friends in Germany and she had been very close to them all her life. 'You should go back to England,' she told me. 'You have got things to do for your exhibition.' She was right – I did have an exhibition coming up later in the year. There was also a lot to do with the studio – dealing with the builders and all the work that was in progress. She felt that it was best that I came back, while she went and stayed with her friends.

I'd been back about six days and was trying to get some work done. I'd managed to get hold of a model and had a big painting on the go in which I'd got quite interested. Then suddenly I got a phone call from Franz and Constanza in southern Germany. They told me that Chrissie had had a bad turn and had to go immediately into hospital for an operation. I dropped everything, got into the car and drove like mad to Gengenbach, where Franz and Constanza lived. I went to the hospital immediately and Chrissie was getting over the operation when I arrived. It was a hospital run by nuns and some very good doctors, and one of the doctors got me in straightaway to tell me about Chrissie's condition. Although his English was not very good and my German was pretty basic, I gathered that he was extremely concerned about Chrissie's condition. When he had operated on her he discovered that the cancer was running through her body; he more or less told me that there was only a limited time left. Chrissie's main concern was that she couldn't eat – this was the one thing that she wanted to do, because if she could eat she could get stronger and she would know that she was getting better. She also realised that she must eat to have the strength to continue the chemotherapy, which by this time she saw as one of her main hopes. But when she recovered from the operation in Offenberg, she still couldn't eat at all. My days were spent running back and forth to the hospital, spending as much time with her as possible. Meanwhile I slept at Franz and Constanza's house in Gengenbach.

This was a particularly bad time. Christmas was approaching and I knew how much Chrissie loved Christmas, but for once its festivities were the last thing on her mind. About this time I had an opening in London, a one-man exhibition, and Chrissie insisted that I came back for the private view. I had no real interest in going back, but she said, 'You just must go back for that evening.' So I managed

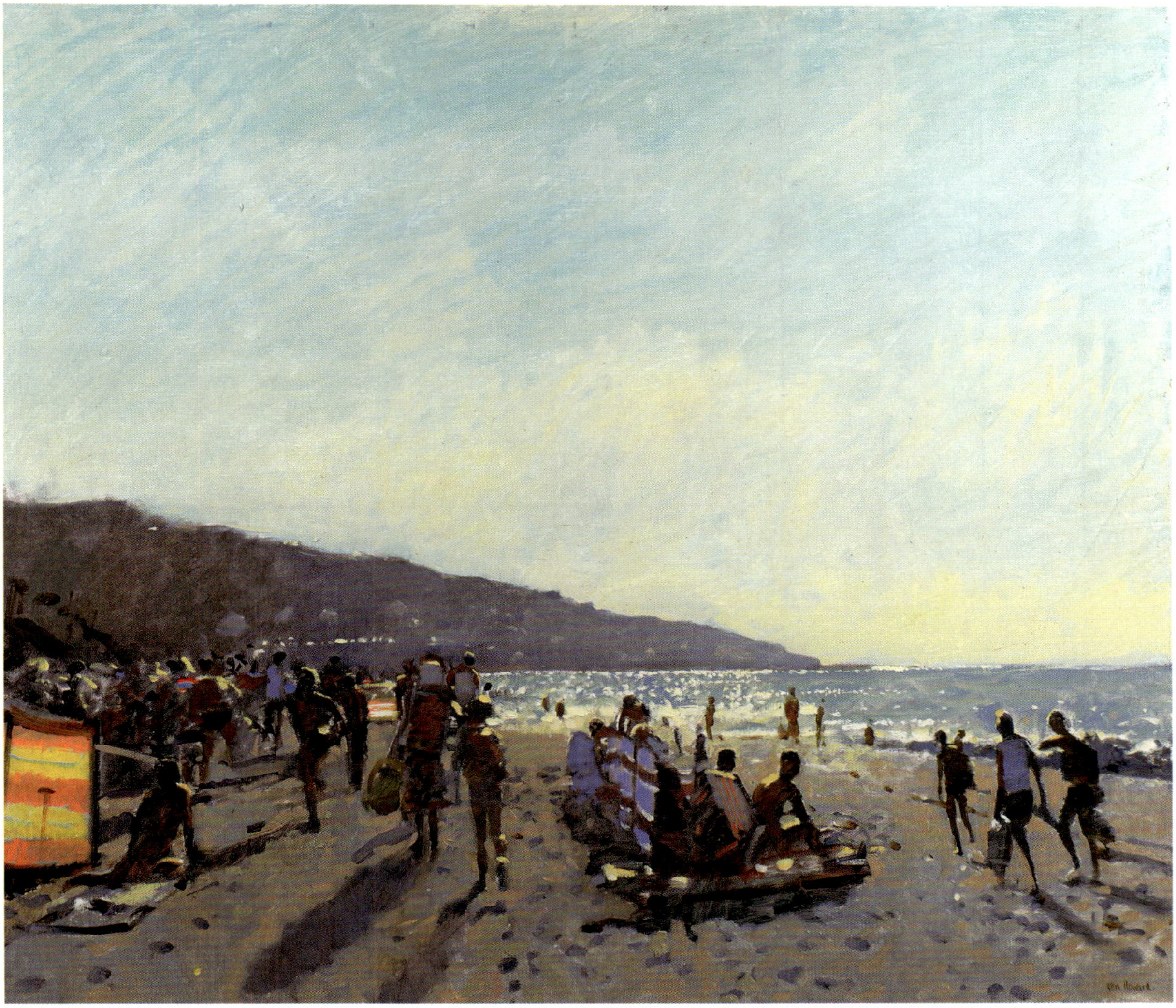

to get a flight out of Strasbourg for the afternoon of the exhibition opening and flew into London. I went to the opening, slept in the studio overnight and returned to Strasbourg by plane early in the morning. By the time I got back to Gengenbach Chrissie wasn't able to eat at all. She was beginning to throw up a sort of green bile that really frightened her. As Christmas approached she said, 'I just must have Christmas Day with Franz and Constanza and you out of the hospital.'

Meanwhile, she was thinking of another operation because her one idea was somehow to start eating again. I didn't want her to go through the hell of another operation, but as long as she believed she could beat this cancer I felt I had to go along with it. However, the doctors at the hospital in Offenberg said that they wouldn't operate: there was no point. Chrissie had, in the interim, met a friend who had told her about a clinic in Bonn that achieved very good results for patients with terminal cancer. She was determined to get there as soon as Christmas was over.

I think it was the worst Christmas Day of my life. I drove to the hospital and picked up Chrissie. On the way back I had to stop the car while she threw up in the countryside, but we finally got to Franz and Constanza's. Chrissie sat with us for about an hour while we all talked and tried to be as light-hearted and 'Christmasy' as possible – but by this time she was obviously very, very ill. In the end she said she couldn't take it any more and would I take her back to hospital.

As soon as Christmas was over we made plans to get Chrissie up to Bonn. My birthday happened to be on Boxing Day, but there was no question of celebrating that. We managed to get an ambulance team to take her and I followed behind in my car. I will remember that journey until the end of my life. It was a cold, drizzly winter's day, the trees were bare and the vineyards that we drove past as we made our way up to Bonn were all desolate – there were no signs of life at all. I remember we stopped in a small lay-by – the ambulance pulled over to allow Chrissie to be sick again and I pulled in behind it. She was very ill and just throwing up all the time, but she was still determined to get to Bonn. They gave her a check-up when they got there, and told her that they thought she had a 50/50 chance of surviving. I have to confess that after what I had been told by the doctors at Offenberg and the report that they had given me to hand to the hospital (although I hadn't actually read the report, I knew very well what would be in it), I thought it was almost cruel to obviously lie to her. Chrissie had a private room in the hospital and we spent New Year's Eve together; at midnight she said would I go and spend some time with a very good friend of hers who lived in Bonn, a friend from her past. But the last thing I could think about was fireworks and the New Year celebrations that were going on all around us.

The following day we gave up on the hospital in Bonn – Chrissie wasn't eating and as long as she wasn't eating and kept on losing weight there was no way that the hospital could treat her. This time I tried to convince her to spend a few weeks in a hospice to get her strength back, rather than go straight back to a hospital environment. She wouldn't hear of that, however, and insisted that she went into the hospital in Cologne. They were asked to operate on her yet again in order to get her eating so that she could go back on the chemotherapy. That next operation was a complete nightmare and afterwards I started to live in the hospital all the time. I managed to get a bed put in the room with Chrissie and spent all the time with her. I remember we covered the mirror there because whenever Chrissie got up and tried to go to the loo or leave the room for some reason, her reflection showed her how gaunt and thin and ill she looked.

To begin with we spent our time playing games such as backgammon, and I used to read books to her. I remember reading *The French Lieutenant's Woman* and *Watership Down* to her, among others, and Chrissie lay in bed and enjoyed the fact that I was reading. Eventually, even the effort of concentrating on my voice as I read became too much and she began to slide into a semi-conscious state. The last operation that she had in Cologne had been completely unsuccessful and once again the doctors told me what very bad shape she was in. I will never forget when they told me that she only had a few days left to live. They touched on the idea of letting her have more morphine to combat the very real pain she was in. In a way they were suggesting helping her to die. I didn't fully understand what they were talking about and was incredibly shocked when I got the gist. Straightaway I said no, they mustn't do anything like that. I wanted Chrissie to live as long as possible, and believed in the possibility of her beating the cancer.

One evening, about three days before the end, Chrissie turned to me and said, 'I'm dying, aren't I?' It was the first time that we had talked about it and I couldn't actually deny the fact. I wouldn't say she was, but nor could I say she wasn't. My silence told her, I think, and for the first time she started talking about what would happen after she died. Until then we had both been in a state of denial, unable to talk really closely or very intimately. Once Chrissie had accepted that she was dying, however, we began to talk about everything. She found the energy to talk to tell me that I had given her the happiest ten years of her life. Typical of Chrissie, she was already thinking of me by this time – she had given up on herself, but she was preparing me for what was to come. She told me that those years in England and Cornwall and travelling had been the happiest of her life, and she talked at great length. Eventually I broke down and asked what I would do on my own. 'You will marry again,' she said to me. 'You must marry again. You are not a person to live by yourself.' And then, with typical Chrissie insight, she said, 'But don't marry again too soon.' Again she was thinking of me and knew me well enough to guess that I would try and cover my grief and start something else, probably too impetuously. Her words remained with me, 'You will marry again, but don't marry again too soon.'

During those last two weeks she was surrounded by other loved ones, as well as myself. Her daughters, Tina and Babs, were in and out constantly, and Hartmut came in every day. In the evening he would say to me, 'Now you had better go and eat something,' aware that I had been in the hospital all day. He would offer to sit with Chrissie until I returned, which I thought was wonderful. Here was a man who had lost the woman that he had loved and had recently re-married, but he was prepared to be completely with her, and to a degree with me. I thought this was very, very generous. Whenever I needed to get out Hartmut was always there to take over; we were determined not to leave Chrissie alone as long as she was conscious.

I remember very little about the last day of Chrissie's life. She was in a sort of semi-coma and I just sat in the room and watched her. All I remember is that at three o'clock in the morning on 26 January 1992, Chrissie died. I was sitting by the bed at the time and all of a sudden I saw liquid run out of her mouth. Somehow I knew that her lungs had filled and she had passed away.
A very good nurse who was looking after Chrissie had been in and out of the room constantly; she was very understanding and I think she knew almost to the hour when Chrissie would die. She came in at just about three o'clock to find me weeping. She got me out of the room and I left the hospital to go back to Chrissie's Cologne house to sleep from sheer exhaustion. I emerged from the hospital at about four o'clock into the grey, cold, north German winter. Everything seemed to be there to express one's grief and despair – the weather and the whole atmosphere seemed to know that Chrissie had died.

The following days were obviously busy. Tina and Babs were both very supportive in the preparations for Chrissie's funeral as, once again, was Hartmut. We had been keeping in touch throughout Chrissie's illness with people in England, particularly with friends in Mousehole and, of course, in London. Brian and Mavis, Geoff and Marie Holt and others had been constantly in touch, and I had to let them all know about the funeral arrangements. Brian and Mavis and Geoff and Marie decided to come to Cologne for the funeral. It all seems a bit of a dream now; I suppose eventually you try and put things out of your mind. Anything that makes you that wretched has eventually to be pushed back in your mind, and those days of preparation for the funeral are now vague to me.

There was an enormous turnout of Chrissie's friends on the day of her funeral. Although she hadn't been living in Germany for some years, her friends had all been very close. Her many friends were joined by mine from England, obviously fewer in number. Hartmut and I were very close on that day, walking together behind the coffin. Tina had found a grave with a sculpture above it – and this sculpture was incredibly, uncannily like Chrissie. It had the feel of Chrissie, capturing her gentleness and tranquillity. So we laid her to rest, and in the following weeks Tina planted flowers and shrubs and made the grave fit for Chrissie – I suppose it symbolised her. After the funeral Brian drove me back to England in my little Volkswagen Polo. The car had been left in Germany all that time because I had needed it to get me backwards and forwards from the hospitals and from southern to northern Germany.
I remember on the way back we spoke little and listened to music; I am very keen on opera and we played a tape of *La Bohème,* but I couldn't listen to the end of it without weeping in the car. I suppose I was in a very fragile state at that time.

But now, nearly two decades later, I can appreciate what we had together – eleven of the most wonderful years that anyone could have. I had lived with Chrissie and there had been very little tension or argument. We had relished everything together – her work, my work, our travel. She and I had enjoyed very similar tastes in music and reading, and we had a very good group of friends whom we both loved dearly. Our painting had been reasonably successful, which I suppose makes life that little bit richer. They had been a wonderful eleven years. At first I was very angry that this had all been taken away.

When I got back to England there was a pile of post waiting for me. One of the letters I opened was from Cancer Research, to which I had given modest amounts over the years. It was a questionnaire about lifestyle choices if you were to avoid cancer, and Chrissie could have given the correct answer to everything that it asked. 'Do you smoke?' No, she did not. 'Do you drink alcohol?' No, she did not. 'Do you eat healthily?' Yes, she did. 'Do you take regular exercise?' Yes, she did. 'Are you basically a calm person and without stress?' Yes, she was. Apparently if you could fulfil all these it would help to combat cancer. I remember answering this questionnaire and then writing a letter – it was a ridiculous thing to do. I enclosed the letter to explain that I had answered the questionnaire on behalf of my wife, who had just died of cancer.

The next weeks were as if I was dead. I didn't paint. I didn't do anything, except mope around. I really felt that my life was over – I couldn't see any way forward at all.

And then there was Dora.

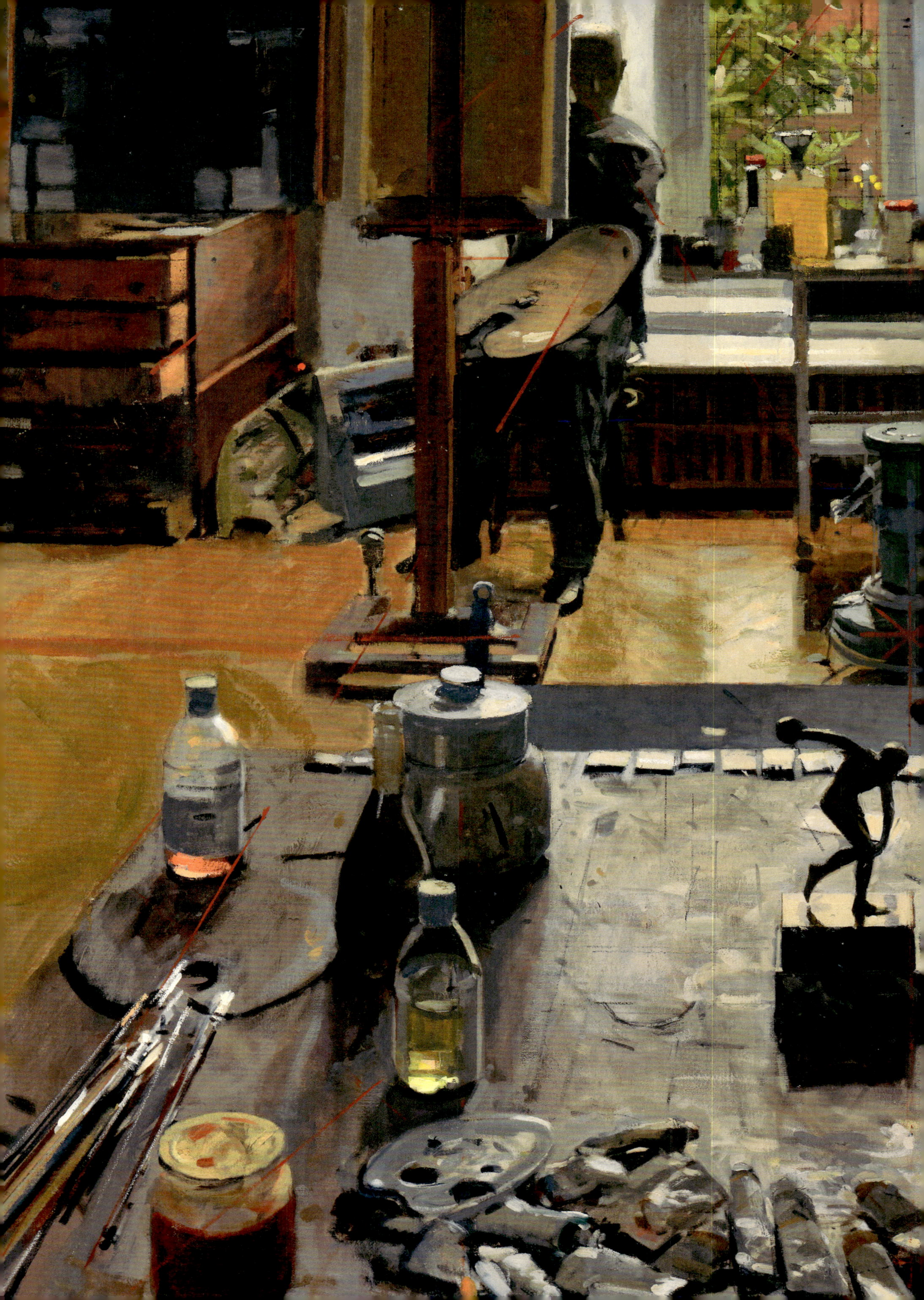

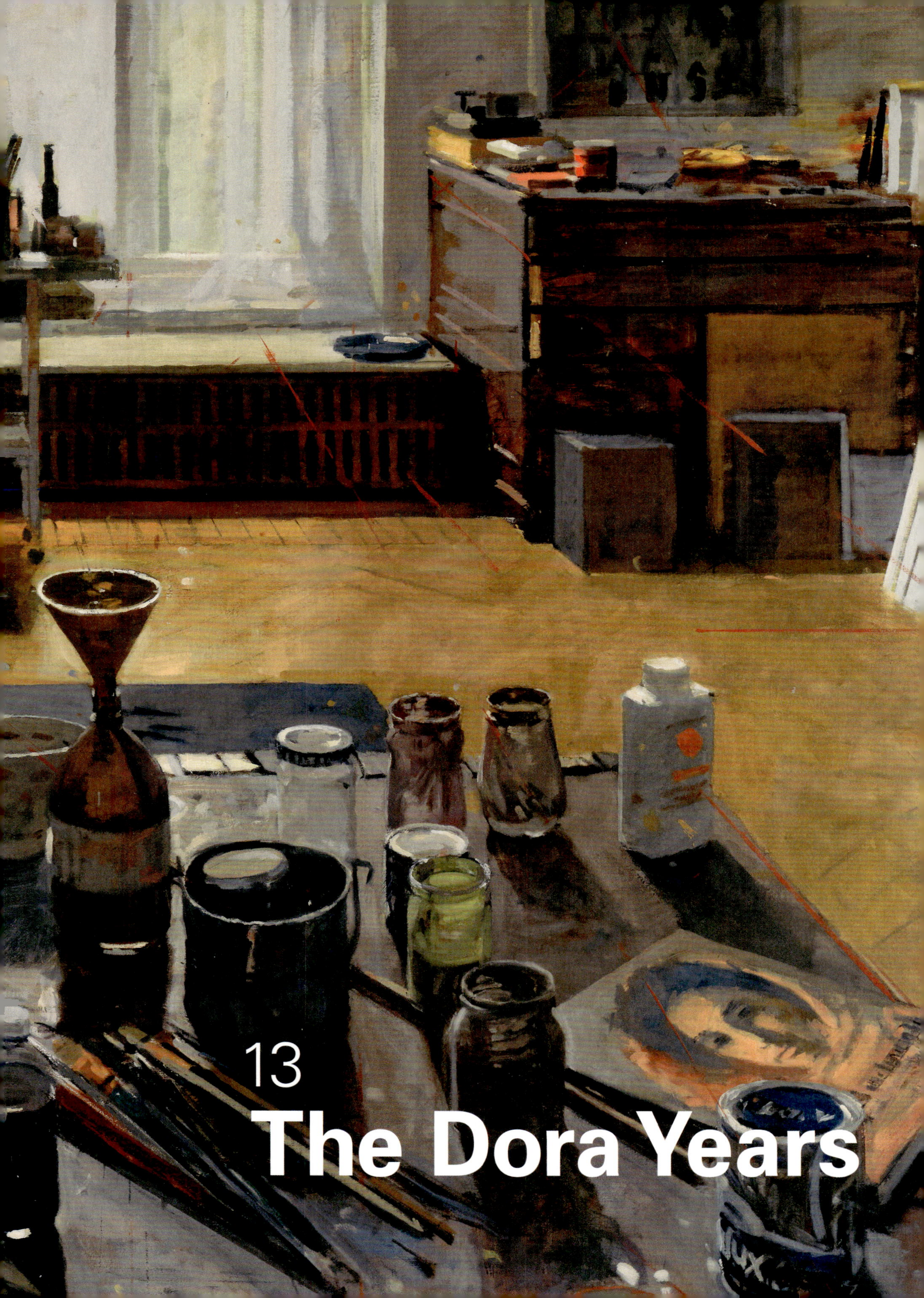

13

The Dora Years

Lunch at Campo Sant'Angelo, 1988
Watercolour, 27.5 x 22.5 cm

This was the painting I was working on the day I met Dora for the first time. Once again, the scale of the figure is paramount: if I had made her any larger or smaller, the composition would not have worked. As so often in Venice, it was working against the light that I found so exciting.

In 1958, when I was studying in Florence on an Italian government scholarship, little did I know that in Friuli, in Italy's northeast corner, a two-year-old girl was living in the city of Udine. That girl was to be very important to me – 42 years later she became my present wife. We first met years before, when I was working in Venice with Chrissie in 1988. I remember that I was painting in a square, the Campo Sant'Angelo, when a young woman in a purple tracksuit came into the square. She sat down by the fountain to eat a sandwich and feed the pigeons. When I saw her I realised immediately that I needed a figure there in the watercolour and quickly added her to the composition.

A little later she came over and looked at what I was doing. She said she liked the painting and asked if she could buy it, but I explained that she would probably find the price a bit funny if I told her (most people do not expect to pay a high price for work from artists working in the streets). Nevertheless, Dora, for that was her name, continued to talk to me. She said she had just been to England and been to see the Royal Academy. I told her I was an exhibitor there and she wrote down my name and went on her way. That evening I told Chrissie that I had met this rather attractive Italian girl in the Campo Sant'Angelo; I thought that we might see her when we were on our *passeggiata* that evening. We didn't, however, and our life continued as it had been. In 1990 Chrissie and I got married, and then in 1992 Chrissie died.

After spending the last four months of Chrissie's life in Germany, I returned to England. I was emotionally shattered, tired and depressed. I came back to an enormous amount of post, of course, as I had been away for four months, and among the letters was one from Dora Bertolutti. She was asking if I still had the watercolour that I had done four years earlier. That year she had visited the Summer Exhibition at the Royal Academy and seen the type of paintings that she liked so much. On looking up the artist in the catalogue, she realised it was the man who had painted her in Venice a few years ago. Dora then decided to find out if I still had the watercolour, as now she felt that she would be able to afford it.

She was in luck. Although I didn't have the original watercolour, which had sold quite quickly on my return from Venice, I did in fact have a reproduction. It was featured in a book about my work that was being prepared at the time and I had a set of proofs with me in the studio. I sent a proof of the painting to her in Italy and some weeks later I got a phone call. Dora told me she was in England with a painting that she wished to send to the Summer Exhibition at the Royal Academy that year. In fact it was a bit early, but I told her to come to the studio with the picture. I thought perhaps we could hand it over to my art handlers, who would then give it in at the time of the submission.

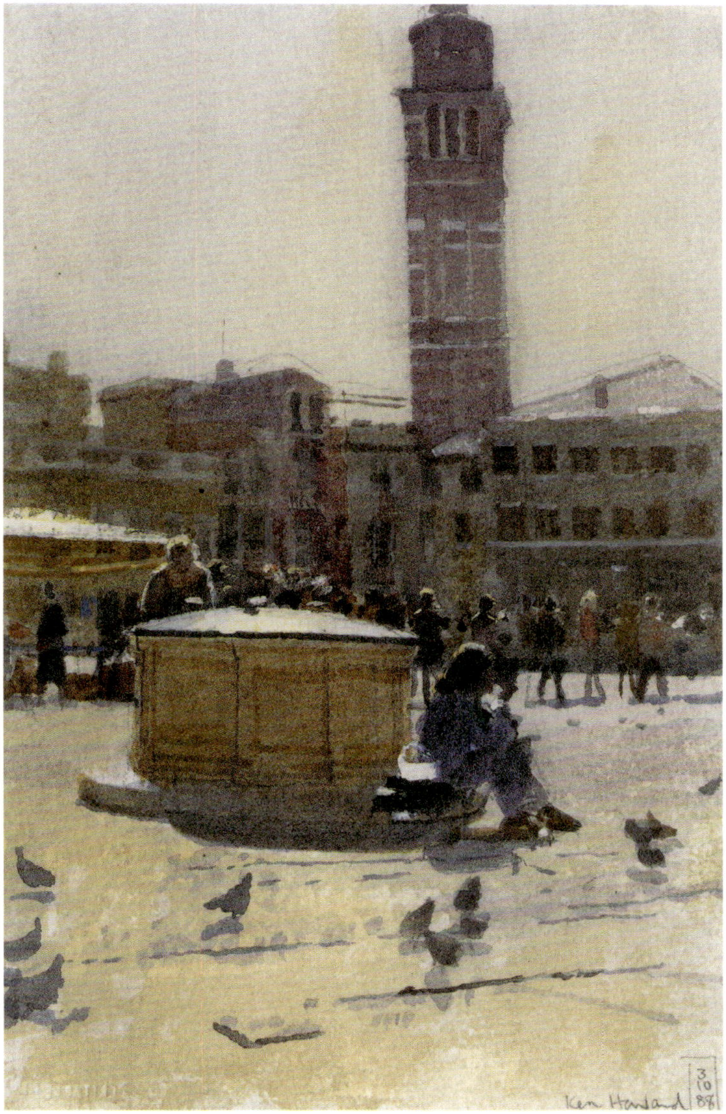

I have to confess that I wasn't particularly interested in seeing anybody at that time in my life. On returning from Germany I had withdrawn into my shell. I wasn't painting at all, and in fact the only thing that I put into the Royal Academy that year was an old painting of a graffiti wall – the painting that I had presented to the Academy as my Diploma Work. I also contributed one of Chrissie's watercolours along with it. I wasn't painting, I was depressed and I can't have been the most exciting person to meet, I must admit.

Anyway, Dora came to the studio with her painting and we took it to Art Moves of Chelsea, then I dropped her off at Ladbroke Grove where she was staying with a friend called Joan. When I dropped Dora off I suggested that if she wasn't busy that evening she might like to have supper with me. I was feeling somewhat lonely, so later that evening I rang her. She agreed to come out and afterwards we came back to the studio. In the end Dora stayed the night and it was the beginning of our relationship. The next two days were very intense and we spent a lot of time together. We either went to exhibitions or I met her friends, but when I drove her down to the airport at Gatwick I couldn't really imagine that it would go on. Dora too, some years later, admitted that she just thought of me as a bit of an adventure. We were both proved very wrong!

At that time Dora was 35 years old and I was a rather worn 60, so naturally she was very exciting for me. When we first met I couldn't believe my luck that she was in any way attracted to me. Physically she was my ideal – dark, very Italian-looking, voluptuous and generally beautiful. We could communicate, although we couldn't speak on any deep level as my Italian was non-existent and Dora's English fairly basic (although very good compared to my Italian). Dora was from very much the same background as myself; she had been born into what you would, I suppose, call a working-class family.

They had a smallholding in the north of Italy and her parents had separated, something fairly rare at that time. When she was still quite young, I think about 21, Dora had married Enzo, a young farmer in that area of Friuli. She was in fact still married when we met, but the relationship had broken down and she and Enzo lived separate lives. When Dora finished full-time school at fourteen she started a secretarial course and later attended evening classes to study for A-levels in order to become a surveyor and work with a building company.

Dora was also very interested in painting and etching, and she attended evening classes to improve them. Two things in her young life had affected Dora's whole outlook. One was the loss of her sister, who was killed aged only 21. She was riding a bike with her young son on the back when a car ran off the road and smashed into the two of them. Both were killed instantly. This had a huge effect on Dora and she said that after that she just lived for the day; she no longer thought that life would go on for ever. The very severe earthquake that devastated Northern Italy in 1976 also had a lasting effect. Among other places it hit Faedis, the village outside Udine where Dora lived. She and her family had to sleep outside after the earthquake for fear of the houses collapsing, and she always remained somewhat cautious about where she was, where she stayed and what floor she was on.

So those two events had affected Dora extremely, making her both excessively cautious of what life could bring and eager to make the most of it while she was alive. When she married Enzo they originally struggled, but then they gradually built a large house in the country outside Udine. Enzo was extremely successful, his farm flourished and I suppose they became what one would call 'comfortably off'. Unfortunately their personalities, much like Annie's and mine, grew apart rather than closer together. Gradually the marriage broke down and they started to lead separate lives. It was then that I was fortunate enough to meet Dora.

When we first got together and Dora showed her mother a photograph of us, her mother's first reaction was that 'even for me he is old'. I have always been sorry that my mother never knew Dora – she died before Dora came into my life, but I think she would have approved of her. My mother didn't approve of my first two wives for various reasons – I think mothers often find the wives of their sons quite difficult. They don't fit the image of the women they have imagined. Nevertheless, I think that in Dora's case my mother would have approved greatly. She is very hard working, direct and down to earth; Dora says exactly what she thinks, and my mother did just the same. My mother was also very conscious of what we used to call in those days 'class', and she always felt that my first two wives were 'above' me socially, whereas she would have felt that Dora and I were well-suited in our backgrounds. Working-class people of her generation often revealed a strange, inverted snobbery. They felt strongly that their children should stay within the same class and not 'get above themselves'.

Some time ago I was asked to write an article for a magazine on 'what the artist needs'. When I was first approached to do this I asked what the last artist had said. Apparently he needed Naples yellow, which I thought rather boring. At first I told them to give me some time to think about it, but then I changed my mind. 'No, I don't need any time. I know exactly what every artist needs. Every artist needs a Dora.' Once Dora came to live with me I realised that she did everything for me, other than paint the pictures. When we travel she always does all the driving, partly because she suffers from travel sickness, but also because she enjoys it. Dora likes being in control of things and she does feel so when she is driving a car. She also wanted very much to enter into my working life and so she became in effect my studio assistant. In other words she prepares the grounds for the canvases when they arrive from the canvas-maker, which is a great time-saver for me. When I need a model she will pose, which is an incredible advantage. I also enjoy painting her probably more than my other models – partly because it helps to know a model you are painting. I don't mean that in any deep philosophical sense – it is simply that I have become very familiar with Dora visually through living with her and being with her so much, and that really helps. On the whole, however, Dora would rather have me employ a model – she doesn't enjoy doing nothing, as it were.

Dora's way of looking after the house seems to me very Italian, as Italian women have a particular feeling for cleanliness (not necessarily tidiness). Dora doesn't interfere too much in the studio, but she certainly wants the house to

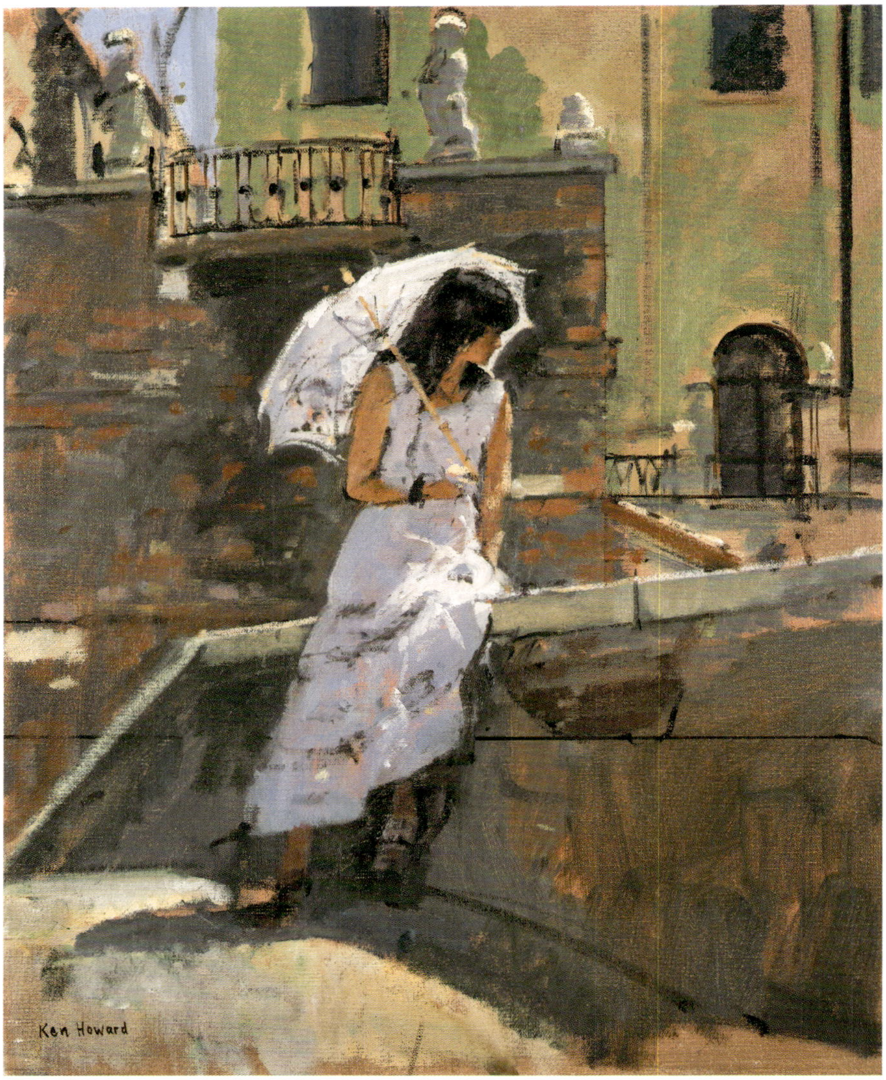

be clean, whereas I, although naturally a tidier, am not particularly bothered about cleanliness. Dora makes sure that my clothes are freshly laundered, and she loves preparing everything for me. For the first time in my life I find that breakfast is ready on the table when I get up in the morning. She prepares it the night before, and she also enjoys making lunch and cooking dinner in the evening. Italian women know how to look after their men, and I suppose I really do appreciate that. I admit that I am basically selfish. I think anyone who paints or is creative has to be relatively selfish. Life has to fit around your work – you can't fit your work around your life. So as your partner is very much part of an artist's life, she has to fit life around your work as well. Dora finds no problem in doing that.

On the contrary, Dora would be concerned if I didn't work. She's always asking when am I going out or where am I going to work. When we are in Venice she always comes with me in the morning and carries my materials to wherever I am going, which I appreciate, I suppose because I am getting a little older now.

She comes to meet me at lunchtime and brings the materials back to the studio, then gives me a good lunch. If it's the middle of summer I'll maybe have a siesta and then go out again in the evening, which some partners might feel is a bit antisocial. But Dora has no problem with this work ethic and wants very much to fit in and be part of it herself. She loves being involved in projects, such as the garden down in Cornwall where we have a meadow. This used to be completely overgrown with brambles and goodness knows what, but it has been transformed into a large, wonderful field with 50 trees in it, as well as vegetables, flowers and a summer house at the top. I had really nothing to do with that, apart from paying a few bills; it is Dora's creation and she keeps the whole thing going.

One of my regrets in life – and I haven't really had very many – is that I sold St Clement's Hall in Mousehole; I know that Dora would have loved to have had that house. When we first got together in 1993 I still owned the house as well as the studio, but I sold the house soon afterwards. I know that Dora regrets that very much, and I do now as well. It's no good looking back on things, but if I had my time again I wouldn't sell St Clement's. There was no real need to, but it was just that after Chrissie's death I lost interest – it had been a special place for us and that was all over. I bought the second studio in London, the one next door, and I had taken on debts to do so, which I didn't really enjoy. I felt that if I sold the house in Cornwall I could pay off the debts in London and not feel pressurised by them any more.

I think most artists don't like feeling pressurised as this means you have to take on commissions you would not choose to do. This is, of course, one of the problems of earning your living through painting if you don't already have money in the family. Often artists came from relatively prosperous backgrounds, or found rich patrons. Many of the Impressionists, for example, did not come from poor families in which it was essential to earn a living from their work, despite the general belief that they were bohemians. Monet and Pissarro may not have been born wealthy, but Degas was from quite a rich family, Cézanne's father was a banker and Toulouse-Lautrec had a title. When I was young I felt it was an advantage to have to earn money; it made you get up in the morning and concentrate on your work. I didn't think I necessarily required this stimulus, but the necessity focused my inspiration and my innate desire to paint. I thought it was helpful to have to work every day according to a certain discipline.

But life was different then. When I was young I had very little money, so there was no problem with overindulgence on food and wine. Work was all absorbing to me and filled my life totally, so in a way I worked much harder and my mind was sharp and clear. Later on in life one inevitably gets committed to

Dora and the White Parasol, 1997
Oil on canvas,
180 x 150 cm

I painted Dora on this bridge in the Calle Lunga, San Barnaba. She posed for me on the spot, much in the tradition of the Newlyn painters.

things. You belong to societies and may be President or Patron or Vice-President of them. Such responsibilities take up your life, and can become an obstacle to getting your work done – something easier to see in other people's lives than in one's own. One of the Academicians I knew very well, for example, had a studio in Chelsea. Soon after I was elected to the Academy, I remember, I asked him if I could paint his studio as I was doing a series of other people's studios, and he agreed. We arranged that I should come at the end of the morning so as not to disturb his working day. He then went to the Chelsea Arts Club for lunch and did not return till about four in the afternoon, so I could paint for about five hours while he was away.

What I inevitably observed when I arrived at his studio in the late morning was that dealing with letters and making phone calls were always making demands on his time. Then he would go to the Chelsea Arts Club for lunch, where he met friends, had a good meal and probably a nice bottle of wine – all disruptive to the working day. I had no such temptations when I was young, but now I know that if somebody asks me to do something I will generally oblige (I am quite bad at saying no to things). This can lead you into all sorts of situations where your time is sapped.

Now, in fact, I find that the best time for work is when I leave London. When I go to Venice I can honestly say that I still work six days out of seven, for maybe twelve hours a day. In Cornwall, too, I still work six days out of seven throughout the daylight hours. I start early in the morning and continue until late into the evening. In London, because of all the other commitments, I just can't do that. I have to deal with things at the Academy and matters arising from other societies and projects with which I am involved.

I met a young student recently and my advice to him was to keep away from distracting commitments. I know that sounds incredibly selfish, but in the end it's the only way to be productive and get work done. After all, the most important thing in any painter's life is work. All the rest may be flattering and good for one's ego, but it doesn't do anything for your art. I always remember seeing how my friend was caught up with letters and calls in his studio. I swore to myself that I would never let this happen to me. I vowed that I would always leave other involvements until the evening; the first priority every day would be painting, and everything else would have to fit around it. My life, in other words, would have to fit around my work. Now I've reached a certain age and when I'm in London I have to look to myself, which isn't easy; very often my work has to fit around my life. This is hard to avoid, but I know that it isn't a good thing.

Now to return to my early days with Dora. When she went off to Gatwick after we first got together, I imagined that would be the end of things. Dora admitted later that she had felt exactly the same way. But we began to miss each other when we were apart; we started to talk on the phone and she started to mention coming to England from time to time. Then I started going to Italy every so often, and slowly my life started to take off again. I began to emerge from the hole I'd gone into after Chrissie died, when all ambition for exhibiting disappeared. In fact, my paintings became very dark, very black, as they had done for a time after my mother died. I think emotionally one experiences a great deal that one doesn't necessarily recognise at the time, but it still finds expression in one's work.

That first year after Chrissie's death was pretty chaotic for me, partly because I was involved in all sorts of things. I was on the Council of the Royal Academy, for instance, which was quite invasive. I became President of a couple of societies which also took up a lot of time. I started travelling a lot, not only to Italy, including Venice, but also going to Norway to spend time with Bibi and Haakon, Chrissie's half-sister and brother-in-law. When people lose someone, they react to it in different ways. Some people are completely shattered and accept it totally at once, whereas others may become extremely active in an attempt to deny what has happened. I think that was what happened to me, in a strange way. I went into a state of denial after Chrissie's death, and I had one hell of a year. My work went to pot and I didn't exhibit very much. I drank too much and spent far too much time at the Chelsea Arts Club, with all that involved. I had what the Germans euphemistically call 'a friend' in London and another in Cornwall; I was also seeing Dora in Italy. I didn't deny to any of these friends what my life was, but obviously it wasn't very good for me. I had just reached a complete state of denial about what was going on in my life.

Dora, with her usual sense of humour, once said to me, 'When I met up with you I thought you were old and you would be faithful, but now I realise that you are just old.' This is typically Dora, she never gets excessively jealous about anything. Somehow she stuck with me through all this and gradually I came to realise that I wasn't just attracted to her physically; I was responding to her as a whole person. I began to realise that I couldn't live without her and that I loved her, and it was then that she became a stabilising influence in my life. I began to lead a more coherent life and concentrated on her and our relationship. In so doing I got back into my work again. Painting once again became the centre of my life, rather than a frenetic rushing around like a headless chicken, trying to ignore or overcome what had happened.

Street Scene in Udaipur, 1993
Oil on canvas, 100 x 120 cm

As I have grown older I have become more and more obsessed by light. This painting was made in London soon after I returned from a trip with Spencer Scott Travel. It was painted from a series of watercolours I made from a rooftop in Udaipur, just after midday. The light reflects directly off the road, casting relatively short shadows, and tones again were orchestrated using red, green and earth colours.

During that first year after Chrissie's death I also travelled a lot. As well as going to Italy on a regular basis I was commissioned to go down to Dubrovnik during the Bosnian War. The idea was that I would do watercolours of the old city, which had been virtually destroyed by shelling. The watercolours would then be exhibited in London, and the commission from them would all go to a charity raising money to rebuild Dubrovnik. I did a similar thing with a group of artists in Israel. We had a show when we got back and the commission from the paintings went to a scheme to grow trees in swamp areas in Palestine, helping to reclaim the land.

I was also taken up by a travel company called Spencer Scott Travel. When Chrissie was alive I had often received phone calls from travel companies asking if I would go on trips as the attraction: 'Paint in Cuba with Ken Howard' or 'Paint in Rajasthan with Ken Howard' and so forth. I always said no when Chrissie was alive because she wasn't keen. When I asked her, she always replied, 'Why would we want to do that, when we can afford to do it by ourselves anyway?'

But when she died I suddenly felt that all my time had to be filled up. When I was approached to do such a trip I initially said no, out of habit, but then I reflected and asked, 'Well what does it involve?' They told me I could choose anywhere in the world that I wanted to go. Expenses would be paid and I didn't need to commit myself to teaching. All I had to do was paint with the people on the trip. So I agreed, feeling that it was another way of travelling and getting through this time in my life. In a strange sort of way, I suppose it was similar to what happened when Annie and I divorced, when I started going to Northern Ireland, then to India and finally all over the Far East, Middle East and America. Travel for me has always been a sort of cleansing thing.

Anyway, I agreed to do these trips. In the end I did them for several years – one a year – and they included Cuba, Turkey and South Yemen. Obviously I did a trip to Venice and various other parts of the world – I remember going to Morocco, for example – and generally travelled around. They were good trips really; all I had to do was paint, and the people on the trips also painted. I didn't have to give them instructions or anything; our contact was mainly social. In the evening I would always have two different people each side of me to talk to over dinner, and a couple of times during the trip I did lectures in the evening as I always took slides with me. Basically these were painting trips, and they were very good business. Not only did I get paid for going on the trip, plus all my expenses, but at the end of the trip people very often bought my work. It had begun in a dark time, but it became quite an enjoyable way of earning part of my living.

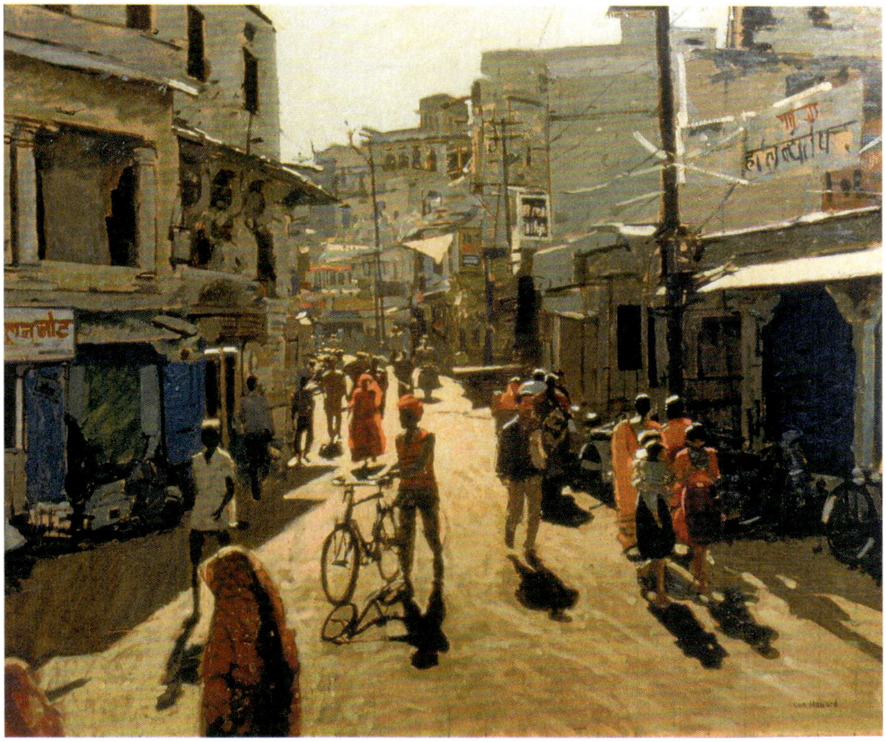

When I worked in Dubrovnik I was resting one day and met some soldiers who had come down from Mostar in Bosnia and Herzegovina. They were part of the multi-national forces that were there at the time and they recognised me from Northern Ireland. They asked what I was doing and invited me to come up to Mostar and do some work for them there. I explained that I couldn't because I was already committed, but I did offer to come back out and I did in fact return. It was an incredible experience. War is certainly terrible, in the right sense of word, yet it does create beautiful, exciting and arresting images. Mostar in many places was what France must have been like in the First World War. The devastation reminded me very much of when I had worked in Beirut, in the sense of Yeats's 'terrible beauty', and it took me back to my experience of Northern Ireland. I did some quite good paintings in Mostar. I exhibited a large one made up of graffiti and various images in the Royal Academy that year and I think that it was quite a jolt for some, who had got so used to my paintings of Venice and studios and beaches. Many were quite surprised to find me doing such tough, raw painting. They were people who hadn't known my Northern Ireland images and the work I had done when I was a war artist.

All of this time, of course, Dora was becoming more and more a part of my life. I did go through a stage where I felt that it was all too early, that I hadn't really got over the loss of Chrissie. I remember meeting Dora in Paris one weekend and telling her that I wasn't going to see her any more. She was very upset and I realised afterwards that I was stupid, but at the time it felt the right thing. I went back to England and missed her dreadfully, and after a few weeks I rang her, trying

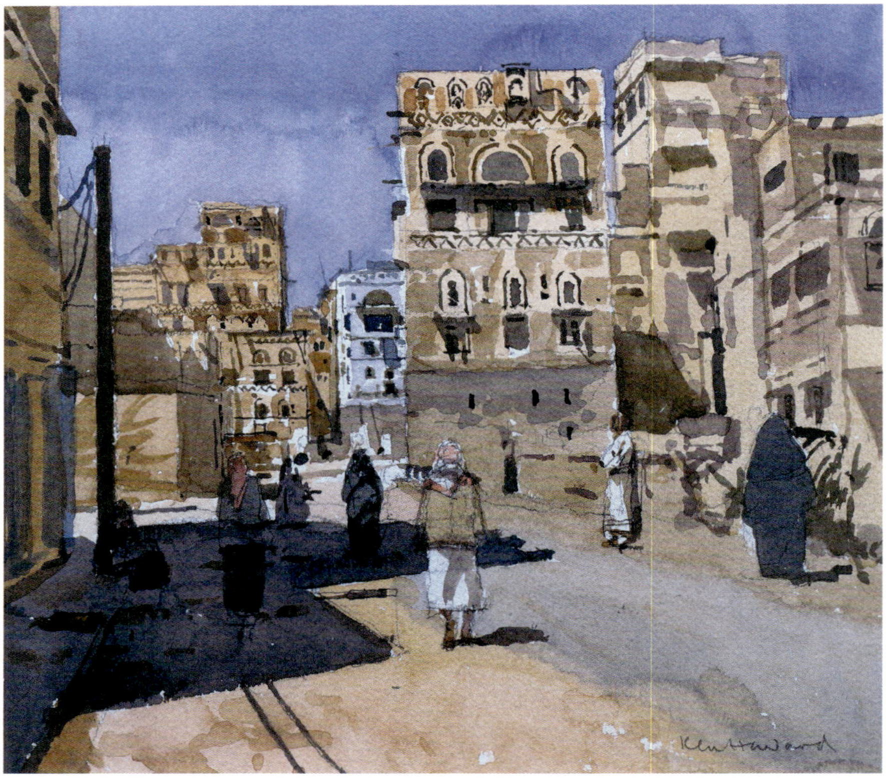

to pretend that it was just a conversation. Really, of course, I wanted to know all that had been happening to her and wanted very much to see her again. When I asked her if she had been seeing anyone else, Dora told me that she had been seeing a photographer and that they had gone for a long weekend down to Brioni in Croatia – one of the places that Dora and I had visited at the beginning of our relationship. Of course, being a typical man, that really got to me. I asked if I could come down to Italy the next weekend and she said yes, I could come if I wanted to. Dora was, typically, just being honest. She obviously still liked me and had been missing me, although she didn't say so directly.

That weekend was quite funny really, because when I got there the one thing I wanted to do was to go back to the hotel and be with her. I flew to Venice and got the train up to Udine, where Dora met me at the station. I asked where we were booked in, but she wanted to go round Udine for a walk. I was longing to get back to the hotel. We passed a shop with some beautiful clothes. Dora said, 'I've always wanted clothes from that shop,' and I suggested that we went in to get some. She tried on various clothes, while I said this looks great, that looks great – all the time desperately wanting to get back to the hotel. When we emerged she mentioned a restaurant at Cividale that she'd always wanted to eat at and wondered if we could go. And I thought, well yes, all right, and we went to the restaurant at Cividale and had a great big meal. By the time we got back to the hotel it must have been about eleven o'clock in the evening; I had drunk a fair bit and my original desire was somewhat waning. Yet, without being conscious of it, Dora knew how to treat a man if you like. She knew just what to do, and it was after that weekend, really, that I straightened my life out and became committed to her.

The weeks went by and I became aware of how much I enjoyed being with Dora. I realised the complexity of her character and how it fascinated me, and it wasn't all that long after that she left Italy and came to London to live with me. On the New Year's Eve of the Millennium I had a black-tie dinner in the studio for friends of mine – not typical of me, but it was a special time. I asked Dora to marry me that evening and she agreed. We got married in the September of that year.

Our wedding was a great experience. Friends came over from Italy to mix with others from across London and generally around England – including people whom I'd known almost all my life. We were married in Chelsea Registry Office as we'd both been married before, and we had the blessing in the Boltons Church just round the corner from my studio. Two different priests officiated – the priest of the church itself and also a great friend of mine, Paul Abram, whom I had met in Northern Ireland when he was the padre of the Parachute Regiment. When Dora and I married he was the padre of the Tower of London. They did the blessing between them, and we had lunch in the Chelsea Arts Club for all the Italians. In the evening the Academy gave us the private rooms and we had a wonderful reception with friends who came from everywhere. And the painting that I'd done in Campo Sant'Angelo on the day that I'd met Dora all those years ago was loaned to us by its owners. They liked it too much to let me have it back, but they loaned it to us for that evening. We displayed it prominently to show the beginning of our story.

After we were married Dora became, if anything, more caring. Maybe it was with me getting older, I don't know, but she seemed to want to look after me even more. She has a natural desire to look after people – I noticed during my life that whenever we were in Italy, if one of her family was in hospital, or maybe an elderly member of the family was in an old people's home, Dora made a point of going to see them. She genuinely wanted to visit them. And she would be the first to go if anyone she knew was in hospital in Venice. I feel very fortunate that when I do eventually slow down and perhaps become somewhat incapable, I am sure Dora will look after me; that is her natural response to everybody she loves. When her father was dying of cancer she took him home from the hospital and looked after him right up until the day he died, dealing with all the difficult things that arose. Dora seems to do those things instinctively, without question.

It may seem strange that someone who has such a natural nurturing bent has not had children of her own, but Dora never really felt the need or the desire.

Morning Light, Yemen, 1997
Watercolour, 17.5 x 25 cm

This watercolour was made in Sana'a, the main city in the Yemen, during a trip for Spencer Scott Travel. My favourite medium is watercolour, which is like playing a single musical instrument, whereas oil painting is like trying to conduct an orchestra. Painting a watercolour is like balancing on a tightrope – you can fall off at any moment.

I would say this is strange, except that I feel very much the same way myself. I enjoy children when they're around, but don't really feel that I have missed out in life through not having them – though I suppose that may just be because I haven't experienced it! Dora was pregnant for a short time in our relationship, although she hadn't been trying for a child when she conceived. It was a very short period, but I do remember that psychologically I changed completely. By this time I was already in my late sixties, yet the idea of having to support a child, bring it up, put it through school and so forth didn't deter me at all. Instead I felt a certain excitement. When the child didn't happen I was disappointed, but I didn't feel we must try again. It was exactly the same with Dora, who is very practical and not one for getting over-emotional about such things. How she is so balanced I don't know, but it is the way she is. Dora has in fact been involved with a child already, because a friend of hers sadly died when her son, Andrea, was aged only six. As the father did not take responsibility for the boy, Dora and her husband brought him up as their own, although the father would not let them adopt him formally. Nevertheless, Dora brought him up as her son and maybe that fulfilled her natural mothering instinct. They were closely involved throughout his time at school, but he later became very independent – as children do when they grow up. Dora was involved with me by then; I suppose I filled the vacuum when Andrea,

Dora and I preparing to leave the studio for our marriage in September 2000.

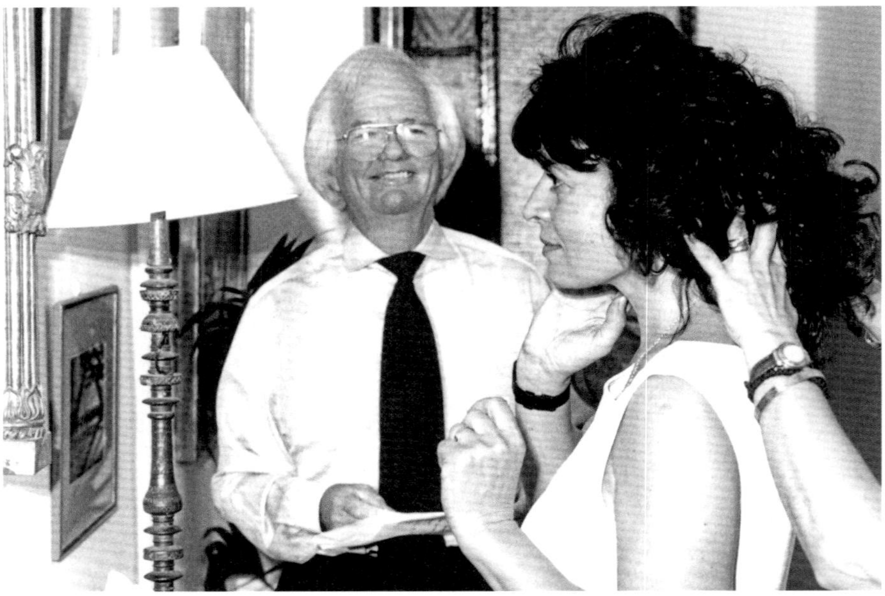

now in his late teens and early twenties, no longer needed Dora as he had done when he was a child.

Immediately after Chrissie's death I lost the impetus for work. Both the drive and the need to paint vanished, but when they returned I continued with the New Grafton Gallery. David Wolfers died just after Dora and I were married, and I was flattered to be approached by Richard Green to join his gallery. I felt that it was time for me to get back into Bond Street and the West End properly, and Richard Green's gallery had such a very good reputation. I was in fact the first living artist to be 'acquired' by him on that sort of permanent basis.

As I have mentioned, part of the deal was exclusivity. When I was young I had always resisted becoming exclusive to anyone; I enjoyed the cut and thrust of dealers and people coming to the studio and buying. My work has always been relatively popular so I had never felt the need to be exclusive to anyone, but by the time Richard Green asked me to join his gallery I was approaching 70. I felt that it was probably time for a more organised professional life and that having one person to handle everything would leave me more peace for work. My life was complicated in many ways at that time, so cutting out all the different dealers who requested work would at least simplify that aspect of things. I told Richard that I would like to have one show a year with him if I was to be exclusive – I naturally produce quite a lot when I'm working in Venice and Cornwall, for example. If you are concerned with the effect of light you are obliged to work quickly and on a small scale, so you do end up producing quite a lot. So a show a year seemed a reasonable request for me to make.

After four years, however, I realised that it was too much. We cut back to every eighteen months which, combined with the Royal Academy Summer Exhibition (by then a regular source of income), was enough for me to live on. I had also been elected to practically everything you could belong to by that time – the Royal Institute of Oil Painters, the Royal Watercolour Society, the Royal Society of British Artists, the Royal West of England Academy and the Royal Academy. I was President of the New English Art Club, and I still needed to show with all these groups. My exclusivity to Richard Green was useful as it started to limit the amount of work I had to find for exhibitions and dealers. Richard's is, of course, a very professional gallery; he invested in me in terms of advertising and catalogues, and got my name around, even though previously I'd exhibited much more widely. In these ways the change suited me very well.

Probably one aspect that I didn't enjoy as much was that once I was with Richard the price of my work went up. That impacted somewhat on the breadth of my following – before then, many more people could afford what I did and I liked the idea of my paintings finding a home. I always remember that one of my heroes, Walter Sickert, said that the utilitarian purpose of painting is to decorate walls – and although this may not be the thing to say in the early twenty-first century, I think it is still very relevant today.

Painting has decorated the walls of caves, the palaces of Greeks and Romans, the magnificent homes of the Medici and, later on, the houses of the burghers of Holland. It has to speak to people and have emotional impact, as well as many other things, of course, but I do believe its decorative purpose is important. It is for me a concern that art today is made for museums and exhibitions rather than for domestic consumption. I love to go to people's houses and see my work on their walls – it's like seeing that your children have come home. One particular couple in the West Country, Sir Peter and Nancy Whiteley, have nearly 50 of my paintings. Others may have 25, 30 or 35 – rather like in music when you buy several pieces from a particular composer if you like his or her work. If you like a person's paintings and they are affordable, people want to own several. I know that I very seldom buy just one piece from an artist I admire. I usually buy four or five, which is quite logical to me.

I have always had a great love of music, and the connection between it and painting has become more important in my later years. Now if someone asks me what I feel painting is about, one of my newer responses is that it is about orchestrating tone, colour and light. That might sound a bit ethereal, but for me it is the truth. My work is about form as much as content, and form requires this orchestration, the fitting together of parts into a unified whole. This is in the end what composition is about, and what painting really means to me. In terms of composition painting is not that different from music in form, but the content affects us in a different way. I often wonder why I never cry when looking at a painting, whereas music can move me sometimes to tears. I have been known to weep when I see certain films, but painting doesn't have this effect. I think the reason for this is something to do with the content of the work. Yet I believe the analogy is valid in terms of the creative process. The form of painting in the end is not that different from the form of music or the form of writing.

My love of music is perhaps one way in which Dora and I are different. She is much younger than I am and favours more popular music, whereas over the years I have become very committed to opera. I sometimes drag Dora down to Bayreuth in northeast Bavaria or to Plymouth to hear Glyndebourne on Tour. She is very good about it and I think that she enjoys opera more and more as she gets older. I always play music when I have a model and some of them have told me that they started to listen to opera and classical music as a result of posing for me. I am quite selective in the music I choose – pop music is far too disturbing, as are Wagner and Beethoven. I can paint to musicians such as Bach, Mozart or Vivaldi, however, and I can paint to a background of opera by Puccini or Verdi. I use music as a way of keeping a distance between myself and the model. I don't like to talk when I work and without music I would have to say something to the model from time to time. If you play music it fills that void and there is no oppressive quiet. You don't need to speak to the model from one rest to the next and that is a great advantage.

The latest place that I use as a studio is in Venice. It is not new for me – in the course of the past 30 years I must have been to Venice about 50 times, I suppose. Back in the '70s I used to go maybe once, possibly twice a year, and gradually my visits increased. Dora comes from Udine to the northeast of Venice and when we got together we started to go to the city on a very regular basis. First we stayed with a friend who had a studio, then we rented apartments – a much more reasonable way of staying in the city than in hotels, as Venice is an extremely expensive place to stay (almost as expensive as living in London). Eventually I realised that bringing my materials and clothes down every time was getting too much. I was about 65 by then and didn't really want to be carrying this gear there all the time. I had found ways of managing by making several friends in Venice, some of whom had shops; I used to leave my painting equipment with them when I went home and then just pick them up the next time I was back.

But eventually it was inevitable that Dora and I should consider trying to find a permanent base in Venice. My first wish was to get a floor in a *palazzo*, a typical Venetian apartment if you like. We looked around and found a floor in the Palazzo Berlendis, located on the Fondamente Nuove near to San Giovanni e Paolo. Dora and I decided that we would go for this property. It was on the first floor, not the ground floor – you never buy anything on the ground floor in Venice because of the *acqua alta* (high water). Most places in Venice flood – it's not the case absolutely everywhere, but certainly most places. The first floor is the ideal. When people in the past owned a whole *palazzo* they used to live on the first floor in the winter; the ceilings were lower and the rooms smaller, so you could keep warmer than on the upper floor.

I fell in love with this flat as nothing had really been done to it. The ceilings were original seventeenth-century, as were the windows and doors. The floors did slope, I must admit, so that you had to climb up the living room – well, that's a slight

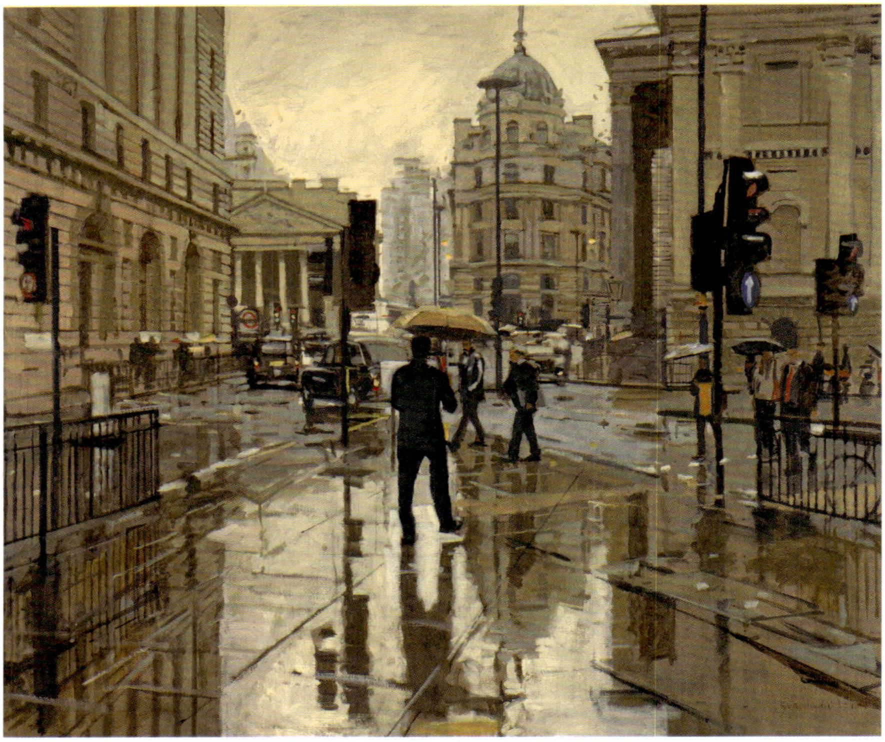

The City of London, Rain Effect, 2005
Oil on canvas, 100 x 120 cm

This work was made from studies that I painted while sheltering in a doorway by the Mansion House, looking towards the Royal Exchange. The work was painted entirely in the studio using a very limited earth palette of blue-black, titanium white, raw umber, raw sienna, burnt sienna and yellow ochre.

exaggeration, but there were structural problems. However, I fell in love with the place as soon as I saw it and wanted very much to buy it. It belonged to an elderly admiral who'd commanded the Italian Navy during the first Gulf War. He and his wife lived in Rome, but they kept this apartment in Venice and had now decided to sell it. The admiral agreed to sell it to us, we fixed the price and sorted out details of the furniture; everything seemed fine. Eventually he invited us to go and have lunch with him at the Officers' Club near the Arsenale in Venice, which I thought was to settle the final details of the sale. When we met, however, he informed us that his wife had decided not to sell the apartment after all. I must admit that I was absolutely shattered – in my dreams I was already living in this apartment in the Venetian *palazzo* and suddenly it was taken away.

I was now determined to find and buy a property in Venice, so I told Dora to carry on looking. I went off each day and got on with my painting, while Dora visited various properties and reported back. We looked at several and eventually she said, 'I think I've found exactly what we want. It's an apartment in Cannaregio, away from all the tourism, up near the Fondamente Nuove and just around the corner from the Palazzo Berlendis.' It wasn't exactly the typical Venetian apartment although it was very large – about 300 square metres. Actually, it was a *mansarda*, or roof space. I had told Dora not to consider anything above the second floor because I was already beginning to be conscious of the long climb when we had been to some apartments on the fourth floor. It was a quite a slog getting up four floors with all your equipment and one had to consider how many times one went back and forth in the day. I'd asked her to try and find something on the first floor,

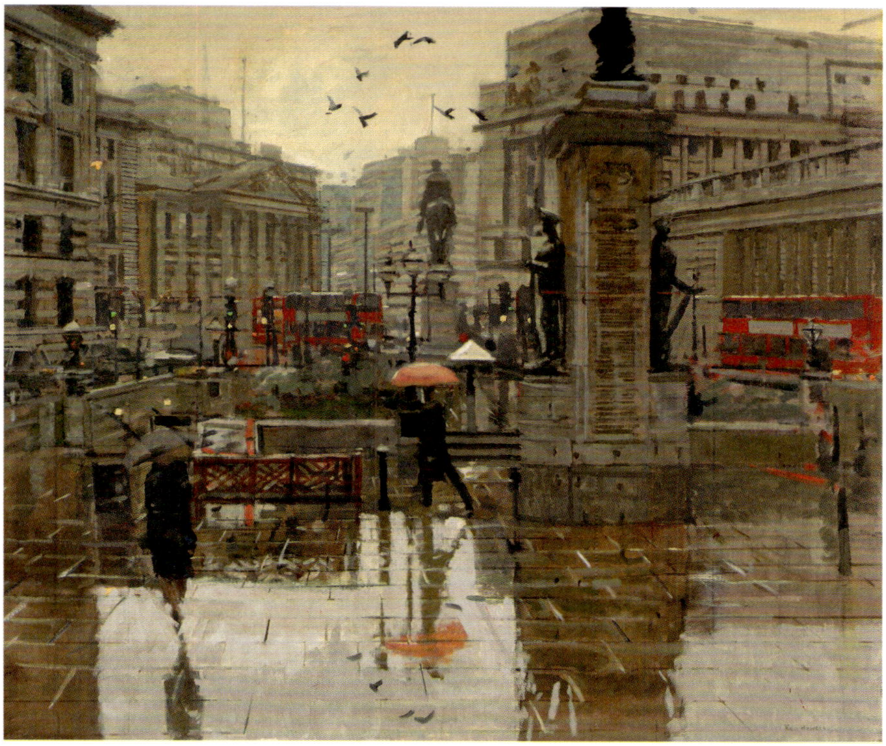

which in fact this was: a *mansarda* over a couple of shops. It was an absolutely wonderful, very large space that had been beautifully converted by the family who owned the business below. Ideally we wanted our own front door, because in Venice a floor in a *palazzo* usually means sharing the entrance and the cost of its upkeep, with other people. Dora, very wisely, preferred to find a place that had its own front door and didn't depend on anyone else.

And this she had discovered in the little Ramo e Corte del Paludo. The properties underneath belonged to a plumber and his son, who ran the business from below and lived in a *mansarda* above. When he divorced we bought it lock, stock and barrel – the knives, forks, spoons, even the linen, all the furniture and everything. It is an unusual apartment as the bathroom is fairly large; I considered covering the floor and making it into my studio because it had a skylight, but in the end we left it as a bathroom. It is a rather grand bathroom, appropriate to a plumber, with a jacuzzi almost large enough to swim in, as well as a sauna, bath and shower. It is rather too much for us, but I'm not a great one for knocking places about; I prefer to preserve spaces as they have been planned.

The great thing about the property is that it has three skylights in the roof, as well as normal windows, giving the rooms a lot of light. This is very unusual in Venice, where interiors are often quite dark. When you think of the paintings of John Singer Sargent, for example, they very often show dark interiors. Walter Sickert, who also painted interiors in Venice, used low tones and strong contrasts. This was also an ideal purchase for me because nothing needed doing to it. We literally moved in on Tuesday and I was painting by Wednesday – not something

From the Royal Exchange, Rain Effect, 2005
Oil on canvas, 100 x 120 cm

Reflections have fascinated me all my life, so rain has always been an inspiration. Whether in Northern Ireland, Venice or London, as soon as it rains the world seems full of subjects. This painting, made in the studio, derived from a series of studies I made sheltering under the portico of the Royal Exchange on an overcast day.

you can say of many places. The longer I've stayed in our Venetian house, the more I have fallen in love with it. Once I had got the Palazzo Berlendis out of my system, I developed a real affection for the Ramo e Corte del Paludo.

When I am in Venice we have a very strict working pattern. I like working early in the morning and in the evening, and tend to go out at around six or seven in the morning. I return about eleven and have a siesta until around four, then go back to work from four till eight depending on the time of year. In the winter I obviously start later, and right in the middle of winter I just go home for a bit of lunch and then go straight out again, because even in Venice the days get very short.

The wonderful thing about painting in Venice, though, is that it is always beautiful. It is exquisite at all times of year, in all lights, atmospheres and weather conditions. When it rains the effects are absolutely incredible and you can go and paint under the arches in San Marco or in the Piazzetta. In sunlight the light is very strong and full of vibrancy; it bounces off the water. Even on one of those grey, flat days, Venice is always lovely.

I suppose I look a little bit like a bagman when I work in Venice. My clothes are always daubed with paint, I'm usually covered with it too, and I suppose at my age I do look a bit decrepit. Indeed I know I do: a few weeks ago when I was working there I sat down for a rest by one of the bridges and some kind soul immediately came up and offered me some money. He obviously thought that I was a down and out who had fallen on hard times in Venice. Dora always finds this quite amusing; she quite likes my indifference to this aspect of my work.

With Tom Stoppard at my Richard Green Exhibition in 2002.

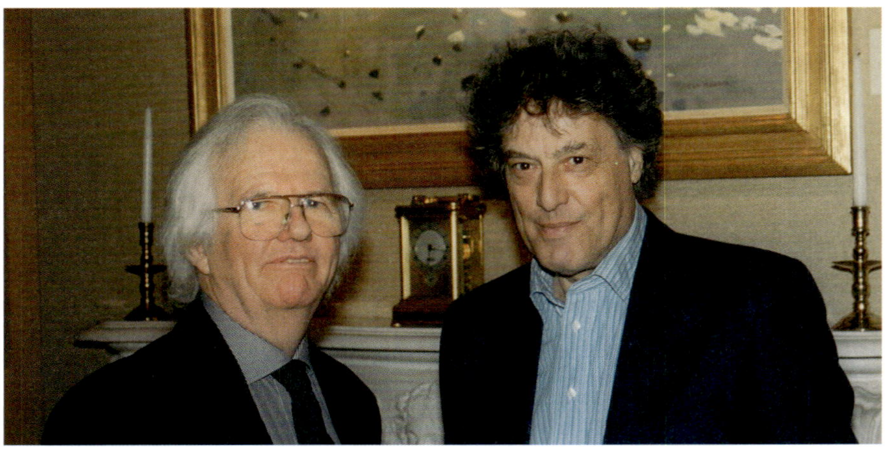

We eventually got things sorted, bringing down the paintings and books and possessions that we needed to make it an actual home. One of my priorities was to get my studio corner sorted out. If you are a painter your life must revolve around your work, and for me I confess a property really centres round the area that I work in.

Having got the studio in Venice sorted out, Dora felt the need of another project to take on. She had been a surveyor as a young woman and still loves having an involvement in properties. In a rather complicated process she had inherited the house in Faedis where she had lived as a child. It essentially consisted of a house at the foot of the mountains with a barn at the side where the cows lived and pigs in pigsties. Since those days there has inevitably been development around their house, as in every small town – or every large one for that matter. However, the house itself, when she inherited it, remained very much the home that she had lived in as a child. Dora embarked on the project of renovating the whole house. She had to put a new roof on and decided to convert the barn area into a three-storey flat and completely modernise the property. Obviously this doesn't involve me in the least, nor does Dora expect it to. She manages the whole process of dealing with builders, which unless you speak Italian and understand how Italians do business would be very difficult, and probably much more expensive. My only involvement in the renovation has been to finance the project. But I'm quite happy to do that if I am left in peace for the rest of the time to get on with my work. Sometimes Dora asks my opinion about something, but basically she makes the decisions about what is going to happen. She has done a great job and we have gained a rather wonderful house in Faedis as a result.

I haven't worked in Faedis a lot because landscape has never particularly inspired me. I have always been a vertical and horizontal man, focusing on studio interiors, cityscapes and so forth. Although my beach scenes have a lot of movement and light in them, I still see them basically in vertical and horizontal terms, with windbreaks, people, or a village in the background providing the vertical accents. But I have the feeling that as the years go by and I begin to see Faedis (because in a strange way it is still all too new to me as an experience) I will. Learning how to see your surroundings as a subject for painting does take time. When I moved into South Bolton Gardens, which eventually became the most interesting subject that I had ever found, I didn't initially see it at all. I lived there for six or seven years without actually seeing it in terms of paintings. The first three or four years I worked in Venice were the same. I was always very dissatisfied with the work I produced there – only after four or five years did I begin to see Venice as I see the city now.

Self-portrait at Seventy-six, 2009
Oil on canvas, 61 x 30 cm

This is the last of many self-portraits that I have done over the years. If I had my life again, I would make a portrait every year, almost like keeping a diary.

One of the nicest compliments I have received came from a Venetian friend of ours called Francesco da Mosto who presents films on Italy for the BBC. He very kindly came over to open one of my Richard Green exhibitions and warned me when he arrived that he wasn't going to say too much. I said, 'I think that's a good idea, Francesco, because at openings people don't want speakers to rabbit on too much.' Anyway when he came to open the exhibition he said something that was simple, but which to me couldn't have been more important. Francesco has lived in Venice all his life; his family was one of the earliest in the city and he is actually a Count. He knows the city really well, so when he said, 'Ken Howard has given me a new way of seeing Venice,' it was probably the most flattering thing that he could have said.

And so we return to my first realisation about painting all those years ago. I recognised that above all else painting must reveal things to people – it must show them a way of seeing the world, a perception individual to that particular artist. And I have consistently tried to do this in my work. It hasn't always been easy, ironically in part because life has probably been too good to me. My mother's comment when I was very young, that if I fell down the loo I would emerge with a bar of chocolate, has been proved right many times. This isn't necessarily the best thing for an artist because, whether you like it or not, you do your best work when you are struggling or in emotional turmoil, as I was when I first went to Northern Ireland. Some of your best paintings are created when you are discovering yourself, when things are dark, when life is not that good to you. In other words, when you are suffering – but this has to be genuine, you can't manufacture the grief or pain.

And now, because of the direction my life has taken, I am, at 77 years old, a relatively happy man. So I should be. I live with a younger woman who looks after me wonderfully and who excites me still. I am fortunate enough to have a decent gallery, as well as studios in Cornwall, Venice and London, and I make a reasonably good living doing what I really enjoy. And yet all this doesn't necessarily mean that I paint much better pictures; it could even mean the opposite.

I am often asked about what I paint, and why, and what in essence my work is about. I have a very simple answer to that – the words of a lecturer when I was at the Royal College of Art. He said that an artist should think of himself as a musical instrument: his life is spent in tuning his instrument in order to express the beauty of nature. It caught my imagination then, and it has run through my life ever since. I have never been particularly interested in trying to be innovative for the sake of it. My journey, in a way, is to become increasingly sensitive to the beauty of nature, and hopefully to produce work that is more and more expressive of this. I have been very fortunate in having the chance to follow such a path.

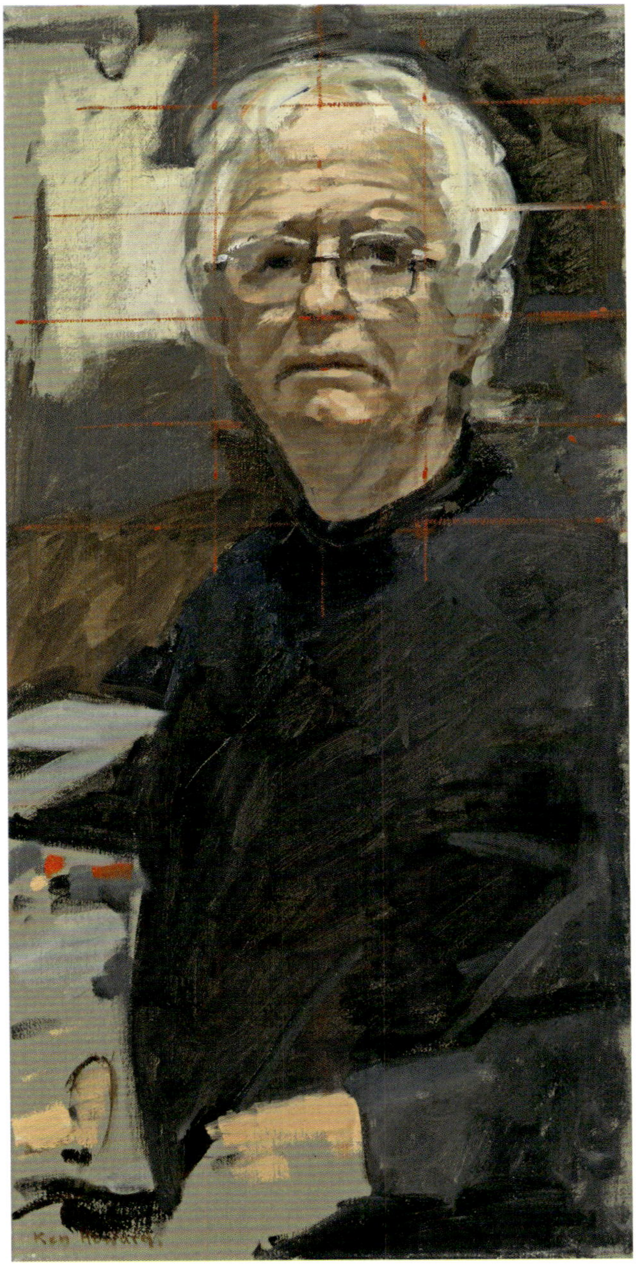

While compiling this book I have had the honour of being awarded an OBE for services to the arts in the 2010 Queen's Birthday Honours list. I have had the pleasure of countless letters of congratulation from generous friends – and I have also, I suppose, felt some sadness that neither of my parents lived to see it. I know they would have been pleased, and maybe they would have seen it as a justification for all the sacrifices they made when I was young. To them I am eternally grateful that they nurtured what talent I had and gave me many opportunities that they were denied. My life has been a blend of both light and dark – reflected in the title I have chosen for this book – but above all else it has been full.

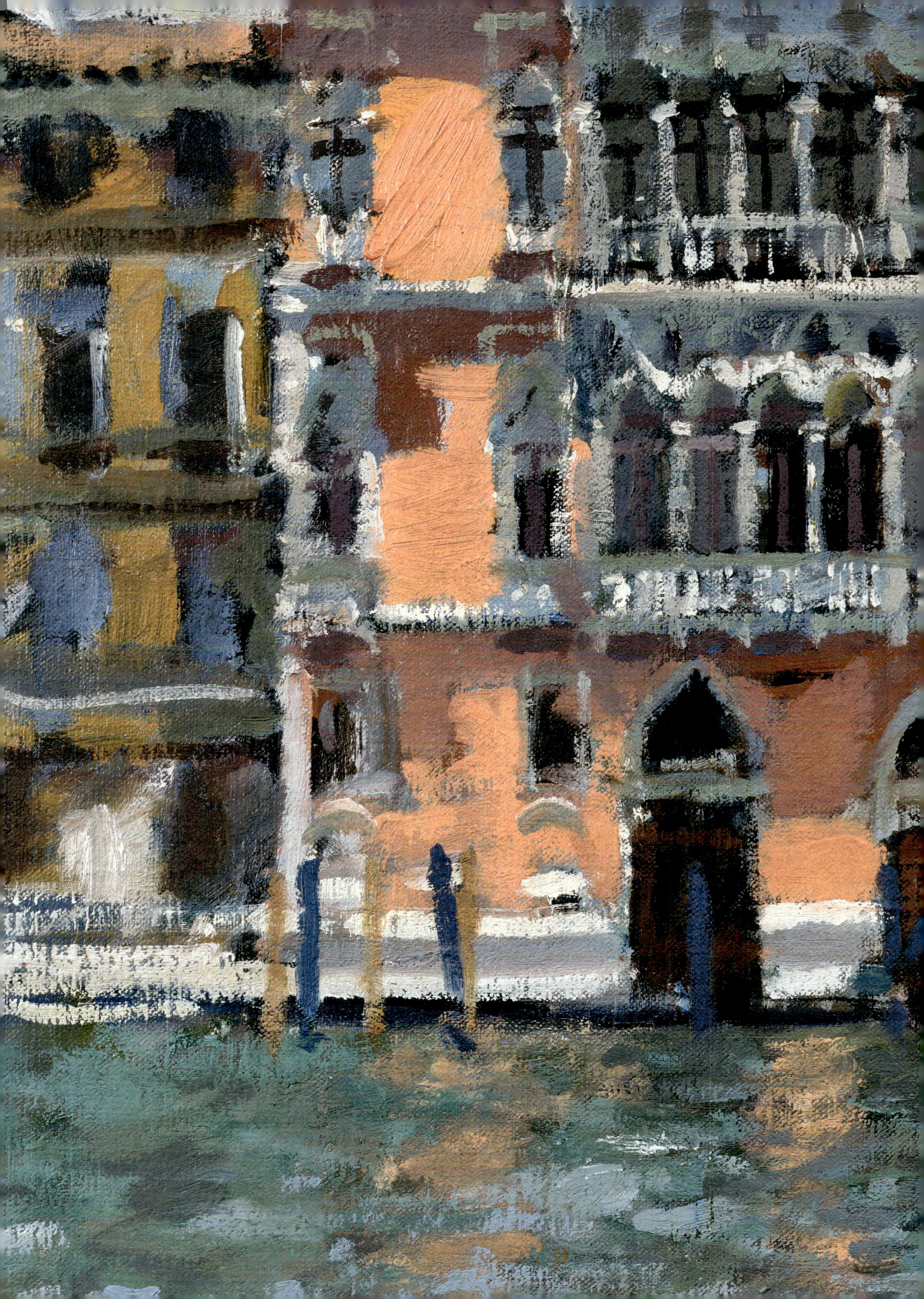

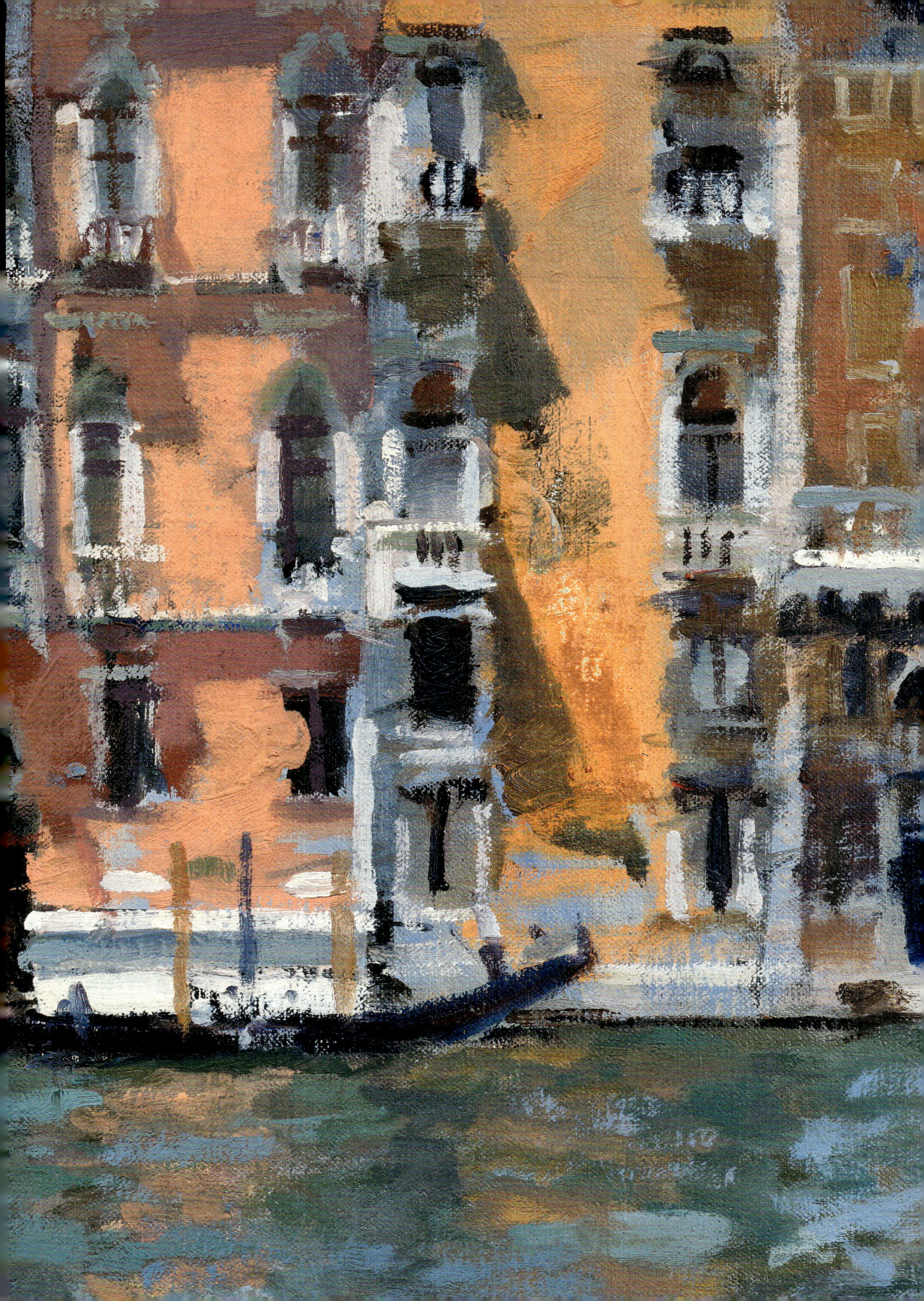

Index

Page numbers in *italic* refer to the illustrations

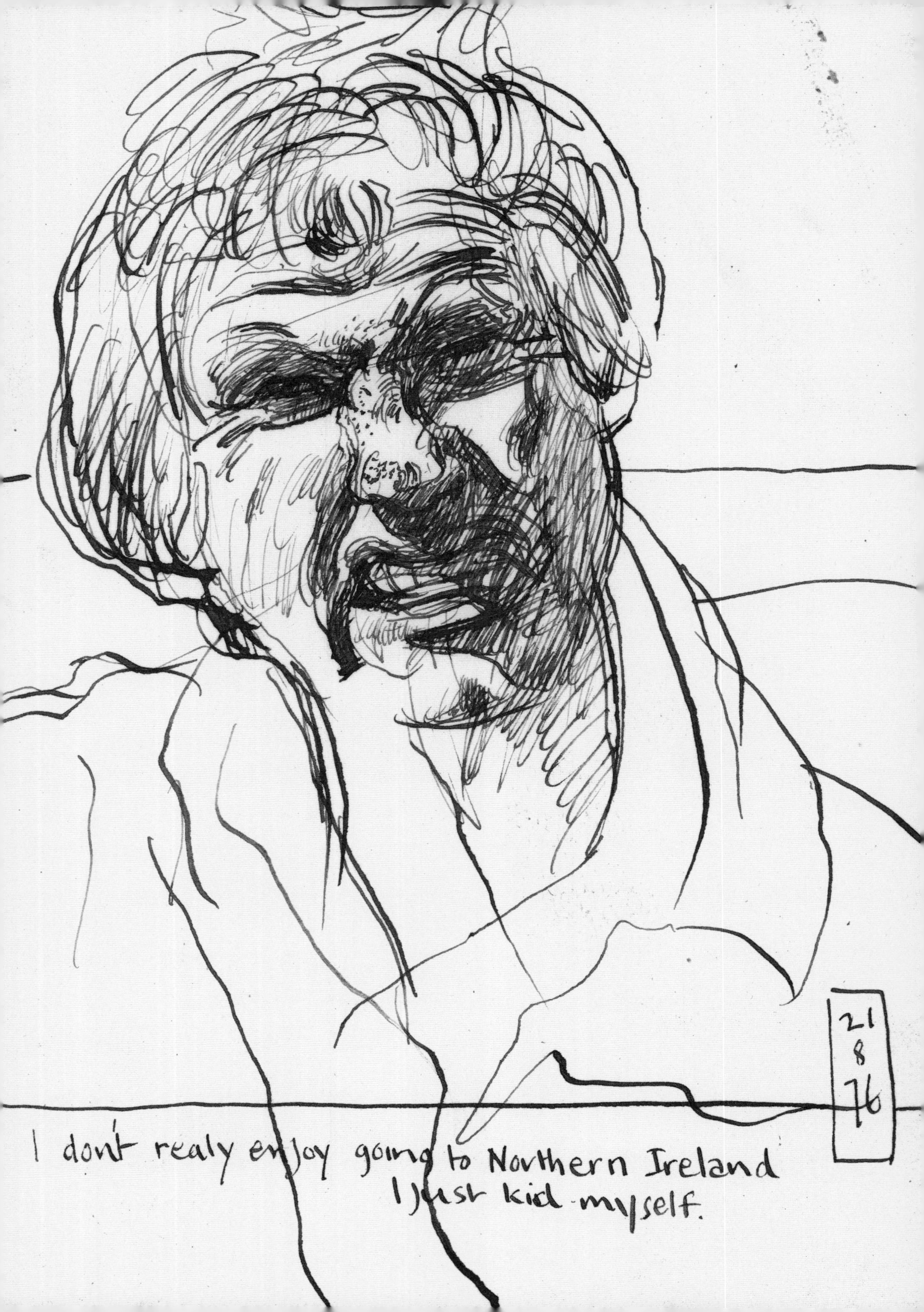
21
8
76
I don't realy enjoy going to Northern Ireland
I just kid myself.